YOUR SOUL LIVES FOREVER

THE LOCHLAINN SEABROOK COLLECTION

AMERICAN CIVIL WAR
Abraham Lincoln Was a Liberal, Jefferson Davis Was a Conservative: The Missing Key to Understanding the American Civil War
Confederacy 101: Amazing Facts You Never Knew About America's Oldest Political Tradition
Confederate Blood and Treasure: An Interview With Lochlainn Seabrook
Everything You Were Taught About African-Americans and the Civil War is Wrong, Ask a Southerner!
Everything You Were Taught About the Civil War is Wrong, Ask a Southerner!
Give This Book to a Yankee! A Southern Guide to the Civil War For Northerners
Heroes of the Southern Confederacy: The Illustrated Book of Confederate Officials, Soldiers, and Civilians
Lincoln's War: The Real Cause, the Real Winner, the Real Loser
Seabrook's Complete Battle Book: War Between the States, 1861-1865
The Great Yankee Coverup: What the North Doesn't Want You to Know About Lincoln's War!
The Hampton Roads Conference: The Southern View
The Ultimate Civil War Quiz Book: How Much Do You Really Know About America's Most Misunderstood Conflict?
Women in Gray: A Tribute to the Ladies Who Supported the Southern Confederacy

CONFEDERATE MONUMENTS
Confederate Monuments: Why Every American Should Honor Confederate Soldiers and Their Memorials

CONFEDERATE FLAG
Confederate Flag Facts: What Every American Should Know About Dixie's Southern Cross
What the Confederate Flag Means to Me: Americans Speak Out in Defense of Southern Honor, Heritage, and History

SECESSION
All We Ask Is To Be Let Alone: The Southern Secession Fact Book

RECONSTRUCTION
Twelve Years in Hell: Victorian Southerners Debunk the Myth of Reconstruction, 1865-1877

SLAVERY
Everything You Were Taught About American Slavery is Wrong, Ask a Southerner!
Slavery 101: Amazing Facts You Never Knew About America's "Peculiar Institution"
The Bittersweet Bond: Race Relations in the Old South as Described by White and Black Southerners

NATHAN BEDFORD FORREST
A Rebel Born: A Defense of Nathan Bedford Forrest -Confederate General, American Legend (winner of the 2011 Jefferson Davis Historical Gold Medal)
A Rebel Born: The Screenplay (film about N. B. Forrest)
Forrest! 99 Reasons to Love Nathan Bedford Forrest
Give 'Em Hell Boys! The Complete Military Correspondence of Nathan Bedford Forrest
I Rode With Forrest! Confederate Soldiers Who Served With the World's Greatest Cavalry Leader
Nathan Bedford Forrest and African-Americans: Yankee Myth, Confederate Fact
Nathan Bedford Forrest and the Battle of Fort Pillow: Yankee Myth, Confederate Fact
Nathan Bedford Forrest and the Ku Klux Klan: Yankee Myth, Confederate Fact
Nathan Bedford Forrest: Southern Hero, American Patriot -Honoring a Confederate Icon and the Old South
Saddle, Sword, and Gun: A Biography of Nathan Bedford Forrest For Teens
The God of War: Nathan Bedford Forrest As He Was Seen By His Contemporaries
The Quotable Nathan Bedford Forrest: Selections From the Writings and Speeches of the Confederacy's Most Brilliant Cavalryman

QUOTABLE SERIES
The Alexander H. Stephens Reader: Excerpts From the Works of a Confederate Founding Father
The Quotable Alexander H. Stephens: Selections From the Writings and Speeches of the Confederacy's First Vice President
The Quotable Jefferson Davis: Selections From the Writings and Speeches of the Confederacy's First President
The Quotable Nathan Bedford Forrest: Selections From the Writings and Speeches of the Confederacy's Most Brilliant Cavalryman
The Quotable Robert E. Lee: Selections From the Writings and Speeches of the South's Most Beloved Civil War General
The Quotable Stonewall Jackson: Selections From the Writings and Speeches of the South's Most Famous General
The Unquotable Abraham Lincoln: The President's Quotes They Don't Want You To Know!

CIVIL WAR BATTLES
Encyclopedia of the Battle of Franklin -A Comprehensive Guide to the Conflict that Changed the Civil War
Nathan Bedford Forrest and the Battle of Fort Pillow: Yankee Myth, Confederate Fact
Seabrook's Complete Battle Book: War Between the States, 1861-1865
The Battle of Franklin: Recollections of Confederate and Union Soldiers
The Battle of Nashville: Recollections of Confederate and Union Soldiers
The Battle of Spring Hill: Recollections of Confederate and Union Soldiers

CONSTITUTIONAL HISTORY
America's Three Constitutions: Complete Texts of the Articles of Confederation, Constitution of the United States of America, and Constitution of the Confederate States of America
The Articles of Confederation Explained: A Clause-by-Clause Study of America's First Constitution
The Constitution of the Confederate States of America Explained: A Clause-by-Clause Study of the South's Magna Carta

CHILDREN
Honest Jeff and Dishonest Abe: A Southern Children's Guide to the Civil War
Saddle, Sword, and Gun: A Biography of Nathan Bedford Forrest For Teens

VICTORIAN CONFEDERATE LITERATURE
I, Confederate: Why Dixie Seceded and Fought in the Words of Southern Soldiers
Rise Up and Call Them Blessed: Victorian Tributes to the Confederate Soldier, 1861-1901
Support Your Local Confederate: Wit and Humor in the Southern Confederacy
The Bittersweet Bond: Race Relations in the Old South as Described by White and Black Southerners
The God of War: Nathan Bedford Forrest As He Was Seen By His Contemporaries
The Old Rebel: Robert E. Lee As He Was Seen By His Contemporaries
Victorian Confederate Poetry: The Southern Cause in Verse, 1861-1901

ABRAHAM LINCOLN
Abraham Lincoln: The Southern View -Demythologizing America's Sixteenth President
Lincolnology: The Real Abraham Lincoln Revealed in His Own Words -A Study of Lincoln's Suppressed, Misinterpreted, and Forgotten Writings and Speeches
Lincoln's War: The Real Cause, the Real Winner, the Real Loser
The Great Impersonator! 99 Reasons to Dislike Abraham Lincoln
The Unholy Crusade: Lincoln's Legacy of Destruction in the American South
The Unquotable Abraham Lincoln: The President's Quotes They Don't Want You To Know!

NATURAL HISTORY
North America's Amazing Mammals: An Encyclopedia for the Whole Family
The Concise Book of Owls: A Guide to Nature's Most Mysterious Birds
The Concise Book of Tigers: A Guide to Nature's Most Remarkable Cats

FAMILY HISTORIES
The Blakeneys: An Etymological, Ethnological, and Genealogical Study -Uncovering the Mysterious Origins of the Blakeney Family and Name
The Caudills: An Etymological, Ethnological, and Genealogical Study -Exploring the Name and National Origins of a European-American Family
The McGavocks of Carnton Plantation: A Southern History -Celebrating One of Dixie's Most Noble Confederate Families and Their Tennessee Home

MIND, BODY, SPIRIT
Autobiography of a Non-Yogi: A Scientist's Journey From Hinduism to Christianity (Dr. Amitava Dasgupta, with Lochlainn Seabrook)
Britannia Rules: Goddess-Worship in Ancient Anglo-Celtic Society—An Academic Look at the United Kingdom's Matricentric Spiritual Past
Carnton Plantation Ghost Stories: True Tales of the Unexplained from Tennessee's Most Haunted Civil War House!
Christ Is All and In All: Rediscovering Your Divine Nature and the Kingdom Within
Christmas Before Christianity: How the Birthday of the "Sun" Became the Birthday of the "Son"
Jesus and the Gospel of Q: Christ's Pre-Christian Teachings As Recorded in the New Testament
Jesus and the Law of Attraction: The Bible-Based Guide to Creating Perfect Health, Wealth, and Happiness Following Christ's Simple Formula
Mysterious Invaders: Twelve Famous 20th-Century Scientists Confront the UFO Phenomenon
Seabrook's Bible Dictionary of Traditional and Mystical Christian Doctrines
Sea Raven Press Blank Page Journal: For Reflections, Notes, and Sketches
Secrets of Celebrity Surnames: An Onomastic Dictionary of Famous People
The Bible and the Law of Attraction: 99 Teachings of Jesus, the Apostles, and the Prophets
The Book of Kelle: An Introduction to Goddess-Worship and the Great Celtic Mother-Goddess Kelle, Original Blessed Lady of Ireland
The Goddess Dictionary of Words and Phrases: Introducing a New Core Vocabulary for the Women's Spirituality Movement
The Martian Anomalies: A Photographic Search for Intelligent Life on Mars
UFOs and Aliens: The Complete Guidebook
Victorian Hernia Cures: Nonsurgical Self-Treatment of Inguinal Hernia
Vintage Southern Cookbook: 2,000 Delicious Dishes From Dixie
Your Soul Lives Forever: Documented Victorian Case Studies Proving Consciousness Survives Death

WOMEN
Aphrodite's Trade: The Hidden History of Prostitution Unveiled
Princess Diana: Modern Day Moon-Goddess - A Psychoanalytical and Mythological Look at Diana Spencer's Life, Marriage, and Death (with Dr. Jane Goldberg)
Women in Gray: A Tribute to the Ladies Who Supported the Southern Confederacy

REPRINTS
A Short History of the Confederate States of America (author Jefferson Davis; editor Lochlainn Seabrook)
Prison Life of Jefferson Davis (author John J. Craven; editor Lochlainn Seabrook)
Life of Beethoven (author Ludwig Nohl; editor Lochlainn Seabrook)
The New Revelation (author Arthur Conan Doyle; editor Lochlainn Seabrook)
The Rise and Fall of the Confederate Government (author Jefferson Davis; editor Lochlainn Seabrook)

Lochlainn Seabrook does not author books for fame and glory, but for the love of writing and sharing his knowledge.

SeaRavenPress.com

YOUR SOUL LIVES FOREVER

Documented Victorian Case Studies Proving Consciousness Survives Death

---

CONCEIVED, COLLECTED, EDITED, ARRANGED, & DESIGNED WITH AN INTRODUCTION BY
HISTORIAN, CHRISTIAN MYSTIC, & ANOMALOUS RESEARCHER, COLONEL

LOCHLAINN SEABROOK

JEFFERSON DAVIS HISTORICAL GOLD MEDAL WINNER

Diligently Researched and Generously Illustrated
by the Author for the Elucidation of the Reader

2024

Sea Raven Press, Park County, Wyoming, USA

YOUR SOUL LIVES FOREVER

Published by
Sea Raven Press, Cassidy Ravensdale, President
Park County, Wyoming, USA
SeaRavenPress.com

Copyright © all text and illustrations Lochlainn Seabrook 2024
in accordance with U.S. and international copyright laws and regulations, as stated and protected under the Berne Union for the Protection of Literary and Artistic Property (Berne Convention), and the Universal Copyright Convention (the UCC). All rights reserved under the Pan-American and International Copyright Conventions.

PRINTING HISTORY
1st SRP paperback edition, 1st printing, February 2024 • ISBN: 978-1-955351-38-6
1st SRP hardcover edition, 1st printing, February 2024 • ISBN: 978-1-955351-39-3

ISBN: 978-1-955351-38-6 (paperback)
Library of Congress Control Number: 2024932644

This work is the copyrighted intellectual property of Lochlainn Seabrook and has been registered with the Copyright Office at the Library of Congress in Washington, D.C., USA. No part of this work (including text, covers, drawings, photos, illustrations, maps, images, diagrams, etc.), in whole or in part, may be used, reproduced, stored in a retrieval system, or transmitted, in any form or by any means now known or hereafter invented, without written permission from the publisher. The sale, duplication, hire, lending, copying, digitalization, or reproduction of this material, in any manner or form whatsoever, is also prohibited, and is a violation of federal, civil, and digital copyright law, which provides severe civil and criminal penalties for any violations.

Your Soul Lives Forever: Documented Victorian Case Studies Proving Consciousness Survives Death, by Lochlainn Seabrook. Includes an introduction, illustrations, index, endnotes, appendices, and bibliography.

ARTWORK
Front and back cover design and art, book design, layout, font selection, and interior art by Lochlainn Seabrook
All images, image captions, graphic design, and graphic art copyright © Lochlainn Seabrook
All images selected, placed, manipulated, cleaned, colored, tinted, and/or created by Lochlainn Seabrook
Title page soldier image from Lochlainn Seabrook's book, 'Heroes of the Southern Confederacy'
Cover image: "Resurrection Stairway," Romolo Tavani

All persons who approve of the authority and principles of Colonel Lochlainn Seabrook's literary work, and realize its benefits as a means of reeducating the world about facts left out of mainstream books, are hereby requested to avidly recommend his titles to others and to vigorously cooperate in extending their reach, scope, and influence around the globe.

The views documented in this book concerning spirituality are those of the publisher.
WRITTEN, DESIGNED, PUBLISHED, PRINTED, & MANUFACTURED IN THE UNITED STATES OF AMERICA

DEDICATION

To the open-minded Victorian Christian researchers who withstood mockery, contempt, and censure in order to scientifically investigate the paranormal realm so familiar to Jesus, Saint Paul, and Saint John.

Epigraph

Man lives on earth not once, but three times: the first stage of his life [in the womb] is continual sleep; the second, sleeping and waking by turns; the third, waking for ever.... The act of leaving the first stage for the second we call Birth; that of leaving the second for the third, Death.

Our way from the second to the third is not darker than our way from the first to the second: one way leads us forth to see the world outwardly; the other, to see it inwardly.... death is merely a second birth into a happier life, when the spirit, breaking through his narrow hull, leaves it to decay and vanish, like the infant's hull [the womb] in its first birth. And then all those things which we, with our present senses, can only know from the outside, or, as it were, from a distance, will be penetrated into, and thoroughly known, by us.

Then, instead of passing by hills and meadows, instead of seeing around us all the beauties of spring, and grieving that we cannot really take them in, as they are merely external: our spirits shall enter into those hills and meadows, to feel and enjoy with them their strength and their pleasure in growing; instead of exerting ourselves to produce, by means of words or gestures, certain ideas in the minds of our fellow-men, we shall be enabled to raise up and influence their thoughts, by an immediate intercourse of spirits, which are no longer separated, but rather brought together, by their bodies; instead of being visible in our bodily shape to the eyes of the friends we left behind, we shall dwell in their inmost souls, a part of them, thinking and acting within them and through them.

Gustav Theodore Fechner, 1882

CONTENTS

Notes to the Reader, by Lochlainn Seabrook: page 11
The Basic Tenets of Spiritualism: page 13
"Haunted Houses," By Henry Wadsworth Longfellow: page 16
Introduction, by Lochlainn Seabrook: page 17

1: VISUAL ACCOUNTS
CASES OF APPARITIONS, GHOSTS, & PHANTASMS: page 23

2: TELEPATHIC ACCOUNTS
CASES OF THOUGHT TRANSFERENCE,
AUTOMATIC WRITING, & ESP: page 163

3: ONEIROLOGICAL ACCOUNTS
CASES OF PERCIPIENT DREAMS: page 211

4: AUDITORY ACCOUNTS
Cases of Spectral Voices & Sounds: page 261

5: OLFACTOROUS ACCOUNTS
Cases of Paranormal Smells: page 297

6: CLAIRVOYANCE ACCOUNTS
Cases of Visions & Mirages: page 299

7: PARANORMAL ACCOUNTS
Cases of Haunted Houses & Poltergeists: page 315

8: TANGIBILITY ACCOUNTS
Cases of Tactile Spirits: page 349

9: PARAPHYSICAL & PARAPSYCHOLOGICAL ACCOUNTS
Cases of Unknown Forces, Mental Healing, Strange Powers, & Unusual Experiences: page 355

10: PRECOGNITIONARY ACCOUNTS
Cases of Premonition & Omens: page 393

Appendix A - Spiritualism and the Gospel of Jesus: page 397
Appendix B - Ashes to Ashes, Dust to Dust: page 403
Notes: page 405
Bibliography: page 413
Index: page 417
Meet the Author-Editor: page 429
Learn More: page 431

NOTES TO THE READER

A WORD ON MY VICTORIAN MATERIAL
❦ In order to preserve the authentic historicity of the Victorian material I have collected for this book, I have retained the original spellings, formatting, and punctuation of the 19th-Century individuals I quote. These include such items as British-English spellings, obsolete words, and various literary devices peculiar to the time. However, I have done away with long-running paragraphs (for easier reading), as well as corrected misspelled names to prevent confusion, and also *where possible*, inaccurate dates and locations (the inevitable result of aging faulty memories). Bracketed words are *always* my additions and clarifications (added mainly for my new, foreign, and young readers), while italicized words are (where indicated) my emphasis.

WHY MANY OF THE CONTRIBUTORS ARE ANONYMOUS
❦ When giving their paranormal accounts the Victorian participants understandably often withheld full names from the public, not only for privacy reasons, but also for fear of jeopardizing relationships, reputations, and jobs.

THE MEANING OF "DOCUMENTED"
❦ As this word is significant, and as it appears in my subtitle, it deserves an explanation. The majority of my selected case studies derive from Britain's prestigious—and happily, still operating—Society for Psychical Research, which has always placed a premium on approaching its study of the paranormal scientifically.

The Victorian Era S.P.R. specifically (which began its work in 1882) not only *personally* visited and interviewed its subjects, but also everyone else involved, including relatives, neighbors, shop-owners, police, etc. This intense hands-on process could take days, weeks, even months to complete, and almost always included the procurement of signed affidavits and corroborative letters and statements from witnesses to the paranormal phenomena in question.

Though an S.P.R. investigation, as thorough and honest as it was, did not and could not always rule out misidentifications and hoaxing, when such was discovered, the case was immediately dropped. Those cases that passed the S.P.R.'s rigorous screening process, many which I collected for this book, remain an important and objective record of early scientific research into the paranormal; results that have greatly added to both our understanding of *and* evidence for the reality of life after death.

In accordance with the First Law of Thermodynamics—that is, *energy cannot be created or destroyed; only transferred or converted from one form to another*—our souls cannot and never truly die, but journey on an endless adventure through eternity. This book proves it.

LOCHLAINN SEABROOK

YOUR SOUL LIVES FOREVER

Keep Your Body, Mind, & Spirit Vibrating at Their Highest Level

YOU CAN DO SO BY READING THE BOOKS OF

SEA RAVEN PRESS

There is nothing that will so perfectly keep your body, mind, and spirit in a healthy condition as to think wisely and positively. Hence you should not only read this book, but also the other books that we offer. They will quicken your physical, mental, and spiritual vibrations, enabling you to maintain a position in society as a healthy erudite person.

KEEP YOURSELF WELL-INFORMED!

The well-informed person is always at the head of the procession, while the ignorant, the lazy, and the unthoughtful hang onto the rear. If you are a Spiritual man or woman, do yourself a great favor: read Sea Raven Press books and stay well posted on the Truth. It is almost criminal for one to remain in ignorance while the opportunity to gain knowledge is open to all at a nominal price.

We invite you to visit our Webstore for a wide selection of wholesome, family-friendly, well-researched, educational books for all ages. You will be glad you did!

Artisan-Crafted Books & Merch From the Rocky Mountains!

SeaRavenPress.com

LochlainnSeabrook.com
TheBestCivilWarBookEver.com
AmbianceGoneWild.com
Pond5.com/artist/LochlainnSeabrook

The Basic Tenets of Spiritualism
[AS ESPOUSED BY THE VICTORIANS IN THIS BOOK]

Spiritualism, in the general acceptation of the term, implies a recognition of God as the infinite spirit-presence of the universe, and of a present as well as past intercourse and communion between the inhabitants of earth and those peopling the world of spirits. It is a fact, and a life; in method it is phenomenal and philosophical, corresponding to the inductive and deductive methods of reasoning. As the administration of law has little to do with essential justice, and theology little to do with religion "pure and undefiled," so creeds and church dogmas have, legitimately, nothing to do with Spiritualism. The angels never designed the introduction of a new sect upon earth through the agency of Spiritual manifestations. Those are Spiritualists, then, who from personal, or otherwise well-attested evidences, believe in present interviews with, and communications from, immortalised spirits, and strive so far as in them lies to live pure and spiritual lives.[1] — Dr. James Martin Peebles, 1869

SPIRITUALISTS MAINTAIN

1. That man has a spiritual nature as well as a corporeal; in other words, that the real man is a spirit; which spirit has an organized form, composed of sublimated material, with parts and organs corresponding to those of the corporeal body.

2. That man, as a spirit, is immortal. Being found to survive that change called physical death, it may be reasonably supposed that he will survive all future vicissitudes.

3. That there is a spiritual world, or state, with its substantial realities, objective as well as subjective.

4. That the process of physical death in no way essentially transforms the mental constitution or the moral character of those who experience it, else it would destroy their identity.

5. That happiness or suffering, in the spiritual state, as in this, depends not on arbitrary decree or special provision, but on character, aspirations, and degree of harmonization, or of personal conformity to universal and divine law.

6. Hence that the experience and attainments of the present life lay the foundation on which the next commences.

7. That since growth (in some degree) is the law of the human being in the present life, and since the process called death is in fact but a birth into another condition of life, retaining all the advantages gained in the

experiences of this life, it may be inferred that growth, development, expansion, or progression is the endless destiny of the human spirit.

8. That the spiritual world is not far off, but near around, or interblended with our present state of existence; and hence that we are constantly under the cognizance of spiritual beings.

9. That, as individuals are passing from the earthly to the spiritual state in all stages of mental and moral growth, that state includes all grades of character, from the lowest to the highest.

10. That, as heaven and hell, or happiness and misery, depend on internal state rather than on external surroundings, there are as many gradations of each as there are shades of character, each one gravitating to his own place by natural Law of Affinity. They may be divided into several general degrees or spheres; but these must admit of indefinite diversifications, or "many mansions," corresponding to diversified individual characters—each individual being as happy as his character will allow him to be.

11. That communications from the spiritual world, whether by mental impressions, inspirations, or any other mode of transmission, are not necessarily infallible truth, but, on the contrary, partake unavoidably of the imperfections of the minds from which they emanate, and of the channels through which they come, and are, moreover, liable to misinterpretation by those to whom they are addressed.

12. Hence that no inspired communication, in this or any other age (whatever claims may be or have been set up as to its source), is authoritative any further than it expresses *truth* to the individual consciousness,—which last is the final standard to which all inspired or spiritual teachings must be brought for judgment.

13. That inspiration, or the influx of ideas and promptings from the spiritual realm, is not a miracle of a past age, but a *perpetual fact*,—the ceaseless method of the divine economy for human elevation.

14. That all angelic and all demonic beings which have manifested themselves, or interposed in human affairs in the past, were simply disembodied human spirits, in different grades of advancement.

15. That all authentic miracles (so called) in the past—such as the raising of the apparently dead, the healing of the sick by the laying on of hands or other simple means, unharmed contact with poisons, the movement of physical objects without visible instrumentality, etc., etc., have been produced in harmony with universal laws, and hence may be repeated at any time under suitable conditions.

16. That the causes of all phenomena—the sources of all Life, Intelligence, and Love—are to be sought in the internal, the spiritual, realm, not in the external or material. [See Luke 17:20-21. L.S.]

17. That the chain of causation leads inevitably upward or inward to an Infinite Spirit,—who is not only a Forming Principle (Wisdom), but an Affectional Source (Love), thus sustaining the dual parental relations of Father and Mother to all finite intelligences, who, of course, are all brethren.

18. That Man, as the offspring of this Infinite Parent, is his highest representative on this plane of being,—the Perfect Man being the most complete embodiment of the Father's "fulness" which we can contemplate; and that each man is, or has, by virtue of this parentage, in his inmost a germ of Divinity, an incorruptible portion of the Divine Essence, which is ever prompting to the right, and which in time will free itself from all imperfections incident to the rudimental or earthly condition, and will triumph over all evil.

19. That all evil is disharmony, greater or less, with this inmost or divine principle; and hence whatever prompts and aids man to bring his more external nature into subjection to and harmony with his interiors—whether it be called "Christianity," "Spiritualism," or "The Harmonial Philosophy"—whether it recognizes "the Holy Ghost," "the Bible," or a present Spiritual and Celestial Influx—is a "means of salvation" from evil.[2] — Mr. A. E. Newton

A Victorian Spiritualist camp meeting at Onset Bay, Massachusetts, 1800s.

HAUNTED HOUSES

All houses wherein men have lived and died
Are haunted houses. Through the open doors
The harmless phantoms on their errands glide,
With feet that make no sound upon the floors.

We meet them at the doorway, on the stair,
   Along the passages they come and go,
   Impalpable impressions on the air,
A sense of something moving to and fro.

There are more guests at table than the hosts
   Invited; the illuminated hall
Is thronged with quiet, inoffensive ghosts,
   As silent as the pictures on the wall.

The stranger at my fireside cannot see
   The forms I see, nor hear the sounds I hear;
   He but perceives what is; while unto me
All that has been is visible and clear.

We have no title-deeds to house or lands;
   Owners and occupants of earlier dates
From graves forgotten stretch their dusty hands,
And hold in mortmain still their old estates.

The spirit-world around this world of sense
   Floats like an atmosphere, and everywhere
Wafts through these earthly mists and vapours dense
   A vital breath of more ethereal air.

And as the moon from some dark gate of cloud
   Throws o'er the sea a floating bridge of light,
Across whose trembling planks our fancies crowd
   Into the realm of mystery and night,—

So from the world of spirits there descends
   A bridge of light, connecting it with this,
O'er whose unsteady floor, that sways and bends,
   Wander our thoughts above the dark abyss.

Henry Wadsworth Longfellow, 1878

INTRODUCTION
The Bridge Between Two Worlds

> "And God shall wipe away all tears from their eyes; and there shall be no more death, neither sorrow, nor crying, neither shall there be any more pain: for the former things are passed away." — Book of Revelation 21:4

RATIONALISTS, MATERIALISTS, AND ATHEISTS would probably not consider reading this deeply eschatological work—except to criticize and ridicule its contents. But it was not written for them. On the other hand, if you are an on-the-fence skeptic this book may begin to erode some of your preconceived notions, perhaps even completely overthrowing your views on the topics of the survival of consciousness and eternal life.

Naturally, believers will not find the 385 Victorian case studies of "paranormal" occurrences contained in this work disturbing or even surprising; in fact, my collection of 150 year old accounts will no doubt actually strengthen their already deeply held beliefs in Spirit, resurrection, and life after death.

MY PARANORMAL LIFE

I myself certainly do not need convincing, proof, or evidence for what society refers to as "supernatural activities," for I have experienced, at one time or another in my life, nearly every phenomena chronicled in this book—and some that are not. Always intriguing, never frightening, these types of things are daily occurrences in my life, and as a mystical Christian I have come to accept and even appreciate them as purposefully manifested spiritual signs of other realities; of, in other words, immortal life.

Yes, materialists have ready and clever psychological and physiological rationales for *all* paranormal experiences, beliefs, and events; though most of these theories are unconvincing and even ludicrous in the extreme, and do not begin to actually explain them—as most believers will agree who have examined them.

Being logically minded, I have investigated my own otherworldly encounters using the scientific method. I am only occasionally able to debunk them, however, with well over 90 percent falling outside our currently accepted understanding of the laws of physics.

SPIRITUALISM: AN ANCIENT REALITY

The "supernatural" case studies I have included in the following pages are not new. In fact, ghostly spirit beings, as just one example, can be found in stories and myths thousands of years old. Our Christian Bible itself contains countless references to psychic powers, other-worldly forces, supernatural events, and non-physical beings (known in the Good Book as "familiar spirits").

A small sampling of these would include: God's creation of the world, Moses parting the Red Sea, Enoch's "translation" into the heavens, Lot's wife turning to salt, the burning bush, Aaron's rod turning into a serpent, the plagues on Egypt, the appearance of manna, Moses bringing forth water from a rock, the fall of Jericho, the feeding of Elijah by God, God speaking to Job from a whirlwind, Ezekiel witnessing a flying saucer like craft, an angel appearing to Mary, and the virgin birth of Jesus. The list goes on.

JESUS & THE PARANORMAL

Of all our biblical figures none was more familiar with the unseen world of Spirit than Jesus, the fully enlightened Christ being who taught eternal life, turned water into wine, multiplied loaves of bread, healed the sick, and walked on water.[3] Unlike many modern mainstream Christians, however, Jesus did not preach against using one's paranormal abilities, nor did He claim these powers for himself. Instead, He taught that

> "whoever believes in me will also do the works that I do; and greater works than these will he do."[4]

One of Jesus' more notable paranormal teachings concerns the Law of Reciprocity, or what is now more commonly known as the Law of Attraction. In the Gospel of Mark our Lord makes this remarkable statement:

> "What things soever ye desire, when ye pray, believe that ye receive them, and ye shall have them."[5]

If an ancient Pagan had preached this occult formula it would be considered a form of "white magic." Even so, those who are familiar with authentic ancient spiritual teachings will perfectly comprehend such statements, for they are universal and timeless—which is why this exact same doctrine was taught by Buddha and numerous other spiritual leaders hundreds of years before Jesus was born.[6]

Yet both modern science and modern mainstream Christians reject such teachings, even when they come directly from our Lord. Why?

BIBLICAL WARNINGS: THE TRUTH
It is a fact that certain Old and New Testament passages warn us against getting involved with the paranormal. For example:

> "Do not defile yourselves by turning to *mediums* or to those who consult the spirits of the dead."[7]

But the truth is, as my mystical English cousin, spiritualist Arthur Conan Doyle (creator of Sherlock Holmes) wrote in 1918:

> ". . . the list of gifts which St. Paul gives as being necessary for the Christian Disciple, is simply the list of gifts of a very powerful *medium*, including prophecy, healing, causing miracles (or physical phenomena), clairvoyance, and other powers.[8] The Early Christian Church was saturated with spiritualism, and they seem to have paid no attention to those Old Testament prohibitions which meant to keep these powers only for the use and profit of the priesthood."[9]

And to those who believe Christianity and Spiritualism are incompatible, Victorian Christian Dr. James Martin Peebles directed the following:

> "The primitive Christians were religious Spiritualists. They often saw Christ in visions, and in His name they healed the sick. Spiritualism, the complement of Christianity, sweetens the bitterest cup, helps bear the heaviest burden, lightens the darkest day, comforts the saddest heart, and gathering up the kindly efforts we make in behalf of our fellow-men, transfigures them with its brightness, ennobles them with its moral grandeur, and throws around them the circling aureole of fadeless splendours. And further, by and through its holy ministries, we know that the grave is no prison house for the soul, but that life, progressive life, is ours, eternal in the heavens."[10]

Whatever one's personal beliefs, we must bear in mind that the unseen world often imposes itself upon us, whether we like it or not. Nearly 100 percent of the Victorian individuals recorded in this book, for instance, were Christians, many who did not pursue the paranormal or believe in things like Spiritualism, ghosts, or precognitive dreams—many actually flatly rejecting it all. Despite this, the supernatural eventually impinged on their lives in a variety of manifestations—almost always, as the reader shall see, in the form of beneficent spirits (usually, though not always, of deceased husbands, wives, brothers, sisters, or close relatives) seeking to help, inform, alert, relieve, or reassure their still living earthly human contacts. Mystical Christians, such as myself, do not "dabble in the occult arts." We simply seek to understand these amazing and always life-altering anomalous experiences rather than ignore them out of fear, philistinism, nescience, or confirmation bias.

SPIRITUALISM: THE SCIENTIFIC EVIDENCE
One might ask, "what do Victorian 'ghost stories' have to do with the topic of immortal life?"

Although I believe that one day quantum physics will prove—through, for example, the ongoing discovery and exploration of extra spatial dimensions—that *consciousness continues forever*, current conventional science is purely atheistic. Therefore,

from my perspective, anything that counters this myopic, spiritless worldview lends credibility to the idea of life after death. This would include scientifically unexplainable apparitions (humans and animals), deathbed visitors, thought transference, premonitionary dreams, spectral voices and sounds, visions, mirages, poltergeists, hauntings, invisible touching, séances, mental healing, levitation, cryptids, autonomous lights, unknown forces, unusual powers, omens, and unaccountable odors, examples of each which I have collected for this book.

Of all the items listed above, none has been more definitively proven scientifically than ESP, as anyone is aware who has read the works of J. B. Rhine and other forward-thinking scientists.[11] Canadian author and psychical researcher H. Addington Bruce wrote in 1908:

"It is quite true that we are sadly ignorant of the laws of telepathy; but it would seem equally certain that telepathy itself is an established fact—established by the experiments of the psychical researchers and by the thousands upon thousands of spontaneous instances recorded by individuals."[12]

Mental telepathy, of course, proves the existence of an extra-dimensional reality not currently recognized by conventional science, which in turn connects it with the idea of immortality.

While it is true that, just as with existence of God, one cannot *scientifically prove* the concept of eternal life to everyone's satisfaction, it is also true that one cannot *scientifically disprove* it to everyone's satisfaction. However one defines the unseen, the hidden, the paranormal, it continues to stand outside both science and religion, thus the meaning of the word itself: "beyond the norm."

SUMMATION
When and if it is ever finally proven by science, it will become what enlightened individuals have always considered the paranormal to be: *normal*, that is, abilities and energies that fall squarely within everyday physical laws—just as Jesus taught. Until then, we, the curious and the unbiased, must content ourselves with researching, investigating, and attempting to understand both our own extraordinary experiences and talents and those of the many individuals who have come before us.

It is in this spirit that I offer this volume of hand-selected case studies—a bridge between two worlds—which I have entitled, *Your Soul Lives Forever*. It will serve not only as a reminder that we still have yet to establish an accurate and universally consensual definition of reality, but more importantly, as a paranormal, thanatological, pneumatological, and eschatological handbook meant to educate, console, uplift, and illuminate. Let us remember the cosmic words of Christian mystic Saint Paul of Tarsus: "Whatsoever doth make manifest is light."[13]

Lochlainn Seabrook
Park County, Wyoming USA
February 2024
In Nobis Regnat Christus
John 1:9 KJV

"Books invite all; they constrain none."
Hartley Burr Alexander (1873-1939)

Chapter One
VISUAL ACCOUNTS
Cases of Apparitions, Ghosts, and Phantasms

☞ CASE #1: In 1739 Mrs. Birkbeck, wife of William Birkbeck, banker, of Settle, and a member of the Society of Friends, was taken ill and died at Cockermouth, while returning from a journey to Scotland, which she had undertaken alone—her husband and three children, aged seven, five, and four years respectively, remaining at Settle. The friends at whose house the death occurred made notes of every circumstance attending Mrs. Birkbeck's last hours, so that the accuracy of the several statements as to time as well as place was beyond the doubtfulness of man's memory, or of any even unconscious attempt to bring them into agreement with each other.

One morning, between seven and eight o'clock, the relation to whom the care of the children at Settle had been entrusted, and who kept a minute journal of all that concerned them, went into their bedroom as usual, and found them all sitting up in their beds in great excitement and delight. "Mamma has been here!" they cried, and the little one said, "She called, Come, Esther!" Nothing could make them doubt the fact, and it was carefully noted down to entertain the mother on her return home. That same morning as their mother lay on her dying bed at Cockermouth, she said, "I should be ready to go if I could but see my children." She then closed her eyes, to reopen them, as they thought, no more. But after ten minutes of perfect stillness she looked up brightly and said, "I am ready now; I have been with my children;" and then at once peacefully passed away. When the notes taken at the two places were compared, the day, hour, and minutes were the same.

One of the three children was my grandmother, née Sarah Birkbeck, afterwards the wife of Dr. Fell, of Ulverstone. From her lips I heard the above almost literally as I have repeated it. The elder was Morris Birkbeck, afterwards of Guildford. Both these lived to old age, and retained to the last so solemn and reverential a remembrance of the circumstance that they rarely would speak of it. Esther, the youngest, died soon after. Her brother and sister heard the child say that her mother called her, but could not speak with any certainty of having themselves heard the words, nor were sensible of more than their mother's standing there and looking on them.[14] — MRS. CHARLES FOX

☛ CASE #2: I was a boy in the Sixth Form at Harrow; and, as head of Mr. Rendall's house, had a room to myself. It was in the summer of 1858. I woke about dawn, and felt for my books upon a chair between the bed and the window; when I knew that I must turn my head the other way, and there between me and the door stood Dr. Macleane, dressed in a clergyman's black clothes. He bent his sallow face a little towards me and said, "I am going a long way—take care of my son." While I was attending to him I suddenly saw the door in the place where Dr. Macleane had been. Dr. Macleane died that night (at what hour I cannot precisely say) at Clifton. My father, who was a great friend of his, was with him. I was not aware that he was more than usually ill. He was a chronic invalid.[15] — JOHN ADDINGTON SYMONDS

☛ CASE #3: I was at home for my holidays, and residing with my father and mother, not here, but at another old family place in Mid-Lothian, built by an ancestor in Mary Queen of Scots' time, called Inveresk House. My bedroom was a curious old room, long and narrow, with a window at one end of the room and a door at the other. My bed was on the right of the window, looking towards the door. I had a very dear brother (my eldest brother), Oliver, lieutenant in the 7th Royal Fusiliers. He was about nineteen years old, and had at that time been some months before Sebastopol.

I corresponded frequently with him, and once when he wrote in low spirits, not being well, I said in answer that he was to cheer up, but that if anything did happen to him he must let me know by appearing to me in my room, where we had often as boys together sat at night and indulged in a surreptitious pipe and chat. This letter

(I found subsequently) he received as he was starting to receive the sacrament from a clergyman who has since related the fact to me. Having done this he went to the entrenchments and never returned, as in a few hours afterwards, the storming of the Redan commenced.

He, on the captain of his company falling, took his place, and led his men bravely on. He had just led them within the walls, though already wounded in several places, when a bullet struck him on the right temple and he fell amongst heaps of others, where he was found in a sort of kneeling posture (being propped up by other dead bodies) thirty-six hours afterwards. His death took place, or rather he fell, though he may not have died immediately, on the 8th September, 1855.

That night I awoke suddenly, and saw facing the window of my room, by my bedside, surrounded by a light sort of phosphorescent mist as it were, my brother kneeling. I tried to speak but could not. I buried my head in the bedclothes, not at all afraid (because we had all been brought up not to believe in ghosts or apparitions), but simply to collect my ideas, because I had not been thinking or dreaming of him, and indeed had forgotten all about what I had written to him a fortnight before. I decided that it must be fancy, and the moonlight playing on a towel, or something out of place.

But on looking up there he was again, looking lovingly, imploringly, and sadly at me. I tried again to speak, but found myself tongue-tied. I could not utter a sound. I sprang out of bed, glanced through the window, and saw that there was no moon, but it was very dark and raining hard, by the sound against the panes. I turned, and still saw poor Oliver. I shut my eyes, walked through it and reached the door of the room. As I turned the handle, before leaving the room, I looked once more back. The apparition turned round his head slowly and again looked anxiously and lovingly at me, and I saw then for the first time a wound on the right temple with a red stream from it. His face was of a waxy pale tint, but transparent-looking, and so was the reddish mark. But it is almost impossible to describe his appearance. I only know I shall never forget it.

I left the room and went into a friend's room and lay on the sofa the rest of the night. I told him why. I told others in the house, but when I told my father he ordered me not to repeat such nonsense, and especially not to let my mother know.

On the Monday following he received a note from Sir Alexander Milne to say that the Redan was stormed, but no particulars. I told my friend to let me know if he saw the name among the killed and wounded before me. About a fortnight later he came to my bedroom in his mother's house in Athole Crescent, in Edinburgh, with a very grave face. I said, "I suppose it is to tell me the sad news I expect;" and he said, "Yes."

Both the colonel of the regiment and one or two officers who saw the body confirmed the fact that the appearance was much according to my description, and the death wound was exactly where I had seen it. But none could say whether he actually died at the moment. His appearance, if so, must have been some hours after death, as he appeared to me a few minutes after two in the morning.

Months later his small prayer-book *and the letter I had written to him* were returned to Inveresk, found in the inner breast pocket of the tunic which he wore at his death. I have them now.[16] — CAPTAIN G. F. RUSSELL COLT

☛ CORROBORATION LETTER BY MR. COLT'S SISTER, SEE PREVIOUS ENTRY): On the morning of September 9th, 1855, my brother, Mr. Colt, told myself, Captain Ferguson of the 42nd Regiment, since dead, and Major Borthwick of the Rifle Brigade (who is living) and others, that he had during the night wakened from sleep and seen, as he thought, my eldest brother, Lieut. Oliver Colt of the Royal Fusiliers (who was in the Crimea), standing between his bed and the door; that he saw he was wounded in more than one place—I remember he named the temple as one place—by bullet-wounds; that he roused himself, rushed to the door with closed eyes and looked back at the apparition, which stood between him and the bed. My father enjoined silence; lest my mother should be made uneasy; but shortly afterwards came the news of the fall of the Redan and my brother's death.

Two years afterwards my husband, Colonel Hope, invited my brother to dine with him; the former being still a lieutenant in the Royal Fusiliers, the latter an ensign in the Royal Welsh Fusiliers. While dining, they were talking of my eldest brother. My husband was about to describe his appearance when found, when my brother described what he had seen, and to the astonishment of all present, the description of the wounds tallied with the facts. My husband was my eldest brother's greatest friend, and was among those who saw the body as soon as it was found.[17] — MRS. HOPE

☛ CASE #4: My mother married, at a very early age, without the consent of her parents. My grandmother vowed that she would never see her daughter again. A few months after her marriage my mother was awakened at about 2 a.m. by a loud knocking at the door. To her great surprise my father did not wake. The knocking was resumed; my mother spoke to my father, but, as he still slept, she got up, opened the window and looked out, when, to her amazement, she saw her mother, in full Court dress, standing on the step and looking up at her. My mother called to her, but my grandmother, frowning and shaking her head, disappeared.

At this moment my father woke, and my mother told him what had happened. He went to the window, but saw nothing. My mother was sure that my grandmother, even at that late hour, had come to forgive her, and entreated my father to let her in. He went down and opened the door, but nobody was there. He assured my mother that she had been dreaming, and she at last believed that it was so.

The next morning the servants were questioned, but they had heard nothing, and the matter was dismissed from the minds of my parents till the evening, when they heard that my grandmother had been, in Court dress, at a ball the night before—I think at Kensington Palace, but of this I am not sure—that, feeling unwell, she had returned home, and after about an hour's illness, had died at 2 a.m. She had not mentioned my mother's name during her short illness.[18] — MISS SUMMERBELL

☛ CASE #5: In December, 1880, Mr. J. G. Keulemans was living with his family in Paris. The outbreak of an epidemic of small-pox caused him to remove three of his children, including a favourite little boy of five, to London, whence he received, in the course of the ensuing month, several letters [from their caretakers] giving an excellent account of their health.

> "On the 24th of January, 1881, at half-past seven in the morning, I was suddenly awoke by hearing his voice, as I fancied, very near me. I saw a bright, opaque, white mass before my eyes, and in the centre of this light I saw the face of my little darling, his eyes bright, his mouth smiling. The apparition, accompanied by the sound of his voice, was too short and too sudden to be called a dream: it was too clear, too decided, to be called an effect of imagination. So distinctly did I hear his voice that I looked round the room to see whether he was actually there. The sound I heard was that of extreme delight, such as only a happy child can utter. I thought it was the moment he woke up in London, happy and thinking of me. I said to myself, 'Thank God, little Isidore is happy as always.'"

Mr. Keulemans describes the ensuing day as one of peculiar

brightness and cheerfulness. He took a long walk with a friend, with whom he dined; and was afterwards playing a game at billiards, when he again saw the apparition of his child. This made him seriously uneasy, and in spite of having received within three days the assurance of the child's perfect health, he expressed to his wife a conviction that he was dead. Next day a letter arrived saying that the child was ill; but the father was convinced that this was only an attempt to break the news; and, in fact, the child had died, after a few hours' illness, at the exact time of the first apparition.[19]

☛ CASE #6: I give the annexed narrative of the apparition of a deceased or dying person on the authority of my mother, the late Mrs. Elizabeth A. Grignon, wife of the late William Stanford Grignon, of Upton, near Montego Bay, Jamaica, Esq., and youngest sister of the well-known counsel, Sir James Scarlett, afterwards the first Lord Abinger. I received the account from her, and have had it confirmed by my late sister, Miss Elizabeth Scarlett Grignon, who had often heard it from our mother. I may say that my mother was a cool-headed, accurate person.

About the year 1820 she was resident at Upton, in Jamaica, and had as an upper nurse in her family a Mrs. Duchoux, an English woman who had married a Frenchman; with the exception of this nurse, every servant in the house was black or brown. One morning my mother observed that this woman seemed much depressed, so much so that she pressed her for the reason. She said she was sure she should hear of the death of an aunt of hers resident in England. Her statement was as follows:

She had got into bed, but not yet fallen asleep, and had before this locked the door of her bedroom. A negro girl was sleeping on a mattress on the floor of her room. Near the foot of her bed was a small table on which stood a candle under a shade. Looking up, she saw a female figure in a night-dress, standing with its back towards her at the foot of the bed, near the table with the light on it, and holding a roll of paper in its hand. As she looked, the figure turned its face round towards her, and she at once recognised an aunt then living in England. The figure then moved towards the door and seemed to pass out of it or disappear.

Mrs. Duchoux was not at all frightened, but jumped out of bed and found the door still locked on the inside, and the negro girl asleep. She was quite sure that it was her aunt's and no other face which she saw, and that she should hear of her death. My mother told her that she must have dreamed the whole scene; but nevertheless was so far impressed by the woman's reiterated assurance that she had been wide awake, that she at once made a note of the statement, with the date.

On the arrival of the packet [ship] which left England shortly after the date of the apparition a letter reached Mrs. Duchoux, informing her that her aunt had died just about the date of the vision, and had in her will left her £100. I cannot say that the time of the apparition coincided exactly with the last moments of the deceased. I doubt if this was inquired into at the time. But I remember that my mother stated that the woman had not previously heard anything to make her anxious about her aunt.[20] — REV. W. S. GRIGNON

☛ CASE #7: In 1833, Sarah and Margaret Jardine, daughters of a barrister on the Western Circuit, were girls of about ten and twelve respectively. They lived with their parents in a house in the suburbs of London, and their grandfather and grandmother on the opposite side of the road. Their grandmother was a woman of decided character and very firm will, and between her and the children there was strong affection.

One night as the children lay in their four-post bed, sleeping as they did with a rush light in the room, Sarah saw her grandmother in her night-dress standing at the foot of the bed, looking at them with a pleased smile on her face. She moved round the bed, keeping her eyes constantly fixed upon the children, till she passed behind the curtain at the head of the bed on Sarah's side, and seemed to sit down on the chair that was placed there. Sarah raised herself up and drew back the curtain in order to speak to her, when, to her great surprise, she saw no one there. She was not at all frightened, and awoke her sister, saying, "Grandmamma is in the room." They both got up and looked about for her, and finding that there really was no one in the room, Margaret said that her sister must have been dreaming, and scolded her for awaking her.

In the morning they were awoke by their father, who told them that a dreadful thing had happened, that their grandmamma had died in the course of the night. She had been ailing, but nothing serious had been apprehended until her son was sent for, after the children had gone to bed. On hearing that her grandmother was dead, Sarah became much terrified at the thought of having seen a ghost and gave a violent scream, without saying anything of the cause of her fright.

A day or two afterwards her sister told what Sarah had seen, and in order to reassure her they tried to persuade her that it had been a dream. But she herself was quite certain that it was not; and for long afterwards she had such a dread of seeing the apparition again that they dared not leave her alone at night. After the lapse of more than forty years she still retains the most vivid remembrance of the whole incident.[21] — MISS SARAH JARDINE

☛ CASE #8: (Mrs. Hunter had had a friend from whom she had parted in coldness, and whom she had not since seen or corresponded with.)

Poor Z. was very far from my thoughts, when one night I had just got into bed. The fire burned brightly, and there was my usual night-light. I was placing my head on the pillows, when I beheld, close to the side of the bed, and on a level with it, Z.'s head, and the same wistful look on his face which it had worn when we parted years before.

Starting up, I cried out, "What do you want?" I did not fear; anger was my feeling. Slowly it retreated, and just as it disappeared in the shadow of the wall, a bright spark of light shone for a few seconds, and slowly expired.

A few days after my sister wrote, "You will have heard of poor Z.'s death, on his way to the South of France." I had heard nothing about him for years. Special reasons prevented my inquiring particularly into the precise moment of his death. Strange to say, my bedfellow [a dog] was his great pet among my children; she, however, slept through this strange interview.[22] — MRS. HUNTER

☛ CASE #9: (Mrs. Hunter's husband had had a Scotch wet-nurse of the old fashioned sort, more devoted to him than even to her own children. Mrs. Hunter, soon after her marriage, made acquaintance with this nurse, Mrs. Macfarlane, who paid her several visits during Mr. Hunter's absence in India. In June, 1857, Mrs. Hunter, who was travelling to a health-resort, confided to Mrs. Macfarlane's keeping a box of valuables. One evening in the following August Mrs. Hunter was entertaining some friends; but having occasion to return to the dining-room for a moment, she passed the open door of her bedroom, and felt irresistibly impelled to look in; and there on the bed was a large coffin, and sitting at the foot of it was a tall old woman steadfastly regarding it.)

Returning to my friends, I announced the vision, which was received with shouts of laughter, in which after a time I joined. However, I had seen what I have described, and, moreover, could have told the very dress the old woman wore. When my friends left, and I had paid my usual last visit to the nursery, my nurse looked odd and *"distraite,"* and to my astonishment followed me onto the landing.

"O ma'am," she began, "I feel so queer, such a strange thing happened. At seven o'clock I went to the kitchen for hot water, and when I came out I saw a tall old woman coming downstairs, and I stopped to let her pass, but, ma'am, there was something strange about her, so I turned to look after her. The hall door was wide open, and she was making for it, when in a moment she melted away. I can swear I saw her, and can tell you her very dress, a big, black poke bonnet and a checked black and white shawl."

(This description of the dress exactly corresponded with what Mrs. Hunter had herself seen. Mrs. Hunter laughed the matter off, and did not even think of connecting her own vision with the nurse's. About half-an-hour afterwards, when in bed, she heard a piercing scream from her little daughter, aged five, followed by loud, frightened tones, and she then heard the nurse soothing the child.)

"Next morning little E___ was full of her wrongs. She said that a 'naughty old woman was sitting at the table and staring at her, and that made her scream.' Nurse told me that she found the child wide awake, sitting up in bed, pointing to the table, and crying out, Go away, go away, naughty old woman!' There was no one there. Nurse had been in bed some time and the door was locked. My child's vision I treated as I did her nurse's, and dosed [dismissed] both. However, a day or two afterwards, I received a letter from Mrs. Macfarlane's son, announcing her death, and telling me how her last hours were disturbed by anxiety for my husband and his family. My nurse, on being told the news, exclaimed, 'Good Lord, it was her I saw that night, and her very dress!' I never ascertained the exact hour of her death. My letter of inquiry and condolence was never answered, though my box was duly sent to me."[23] — MRS. HUNTER

☛ CASE #10: Forty-two or three years ago my father was with a detachment of his regiment, the Royal Artillery, stationed at Montreal, Canada. He had left his mother some months before in England in an indifferent state of health. One evening he was sitting at his desk, writing to her, when my mother, looking up from her work, was startled to see his mother looking over his shoulder, seemingly intent on the letter. My mother gave a cry of alarm, and on my father turning round the apparition vanished.

On the same evening I and my brother (aged about six and five years) were in bed, watching the bright moonlight, when suddenly we saw a figure, a lady with her hands folded on her breast, walking slowly, between the bed and the window, backwards and forwards. She wore a cap with a frill tied under her chin, and a dressing-gown of the appearance of white flannel, her white hair being neatly arranged. She continued to walk, it seemed to me, fully five minutes, and then was gone. We did not cry out, and were not even alarmed, but after her disappearance we said to each other, "What a nice, kind lady!" and then went to sleep.

The children mentioned what they had seen to their mother next morning, but were told not to talk about it. The news of their grandmother's death on that same evening arrived a few weeks afterwards. "I may add," Mr. Colchester concludes, "that neither I nor my brother had ever seen our grandmother till that evening, nor knew of what my mother had seen till years after. The apparition I saw is as palpably before me now as it was forty years since."[24] — MR. C. COLCHESTER

☛ CASE #11: The passage from Bermuda to Halifax is in certain seasons hazardous, and in 1830 a [British military] transport, containing some two hundred and twenty men, was lost at sea between these two ports. Two officers of the regiment [Lieutenants Creigh and Liston] to which the detachment had belonged had, in a half-jesting way, made a sort of promise that whoever died first should come back if he could and let the other know whether there was another world. This conversation was heard by the narrator, as it took place in his presence, perhaps a year before the events happened, though not remembered till afterwards.

Liston embarked in charge of the detachment, and had been gone about a fortnight, when Creigh, who had one night left the mess early and retired to bed, and was beginning to close his eyes, saw his door open and Liston enter. Forgetting his absence and thinking he had come to pull him out of bed (for practical joking was then more common in the army than it is now), he cried, "No, no, damn it, Liston, don't, old fellow! I'm tired! Be off!"

But the vision came nearer the bed foot, and Creigh then saw that Liston looked as if very ill (for it was bright moonlight), and that his hair seemed wet and hung down over his face like a drowned man's. The apparition moved its head mournfully; and when Creigh in surprise sat up, rubbed his eyes, and looked again, it was gone.

Still Creigh avers that all this time he had no idea of its being a spectre, and, believing that he had seen Liston himself, he went to sleep. In the morning he related the occurrence, when he recollected, but not till then, Liston's absence on duty from the island.[25] — MR. COLCHESTER [FATHER OF THE NARRATOR IN THE PREVIOUS ACCOUNT]

☛ CASE #12: Some years ago, when residing at Walthamstow, in Essex, my wife and self became intimate with a lady and gentleman who had become temporarily our near neighbours. On one occasion, when they were dining with us quite *en famille*, my friend and I, on repairing to the drawing-room, not long after the ladies had left us, were surprised to find that his wife had been suddenly taken with a kind of fainting fit, and had been obliged to return home accompanied by one of our female servants.

My wife, as a matter of course, went the next day to inquire after her friend, who then told her that the cause of her sudden indisposition had been the appearance, as if in her actual person standing before her, of one of her two sisters, who were then residing with their mother at Beyrout [Beirut], in Syria, which had greatly alarmed her. Communication by telegraph had not then been established, and by post it was much slower than at present.

Many days had therefore elapsed before the lady received letters from Beyrout, but on their arrival they conveyed the intelligence that her sister had died on the day and, allowing for the difference in the time, at about the hour of her appearance to our friend.[26] — MR. P. H. BERTHON

☛ CASE #13: Some thirty years ago, or more, an English regiment was quartered in Upper Canada. One of the officers, a Mr. W., admired a young Canadian lady very much, and was a great deal at her father's house. He was a great rider, and in one race had received an injury to his leg which crushed the bone, and produced a slight halt.

On a certain day Mr. W. rode and won a hurdle race; the young lady, Miss H., had been present at the race. She then wore a very pretty rose, and Mr. W. suggested beforehand that it should be given to the winner. He claimed it immediately, and also engaged her for two or three dances at a ball to be given by her father that evening.

Evening came and the guests arrived, but no Mr. W. Miss H. was rather vexed at his lateness, and spoke of it to one or two gentlemen, particularly when the dances began which she had promised to give him. But as she felt sure he would appear, she refused to dance them with others. Presently, as she was standing and talking to three of these gentlemen, Mr. D. A., Mr. R. P., and another, they all saw Mr. W. come into the room, look steadily and calmly at her, and pass into the dining-room. He was dressed in ordinary evening dress, in his red shell jacket, and there was nothing remarkable about his appearance. She thought it strange that he did not come to speak to her, and alluded to it to the other gentlemen, saying she thought Mr. W. was really the rudest man she ever saw, and laughing, followed him into the dining-room. There, however, he was not. The other gentlemen had seen him as well as she, and, I believe, her mother also. The time was quarter-past ten.

The whole affair piqued and vexed her a good deal. The next morning her father came hastily into the room, and asked her if she had not seen Mr. W. the night before. She said "yes," and that he had acted very oddly in only just appearing for a moment, and in not even speaking to her. Her father then told her that on that morning his body had been found in the river. His watch had stopped at quarter-past ten, which was the hour at which he had been seen in the ball-room. The rose Miss H. gave him was still in his button-hole.[27] — MISS PEARD

☛ CASE #14: On the 5th of September, 1867, there was a [sailing] regatta on the Shannon [River]. Two young friends of ours (Irwin and Charles Coghlan) had a yacht to sail. On the 4th (a stormy day), they sailed to the opposite shore for a young friend they expected; in midway the squall upset their yacht, and they, with their boy, were drowned. The writer of the subjoined account [see the next entry below] is my daughter. She and her sister thought the two young gentlemen were coming to bring them in their yacht to their father's, for a party there next evening.

On the 5th my daughters were going in my carriage—a distance of ten miles; when half-way they were stopped by Mr. Coghlan's servant with a hurried note, giving the sad report of the loss of his two sons, the boy, and the boat. The apparition was at the same hour as their loss. They also appeared to their mother, who now lives in Rathgar, Dublin [Ireland], a widow.[28] — REV. CANON EYRE

☛ CORROBORATION LETTER [SEE PREVIOUS ENTRY]: With reference to the apparition of the two gentlemen which I saw, the facts are as follows: I was in our dining-room (Portumna Rectory) about eleven o'clock on the morning of the 4th September, 1867, when, on looking out of the window, I saw the two young [yachting] gentlemen in question coming in at the avenue gate, and a boy with them. I then left the room to tell my mother they were coming. My sister, who was in the room at the time, did not see them. It was about the time they met with their sad end.[29] — MISS EYRE

☛ CASE #15: During the Indian mutiny my brother was serving (as ensign) in the 72nd Highlanders. At that time I was an undergraduate of T.C.D. and living at Sandycove, near Kingstown. One night, about two o'clock, I was reading by the fire when I heard myself distinctly called by my brother, the tone of his voice being somewhat raised and urgent. Looking round I saw his head and the upper part of his body quite plainly. He appeared to be looking at me, and was about seven or eight feet distant. I looked steadily at him for about half a minute, when he seemed gradually to fade into a mist and disappear.

The date of this occurrence I unfortunately lost note of, but upon my brother's return from India, and my casually mentioning that I had so seen him, we talked the matter over, and both came to the conclusion that the apparition coincided with a dangerous attack of illness in which my brother suddenly awoke with the impression that he was suffocating, at which moment he thought of me. The attack was brought on by sleeping during a forced march through a country great part of which was under water.

This is the only apparition that I have experienced, and there was no anxiety on my mind which could have given rise to it, as we had quite recently had a letter from my brother, written in good health and spirits.[30] — CANON SHERLOCK

☛ CASE #16: When my son H. was a boy, I one day saw him off to school, watching him [walk] down the grove, and then went into the library to sit, a room I rarely used at that time of the day. Shortly after, he appeared, walking over the wall opposite the window. The wall was about thirteen feet distant from the window, and low, so that when my son stood on it, his face was on a level with mine, and close to me. I hastily threw up the sash, and called to ask why he had returned from school, and why he was there; he did not answer, but looked full at me with a frightened expression, and dropped down the other side of the wall and disappeared.

Never doubting but that it was some boyish trick, I called a servant to tell him to come to me, but not a trace of him was to be found, though there was no screen or place of concealment. I myself searched with the same result.

As I sat still wondering where and how he had so suddenly disappeared, a cab drove up with H. in an almost unconscious state, brought home by a friend and schoolfellow, who said that during a dictation lesson he had suddenly fallen backward over his seat, calling out in a shrill voice, "Mamma will know," and becoming insensible.

He was ill that day, prostrate the next; but our doctor could not account for the attack, nor did anything follow to throw any light on his appearance to me. That the time of his attack exactly corresponded with that at which I saw his figure, was proved both by his master and class-mates. (The Rev. H. Swithinbank, eldest son of the writer of the above, explains that the point at which the figure was seen was in a direct line between the house [situated in Summerhill Terrace, Newcastle-on-Tyne] and the school, but that "no animal but a bird could come direct that way," and that the walking distance between the two places was nearly a mile. He describes his brother as of a nervous temperament, but his mother as just the opposite, a calm person, who has never in her life had any other similar experience.)[31] — MRS. SWITHINBANK

☛ CASE #17: [Author-editor's note: The anonymous individuals named A., X., Y., and Z., in the following case were then living in four separate European countries. L.S.]

On the night of August 23-24, 1882, "I woke," says A, "after midnight with a sense of great anxiety, a sense that a spiritual message of vital importance had gone to X. by mistake." A.'s first letter, written to X. early in the morning of August 24th, cannot be found; but on the receipt of that letter, X. wrote, "Your letter astonished me. Yesterday morning early, before it was light, I woke up at with just this feeling of warning. Something was saying to me,

'This is for the last time; it is wrong and must not be.' In the darkness it gave me a horrible feeling.

This feeling of moral warning was vaguely connected with A. in X.'s mind. The same post which brought X.'s letter to A., brought also letters from Y. and Z. Y., a correspondent from whom A. only heard about once a year, wrote soon after midnight of August 24-25. His letter, which was in metre, expressed a vague but strong feeling of anxious sympathy. In point of date Z.'s letter was more precisely coincident with A.'s primary impression; for it conveyed an inquiry as to A.'s well-being, prompted by an alarming dream which had visited Mrs. Z. on the night of August 23-24.

"I seemed first," says Mrs. Z. in a subsequent letter, "to have a vague feeling of your presence; then to see you in a central spot of light with darkness everywhere else. I stood in the edge of the darkness, looking at you with sympathy, pity, and a little morbid curiosity which disturbed me, and made me wish that you would speak and break the spell that held me waiting (as I felt) for a clear revelation of what was lying heavily upon your soul. You raised your head as I watched you, and turned unseeing eyes towards me. The expression was of hopeless, despairing bewilderment. You had the appearance of a person who knows himself to be alone. As your eyes passed over me again, still unseeing, I knew that I was there in spirit only, and was about to hear and see and know things that I should not. I forced myself away into the darkness, and then into waking."

"To me alone, perhaps," says A., "these matters carry much significance. I was greatly troubled at that time about a case of conscience, which I could not solve, and which all my will prompted me to solve wrongly." (We may add that none of these friends, though linked with A. by close bonds of sympathy, were cognisant of the case of conscience in question.)[32] — NAMES WITHHELD BY THE S.P.R.

☛ CASE #18: It was a very wet Sunday afternoon in 1835 or '36, Mrs. Clay being at home and Mr. Clay at service in the gaol where he was chaplain.
   Rather before his usual time Mrs. Clay heard her husband return, enter the house by the back door under the window of the room she was in, hang up his coat and hat, saw him enter the room, and, standing at the door, heard him remark what a wet day it was, and then, after her reply, he went upstairs. As he did not return, Mrs. Clay ran upstairs to seek him, and concluded he had gone out again as she could not find him.
   A little later the whole occurrence was re-enacted, and on her asking her husband why he had gone out again, he assured her he had not done so, but had then only just come back from service. This time it was the real Mr. Clay.[33] — MRS. CLAY

☛ CASE #19: On one occasion . . . Mr. P. saw a figure in his studio. He was sitting before his easel with his back to the door one winter's morning, when, as he assured us, he felt that someone was in the room, and, turning round, he saw the apparition a few feet from him. This intrusion appears to have annoyed him, and he uttered an impatient exclamation, upon which the figure slowly vanished.[34] — THE JOURNAL

☛ CASE #20: Two gentlemen were travelling together in a post chaise one Christmas Eve, on some date between 1820 and 1830. The country was not known to them, and the difficulty of finding their way was increased by a heavy fall of snow. The coachman appears to have taken the wrong turning at some cross-roads, and only discovered his mistake on arriving at a house whose brilliantly lit up interior betokened that some Christmas festivities were being carried on within.
   The elder of the two gentlemen walked up to the door, and asked his way of the master of the house, who came out to meet him. He was courteously invited to enter, and, on his declining, a servant was sent with him to conduct the chaise into the right road. When, on his leaving them, one of the occupants of the carriage placed a crown piece in the servant's hand, it appeared to them both to fall through the hand on to the snow, and the man, at the same time, mysteriously to vanish.
   On arriving at their destination, the travellers learnt that no house now stood in the locality, which they described; the house, which had formerly occupied the spot, had been pulled down after a terrible crime which had been committed there on Christmas Eve

many years before. On examining the scene of their night's adventure on the day following, the travellers found in the snow the wheel marks of their carriage leading up to the spot where this house had once stood.[35] — *THE JOURNAL*

☛ CASE #21: In the early spring of 1852, Mr. X. Z. went to reside in a large old house near C____. Mr. X. Z. only occupied part of the house, the remainder being inhabited by a friend of his own, Mr. G____ and some pupils. Mr. G____ had occupied the house about a year before Mr. X. Z.'s arrival; and two servants had, in that interval, given him warning, on account of strange noises which they had heard. The house, which is a large one, was let at an extremely low rent.

On the night of the 22nd September, 1852, at about one a.m., Mr. X. Z. went up to his bedroom. The house was in complete darkness, and he took no candle with him; but on opening a door which led into the passage where his room was situated, he found the whole passage filled with light. The light was white like daylight, or electric light, and brighter than moonlight. At first Mr. X. Z. was dazzled by the light, but when his eyes became used to it he saw, standing at the end of the passage, about 35 feet from him, an old man in a figured dressing-gown. The face of this old man, which Mr. X. Z. saw quite clearly, was most hideous; so evil was it that both expression and features were firmly imprinted on his memory. As Mr. X. Z. was still looking, figure and light both vanished, and left him in pitch darkness.

Mr. X. Z. did not, at that time, believe in ghosts, and his first thought was (he had lately read [David] Brewster's *Natural Magic*, and had been much impressed with the striking cases of spectral illusion recorded in that work) that he was the subject of a hallucination. He did not feel at all frightened, but resolved to take a dose of physic in the morning.

The next day, however, remembering the tales told by the two servants who had left, he made inquiries in the village as to the past history of the house. At first he could find out nothing, but finally an old lawyer told him that he had heard that the grandfather of the present owner of the house had strangled his wife and then cut his own throat, on the very spot where Mr. X. Z. had seen the figure. The lawyer was unable to give the exact date of this occurrence, but Mr. X. Z. consulted the parish register, and found the two deaths recorded as having taken place on the 22nd September 179?,—(the precise year he could not now [in 1882] remember). The lawyer added he had heard that the old man was in the habit of walking about the house in a figured dressing-gown, and had the reputation of being half an imbecile.

On the 22nd September, 1853, a friend of Mr. G____'s arrived to make a short stay. He came down to breakfast the following morning, looking very pale, and announced his intention of terminating his visit immediately. Mr. G____ rather angrily insisted on knowing the reason of his sudden departure; and the young man, when pressed, reluctantly explained that he had been kept awake all night by the sound of cryings and groanings, blasphemous oaths, and cries of despair. The door of his bedroom opened on to the spot where the murderer had committed suicide; and it was in the bedroom which he had occupied that the murder had been committed.

In 1856 Mr. X. Z. and his friend had occasion to call on their landlord, who lived in London. On being shewn into the room Mr. X. Z. at once recognised a picture above the mantel-piece as being that of the figure which he had seen. The portrait, however, had been taken when the man was younger, and the expression was not so hideous. He called Mr. G____'s attention to the painting, saying: "That is the man whom I saw."

The landlord, on being asked whom the portrait represented, replied that it was the portrait of his grandfather, adding that he had been no credit to the family.

Doors also opened and shut in the house without apparent cause; bells were rung in the middle of the night, causing all the household to turn out and search for burglars; and the inmates of the house declared that unseen footsteps had followed them down the whole length of the passage already mentioned.[36] — MR. X. Z. [NAMES WITHHELD BY THE S.P.R.]

☛ CASE #22: The [haunted] house [in question] itself is an old rectory in the north of Ireland [in the town of D____]. In 1818 or 1819, Miss A____, the eldest daughter of the then incumbent, died, and it is this lady whom the apparition which has been seen in the house is supposed to represent. Into the circumstances attending her death, which lend a tragic interest to the commonplace details of the following narrative, we are not at liberty to enter. But this much is clear, that Miss A____'s life had been an unhappy one—narrow in its interests, and repressed in its sympathies.

After Dr. A____ left there had been six rectors in succession before Mr. G____, the father of our informants. Miss H. G____ informed us that she had heard from Mr. H____, one of their predecessors, that strange noises, which he attributed to rats, were heard in the house during his residence there. Since this gentleman's departure, however, the house had been partially rebuilt, and there appear to have been no rats in Mr. G____'s time.

Miss H. G____ and her sister had heard when they first came to the house that it was haunted by Miss A____'s ghost; but nothing unusual appears to have been *seen* in the house until 1861 or 1862. The old rectory is at the present date (1882) occupied by a respectable farmer and his family. We understand that these persons have not witnessed anything unusual in the house, but we have as yet found no opportunity for detailed investigation.

The following is a copy of a letter written to us by Miss G____, one of four sisters.

> We lived for twelve years in what was considered to be a "haunted house." It was an old country rectory, in which, forty years before, a terrible tragedy had occurred. We took possession of the place in October, and nothing remarkable occurred until one evening about Christmas time—I forget the exact date. After family prayers, when all our party, except my mother and father and myself, had retired, I left the dining-room, and went across the hall into the drawing-room. There was no light in the front hall, but a hanging lamp in the back passage gave some little light. The drawing-room fire was almost, but not quite, out. There was a white marble mantelpiece, and before the fire-place stood a chair, in which one of us had been sitting before tea. As I entered the room, a figure rose up quietly from that chair and approached me. I thought I recognised my sister, and said, "Are you here, H____? I thought you had gone to bed." The figure advanced and came so close to me that I put out my hand and said, "Don't knock me down." Still no answer, and the figure was gone.
>
> I returned to the dining-room and said to my father and mother, "If there is a ghost in D____ I have seen it just now." They laughed at the idea, but I insisted that I had seen something for which I could not account, and was determined to investigate it. I therefore took a lamp and searched drawing-room, hall, and passages, satisfied myself that the servants had gone to bed, and then went to the rooms upstairs occupied by my sisters and by some friends who were staying with us at the time. Not one of them had been in the drawing-room after prayers.
>
> . . . A few evenings afterwards I opened a door which led from the back passage to the top of the kitchen stairs. A figure seemed to rush up the stairs to meet me, went past me, and when I looked after it into the lighted passage behind me, it was gone. For this incident also I could not satisfactorily account.
>
> This is all I saw, but I, as well as other members of our household, often heard strange noises, as of dragging furniture, heavy footsteps,

etc., especially at night.

We investigated these over and over again, and once I detected that the sound of a clanking chain was caused by a reverberation from the stable. There were no rats in the house while we were there. June 7th, 1882.

Three other points I should note before leaving this subject.

1st. The figure at D_____ was generally seen about the shortest and longest days of the year.

2nd. Some old parishioners who remembered Miss A_____, the Archdeacon's daughter, whose mysterious death occurred in 1819, remarked to us that my sister H_____'s figure was singularly like hers.

3rd. We came by degrees to consider the mysterious figure which occasionally appeared, as a personage in the house, friendly toward us, but quite unconnected with our concerns. We always spoke of her as "Miss A_____." She never came to warn us, nor to communicate with us. We had towards her a kindly feeling, perhaps mixed with awe, but we were not in the least afraid of her. Servants who were at different times in our employment could give information about the appearances and sounds in that house, but it would be vain to expect them to reply to letters. June 19th, 1882. — I. F. G.

Mrs. B_____, the writer of the letter given below, is a friend of the G_____ family, and has, at their request, communicated to us the following incident.

I am not quite sure what year it was that during one of many visits to my friends at D_____, I saw the "ghost" of the house. It was, I think, 1861, about the end of September. We were a large merry party just finished tea in the dining-room, and were all proceeding from it across the hall to the drawing-room; the doors of the rooms facing each other. I, being the guest, was the first to leave the dining-room and enter the drawing-room, the last of the party following, carrying the lamp, so that all the light was behind us, though still very strong.

When I opened the drawing-room door I started back on seeing what I thought was a lady, or one of the daughters of the house, seated on a sofa by the fire on the opposite side of the room from the door (although I knew everyone staying in the house was immediately behind me), and said, "Who's that?" "Oh!" said someone, "it must be Miss A_____," the name by which the ghost of the house was known.

In a minute the room was full of bright light, and there was nothing to be seen of the appearance which a moment before looked so like a lady comfortably seated by the fire. I had never been much of a believer in what I had been told of the ghost of this house, and even still think it may have been a combination of shadows and reflections; and the seeing of it thus did not inspire me with any feeling of alarm, as I have often stayed in the house since; but I have never, either before or since, seen any shadows take so tangible and substantial a form as that did.

During several of my visits I have heard various people, both visitors and inmates, say they had either seen or heard, or rather I should say felt, the presence of the same shadowy lady at all hours and places in the house. July 25th, 1882 — T. M. B

Next, we have Miss H. G____'s evidence, as given to Mr. Sidgwick and Mr. Podmore.

Some time in June, 1861 or 1862, I was coming up the stairs, in the dusk, about nine p.m. As I reached the first landing, I saw just in front of me, apparently about two yards off me, or nearer, standing against the light—which came through the landing window—a grey figure, which I supposed to be one of my sisters. I stopped, and said, "Are you coming on?" No reply; and I made a step forward. The figure vanished; and I felt a slight shock. It was as if I had suddenly come upon my own figure in a mirror. Had there been a mirror there, I should have certainly supposed that to be the case. I went upstairs, and told the others what I had seen.

Miss L. G____, who never saw the apparition herself, has communicated by letter her recollection of what she heard from her brother and others. We have been unable to trace the two servants herein referred to.

In the year 1862 I was staying at Broomfield, after my grandmother's death. Some time towards the end of September my brother John found us there, and told us he had seen the "ghost at D____," but had not told them at home.

He said that one evening he had driven my eldest brother, William, to the station at D____ for the 6:20 train. On his return he left the horse and car, as usual, in the stable-yard with the servant, and was going into the house, when, on passing the drawing-room windows, he saw, standing in that next [to] the hall-door, a figure which he at first took to be one of his sisters. Suddenly he thought that the figure was not dressed in mourning, as his sisters would be, and he stepped back off the doorsteps to look at it again. She was standing with her hands up, as if she had just shut down the lower sash of the window, and was looking out between her arms. He could not in the dusk discern the features, but saw the hair parted on the forehead, and that the dress was *grey*. It was not any of his sisters, or any of the servants. He left the figure standing in the same attitude, and went into the house, and into the drawing-room direct. No one could have left the room without meeting him in the hall. The room was vacant, and when he went into the parlour opposite he found all the members of the family who were at home seated round the tea-table. The servant whose business it was to close the drawing-room windows (who was also in black) and all the other servants were, he satisfied himself, below stairs. The breadth of the area, close to the edge of which he stood to look at the figure, was, I fancy, about eight feet; it could not have been more than ten.

The hour was about, probably after seven o'clock, the date about the 18th September—I am not sure of the exact day. John was eighteen, in good health and spirits. He died in 1865. He did not tell anyone at home at the time, as he said, when he found the room empty, he felt "eerie," but he told me he wandered through the house the rest of the evening trying to see the figure again, but could not. The only other time he was conscious of a "presence" was, he told me, one day when, coming out of one of the rooms on the upper lobby, he felt as if some person brushed closely by him, but he saw nothing.

Several years afterwards—I think about 1868—we had a girl named Susan Taylor living with us as our maid. We were annoyed by a little girl from the village of _____, whom we were trying to train as a servant, telling the servants that the house was haunted, and saying she was afraid to go upstairs in the evening.

Speaking of this to me, Susan said that she did not believe in ghosts; that she had been washing out the upper lobby one evening towards dusk, hurrying to get it done, as she thought I should be displeased at her doing it so late; she looked up, and saw, as she thought, my youngest sister cross the lobby. She said, "I thought I saw Miss Caroline go from your room into Miss H_____'s, with a shawl over her head. I was afraid she had the toothache, and I got up and followed her, but when I went into Miss H_____'s room there was no one there." And she continued: "That shews the nonsense about a ghost in that room, for if there had been one I should have seen it." Susan added that she, like myself, was accustomed to be through the house at all hours of the day and night, sick-nursing. June 13th, 1882. L. E. G_____.

We of subjoin an account, given to us by Miss H. G_____, of phenomena observed by two other persons, with whom it is no longer possible to communicate, and of various strange sounds heard by herself.

Sometime early in the sixties Mr. John H_____ came over to call on us one summer's morning. As he passed the drawing-room windows, of which there were two, to go into the house, he saw, as he thought, myself sitting in the drawing-room. He waved his hand to the figure, went in at the open door, and proceeded straight to the drawing-room. There was no one there. When he met me, Mr. H_____ told me what he had seen.

In October, 1862, Mr. F_____ had been playing by himself in the drawing-room. It had grown dusk, and thinking it was probably time to dress for dinner, he went out into the hall, and groped about on the shelf, where they were usually kept, for a candle. He found a candle, and whilst feeling for the matches, he heard the light step, as he thought, of one of us coming down rapidly from the top of the house. When the step, as he thought, was near him, he called, "Is it one of you girls? Can you find me some matches?" The noise ceased and he found no one there. He at once mentioned the incident to my brother.

([Note added here later:] Mr. F_____ told us that he distinctly saw a girlish figure coming downstairs on the occasion here mentioned, that he addressed her first as one of the ladies of the family, then as a servant; and that it was only when he walked close up to the figure that it vanished. He heard distinctly the rustle of a dress and footfalls, as the figure came quickly downstairs to meet him.)

On another occasion, when I was away from home, and two of my sisters occupied the room next to mine, Mr. F____ occupied the guest-room below mine. In the morning he asked my sisters what they had been about in the night; he heard noises of furniture, etc., being moved in their room, which had prevented him from sleeping.

Strange sounds—generally as of furniture being moved or some person moving about in the room—were frequently heard in my room. The following were the most memorable instances:

1. In 1863, on a summer's morning about 10 a.m., the door of the room being ajar, I heard what I supposed to be the noise made by the housemaid moving about in the room; and accordingly pushed the door further open and stepped into the room, calling out, "Margaret, I want you"; but found no one there.
2. In November, of 1872, about two p.m., when we were on the point of leaving the house, having just gone up to my room, I heard a step come from the room opposite along the passage, and called out, "Who's there?" Finding no one I ran immediately down into the drawing-room and found my sister and brother there (the only persons then in the house, except servants); and then went into the kitchen and ascertained that none of the servants had been upstairs.
3. In the winter of 1864 (I think), while I was sitting in my room with my back to the door, I had a vague impression as of someone entering the room. I then heard a loud noise as of the crack of a whip on wood, three times in succession, as though the whip had been struck first on a wardrobe and then on each of two windows opposite the door—as though the striker were going round the room from the door, towards me, July 6th, 1882.[37] — H. G.

☛ CASE #23: [A case concerning Mrs. A. was of an alarming character.] On the 30th of December, about four o'clock in the afternoon, Mrs. A. came down stairs into the drawing-room, which she had quitted only a few minutes before, and on entering the room she saw her husband, as she supposed, standing with his back to the fire. As he had gone out to take a walk about half an hour before, she was surprised to see him there, and asked him why he had returned so soon. The figure looked fixedly at her with a serious and thoughtful expression of countenance but did not speak. Supposing that his mind was absorbed in thought, she sat down in an arm chair near the fire, and within two feet at most of the figure, which she still saw standing before her.

As its eyes, however, still continued to be fixed upon her, she said after the lapse of a few minutes, "Why don't you speak?" The figure immediately moved off towards the window at the farther end of the room, with its eyes still gazing on her, and it passed so very close to her in doing so, that she was struck by the circumstance of hearing no step nor sound, nor feeling her clothes brushed against, nor even any agitation in the air. Although she was now convinced that the figure was not her husband, yet she never for a moment supposed that it was any thing supernatural, and was soon convinced that it was a spectral illusion.

As soon as this conviction had established itself in her mind . . . the figure had retreated to the window, where it disappeared. Mrs. A. immediately followed it, shook the curtains and examined the window, the impression having been so distinct and forcible that she was unwilling to believe that it was not a reality. Finding, however, that the figure had no natural means of escape, she was convinced that she had seen a spectral apparition . . . and consequently felt no alarm or agitation. The appearance was seen in bright day light, and lasted four or five minutes. When the figure stood close to her it concealed the real objects behind it, and the apparition was fully as vivid as the reality.[38] — DR. BREWSTER

☛ CASE #24: . . . On the 4th of January 1830, at about ten o'clock at night, when Mr. and Mrs. A. were sitting in the drawing-room, Mr. A. took up the poker to stir the fire, and when he was in the act of doing this, Mrs. A. exclaimed, "Why there's the cat in the room!" "Where?" asked Mr. A. "There, close to you," she replied. "Where?" he repeated. "Why on the rug to be sure, between yourself and the coal scuttle."

Mr. A., who had still the poker in his hand, pushed it in the direction mentioned, "Take care," cried Mrs. A., "take care, you are hitting her with the poker."

Mr. A. again asked her to point out exactly where she saw the cat. She replied, "Why sitting up there close to your feet on the rug: She is looking at me. It is Kitty—come here Kitty?" There were two cats in the house, one of which went by this name, and they were rarely if ever in the drawing-room.

. . . When she was asked to touch it, she got up for the purpose, and seemed as if she were pursuing something which moved away. She followed a few steps, and then said, "It has gone under the chair." Mr. A. assured her it was an illusion, but she would not believe it. He then lifted up the chair, and Mrs. A. saw nothing more of it.

The room was then searched all over, and nothing found in it. There was a dog lying on the hearth, who would have betrayed great uneasiness if a cat had been in the room, but he lay perfectly quiet. In order to be quite certain, Mr. A. rung the bell, and sent for the two cats, both of which were found in the housekeeper's room.[39] — DR. BREWSTER

☛ CASE #25: About a month after this occurrence [see previous entry], Mrs. A., who had taken a somewhat fatiguing drive during the day, was preparing to go to bed about eleven o'clock at night, and, sitting before the dressing glass, was occupied in arranging her hair. She was in a listless and drowsy state of mind, but fully awake.

When her fingers were in active motion among the papillotes, she was suddenly startled by seeing in the mirror the figure of a near relation, who was then in Scotland, and in perfect health. The apparition appeared over her left shoulder, and its eyes met her's in the glass. It was enveloped in grave-clothes, closely pinned, as is usual with corpses, round the head, and under the chin, and though the eyes were open, the features were solemn and rigid. The dress was evidently a shroud, as Mrs. A. remarked even the punctured pattern usually worked in a peculiar manner round the edges of that garment.

Mrs. A. described herself as at the time sensible of a feeling like what we conceive of fascination, compelling her for a time to gaze on this melancholy apparition, which was as distinct and vivid as any reflected reality could be, the light of the candles upon the dressing-table appearing to shine fully upon its face. After a few minutes, she turned round to look for the reality of the form over her shoulder; but it was not visible, and it had also disappeared from the glass when she looked again in that direction.[40] — DR. BREWSTER

☛ CASE #26: On the 17th March, Mrs. A. [of the previous entry] was preparing for bed. She had dismissed her maid, and was sitting with her feet in hot water. Having an excellent memory, she had been thinking upon and repeating to herself a striking passage in the *Edinburgh Review*, when, on raising her eyes, she saw seated in a large easy chair before her the figure of a deceased friend, the sister of [her husband] Mr. A. The figure was dressed, as had been usual with her, with great neatness, but in a gown of a peculiar kind, such as Mrs. A. had never seen her wear, but exactly such as had been described to her by a common friend as having been worn by Mr. A.'s sister during her last visit to England.

Mrs. A. paid particular attention to the dress, air, and appearance of the figure, which sat in an easy attitude in the chair, holding a handkerchief in one hand. Mrs. A. tried to speak to it, but experienced a difficulty in doing so, and in about three minutes the figure disappeared.

About a minute afterwards, Mr. A. came into the room, and found Mrs. A. slightly nervous, but fully aware of the delusive nature of the apparition. She described it as having all the vivid colouring and apparent reality of life; and for some hours preceding this and other visions, she experienced a peculiar sensation in her eyes, which seemed to be relieved when the vision had ceased.[41] — DR. BREWSTER

☛ CASE #27: On the 5th October, between one and two o'clock in the morning, Mr. A. was awoke by Mrs. A. [of the previous entry], who told him that she had just seen the figure of his deceased mother draw aside the bed-curtains and appear between them. The dress and the look of the apparition were precisely those in which Mr. A.'s mother had been last seen by Mrs. A. at Paris in 1824.[42] — DR. BREWSTER

☛ CASE #28: On the 11th October, when sitting in the drawing-room, on one side of the fire-place, Mrs. A. [of the previous case] saw the figure of another deceased friend moving towards her from the window at the farther end of the room. It approached the fire-place, and sat down in the chair opposite. As there were several persons in the room at the time, she describes the idea uppermost in her mind to have been a fear lest they should be alarmed at her staring, in the way she was conscious of doing, at vacancy, and should fancy her intellect disordered.

Under the influence of this fear . . . she summoned up the requisite resolution to enable her to cross the space before the fire-place, and seat herself in the same chair with the figure. The apparition remained perfectly distinct till she sat down, as it were, in its lap, when it vanished.[43] — DR. BREWSTER

☛ CASE #29: On the 26th of the same month, about two P.M. Mrs. A. [of the previous case] was sitting in a chair by the window in the same room with her husband. He heard her exclaim, "What have I seen?" And on looking at her, he observed a strange expression in her eyes and countenance.

A carriage and four had appeared to her to be driving up the entrance road to the house. As it approached, she felt inclined to go up stairs to prepare to receive company, but, as if spell-bound, she was unable to move or speak. The carriage approached, and as it arrived within a few yards of the window, she saw the figures of the postillions and the persons inside take the ghastly appearance of skeletons and other hideous figures. The whole then vanished entirely, when she uttered the above-mentioned exclamation.[44] — DR. BREWSTER

☛ CASE #30: On the morning of the 30th October, when Mrs. A. [of the previous case] was sitting in her own room with a favourite dog in her lap, she distinctly saw the same dog moving about the room during the space of about a minute or rather more.[45] — DR. BREWSTER

☛ CASE #31: On the 3rd December, about nine P.M. when Mr. and Mrs. A. [of the cases above] were sitting near each other in the drawing-room occupied in reading, Mr. A. felt a pressure on his foot. On looking up, he observed Mrs. A.'s eyes fixed with a strong and unnatural stare on a chair about nine or ten feet distant. Upon asking her what she saw, the expression of her countenance changed, and upon recovering herself, she told Mr. A. that she had seen his brother, who was alive and well at the moment in London, seated in the opposite chair, but dressed in grave clothes, and with a ghastly countenance, as if scarcely alive.[46] — DR. BREWSTER

☛ CASE #32: Many years ago I awoke suddenly in the middle of the night, as it appeared to me, with a distinct impression of a certain person. Next morning, early, I was informed that she had died during the night. Though it did not occur to me to fix the time of awaking, yet I felt compelled to admit (i.e., as afterwards explained, felt it strikingly probable) that the death coincided with my impression.

The poor woman had been ill of cancer in the village where I was staying, and I had visited her at times, at the request of my aunts. I had thought little about her, the visit over, and certainly never dreamed of her. I am not a believer in dreams, or rather, do not encourage attention to them, and I am in no sense credulous of the supernatural.

The vividness of the impression I refer to is as strong to-day as it was the moment it happened, and I do not think it will ever be effaced from my memory. This must have occurred between the years 1851 and 1858. I was a sound sleeper at the time, rarely awaking through the night. I certainly never had such an impression of a person's presence as the one I wrote about, either before or since. But for the death following, I could have attached no meaning to it.[47] — MRS. CATHERINE WILSON

☞ CASE #33: One evening in the early spring of last year (1883) as I was retiring to bed—but whilst I was in full enjoyment of good health and active senses—I distinctly saw my mother and my younger sister crying. I was here in Carmarthen, and they were away in Monmouthshire, 80 miles distant.

They distinctly appeared to me to be giving away to grief, and I was at once positive that some domestic bereavement had taken place. I said to myself "I shall hear something of this in the morning."

When the morning came the first thing which was handed to me was a letter from my father in Monmouthshire, stating that they had, on the day of writing, had intelligence that my nephew had just died. The little boy was the son of my elder sister, living in North Devon. There was no doubt but that my mother and younger sister had both given way to grief on the day of my strange illusion, and it was in some mysterious manner communicated to my mind—together with a certain presentiment that I was on the eve of intelligence of a death in the family.

I thought it most probable, though, that the imaginative faculty added—in a purely local manner—the idea of speedy intelligence to the communication which the mind received in some strange way from Monmouthshire. It was the only occurrence of the sort I have ever experienced.[48] — JOHN HOPKINS

☞ CASE #34: I may remark first of all I am considered by my friends as possessing iron nerves, am passionately fond of athletics, and certainly not given to letting imagination or fear run off with my senses. But although I can without boasting say I hardly know what fear is, I am peculiarly susceptible to mental impressions, that is, I can often tell what is passing in the minds of others (especially of my wife) when out walking with them, so much so that I have almost frightened one or two people by offering to tell them the subject on which they were thinking, and in some cases exactly what they were thinking about that subject.

However, I dare say that is common enough, but what I am particularly writing you on is to tell you two facts, one of which occurred 10 years ago, and the other seven years ago nearly. It seems along time ago to be produced, but to me the scenes are fresh as if they only happened yesterday.

The first was this. I was going from the house I lived at to a shop kept by my brother, and when about half-way it came on to rain very fast. I called in at the house of a lady friend and waited some time, but it did not clear, and as I was afraid my brother would be leaving, I said I must go. I rose to do so, and went into the hall and my friend rushed away upstairs to get an umbrella, leaving me in the dark. In the higher part of the door was a glass window, and I all at once, in the darkness, saw a face looking through that window. The face was very well known to me, though for the instant I did not associate it with the original, as she was 300 miles away. I instantly opened the door, found nobody there, and then searched the ivy with which the porch and house are covered.

Finding nothing, and knowing it was impossible anyone could have got away, I then for the first time inquired of myself whose was the face I had seen. I at once knew the face was that of a married sister-in-law of my wife's. I told all our family of the circumstance directly I got home, and judge of our dismay when the next day we had a telegram to say she died at the very hour I saw her. February 9th, 1884.[49] — T. W. GOODYEAR

☛ CASE #35: In the year 1849 I was serving [aboard the] H.M.S. *Geyser*, on the east coast of Africa, and in company with H.M.S. *Brilliant*, anchored in Tamatave Roads, Madagascar. The following facts I can vouch for.

Some of our officers were dining on board the *Brilliant*. A boat's crew were ordered to be ready at six bells (11 p.m.) to fetch them on board. The lights were out on the lower deck and everything quiet. A messmate (T. Parker) and I, belonging to the boat, were sitting in the mess, abreast of the cook's galley, and opposite each other, he with his arms on the table, and face resting on them, and, as I thought, fast asleep, when all at once he jumped to his feet, declaring that he saw his mother cross the deck in front of the galley, and was very much excited.

I pointed out to him that it was quite impossible, as his face was towards the table, at the same time laughing heartily at him for being so foolish. Our schoolmaster, Mr. T. Salsbury, was lying awake in his hammock, close by, and in the morning he made a note of the circumstances, putting down time and date.

On our arrival at the Isle of France, some time after, Parker received a letter from home stating that his mother died that very night. I am no believer in ghosts, but think this a very remarkable coincidence.[50] — MR. H. ATKINS

☛ CASE #36: After my marriage, I was sitting one evening in the Birmingham Town Hall with my husband at a concert, when there came over me the icy chill which usually accompanies these occurrences. Almost immediately I saw with perfect distinctness, between myself and the orchestra, my uncle, Mr. Ward, lying in bed with an appealing look on his face, like one dying. I had not heard anything of him for several months, and had no reason to think he was ill.

The appearance was not transparent or filmy, but perfectly solid looking; and yet I could somehow see the orchestra, not through but behind it. I did not try turning my eyes to see whether the figure moved with them, but looked at it with a fascinated expression that made my husband ask if I was ill. I asked him not to speak to me for a minute or two; the vision gradually disappeared, and I told my husband, after the concert was over, what I had seen.

A letter came shortly after, telling of my uncle's death. He died at exactly the time when I saw the vision.[51] — MRS. T.

☛ CASE #37: Mrs. V., whose husband was in the Artillery in India, told me the following occurred to herself. The story is well known in her family. She has been dead some years, and it occurred when she was comparatively a young woman. I heard it from her 23 years ago last Christmas, at Southampton.

One evening, sitting in her drawing-room, she saw distinctly a military funeral procession pass at the further end of the room. The coffin borne on a gun-carriage. The men with arms reversed. Directly it passed away, she noted the circumstance, writing it down, and passed some months in greatest anxiety. It was before the days of overland route.

She heard of her husband's death, which had occurred that day, and allowing for the difference of time, the funeral had taken place at the moment she had seen the vision, death and burial following each other within a few hours in India.[52] — H. G. BLACK

☞ CASE #38: Miss Campbell was at church in London with her mother. They remained to the Sacrament, and while standing in the chancel with her back to the church door, which was shut, Mrs. Campbell caught hold suddenly of her daughter's arm, and in a terrified manner pointed to the wall opposite, directly over the altar. Miss Campbell looked, but could see nothing, and could not get her mother to speak, and was much alarmed by the strange unearthly fear expressed on her countenance, and with her eyes, wide open, fixed on the wall.

She got her quietly back to her seat, and her mother then told her that she had seen distinctly a funeral procession moving along the wall, but she could not tell who the people were.

Next day they heard that Miss Campbell's first cousin, a great friend of theirs, brother to Lady A., had dropped dead suddenly in his room at the exact hour when Mrs. Campbell saw the funeral pass before her eyes. He had no previous illness, but was a very strong man.[53] — A. BOLDERO

☞ CASE #39: About the year 1841 I was in a room with my father in our house in the Isle of Wight, when he exclaimed, "Good God, what is that?" starting up as he spoke, and apparently looking at something. He then turned to me and said that he had seen a ball of light pass through the room, and added, "Depend upon it, Morse Simonds is dead." This was an old servant in London, to whom he had been sending money, in illness. In course of post came information that she passed away at the very time in question.[54] — REV. STEPHEN H. SAXBY

☞ CASE #40: [Here is a case for you,] vouching for it on the veracity of a brother, long dead, whose word was never doubted by any who knew him, and upon whose statement I would rely as confidently as upon the evidence of my own senses.

At the time of the occurrence he was a young man, about 23 years of age, in perfect health, of indomitable courage, and without a taint of superstition. Riding home from hunting, with some friends, to Cheltenham, in the looming he saw, or believed he saw, an undefinable white object keeping pace with them by the side of the road; he drew the attention of his friends to the circumstance, but they could not see the object. They changed their pace, but whether walking, trotting, or cantering, to my brother's mind's eye the object remained with them until they reached the lights of the town.

Thinking this very remarkable, my brother put the time down, and this agreed exactly with the hour of the demise of a much loved aunt in the south-west of Ireland.[55] — MR. H. C. HURRY

☛ CASE #41: Some time ago my son told me that a friend of his, a rough and simpleminded fellow, had returned from Shields, and told him a curious tale.

The man is a sailor, and had served with his father ever since he was a boy in a collier which trades between this port and the North. The youth, having become very proficient in his calling, went on his voyages, leaving his father, now an elderly man, at home.

During a stormy voyage, and not far off the Humber, the young sailor saw his father, whom he had left in excellent health, pacing the deck, and calling out several times, as he was wont to do—

"Mind your helm, Joe!"

The young man wished to speak to his father, but could not; some occult power prevented him. At the end of the voyage a letter awaited the young sailor, announcing the death of the father at the precise time when he appeared to his son; but please to remark (a matter of some importance, I think) that the apparition remained on deck *some three hours*, until the vessel got to Grimsby.

I disbelieved my son's story, and requested him to ask his friend to come and take tea with me, that I might hear the account from his own mouth. He came. The simplicity of his manner, his plain, open-hearted account, and I may even say his stupidity, manifested in his peculiar diction, imparted an impress to his tale.

At our request Mr. Lyons interrogated Edward Sings more formally the next time that the latter visited Folkestone. The following is the *procès-verbal* of the examination:—

"What is your name?"

"Edward Sings."

"When did you leave your father last?"

"About six years ago, on a Good Friday."

"Was he in good health when you left him?"
"Yes."
"What happened on your voyage?"
"We was in a gale of wind, and we was running in the Humber; we carried the main gaff away; I was at the wheel steering her in. He come to me three or four times, tapped me on the shoulder, and told me to mind the helm, and I told the captain my father was drowned, or something happened to him. After we got in, when it was my watch, he was walking to and fro with me, and I went down below and told my mate I could not stop up, and I did not like to. My mate took my watch. I never could speak to my father, for something kept me from doing so. I heard of my father's death a week afterwards. No one else saw my father's spirit. My father stopped on deck with me an hour, and as I could not stand it any longer I went below, and my mate took my place. We cast both anchors, and were towed into Grimsby. My mother and sister were at my father's death-bed, and they told me that my father asked several times whether I was in the harbour. I certify this to be a true account." 29th December, 1882.[56] — EDWARD SINGS

☞ CASE #42: Philip [Spencer, of Holloway, Derbyshire] and his first wife, Martha, who was a cousin of mine, having no children of their own, adopted the little daughter of a young woman, who went to live at Derby. The child called them father and mother as soon as she could speak, not remembering her own parents, not even her mother.

While yet very young, she one day began to cry out that there was a young woman looking at her, and wanting to come to her, and according to her description of the person, it must have been her mother. As no one else saw the apparition, and the child continued for more than half an hour to be very excited, Philip took her out of the house to that of a neighbour; but the apparition kept them company, talking by the way. They then went to another house, where it accompanied them still, and seemed as though it wanted to embrace the child; but at last vanished in the direction of Derby—as the little girl, now a young woman, describes it—in a flash of fire.

Derby is about fourteen miles distant from Holloway, and as in that day there was neither railway nor telegraph, communication between them was much slower than at present. As soon, however, as it was possible for intelligence to come, the news arrived that the poor child's mother had been burnt to death; that it happened about the time when it saw her apparition; and, in short, that she was sorrowing and crying to be taken to the child during the whole of the time between being burnt and her expiration.

This is no "idle ghost story," but a simple matter of fact, to which not only Philip but all his old neighbours can testify; and the young woman has not only related it more than once to me, but she told it in the same artless and earnest manner to my friend, the late Dr. Samuel Brown, of Edinburgh, who once called at the cottage with me—repeating it still more clearly to Messrs. Fowler and Wells, on our recent visit.[57] — DR. SPENCER TIMOTHY HALL

☛ CASE #43: About the year 1834 or 1835 I was in a boarding school at Cadogan Place, Chelsea, kept by ladies named Horn, where, amongst other pupils, there were two sisters with whom I was very intimate. These girls came from a distance, their home being in the North of England, I believe, and travelling then being very different to what it is in these days of railways, they did not always go home for their holidays, and consequently were not impressed by the critical state of their mother's health.

We slept in a large dormitory, in which were several beds, the two sisters occupying a double bed. On a certain night, most of the girls being asleep, and myself in the next bed to one of the sisters, who was already in bed, and, like myself, anxious to be quiet, and allowed to go to sleep; but we were hindered by the frolicsomeness of the younger sister, who sat outside the bed and facing the door at the end of the room, which, I remember, was not quite dark, either owing to moonlight or the time of year.

As the elder sister was urging her to be quiet and to get into bed, the younger one suddenly exclaimed, and, putting her hands over her face, seemed greatly agitated. As there seemed no cause for this sudden excitement, we, thinking it was only another form of her nonsense, and fearing the noise would bring up the governess, who also slept in the room, scolded her well, upon which she got into bed.

Turning again to look towards the door, she uttered another cry, directing her sister's attention to the door; but she saw nothing, and still thought the younger one was joking. But the latter buried her head under the clothes, and I, being very tired, went to sleep and thought no more about this disturbance.

Next morning no notice was taken of it, and no impression seems to have been made on my mind or that of the other girls, probably, as I now think, owing to our being accustomed to the volatile disposition of the younger sister.

However, about two days afterwards, the sisters were summoned into the room of the ladies of the school to receive letters. Shortly after I was sent for, and found them in floods of tears, having just heard the news of their mother's death. Being their chief friend, I was excused from lessons that I might be with them, and try to console them.

As we were approaching our room the younger sister stopped us suddenly, and grasping my arm with violence, she said, "Oh, do you remember the other night when I was frightened? I believe it was dear mamma that I saw. Let us go back and ask more about it," or words to that effect.

We went back to Miss Horn's apartment, and on referring to the letter, we found that their mother had died, as nearly as we could calculate, at the same hour that the incident in the dormitory occurred.

This is what the girl said she saw: A tall, slight figure in white, resembling her mother, as she now thought, though she did not recognise features, who, with outstretched arms, seemed to beckon to her. Talking it over on the same day, she remarked, "Ah, I think I see now why dear mamma appeared to me. She had often reproved me for my giddiness, and as she was dying, she wished to give me one more look and reproof. I will try and be very different. I shall never forget her warning," etc. She appeared deeply impressed, but as the sisters and I were soon parted, and did not correspond, I lost sight of them.

This is a true account, and I believe clearly remembered by me, though so many years ago. Neither I nor the sister saw the appearance, but witnessed the effect on the girl who did see it, both being quite awake.[58] — MRS. RICHARDS

☛ CASE #44: When at Loweswater, I one day called upon a friend, who said, "You do not see many newspapers; take one of those lying there." I accordingly took up a newspaper, bound with a wrapper, put it into my pocket and walked home.

In the evening I was writing, and, wanting to refer to a book, went into another room where my books were. I placed the candle on a ledge of the bookcase, took down a book and found the passage I wanted, when, happening to look towards the window, which was opposite to the bookcase, I saw through the window the face of an old friend whom I had known well at Cambridge, but had not seen for 10 years or more, Canon Robinson, (of the Charity and School Commission).

I was so sure I saw him that I went out to look for him, but could find no trace of him. I went back into the house and thought I would take a look at my newspaper. I tore off the wrapper, unfolded the paper, and the first piece of news that I saw was the death of Canon Robinson![59] — VICAR GEO M. TANDY

☛ CASE #45: We were walking home from Richmond [UK], my husband and I, one bright July day about half-past five, having ordered the boat to meet us and take us up to our own steps. Between Richmond and Twickenham, on the Surrey side, is a splendid avenue of large trees; between the avenue and the river is a long and wide stretch of beach, and at the Twickenham end the ground is very open, and one sees the curve of the river and glimpses of some houses at Twickenham and Teddington; there is no bank or tree to intercept the view, and any one walking along the towing path can be seen for a long distance.

When a little way down the avenue, at the third tree, perhaps, a man passed stealthily behind me, to my left side, and went outside the trees—I was walking the furthest from the river. Two or three times he passed me thus, always in the same stealthy manner, as if not wishing to be seen. I did not draw my husband's attention to him, because, although the last man to commence a quarrel, he never submitted to an impertinence, and this stranger's movements appeared so spy-like.

I did not know my husband had seen him till he passed the third time; then R. said: "What is that fellow dodging about for? the avenue is open to all, why does he not keep in or out of it? he appears anxious to know what we are talking about; as it does not concern him, we will go out into the open." We were then about the seventh or eighth tree down.

As he spoke he stepped on to the open beach, and gave me his hand to help me over some obstruction in the path, a fallen branch, if I remember rightly. Both these movements were made in less time than it would take me to speak of them. As I put my hand in his, I looked round, and saw the stranger standing between the trees. It was the first full look we had, and I said, "He looks as if he had stepped out of an old picture!" We could only see his boots, his cloak, and hat. The boots were peculiar, high, and falling over at the knee, his cloak large and round, and thrown over his left shoulder, in the Spanish fashion, and his hat, apparently a soft felt, had a very wide drooping border, and was worn so much on one side we saw no face.

We both distinctly remember that in all the times we saw him that day, no face was visible. His whole costume was of one tone, and that of a dusty cobweb is the only thing I can liken it to.

We stood looking at him, I wondering if he would resent my husband's speech, but he made no movement, and I put my hand in R.'s to step into the open. As my husband's fingers closed on mine, he started, and as I looked up to see the cause I saw his eyes fixed steadily on the open space at the remote end of the avenue.

There, clearly defined by the bright background of the towing path and the river, stood the figure that, less than an instant before, was by our side, and which we certainly thought to be that of a fellow creature (of rather ill-bred manners, utterly inconsistent with the decided dignity of his appearance).

Had he been shot out of a gun, he could not have gone faster.

The distance I have since measured; it is about 150 yards; the time occupied in traversing it I could not have counted a dozen in, however rapidly.

Now comes the most peculiar part of our experience, that which has made me very chary of telling it, for fear of ridicule.

When we saw the figure standing out there on the open ground, we were simply perplexed; no sensation of fear, or suspicion of the supernatural, entered our minds. We walked towards him with our eyes fixed on him.

There stood the figure, clearly defined, till we got within a certain distance; then it changed. It is so difficult to describe what did take place; the only way I can suggest it even is thus: You have seen a thick volume of smoke come out of a railway engine and gradually become thinner and thinner as it hovers over the ground, till you see through it the objects behind.

That is what took place. The figure stood there still, but, though it did not lose its shape, it gradually became transparent, till we saw the river and the bank and the distant trees through it! Still it was there. Then it got fainter and fainter, till there was not the least suggestion of it left; nothing but the large, bright, open space, without a single object behind which any one could have hidden.

We stood still, and I saw our boat coming. I got into it, feeling rather "dazed," like one does when waking from a too heavy sleep. As my husband pulled past the place where the figure had stood, for the first time a feeling of horror came over me, and I said, "What could it have been?"

He answered, "God only knows, darling, perhaps we never shall."

And so, I suppose, we must leave it.[60] — M. R. L.

☛ CASE #46: About midway between Bath and Bristol is the village of Timsbury. The principal house in the place is one which was built during the reign of Henry VIII, and was known in the time of my boyhood as The Court.

When I was 12 years of age my father moved to the neighbourhood of Bath, and was shortly afterwards requested by an old friend to ascertain whether there was a large house, with grounds attached, in the locality to be let furnished. Timsbury Court was the only one which could be heard of, and as it seemed exactly the kind of place that was wanted, Mr. B. agreed to take it. With his wife and daughter, and a staff of servants he brought with him, he accordingly took up his quarters in the house at the beginning of October. Neither he nor any of his household knew any of the inhabitants of the village, or were in any way acquainted with the neighbourhood.

The following December my brother (who was two years younger than myself) and I went on a visit to our friends at Timsbury. As we were the first guests they had received we were given what was considered the best bedroom in the house to sleep in. It was called the Drab Room, because the walls were hung with drab tapestry, and was approached by a corridor which branched off from the head of the stair. The nearest room to it was occupied by Miss B. [Miss Lily Boyd; see next case]. Opposite the door was a mullioned window. Between the door and the window was the entrance to a recess in the wall which was fitted up as a dressing room.

As my lungs were delicate, and the weather was cold, I was not allowed to leave the house during the week that I spent in it, and a fire was kept burning in the bedroom. On the Thursday afternoon I had been reading a book on mesmerism, a very undesirable one for a weakly boy to get hold of, and when it became too dark for me to read any longer without a light, I went upstairs to prepare for dinner.

While I was standing in the dusk before the looking-glass on the table in front of the window, brushing my hair, I happened to glance towards my right, and there distinctly saw the figure of a man standing at the entrance of the dressing-room, about a yard distant from me, with his eyes fixed upon myself. What he looked like I will state presently. The suddenness of the appearance startled me exceedingly, and I rushed downstairs into the drawing-room in an agony of terror, declaring that I had seen a "ghost." I was well laughed at for my folly, and told that I must not read any more books on mesmerism.

By the time dinner was over I had become reassured, and soon ceased to think any more about what I had seen.

The following Saturday night I chanced to awake when the fire, which had been blazing brightly when I went to sleep, now cast only a slight flickering light over the room, just sufficient to disclose the outlines of things but no more. I then saw distinctly a human figure come out of the dressing-room and walk by the side of the bed. My brother, who was sleeping on that side of the bed, happened to be awake also, and saw the figure as well as myself. I asked him who it was. "Only Lizzie" (that is Miss B.), he said, and satisfied with the answer I turned round and fell asleep again. My brother saw the figure pass to the foot of the bed and there lost sight of it.

In the morning I mentioned to Mrs. B. that her daughter had been in our room during the night, but no further notice was taken of it at the time.

I must not forget to add that on several occasions my brother and I were much disturbed by strange noises which we ascribed to the wind.

The following spring two young ladies who were on a visit to the house, slept in the Drab Room. Early on Sunday morning they awoke suddenly, and saw a figure come out of the dressing-room and walk to the foot of the bedstead, where it stood looking at them. They were greatly alarmed and covered their faces with the bed clothes, but the next morning determined to say nothing from fear of ridicule. In fact they did not mention what they had seen until some months afterwards.

In the course of the summer the room was occupied by Mrs. Hb., a lady of decidedly unimaginative character. On the Sunday morning after her arrival she appeared at breakfast looking pale and unwell, and, after breakfast, asked Mrs. B. if she might have her room changed. Mrs. B. of course assented, but pressed her visitor to tell her what was the matter with the room, as she fancied she might have been annoyed by rats or something similar. After a great deal of hesitation Mrs. Hb. confessed that though she knew her hostess would think her extremely foolish, she felt convinced that she had seen something supernatural that morning. She had been aroused from sleep, she said, by hearing the clock strike 4, and just afterwards saw a human figure come from the dressing-room and pass to the foot of the bed, where it stooped down, so as to be hidden from view. She thought someone was playing her a trick, and jumped out of bed to see who it was; she searched the room and found nothing. Mrs. B. naturally in her mind ascribed her guest's apparition to a nightmare, but nothing would persuade the latter that she had not actually seen it with waking eyes.

In the early part of September, Mr. B. received a visit from his son-in-law, Mr. H. and his wife, who like the five visitors before them, also occupied the Drab Room. I heard the following story from Mrs. H.'s own lips.

On the Thursday night after their arrival, she was sleeping on the side of the bed nearest the dressing-room, and was aroused from her sleep by feeling a cold clammy hand laid all across her face. It prevented her from opening her eyes, though she felt that if she could do so she would see something "uncanny." She kicked violently and awoke her husband, who told her she was suffering from nightmare, that was all. Mrs. H. was convinced that it was otherwise, and refused to sleep another night on that side of the bed.

The following night Mr. H. was prevented from getting any sleep by an attack of toothache, and in the morning again began to laugh at his wife, telling her that if "there were a ghost in the room he must have seen it as he had been awake all night." The toothache disappeared in the course of the morning, and the following (Saturday) night Mr. H. slept additionally soundly in consequence of his want of sleep the night before.

Suddenly he was startled from his slumbers by a cold clammy hand placed upon his forehead. He sprang up and saw a brown-looking figure, crouched up, hieing away from him into the dressing-room. He felt his pulse, which was beating normally, then he got out of bed, poured some water into the basin, and plunged both his face and his hands into it. Then he returned to bed, and sitting up in it looked at his watch, and found it was a little after 4 o'clock.

At ten minutes past 4 the figure came out of the dressing-room, and stood close to his pillow, so close indeed that he might have touched it had he chosen. This time the figure was erect, and he was able to measure its height against the window-frame, from which he discovered that it was not quite his own height. The figure was that of a man, dressed in a dark coat, which was fastened by gold buttons at the throat and wrist. The hair was dark and parted in the middle, the face pale and smooth, and the nose of the Greek type. In both face and dress the figure was precisely the same as that which I had seen. Mr. H. deliberated whether he should speak; while doing so he coughed, and immediately afterwards the figure melted before his eyes "like a mist." After this further sleep was out of the question, and Mr. H. agreed with his wife that they had better change their room.

As the next day, however, was Sunday, they thought they would pass one more night there. In the course of this Mrs. H. was awakened by "horrible shrieks, groans and sighs," that proceeded from some part of the room. Her husband was awake, and she asked him what it meant. He replied that he had been listening to those sounds for more than an hour. Then he sat up and said, "In the name of God I command you to be silent."

After this they heard no more.

The story soon became known in the village, and our friends then learned that the Drab Room had been held to be haunted from time immemorial, though they could hear of no legend to account for the supposed fact. In the time of their predecessors it had been closed inconsequence of the belief about it. So well-known in the village, indeed, was the belief, that some of the old people, as it turned out, refused to venture near the gates of the house itself after dark. Our friends remained there only a year or two after the discovery, as their servants became frightened and were accordingly disinclined to stay with them.[61] — REV. PROFESSOR A. H. SAYCE

☛ CASE #47: [Continuing from the previous entry:] The next instance that has occurred, since we occupied the house, is more remarkable still.

Mr. Sayce's two little boys slept together in the haunted room, when they stayed with us. On their return home their mother said, "You must have been very happy. Had you a pleasant visit?" They replied they were very happy all day, but "they did not think it was kind in Lily to dress up in white and come to their bed at night, and that they did not like it at all." These children had never heard of the Timsbury Ghosts, and never speak of what they saw there as anything but "Lily dressed up."

They told their nurse that "one night Lily went into their room, dressed up in white, to frighten them, but they were so sure it was Lily that they determined not to take any notice of her, as they were very tired."

Was not this most curious?

Frederick Holt, my brother-in-law, was all but frightened out of his senses, by an apparition which he saw in the haunted room. He had been lying awake for more than hour, one night, or rather very early one morning, when, from the corner whence it usually issues, where the dressing closet door opens into the bedroom, a figure appeared, and slowly passed the bed. Frederick felt his pulse and his heart, in order to ascertain whether he was any way excited or fevered, as he thought, at first, it must be an illusion, but his pulse was quite steady.

In about 10 minutes the figure returned, with its hands upraised, and with the most agonised expression of countenance that could be described.

Mrs. F. Holt was asleep by her husband one night when the apparition appeared to him. He says he did not awaken her at first for fear of frightening her, and that when the figure returned he felt completely paralysed. He had himself been awakened that night by what felt to be a hand pressed tightly over his face, and he then saw an elderly gentleman with a fine line of face passing from his bed. He was dressed in brown, in the old style, with a long rounded-off waistcoat, and a light neckcloth which was fastened with a brooch or pin. He passed from the dressing-closet, at one side of the room, to a kind of wardrobe-closet for hanging things in at the other.

Mr. Holt put his hand upon his own pulse to see if anything was the matter with him, and counted 80 beats, when the old gentleman came out of the hanging closet again, and again passed by his bed, but this time it stopped, raised up its arms, and, clasping its hands together, laid them down, pressing them on the bed in which Mr. and Mrs. Holt were lying. It then passed on again to the dressing-closet.

Mr. Holt then told his wife what he had seen. Mrs. Holt saw nothing, but they both of them heard loud whisperings and voices all about the room. Neither of them could understand what the voices said. They described the room as seeming all alive with voices.[62] — MISS LILY BOYD

☛ CASE #48: In the year 1875, Captain A. B. MacGowan, 12th U.S. Infantry, was stationed at Camp Independence, California; having with him his wife. His two sons, Charles, aged 15, and George, aged 12, were at that time at school, at Napa College, California, and boarded in the house; and at the table of one of the instructors, Mr. George.

Mrs. MacGowan was a lady of robust health, almost unacquainted with illness; and at this particular time was arranging to give an entertainment to their friends, military and civil. The station being not only far beyond the railroad, but out of the ordinary line of travel, guests would come to such a party with their own conveyance, and after several days' journey; and arrangements would be made to entertain them over-night and longer. Such a festivity would be quite an event for the outpost and for all those interested in it. There was no telegraphic communication with this camp; and the mails were slow, and the distance long. In fact, from Camp Independence, the school is nearly 600 miles. The boys knew what was going on at home by previous correspondence, and knew that, so far from there being any cause for uneasiness, the prospect was one of active enjoyment.

On the morning of December 23rd, 1875, Charles, the elder of the boys at school, came to the breakfast-table with a disturbed countenance, but denied having any trouble when asked about it by the teacher. He was unable to eat any breakfast, although allowing himself to be helped; but when the teacher, at the meal, insisted on knowing the cause of his distress, fearing he might be ill, he burst into tears, and exclaimed, "My mother is dead." He then went on to say that, having gone to bed and to sleep as usual, and with no premonition of trouble, he was awakened in the night and saw his mother standing by his bedside; who said to him, "Charlie, be a good boy"; and then disappeared.

This occurred between 11 and 12 p.m. He had gone to sleep, not hearing 11 strike; but was awakened by this occurrence, and heard all the other hours strike, including 12 o'clock, till morning.

The teacher endeavoured to make light of it; but the boy would not be comforted.

In a day or two a letter was received, saying his mother was indisposed, but not seriously; this was followed a few days later by the announcement that she had unexpectedly grown worse, and had suddenly died, at 11:20 p.m., of this same night (December 22nd, 1875), in which the apparition was seen. The teacher, Mr. George, made a note of the occurrence, and subsequently informed Captain MacGowan thereof.[63] — CAPTAIN A. B. MACGOWAN

☛ CASE #49: In the early morning of August 29th, 1832, when lying in bed half asleep and half awake, I was suddenly startled by perceiving the form of my brother George, then absent from home, standing beside me. The room was quite light, and my recognition of the figure was complete and clear. He looked at me [for some ten minutes], and then seemed to fade slowly away.

My brother (who had a special warm affection for me) was at that time a sailor on board the merchant ship *Eliza*, bound for the East Indies.

I had no reason to suppose anything was wrong with him, nor was he specially in my thoughts. The vision, for I felt certain that I was awake and not dreaming, made a very strong and painful impression upon me, so much so that the family where I was staying asked the cause of troubled looks. I told them what I had seen, and at my hostess's request made a note of the occurrence.

Months afterwards we received the intelligence that my brother had died at Baroda, near Sumatra, of dysentery. The date and hour of his death (as nearly as could be calculated) coincided exactly with that of his appearance to me at Stroud (Gloucester).

I am of a calm and unimaginative temperament, and have never had any similar experience before or since. The coincidence was well-known to various members of my family, but I do not now remember that I mentioned the matter to anyone else at the time.[64]
— WM. GARLICK

☛ CASE #50: Your favour of August 29th at hand and contents noted, and, in reply, will give you, to the best of my recollection, a full history of the circumstance.

The circumstance of which the *Dream Investigator* speaks was this, and let me assure you it is impressed upon my mind in a manner which will preclude its ever being forgotten by me or the members of my family interested.

My little son, Arthur, who was then five years old, and the pet of his grandpa, was playing on the floor when I entered the house a quarter of 7 o'clock, Friday evening, July 11th, 1879. I was very tired, having been receiving and paying for staves all day, and it being an exceedingly sultry evening I laid down by Artie on the carpet, and entered into conversation with my wife (not, however, in regard to my parents).

Artie, as usually was the case, came and laid down with his little head upon my left arm, when all at once he exclaimed, "Papa papa! Grandpa!" I cast my eyes toward the ceiling, or opened my eyes, I am not sure which, when, between me and the joists (it was an old-fashioned log cabin), I saw the face of my father as plainly as ever I saw him in my life. He appeared to me to be very pale, and looked sad, as I had seen him upon my last visit to him three months previous.

I immediately spoke to my wife, who was sitting within a few feet of me, and said, "Clara, there is something wrong at home; father is either dead or very sick." She tried to persuade me that it was my imagination, but I could not help feeling that something was wrong.

Being very tired soon after retired, and about 10 o'clock Artie woke me up repeating, "Papa, grandpa is here." I looked, and believe, if I remember right, got up, at any rate to get the child warm, as he complained of coldness, and it was very sultry weather.

Next morning I expressed my determination to go at once to Indianapolis. My wife made light of it and over-persuaded me, and I did not go until Monday morning, and upon arriving at home (my father's) I found him buried the day before (Sunday, July 13th).

Now comes the mysterious part to me.

After I had told my mother and brother of my vision, or whatever it may have been, they told me the following:

On the morning of the 11th July (the day of his death) he arose early, and expressed himself as feeling unusually well, and ate a hearty breakfast. Soon after leaving the table he said he believed he would "clean up and put on a clean shirt, as he felt some one was coming to see him that day."

He washed, went upstairs and put on his best clothes, and came down and told mother he would go in to the parlour and read, and if any one called to see him notify him.

He took the Bible (he was a Methodist minister) and went and remained until near noon. He ate a hearty dinner and went to the front gate, and, looking up and down the street, remarked that he could not, or at least would not be disappointed, some one was surely coming.

During the afternoon and evening he seemed restless, and went to the gate, looking down street, frequently. At last, about time for supper, he mentioned my name, and expressed his conviction that God, in his own good time, would answer his prayers in my behalf (I being at that time very wild).

Mother going into the kitchen to prepare supper, he followed her and continued talking to her about myself and family, and especially Arthur (my son).

Supper being over, he moved his chair near the door, and was conversing about me at the time he died. The last words were about me, and were spoken, by mother's clock, 14 minutes of 7. He did not fall, but just quit talking and was dead.

Then mother's dream of the extraordinary large coffin came to her memory. She told me that she was going somewhere and saw the coffin, and asked myself and brother, Who was dead? who that large coffin was for? My brother replied it was for father.

This so impressed her mind that it was a source of much discomfort to her. "To think," she said, "that I was warned so plainly, and yet did not have the least idea of his nearness to death."

Now what was so mysterious to me was the anticipated visit or arrival of someone on that particular day, as though he was impressed with the idea that someone would come. In answer to my inquiries, my son Arthur says he remembers the circumstances, and the impression he received upon that occasion is ineffaceable.[65]

— SAMUEL S. FALKINBURG

☛ CASE #51: Some time at the end of 1868 I was discussing with a lady of my acquaintance the question of making compacts to appear after death. I doubted whether such compacts could be fulfilled; she stoutly maintained that they could be.

Finally we agreed to make such a compact ourselves that whichever of us first died should appear after death to the other.

At the beginning of the next year I went on a voyage in the merchant ship, *Edmund Graham*, of Greenock, to Australia, and, on the 22nd of June, when we were between the Cape of Good Hope and Australia (lat. 40 deg. S., long. 22 E.), and the ship running before a heavy gale of wind, the sea swept over the deck and washed seven of us, myself among the number, overboard.

I gave myself up for lost, and I remember well that I thought of the panorama of their past lives which drowning men are said to see, and hoped that the show would commence.

Then I regretted I was without my oilskin, as the water would have time to wet me through before death, and I expected to find it very cold; as far as I can recollect, this was all that passed through my mind.

The next moment I caught hold of a loose rope that was hanging from the ship, and hauled myself on deck. The others were drowned. This took place between and 4 a.m. on June 22nd.

A few months afterwards I had a letter at Bombay, from my friend, in which she mentioned that on the night of the 22nd June she had seen me in her room. When I saw her again, I received from her a full account of the circumstance.

She told me that she woke up suddenly in the night, and saw me at the other end of the room, and that I advanced towards her. Whether she noticed the dress which I was wearing I cannot say. I have often since heard her describe the incident. As far as I can recollect, she told me the precise time of the appearance; and my belief is that it coincided in time with my being washed overboard.

Though I cannot recollect calculating the difference of time, by reference to the longitude, I think it most likely that I did so and found the times to correspond. I was certainly, at that time, quite alive to the fact that 22 deg. of longitude would make a sensible difference in the apparent time.[66] — CAPTAIN M. P.

☛ CASE #52: In 1856 I was engaged on duty at a place called Roha, some 40 miles south of Bombay, and moving about in the districts (as it is termed in India). My only shelter was a tent, in which I lived for several months in the year. My parents, and only sister, about 22 years of age, were living at K., from which place letters used to take a week reaching me. My sister and I were regular correspondents, and the post generally arrived about 6 a.m., as I was starting to my work.

It was on the 18th April of that year (a day never to be forgotten) that I received a letter from my mother, stating that my sister was not feeling well, but hoped to write to me the next day. There was nothing in the letter to make me feel particularly anxious. After my usual outdoor work, I returned to my tent, and in due course set to my ordinary daily work.

At 2 o'clock my clerk was with me, reading some native documents that required my attention, and I was in no way thinking of my sister, when all of a sudden I was startled by seeing my sister (as it appeared) walk in front of me from one door of the tent to the other, dressed in her night-dress. The apparition had such an effect upon me that I felt persuaded that my sister had died at that time. I wrote at once to my father, stating what I had seen, and in due time I also heard from him that my sister had died at that time.

By the context of the narrative you will see it was 2 p.m., broad daylight. My vision corresponded with the exact time of death. I have never seen any other apparition.

You must excuse my sanctioning my name being appended to the account, though I am as certain of it as I am of my own existence. November 11th, 1884.[67] — J. C. H.

☞ CASE #53: I am head-master of the boys' school and organist of the parish at Weighton. My parents reside in Hull, my father being a cooper and cask merchant there.

My mother's maiden name was Jane Cooling. Several years ago (about 10 or 12) she told me a remarkable story which sank deeply into my mind. I got her to tell me the whole of her story again, and it was exactly the same as that she had told years before. I cross-questioned her, but always got the same answers. My mother is 65 years of age. Her mind is quite clear and her memory very good. The affair happened when she was about 16 or 17 years old, and she maintains that even yet she can see (in imagination) her brother as fairly as she saw him then.

The following is the story, which I have recently taken down carefully from her own lips. Having subjected my mother to some very close questioning, I feel sure that you may depend upon the statements being trustworthy.

Henry Cooling, the brother of Jane Cooling, was a sailor, and had gone on a long voyage. Jane was living in Hull in the house of Mr. Kitching, Mytongate. There was a large cupboard in the house, which was on a kind of landing, approached by two or three steps. Just as she was about to go up to it, she saw distinctly, about 5 p.m., her brother Henry standing in front of the door. His eyes were fixed on her for a short time, and then he disappeared towards the left. He was dressed in his seaman's drawers and shirt. The strings of his drawers were loose; his feet were bare; his hair was untidy; and his whole appearance was like that of one roused suddenly from sleep.

After the vision had vanished, as soon as she recovered herself, she went home to her father and told him what she had seen. He said it was all nonsense, and told her to take no notice of it.

However, some days later, a letter came from the captain of the ship, stating that Henry Cooling had been washed overboard during a gale in the Bay of Biscay, just as he was called on deck to assist in working the ship, and the time he gave us about the time of the accident corresponded approximately to that at which Jane saw the vision.

The above is the story purely as she told it to me, and she confidently affirms that it is perfectly true in every detail. Since the above was written, I have found the exact date of my uncle's death—March 27th, 1836. My mother would, therefore, be 17 within a few days.[68] — MR. E. STEPHENSON

☛ CASE #54: In 1874 I was in England ill in bed, and I distinctly saw my dear mother, who was at that time at Nice, come up to the foot of my bed; and look earnestly and sorrowfully at me; it was broad daylight, and I noticed the shawl she wore, one I had not seen her wear for many years. I started up and she was gone.

I then knew that her last illness must have come, though I was kept in ignorance of it, as I was so dangerously ill myself.

I wrote to her, and her answer told me what I dreaded was true. I was allowed to recover sufficiently to go out to Nice, and be with her to the end. Also, I ought to say, that the morning her dear image appeared to me, a doctor arrived from London whom she had sent to me by telegraphing to him from Nice, and this doctor was the means of saving my life, as I was at that time so ill that he said I could not have lived more than four hours longer.[69] — MRS. C. M. W.

☛ CASE #55: One day in the 1840's, when I was living in the Rectory at Marlborough, my father's house, my mother and sister had gone out, and I was lying on a sofa in the drawing-room, at about 3 p.m. I was reading a book, when the light seemed to be slightly darkened, and looking up I saw, leaning in at the window farthest from me, about three feet from the ground, and beckoning, a gentleman whom I had only seen once, about a fortnight or three weeks previously.

Supposing that my father wanted me to sign my name (as a witness to a lease, or something of that kind) I got up, went out of the window (which led down into the garden), and passed along in front of the house, and up six steps into my father's study, which was empty. I then went into the yard and garden, but found nobody; so I returned to my sofa and my books.

When father came in, two hours afterwards, I said, "Why did you send Mr. H. to call me, and then go away?"

My father replied, "What are you talking about? H. is down in Wales." Nothing more was said.

I did not like to dwell on the subject to either of my parents, and I did not mention the occurrence to any one for several years.

About a fortnight afterwards I was told by my mother that Mr. H. had written, proposing for my hand (some property of his adjoined some property of my father's in Wales). I cannot fix exactly how close the coincidence was; but my strong impression is that the letter was received within 24 hours of my experience.

Before I was told of the contents of the letter, I remember that I found the blue envelope of Mr. H.'s letter (with T. H. on the corner, and with the coat-of-arms on his seal, and with the postmark Llandilo) on the floor in my father's study. When the news was told me, I seemed to receive some explanation of my vision. I have never had any hallucination or vision at any other time . . .[70] — MRS. C. BEAUMONT

☛ CASE #56: About September, 1873, when my father was living at 57, Inverness Terrace, I was sitting one evening, about 8:30 p.m., in the large dining. At the table, facing me, with their backs to the door, were seated my mother, sister, and a friend, Mrs. W.

Suddenly I seemed to see my wife bustling in through the door of the back dining-room, which was in view from my position. She was in a mauve dress. I got up to meet her, though much astonished as I believed her to be at Tenby.

As I rose, my mother said, "Who is that?" not (I think) seeing anyone herself, but seeing that I did.

I exclaimed, "Why, it's Carry," and advanced to meet her. As I advanced, the figure disappeared.

On inquiry, I found that my wife was spending that evening at a friend's house, in a mauve dress, which I had most certainly never seen. I had never seen her dressed in that colour. My wife recollected that at that time she was talking with some friends about me, much regretting my absence, as there was going to be dancing, and I had promised to play [piano] for them. I had been unexpectedly detained in London. February 24th, 1885.[71] — CAPT. ALEX. S. BEAUMONT

☛ CASE #57: [From the wife of A. S. Beaumont, previous case.] In 1872, two or three months after my marriage, Captain Beaumont and I returned from London to Tenby. I went up into my dressing room and gave the keys of my luggage to my servant, Ellen Bassett. I was standing before the looking-glass with my back turned to her, and I heard her utter a little sharp cry. I turned round, saying, "What's the matter," and saw her with my nightcap in her hand. She said, "O, nothing, nothing," and I went downstairs.

The day after my husband saw her [Ellen] taking off the paper which pasted up the [temporarily closed-off] door between my bedroom and the dressing-room. He said, "What are you doing?" She said she was opening that door. He said, "Why, the first night that I slept in this house, I saw your mistress walk through that door."

(I must explain that Captain Beaumont had been a guest in this house on a good many occasions before our marriage. On the occasion mentioned, he had imagined that perhaps someone was ill in the house, and that I had entered his room to get something, thinking him sure to be asleep.)

Then the maid told him that she had seen me the night before we came home—she did not know exactly what day we were coming, and had been sleeping in the same bed as he had been in when he saw me. She was just going to step into bed, when she saw me enter "through the door," with a nightcap on, and a candle in my hand. She was so terrified that she rushed out of the room by the other door, and told the other servants she was sure I was dead. They comforted her as well as they could, but she would not return to the room.

The cause of her crying out, when I heard her do so, was that, in unpacking, she recognised the identical nightcap that the apparition had worn. The curious point is that the nightcap was one that I had bought in London, and had not mentioned to her, and was perfectly unlike any that I had ever worn before. It had three frills. I had been accustomed to wear nightcaps of coloured muslin without frills.

The same servant, some months after the nightcap, went into the kitchen and said to the other servants, "We shall have news of missus to-day; I've just seen her standing in the dining-room door; she'd on a black velvet bonnet and black cloak." (We had been in

London some weeks.) This occurred about 9 o'clock a.m.

About 10:30 she received a telegram from us to say we should be home that evening; the telegram was sent from Paddington station as we waited for our train. The bonnet and cloak had been bought in town without her knowledge. The maid was with me for years, and was certainly not nervous or hysterical. I have now parted with her for some years. February 24th, 1885.[72] — MRS. C. BEAUMONT

☛ CASE #58: In October, 1883, being in Toronto, Canada, at the time, I thought I saw my youngest sister come into the ante-room next to the room where we were seated at lunch. I exclaimed, and then thought I had been mistaken, of course, and that one of my cousins who resembled her somewhat in appearance had come to lunch, but found no one was thereat all, nor had anyone come into the room. I remember remarking at the time that I thought I saw my sister all in brown, and that she had nothing of that colour as far as I knew.

A few days afterwards I received a letter from another sister, in which she mentioned that my youngest sister and she had been getting new winter things, and were dressed in brown from head to foot. I think I was quite well at the time, but my sister was ill, which I was not aware of for some weeks afterwards. August 1884.[73] — MISS E. M. CHURCHILL

☛ CASE #59: In the month of November, 1864, being detained in Cairo, on my way out to India, the following curious circumstance occurred to me:

Owing to an unusual influx of travellers, I, with the young lady under my charge (whom we will call D.) and some other passengers of the outward-bound mail to India, had to take up our abode in a somewhat unfrequented hotel. The room shared by Miss D. and myself was large, lofty, and gloomy; the furniture of the scantiest, consisting of two small beds, placed nearly in the middle of the room and not touching the walls at all; two or three rush-bottomed chairs, a very small washing stand, and a large old-fashioned sofa of the settee sort, which was placed against one-half of the large folding-doors which gave entrance to the room. This settee was far too heavy to be removed, unless by two or three people. The other half of the door was used for entrance, and faced the two beds.

Feeling rather desolate and strange, and Miss D. being a nervous person, I locked the door, and taking out the key, put it under my pillow; but on Miss D. remarking that there might be a duplicate which could open the door from outside, I put a chair against the door, with my travelling-bag on it, so arranged, that on any pressure outside one or both must fall on the bare floor, and make noise enough to rouse me. We then proceeded to retire to bed, the one I had chosen being near the only window in the room, which opened with two glazed doors, almost to the floor. These doors, on account of the heat, I left open, first assuring myself that no communication from the outside could be obtained. (The window led on to a small balcony, which was isolated, and was three stories above the ground.)

I suddenly woke from a sound sleep with the impression that somebody had called me, and, sitting up in bed, to my unbounded astonishment, by the clear light of early dawn coming in through the large window before mentioned, I beheld the figure of an old and very valued friend whom I knew to be in England. He appeared as if most eager to speak to me, and I addressed him with, "Good gracious! how did you come here?"

So clear was the figure, that I noted every detail of his dress, even to three onyx shirt studs which he always wore. He seemed to come a step nearer to me, when he suddenly pointed across the room, and on my looking round, I saw Miss D. sitting up in her bed, gazing at the figure with every expression of terror. On looking back, my friend seemed to shake his head, and retreated, step by step, slowly, till he seemed to sink through that portion of the door where the settee stood.

I never knew what happened to me after this; but my next remembrance is of bright sunshine pouring through the window.

Gradually the remembrance of what had happened came back to me, and the question arose in my mind, had I been dreaming, or had I seen a visitant from another world? the bodily presence of my friend being utterly impossible.

Remembering that Miss D. had seemed aware of the figure as well as myself, I determined to allow the test of my dream or vision to be whatever she said to me upon the subject, I intending to say nothing to her unless she spoke to me.

As she seemed still asleep, I got out of bed, examined the door carefully, and found the chair and my bag untouched, and the key under my pillow; the settee had not been touched, nor had that portion of the door against which it was placed any appearance of being opened for years.

Presently, on Miss D. waking up, she looked about the room, and noticing the chair and bag, made some remark as to their not

having been much use. I said, "What do you mean?" and when she said, "Why, that man who was in the room this morning must have got in somehow."

She then proceeded to describe to me exactly what I myself had seen. Without giving any satisfactory answer as to what I had seen, I made her rather angry by affecting to treat the matter as a fancy on her part, and showed her the key still under my pillow, and the chair and bag untouched.

I then asked her, if she was so sure that she had seen somebody in the room, did not she know who it was?

"No," said she, "I have never seen him before, nor anyone like him."

I said, "Have you ever seen a photograph of him?" She said, "No."

This lady never was told what I saw, and yet described exactly to a third person what we both had seen. Of course I was under the impression my friend was dead. Such, however, was not the case; and I met him some four years later, when, without telling him anything of my experience in Cairo, I asked him in a joking way could he remember what he was doing on a certain night in November, 1864.

"Well," he said, "you require me to have a good memory"; but after a little reflection he replied, "Why that was the time I was so harassed with trying to decide for or against the appointment which was offered me, and I so much wished you could have been with me to talk the matter over. I sat over the fire quite late, trying to think what you would have advised me to do."

A little cross-questioning and comparing of dates brought out the curious fact that, allowing for the difference of time between England and Cairo, his meditations over the fire and my experience were simultaneous. Having told him the circumstances above narrated, I asked him had he been aware of any peculiar or unusual sensation. He said none, only that he had wanted to see me very much.[74] — MRS. E. H. ELGEE

☛ CASE #60: On Thursday night, October 30th, 1884, H. M. and I went to dine at Broadmoor. We stayed till 10 p.m. or so, and on leaving the house were talking of different things, M. being quiet as usual; when after five minutes' walk M. suddenly stopped and said, "Look, look! oh look!" We thought nothing of it at first, but he still kept pointing with his finger at some imaginary thing in the darkness.

The spot we were in was very dark, with a wood on our right and a field on our left, separated from us by a railing. Thinking M. saw somebody hiding behind a bush I went forward, but saw nothing.

M. now, still saying: "Look at her, look at her," fell back against the railing and lay motionless with his back against it. We ran to him, asking him what was the matter, but he only moaned.

After a while he seemed better. We wanted him to come on, but he said "Where is my stick?" which he had dropped.

"Oh, never mind your stick," I said, for I was afraid of not being at the college before the shutting of the doors; but he would look for his stick, which he found by lighting a match.

We walked on together, M., notwithstanding all my efforts to get him into conversation, not saying a word. After walking for about a quarter of a mile, he suddenly said, "Where were they carrying her to? I tell you they were carrying her; didn't you see them carrying her?" I tried to quiet him, but he kept on saying, "I tell you they were carrying her."

In a short time he was pacified and walked quietly on for half a mile or so, when he said, looking round in surprise, "Hullo! we must have come a short cut. I know this house." I said we hadn't; but he said, "We must have run then. It seems only a minute ago since we left the house." He several times expressed his surprise at the quickness we had done the last half-mile in. He was all right from this to the college.

On Sunday morning he told me that something very bad had happened on Thursday night. An old lady who was very fond of him, but whom he hadn't seen for a long time, had died suddenly of heart disease. She had been out somewhere and had come home, when, as she was receiving some friends, she fell dead, and, to use his words, she was carried out.

I immediately asked him at what hour did she die? He said at between 10 and 11. (It was a little after 10 when he saw his vision.) I could not get the exact hour of the lady's death, as he didn't like the subject. When he told me this he knew nothing of what occurred on the walk home. When he was told of it he didn't remember a thing about the vision; but said if he hadn't known that he hadn't drunk anything (which was true), he would have said he had been drunk. He seemed to have been in a sort of stupor all the time.

I think I ought to mention that he told me long before this that he had seen a vision of a girl who had been drowned. This is a true account of what happened.[75] — MR. H. KING

☛ CASE #61: On the morning of my father's death, between 4 and 5 o'clock, I saw a sort of shadowy light at the foot of my bed, and half arose to look at it. I distinctly saw my father's face, smiling at me. I drew the curtains apart, and still saw him looking fixedly at me. I awoke the girl who was sleeping with me, and asked her to draw up the window blind. I then asked her if she saw anything. She said, "Nothing. It is too dark."

I fancy I saw the vision for fully five minutes, and then all was dark again. The face was bound under the chin, as usual in death, and the cloth seemed stained, but not so deep as iron-mould quite.

On looking at my father's corpse, after returning to Hull, I told an old friend, who was with me, that it was just so he looked at me, except that the cloth was discoloured. She at once said: "Then he did come to you, that's certain, for the cloth was stained, and I changed it after daylight."

It was within a few minutes of his death that I saw him, and he was asking God to bless me. He was asking for me continually.[76] — M. C.

☛ CASE #62: What follows was communicated orally to the Rev. J. T. Fowler, Librarian and Hebrew Lecturer in the University of Durham, by Mr. Clarke, one of the principal tradesmen in Hull, on the 9th of October, 1872. Mr. Fowler took notes in writing of what Mr. Clarke told him at the time, which notes he handed to me in the same month of October. I put them into the following form after receiving them, and have no doubt of their substance and details being exactly given. The events related had occurred about four years previously to Mr. Fowler's interview with Mr. Clarke.

Mr. Clarke, of Hull, had known for 20 years a Mrs. Palliser, of the same place. She had an only child, a son called Matthew, who was a sailor. Being of the age of 22, he had sailed from Hull to New York.

About a month after his departure, Mrs. Palliser came to Mr. Clarke in tears, and said, "Oh, Mr. Clarke, poor Mat's drowned."

Mr. C. said, "How have you got to know?"

She replied, "He was drowned last night going on board the ship, in crossing the plank, and it slipped; I saw him, and heard him say, 'Oh mother.'"

She stated that she had been in bed at the time, but was sure she was wide awake, and that she had seen also her own mother, who had been dead many years, at the bed-foot, crying, and making some reference to the event.

Mr. C. said to her, "Oh, it's all nonsense, I don't believe anything of the sort."

She earnestly persisted in her conviction, and called on Mr. C. perhaps half a-dozen times during the ensuing week. In order to pacify her, he undertook to write to the agent of her son's ship at New York. This she had wished him to do, thinking that he, as a business man, would know better how to write than herself. After the despatch of the letter, Mrs. P. kept calling on Mr. C. about every week to ask if he had heard anything.

In about a month's time a letter arrived from New York, addressed to "Mrs. Palliser, care of Mr. Clarke." It was opened by Mr. Clarke's son, in the presence of Mrs. Palliser, who, before it was opened, said, "Aye, that'll contain the news of his being drowned."

The letter conveyed the intelligence that Matthew Palliser, of such a ship, had been drowned on such a night through the upsetting of a plank as he was going aboard the ship. The night specified was that of Mrs. P.'s vision.

Mr. Clarke described Mrs. Palliser as "a well-educated woman, a very respectable old lady who had seen better days," about 65 years of age. She had, he said, been a widow for some years before her son was drowned. She was then living in a passage leading out of Blackfriars Gate, in Hull. He had seen her "the day before yesterday." She had told the story "thousands of times," and it was well-known in Hull.[77] — REV. J. BARMBY

☞ CASE #63: My dear son: You ask me to relate Aunt Lucy's dream; it was not a dream but a reality.

You must know that Uncle Bennet was a small farmer, with a large family of 12 children, consequently some had to go away from home. They lived in a small village at Treylion, near St. Ives, Cornwall. Now what I am going to relate is about their daughter Betsy, who had taken a situation—I think at St. Ives.

One morning aunt woke up and saw, standing by her bedside, this daughter, with her hair streaming all over her face, dripping wet, and she, poor thing, looking half-drowned. Aunt said, "Betsy, where have you come from?" The weather being frightfully bad, she thought she had walked home through the wet. She told her to go and dry herself, but she vanished away. Poor aunt was dreadfully alarmed.

They sent to her [that is, Betsy's] place, and it appears she would go to Plymouth, and went in a little sailing-vessel, and that very morning the vessel was lost and all hands perished.

Now, my dear son, I can vouch for every word being true, for aunt was a true Christian woman. I was a girl when she told me the unhappy incident, but it always made a most vivid impression on me.—Believe me, dear son, your loving mother.[78] — C. YOUNG

☛ CASE #64: On the afternoon of Sunday, December 18th, 1864, my father-in-law, Mr. B., my husband, and I were sitting in the dining-room at D_____ Hall. The room was a large one, about 26 ft. by 30 ft.; on one side was the fireplace, with a door on each side; opposite the fireplace were three windows; standing with your back to the fireplace, at the end of the room, on your right, were two more windows, and on your left a blank wall. These windows were some height from the ground, probably 7 ft. or more, so that no one could look in unless standing on a chair.

It was dark, and we were sitting round the fire, the shutters not having been closed. Mr. B. faced the two windows, I sat on the other side of the fireplace, with my back to the said windows, my husband being in the middle facing the fire. Suddenly Mr. B. said, "Who is that looking in at the window?" pointing to the furthest of the two windows.

We laughed, knowing that no one could look in, as there was nothing there for them to stand on. Mr. B. persisted in his assertion, saying that it was a woman with a pale face and black hair; that the face was familiar to him, but he could not remember her name, and he insisted on my husband going round the outside of the house one way whilst he went the other. They, however, saw no one. As they went out I looked at the clock. The time was 5:45 p.m.

On the following Tuesday I heard of the death of my mother, Mrs. R., who had died at St. Peter's Port, Guernsey, exactly at 5:45 p.m. on Sunday, December 18th, the hour at which the face appeared at the window. She had been delirious before her death, and calling piteously for me.

Directly Mr. B. heard of her death he exclaimed, "It was Mrs. R.'s face I saw at the window on Sunday (he had only seen my mother two or three times).

We were not aware that my mother was seriously ill. I do not presume to offer any scientific explanation of these facts, but I firmly believe that my mother's last thoughts were of me, her eldest child. I had only been married two months, and she had not seen me since my wedding-day. Recorded March 20th, 1885.[79] — E. A. B.

☛ CASE #65: I have for some time felt inclined, according to your request [that is, the S.P.R.] for information on subjects connected with psychical research, to relate to you a peculiar circumstance which happened to some very near relatives of my own.

They were, at the time (as nearly as I can remember in 1844), living in the [Scottish] Highlands, and the gentleman had some years before parted from a brother living in Nottinghamshire on very unfriendly terms.

Sitting at breakfast one morning with his wife (my sister), he saw this brother pass the window, and so fully impressed was he that he jumped up, calling to his wife to come to the hall door to receive him.

They went, but on arriving did not see him, though the grounds were searched and servants questioned. On the arrival of the post bag, a letter came saying this brother was lying dangerously ill and most anxious to see and be reconciled to his brother.

Of course he went, but on arriving heard he had died at the exact time he saw him pass the window.

I have often thought of and spoken of this, to me, very remarkable circumstance, and if at all bearing upon your requirements, you are at perfect liberty to use it, only kindly suppress the names, the son of one brother being still alive and ranking high in the military service in India. I am, sir, yours truly.[80] — C. A. F.

☛ CASE #66: I am not quite clear as to the exact date, but about the middle of June, in the year 1863, I was walking up the High Street of Huddersfield, in broad daylight, when I saw approaching me, at a distance of a few yards, a dear friend who I had every reason to believe was lying dangerously ill at his home, in Staffordshire. A few days before, I had heard this from his friends.

As the figure drew nearer, I had every opportunity of observing it; and, although it flashed across my mind that his recovery had been sudden, I never thought of doubting that it was really my friend. As we met, he looked into my eyes with a sad longing expression, and, to my astonishment, never appeared to notice my outstretched hand, or respond to my greeting, but quietly passed on.

I was so taken by surprise as to be unable to speak or move for a few seconds, and could never be quite certain whether there was uttered by him any audible sound, but a clear impression was left on my mind, "I have wanted to see you so much, and you would not come." Recovering from my astonishment, I turned to look after the retreating figure, but it was gone.

My first impulse was to go to the station and wire a message; my next, which was acted upon, was to start off immediately to see whether my friend was really alive or dead, scarcely doubting that the latter was the case.

When I arrived next day I found him living, but in a state of semi-consciousness. He had been repeatedly asking for me, his mind apparently dwelling on the thought that I would not come to see him. As far as I could make out, at the time I saw him on the previous day he was apparently sleeping. He told me afterwards that he fancied he saw me, but had no clear idea how or where.

I have no means of accounting for the apparition, which was that of my friend clothed, and not as he must have been at the time. My mind was at the moment fully occupied with other matters, and I was not thinking of him. I may add that he rallied afterwards, and lived for several months. At the time of his death I was far from home, but there was no repetition of the mysterious experience. February 3rd, 1885.[81] — REV. W. E. DUTTON

☛ CASE #67: Forty years ago, or thereabouts, when I was about 20 years of age, a lady friend of mine, a distant relative by marriage—age between 40 and 50—had fo*r some time been in a delicate state of health, though not confined to the house. We frequently had quiet conversations together on religious matters. Neither of us was of an excitable turn of mind. The invalid herself was happy, and I felt a calm and comforting conviction of the truth of Christianity.

As well as I can now recollect I last saw my friend alive about a fortnight before her

death. She did not seem at that time to be worse than usual, and apparently might have lived at any rate for a few years.

However, one night when I was in bed—say about 4 o'clock in the morning—I had what I may call a vision [of a spirit]. A figure appeared before me neatly draped, and a certain brightness about it seemed to awake me. I at once felt conscious that someone was near me who wished to make a communication to me. I soon recognised the face of my invalid friend. She seemed to wish to give me time to collect myself evidently intimating that there was no cause why I should be afraid. As a matter of fact I had no fear at all. My then feelings may perhaps be best described as partaking both of wonder (or expectation) and pleasure.

When, apparently, the figure had convinced herself that I recognised her, and that I had satisfied myself that I was under no delusion, she seemed to beckon me cheeringly with one or two fingers of her right hand, and to say to me, "It's all right; come on." She then vanished, and I neither saw nor heard anything more.

Though there was no injunction given to me not to tell what I had seen, I yet felt that the communication was of too solemn a nature to allow me at once to talk of it openly. But I said to my brother at breakfast about 8 o'clock that morning that I had dreamt in the night that Mrs. So-and-so was dead, and it turned out, as we heard about 10 o'clock, that our friend had died during the night.

For some years I never mentioned this experience to anyone, but afterwards I felt no hesitation in talking about it to intimate friends.

To my brother I spoke of what I call the vision as if it had been a dream, but this was because I did not wish to draw his attention very specially to it, although I felt constrained to mention it to him in some way. He tells me now that he has no recollection of my having spoken to him about it, as I did at breakfast on the morning of the death, but before we knew of the death having taken place. I am not, however, surprised that my brother should not now recollect the remark I made to him at that time.

My own strong impression all along has been, and still is, that I was communicated with by the spirit of the departed. I, therefore, infer that in reference to that special communication I was to all intents and purposes awake. I never had any similar experience before, neither have I had since. I had no reason to expect any communication of the kind at any time. February 17th, 1885.[82] —
JOHN MATHWIN

☛ CASE #68: Mrs. Stewart, the wife of a carpenter, living in Abergavenny, Monmouthshire, and who is since dead, was in the year 1874, in bed, and early one morning, being sure she was awake (for she had just heard the railway men being called to their work by the call boy), she looked up to see the time, and in one corner of her room she saw distinctly what she thought was her mother, intently looking at her.

She was startled, and hid her face. On looking again the vision was still there, but on looking up a third time it had disappeared.

Mrs. Stewart come up that day to see a sister-in-law who was in service near the town, to ask if she had had any tidings from her home (the impression the vision had made was so great), but nothing had been heard.

Time passed on, and all seemed forgotten, when some of her friends came up to Abergavenny, to the christening of a little baby, born in the meantime. They were in mourning, and inquiries were made as to the friend mourned for, when it was told that on the night Mrs. Stewart thought she saw her mother, a sister of the mother's, to whom she bore a great likeness, had died about the hour named, at some distance off, but they did not tell Mrs. Stewart of the death until some weeks after it happened, as Mrs. Stewart was in delicate health and much attached to her aunt.[83] — JOHN STEWART

☛ CASE #69: On the 4th May, 1883, when on board the H. M. S. *Spartan*, on my way to Cape Town, I was awoke by hearing someone in my cabin, which I alone occupied, when to my surprise I saw the figure of a friend of mine standing by my berth. It then disappeared, and by the first mail after my arrival at Cape Town, I received the news of my friend's death, which took place at 10:30 p.m. on that day. I told two or three passengers on board, who made a note of it. November 1884.[84] — MISS KATE JENOUR

☛ CASE #70: Some 18 or 19 years ago, I remember calling on a working maltster, whose employer was living at Lincoln. His employer was ill at the time, and I asked the man if he had heard from him lately.

"No," he said, "but I am afraid he is dead."

And on my inquiring why he thought so, he replied that on going out that morning early he had seen his employer standing on the top of the steps that lead up to the kiln door, as plainly as he ever had seen him in his life. It was as he expected; the first news that came reported his employer's death.

I have no doubt the man I speak of either saw this appearance, or believed he saw it. March 5th, 1885.85 — UNNAMED CLERGYMAN

☛ CASE #71: Some time in the year 1862 (I think) I was living with my husband and family of little children, accompanied by our English nurse, in apartments in the city of Brussels. The house we occupied was a large one, and we rented the drawing-room and the floor above. The ground floor was occupied by the owner of the house, a Belgian, and his wife and little children. We had no intercourse with this family; we had our own kitchen on the drawing-room floor, and the upper floor consisted of nursery, with nursery bedroom opening from it. We had a Flemish general servant, who went home about 9 every night.

Our English nurse ["M."] was a very clever girl, about 22 or 23 years of age. She read a good deal, and taught herself French. She was very matter-of-fact, and handy and useful in every way. She had been with me 5 or 6 years. Her parents were labouring people in the neighbourhood of London, and by reading and culture she had raised herself a good deal out of their sphere.

We had been about 12 months away from England, when the circumstance I write of happened.

M.'s mother, after having a large family—the youngest being about 9 or 10—did not tell M., nor did any of the family, that she was again expecting an addition. The wife [Madame Nyo] of our landlord had been confined two days, so was in her own room, on the ground floor of the house we lived in.

One night my husband and myself had been out to dinner. On returning, a little after 10 o'clock, my husband was amazed to find our apartments in darkness, and he ran up to the nursery floor to complain to M. of her inattention; as the other servant had gone home it was her place to light our room. My husband found the nursery lighted, but empty, and going towards the children's room he met M. coming out. She began, "Oh! I am so glad to see you; I have been so frightened that I was obliged to sit on Willie's bed till you came in."

I was in the room by this time, and inquiring into the cause of fear. M. said, "After I put the children to bed I sat down in the nursery to my work, when I heard some one coming up the stairs. I went to the door, and on the first landing by your room, I saw, as I thought, Madame Nyo carrying something heavy. I felt that she ought not to be out of her bed, and I called to her in French '*Je viendrai vous aider,*' running down the stairs to where I supposed she was. When I got there it gave me a queer sensation to find no one. However, I said to myself, it was a shadow, and made myself go back to my work. I had scarcely seated myself when a voice called 'May, May, May' (the name my children called her). I got up, went to the door, and seeing some one, ran half way down the stairs to meet the woman, when a terrible dread came upon me, and I rushed back to the nursery and sat on one of the little beds, feeling that being with even a sleeping child was better than being alone."

My husband laughed at her, told her the *vin ordinaire* [that is, cheap wine] was too strong; that she had been dreaming, etc.

We none of us thought much of it, till the first post from England brought M. a letter to say her mother had been confined and she and the child had died within an hour after. Then we all felt convinced that M.'s mother had been able to come and see her daughter. February 18th, 1884.[86] — HARRIET WALSH

☛ CASE #72: During my college days I had a very dear and intimate chum, R. F. Dombrain. We used to walk together, read together, pray together, and would have thought it wrong to keep any secret from each other.

We hoped to go together into the foreign mission field, but my friend was ready to go before I was, and it was while he was in London making arrangements about going abroad that he was seized with a very bad fever, and his life for some time despaired of.

At last he recovered and returned to Dublin, where I saw him several times. He was not quite restored to health, but I hoped he would soon be so. This was the state of things when I went down to the County Limerick, in the spring of 1853. I received a few letters from my friend which told me of gradually improving health.

I was busily occupied about my mission work at the village of Doon, and felt perfectly at ease about my dear friend's recovery. A few days had elapsed without any tidings reaching me, when on the morning of the 14th of April, I had the most vivid dream I remember ever to have seen. I seemed to be walking with young Dombrain, amidst some beautiful scenery, when suddenly I was brought to a waking condition by a sort of light appearing before me. I started up in my bed, and saw before me, in his ordinary dress and appearance, my friend, who seemed to be passing from earth towards the light above. He seemed to give me one loving smile, and I felt that his look contained an expression of affectionate separation and farewell. Then I leaped out of bed, and cried with a loud voice, "Robert, Robert," and the vision was gone.

In the house there was sleeping a young servant boy, whose name was also Robert. He came running into my room, saying that my loud cry had awakened him from sound sleep, and that he thought I was ill. The whole scene was so impressed upon my mind that I felt the death of my friend just as really as if I had been by his bedside, and seen him pass away. I had looked at my watch and found the time 3 minutes past 5. I knew that at that moment my friend's spirit had passed from his body. I could think of nothing else.

A class of Scripture readers came to me at 10 o'clock that morning. I told them I could not speak to them of the appointed subject, but must tell them what had occurred, and for a long time I lectured them entirely on the subject of the future state, and the separation of the soul from the body. During the whole of the day the same sad gloom weighed down my mind, which I should have felt had I been with my friend at his deathbed.

I wrote to my sister asking for particulars, and I wished to know the exact time the death had taken place. Never once did the slightest doubt cross my mind that my friend had died.

The following morning I received a letter from my sister stating that for a few days Mr. Dombrain had not been so well, and that at 3 minutes past 5 in the morning he had quietly passed away from this world.

Since then I have very often mentioned the circumstance to friends, and the deep impression made by the event can never pass from my mind. I lately wrote to my sister asking her to tell me what she remembered about [my] . . . dream. Her reply is dated 17th July, 1884; she says: "I have not a distinct remembrance of the dream. I have heard you allude to it from time to time, and feel quite confident of its reality."[87] — S. P. BALL

☞ CASE #73: I was on a visit at Colnbrook, in Buckinghamshire, in 1878, and one night when I went to bed, and while yet fully awake, I felt an influence as if someone was in the room. I sat up to see what it was, and saw my grandmother, in the plaid cloak she usually wore, leaning upon my mother's arm. I looked round the room to see whether the vision could have arisen from any reflection from the mirrors in the room, and while doing so I saw the figures walk slowly round the room and disappear.

I afterwards ascertained that my grandmother died in London about the time I had seen the apparition in Buckinghamshire. London, October 1884.[88] — MISS KATE R.

☞ CASE #74: There is now living in the parish where we write—she was at church last Sunday—a widow now in her 78th year, but in full possession of all her faculties, who has more than once told us, with all the fulness of detail, and subject to all the cross-questioning which we could devise, how she was at service some miles from home during her father's last illness, and that one Thursday she felt unable to go on with her work, and after a while, about 1 o'clock, saw a vision of her father; that it turned out afterwards that her father died at that very time, and that just before his death he had been speaking of her; that a letter sent to inform her of his being worse failed to reach her and that though she knew he was ill she was not aware that he was in immediate danger; but that she was so impressed with her vision that she set off home the Saturday following, and learnt on the way that her father was dead, and that his funeral was to take place that very day, so that she arrived only just in time.

Indeed, we must confess that the evidence for "apparitions" at the time of departure is so strong that we cannot but accept it as more probably true than false, leaving, however, the philosophical explanation of what an "apparition" may really be to the future. We have verified one subordinate part of the above narrative; for by reference to the parish register we find that the burial took place on the 31st of May, 1823; and as the Sunday letter for that year was E, which is the letter for the 1st of June, the burial turns out to have been, as stated, on a Saturday. Our informant was then, as shown by the register of her baptism, 25 years old.[89] — REV. J. FOXLEY

☞ CASE #75: When I was about 10 or 12 years old I was sitting one evening, towards dusk, at the piano practising, when I saw an old lady, the grandmother of one of my schoolfellows, enter the room. I was in the habit of seeing her frequently and recognised her perfectly. She was very old, and to the best of my belief had never entered our house at all, so that I was greatly surprised to see her. I heard the next day she had died on the evening I saw her. I never had any other hallucination. Autumn 1884.[90] — MARY C.

☞ CASE #76: When I was about 16 years old (probably about 20 years ago), my father came down to breakfast one morning, and, after saying he had been awake a long time, he said, "and about 5 or 6" (I forget the exact time), "I saw old Mr.____; he came and stood by the bed a minute or two, and then went."

In the course of the day we heard of the death of this old gentleman, of whose illness we had previously known, but whose death we had not anticipated, as it was not thought his complaint was one likely to cause death. On inquiry, we learnt that he had died at the hour that my father had said he had had a visit from him.

My father was a merry, strong-minded man, with a scientific turn of mind and a great scorn of superstition. He is, alas! dead now some years, and I don't think we any of us thought more of the circumstance than that it was odd, but I remembered it.[91] — MRS. B.

☞ CASE #77: In the autumn of 1845 we were a large party of young ones staying in the house, and on one occasion were playing at a species of hide-and-seek, in which we were allowed to move from one hiding-place to another until caught by the opposite side. At the back of the house there was a small fold-yard opening on one side into the orchard, on the other into the stable-yard, and there were other buildings to the left.

I came round the corner of these buildings, and saw my cousin standing under some trees about 20 yards from me, and I distinctly saw her face; my sister, who at the moment appeared on the other side, also saw her and shouted to me to give chase. My cousin ran between us in the direction of the fold-yard, and when she reached the door we were both close behind her and followed instantly, but she had entirely disappeared, though scarcely a second had elapsed; we looked at one another in amazement, and searched every corner of the yard in vain; and when found some little time afterwards, she assured us she had never been on that side of the house at all, or anywhere near the spot, but had remained hidden in the same place until discovered by one of the enemy.[92] — S. F. D.

☞ CASE #78: On the first floor of Leigh Rectory there is a passage which runs the length of the house, terminated at one end by the door of a room that was then the nursery. One morning about 10:30 Caroline came out of the nursery, and walking along the passage had to pass a doorway opening on to the stairs which led down into the front hall. As she passed, she glanced down and saw me (conspicuous by the white handkerchief round my head, and facing her) come out of the drawing-room door and walk across the corner of the hall to the library. She proceeded along the passage, and coming to the foot of the attic stairs met our maid, who said to her, "Do you know where Miss Eden is? I want to go to her room."

"Oh yes," answered Caroline. "I just saw her go into the library."

So they came together up to my room, which was one of the

attics, and found me sitting there, where I had been for at least half-an-hour, writing a letter. After a moment's pause of astonishment, they fled, though I called to them to come in.

When I went downstairs a few minutes afterwards and reached the passage, I saw in the nursery a group of maids, all looking so perturbed that, instead of proceeding down the front stairs, I went on to the nursery and asked what was the matter. But as no one answered, and I saw the nursery maid was crying, I thought they had been quarrelling, and went away quite unconscious that it was on my account they were so disturbed.[93] — MRS. LUCY HAWKINS

☛ CASE #79: In the autumn of 1877, I was living at my father's house, Beyton Rectory, Bury St. Edmunds. The household consisted of my father, mother, three sisters, and three maid-servants. One moonlight night I was sleeping in my room, and had been asleep some hours when I was awakened by hearing a noise close to my head, like the chinking of money. My waking idea, therefore, was that a man was trying to take my money out of my trousers pocket, which lay on a chair close to the head of my bed.

On opening my eyes, I was astonished to see a woman, and I well remember thinking with sorrow that it must be one of our servants who was trying to take my money. I mention these two thoughts to show that I was not thinking in the slightest degree of my mother. When my eyes had become more accustomed to the light, I was more than ever surprised to see that it was my mother, dressed in a peculiar silver-grey dress, which she had originally got for a fancy ball. She was standing with both hands stretched out in front of her as if feeling her way, and in that manner moved slowly away from me, passing in front of the dressing-table, which stood in front of the curtained window, through which the moon threw a certain amount of light. Of course my idea all this time was that she was walking in her sleep.

On getting beyond the table she was lost to my sight in the darkness. I then sat up in bed, listening but hearing nothing, and on peering through the darkness saw that the door, which was at the foot of my bed, and to get to which she would have had to pass in front of the light, was still shut. I then jumped out of bed, struck a light, and instead of finding my mother at the far end of the room, as I expected, found the room empty. I then for the first time supposed that it was an "appearance" [apparition], and greatly dreaded that it signified her death.

I might add that I had, at that time, quite forgotten that my mother had ever appeared to any one before, her last appearance having been about the year 1847, three years before I was born. June 20th, 1885.[94] — EDWARD HAWKINS [SON OF THE WRITER OF THE PREVIOUS CASE]

☛ CASE #80: Some years ago (I cannot give you any date, but you may rely on the facts), on one occasion when I was absent from home, my wife awoke one morning, and to her surprise and alarm saw my likeness standing by the bedside looking at her. In her fright she covered her face with the bedclothes, and when she ventured to look again the appearance was gone.

On another occasion, when I was not absent from home, my wife went one evening to week-day evensong, and on getting to the churchyard gate, which is about 40 yards or so from the church door, she saw me, as she supposed, coming from the church in surplice and stole. I came a little way, she says, and turned round the corner of the building, when she lost sight of me. The idea suggested to her mind was that I was coming out of the church to meet a funeral at the gate. I was at the time in church in my place in the choir, where she was much surprised to see me when she entered the building.

I have often endeavoured to shake my wife's belief in the reality of her having seen what she thinks she saw. In the former case I have told her "You were only half awake and perhaps dreaming." But she always confidently asserts that she was broad awake, and is quite certain that she saw me. In the latter case she is equally confident.

My daughter also has often told me and now repeats the story, that one day when living at home before her marriage she was passing my study door, which was ajar, and looked in to see if I was there. She saw me sitting in my chair, and as she caught sight of me I stretched out my arms, and drew my hands across my eyes, a familiar gesture of mine, it appears. I was not in the house at the time, but out in the village. This happened many years ago, but my wife remembers that my daughter mentioned the circumstance to her at the time.

Now, nothing whatever occurred at or about the times of these appearances to give any meaning to them. I was not ill, nor had anything unusual happened to me. I cannot pretend to offer any explanation, but simply state the facts as told me by persons on whose words I can depend.

There is one other thing which I may as well mention. A good many years ago there was a very devout young woman living in my parish who used to spend much of her spare time in church in meditation and prayer. She used to assert that she frequently saw me standing at the altar, when I was certainly not there in the body. At first she was alarmed, but after seeing the appearance again and again she ceased to feel anything of terror. She is now a Sister of Mercy at Honolulu.[95] — THOMAS LOCKYER WILLIAMS

☛ CASE #81: When a resident near Portsmouth, during a visit made by my late mother to London in the summer of 1858, the year preceding her death, I distinctly saw her walking in the back garden at noon-day. I was not at the time thinking of her, but happening to look from my chamber window, I beheld this figure, which, but for my parent's absence from home, I should have supposed her veritable self.

This incident led me to conjecture something was amiss, and this idea was confirmed when the next morning's post brought me information that my mother had sustained a severe fall and was so badly hurt that at first fatal results were feared, and at the moment I fancied I saw her, her thoughts were bent on telegraphing for me to go to her. February 20th, 1885.[96] — M. W.

☛ CASE #82: About 14 years ago, about 3 o'clock one summer's afternoon I was passing in front of Trinity Church, Upper King Street, Leicester, when I saw on the opposite side of the street a very old playmate, who, having left the town to learn some business, I had for some time lost sight of. I thought it odd he took no notice of me, and while following him with my eyes deliberated whether I should accost him or not. I called after him by name, and was somewhat surprised at not being able to follow him any further, or to say into which house he had gone, for I felt persuaded he had gone into one.

The next week I was informed of his somewhat sudden death at Burton-on-Trent, at about the time I had felt certain he was passing in front of me. What struck me most at the time was that he should take no notice of me, and that he should go along so noiselessly and disappear so suddenly, but that it was E. P. I had seen I never for one moment doubted. I have always looked upon this as a hallucination, but why it should have occurred at that particular time, and to me, I could never make out. January 5th, 1884.[97] — ARTHUR IRELAND

☛ CASE #83: I very well remember my brother, the late Major A. P. Scott Moncrieff telling me of an apparition, as he believed it to have been, of our sister Susan, after the news reached us of her death in Edinburgh, on September 7th, 1852.

I was living in Calcutta at that date; my brother was with his regiment at Dinapore. In the month of November, I was on a visit to his house in Hazareebagh, where he was then living with his wife; and it was then that he told me of the apparition.

As he was a man of a very unromantic, practical character, always ready to ridicule a ghost story, I was the more struck with the depth of the impression left on his mind by the vividness of the apparition, as he believed it to have been, which had led to his taking a note of the date in writing.

He told me that after having been asleep for a time, during the night of that date (which must have been the 7th September), he awoke, feeling the heat rather trying; that he saw, by a light burning in the room, the punkah swinging above the bed, and then saw our sister Susan standing at the foot of the bed, gazing at him very earnestly. That he was so surprised, he sat up, rubbed his eyes, and looked again, seeing her still there. That he exclaimed, "O, Susan!" (I think he added, "what are you doing here?" but I am not certain that these were his words; though I am certain that he did utter some such words after saying, "O, Susan!") That his wife awoke on hearing him speak, and said, "What is it, Alick?" (or words of similar import) but that he, fearing lest in the state of health she was then in, it might prove injurious to her to be told what he believed he had seen, said he had awakened from a dream, but did not tell her how fully he was convinced he had been awake when he saw the apparition of his sister, which had disappeared before his wife had spoken to him.[98] — MISS R. SCOTT MONCRIEFF

☛ CASE #84: A striking illustration, both of veridical hallucination and deferred percipience, is afforded by an experiment tried more than twenty years ago by an English clergyman, the Rev. Clarence Godfrey, who undertook to cause a distant friend, a lady whose identity is not revealed in the records of the case, to see a telepathic apparition of him.

Accordingly, when he retired one evening (at 10:45 P.M., on November 15, 1886), he began intently to "will" that she should see him. His "willing" lasted for less than ten minutes, when he fell asleep. Some hours later his friend had the following uncanny experience:

> Yesterday—viz., the morning of November 16, 1886—about half-past three o'clock [A.M.], I woke up with a start and an idea that someone had come into the room. I heard a curious sound, but fancied it might be the birds in the ivy outside. Next I experienced a strange, restless longing to leave the room and go down stairs. This feeling became so overpowering that at last I arose and lit a candle and went down, thinking that if I could get some soda water it might have a quieting effect.
>
> On returning to my room I saw Mr. Godfrey standing under the large window on the staircase. He was dressed in his usual style, and with an expression on his face that I have noticed when he has been looking earnestly at anything. He stood there, and I held up the candle and gazed at him for three or four seconds in utter amazement, and then, as I passed up the staircase, he disappeared. The impression left on my mind was so vivid that I fully intended waking a friend who occupied the same room as myself, but remembering that I should only be laughed at as romantic and imaginative, I refrained from doing so.[99] — HENRY ADDINGTON BRUCE

☛ CASE #85: . . . Nor does the [previous] case stand alone, the records of the Society for Psychical Research containing a number of similar experiments successfully carried out. Thus, a Mr. Kirk from a distance of several miles caused a telepathic phantasm to appear to a Miss G., and this in broad daylight. Miss G.'s report, published in the society's "Proceedings," informs us:

> A peculiar occurrence happened to me on the Wednesday of the week before last. In the afternoon (being tired by a morning walk) while sitting in an easy chair near the window of my own room, I fell asleep. At any time I happen to sleep during the day (which is but seldom) I invariably awake with tired, uncomfortable sensations which take some little time to pass off, but that afternoon, on the contrary, I was suddenly quite wide awake, seeing Mr. Kirk standing near my chair, dressed in a dark-brown coat, which I had frequently seen him wear. His back was toward the window, his right hand toward me; he passed across the room toward the door . . . but when he got about four feet from the door, which was closed, he disappeared.[100] — HENDY ADDINGTON BRUCE

☛ CASE #86: The significance of this phenomenon [cited above] to our present subject of inquiry may be emphasized by yet another illustration—the experimental production, by means of telepathy, of an apparition not of the living but of the dead.

The experimenter, a certain Herr Wesermann, determined to cause a Lieutenant N. to see in a dream a vision of a lady who had been dead for some years, his purpose being to incite Lieutenant N. thereby to "a good action."

Eleven o'clock was selected by him as the hour for the experiment, nothing of which, of course, was known to N. But at eleven the latter, instead of being in bed and asleep, was conversing with a fellow officer in his room at the barracks. Nevertheless, the experiment, if Herr Wesermann's narrative is to be accepted, was a complete and sensational success. The door of the chamber seemed to open and the "ghost" of the dead lady to walk in. Both of the astounded warriors claimed to have seen her distinctly, and both, upon her disappearance, excitedly summoned the sentinel, who assured them that no one had entered the room.[101]— HENRY ADDINGTON BRUCE

☛ CASE #87: [Let us look at] . . . an old-fashioned "ghost" story of the simpler sort. In this instance the percipient, a Mr. J., was a personal acquaintance of Frederic William Henry Myers [one of the founders of the Society for Psychical Research], who obtained a first-hand account of the experience.

In 1880, it appears, Mr. Q., the librarian of X. library, died and Mr. J. was appointed his successor. Mr. J. had not known Mr. Q. nor had he, to his knowledge, seen any portrait of him when, in 1884, or four years after his death, he made the old librarian's acquaintance under these circumstances:

> I was sitting alone in the library one evening late in March, 1884, finishing some work after hours, when it suddenly occurred to me that I should miss the last train to H., where I was then living, if I did not make haste. . . . I gathered up some books in one hand, took the lamp in the other, and prepared to leave the librarian's room, which communicated by a passage with the main room of the library.

As my lamp illumined the passage I saw apparently at the end of it a man's face. I instantly thought a thief had got into the library. I turned back into my room, put down the books, and took a revolver from the safe, and, holding the lamp cautiously behind me, I made my way along the passage . . . into the main room. Here I saw no one, but the room was large and encumbered with bookcases. I called out loudly to the intruder to show himself several times, more with the hope of attracting a passing policeman than of drawing the intruder.

Then I saw a face looking round one of the bookcases. I say round, but it had an odd appearance as if the body were in the bookcase, as the face came so closely to the edge and I could see no body. The face was pallid and hairless, and the orbits of the eyes were very deep. I advanced toward it, and as I did so I saw an old man with high shoulders seem to rotate out of the end of the bookcase, and with his back toward me, and with a shuffling gait, walk rather quickly from the bookcase to the door of a small lavatory, which opened from the library and had no other access. I heard no noise.

I followed the man at once into the lavatory; and to my extreme surprise found no one there. . . . Completely mystified, I even looked into the little cupboard under the fixed basin. There was nowhere hiding for a child, and I confess I began to experience for the first time what novelists describe as an "eerie" feeling. I left the library, and found I had missed my train.

Next morning I mentioned what I had seen to a local clergyman who, on hearing my description, said, "Why, that's old Q.!" Soon after I saw a photograph (from a drawing) of Q., and the resemblance was certainly striking. Q. had lost all his hair, eyebrows and all, from (I believe) a gunpowder accident. His walk was a peculiar, rapid, high-shouldered shuffle. Later inquiry proved he had died at about the time of year at which I saw the figure.[102] — HENRY ADDINGTON BRUCE

☛ CASE #88: Somewhat similar [to the previous case], but having a coincidental significance, is the story of the "ghost" seen by the Essex gardener, who one morning beheld, as he thought, a lady whom he knew standing by a family tomb. The lady in question was then supposed to be in London, but as she had an almost morbid habit of visiting the tomb, the gardener supposed that she had returned from the city. Later it was learned that at the time he imagined he saw her she was lying dead in London.[103] — HENRY ADDINGTON BRUCE

☛ CASE #89: . . . an unnamed but "well known Irish gentleman" relates that when his wife was dying she affirmed that she saw in a corner of the room a certain Julia Z., who had once sung at a house party given by the dying woman and whose apparition, according to the unhappy percipient, was even then singing. Since Julia Z. was, to the best of his knowledge, alive and well, her husband suspected all this to be "nothing but the fantasies of a dying person."

The day after his wife's death, however, he was astounded to learn that Julia Z. had herself died a fortnight earlier, and on writing to the latter's husband was told that "on the day she died she began singing in the morning, and sang and sang until she died."[164] — HENRY ADDINGTON BRUCE

☛ CASE #90: In 1867 my only sister, a young lady of eighteen years, died suddenly of cholera in St. Louis, Missouri. My attachment for her was very strong, and the blow a severe one to me. A year or so after her death I became a commercial traveler, and it was in 1876, while on one of my Western trips, that the event occurred.

I had "drummed" the city of St. Joseph, Mo., and had gone to my room at the Pacific House to send in my orders, which were unusually large ones, so that I was in a very happy frame of mind indeed . . . . The hour was high noon, and the sun was shining cheerfully into my room. While busily smoking a cigar and writing out my orders, I suddenly became conscious that some one was sitting on my left, with one arm resting on the table. Quick as a flash I turned and distinctly saw the form of my dead sister, and for a brief second or so looked her squarely in the face; and so sure was I that it was she, that I sprang forward in delight, calling her by name, and, as I did so, the apparition instantly vanished.

Naturally I was startled and dumfounded, almost doubting my senses; but the cigar in my mouth, and pen in hand, with the ink still moist on my letter, I satisfied myself I had not been dreaming and was wide awake.

Now comes the most remarkable confirmation of my statement, which cannot be doubted by those who know what I state actually occurred. This visitation, or whatever you may call it, so impressed me that I took the next train home, and in the presence of my parents and others I related what had occurred. My father, a man of rare good sense and very practical, was inclined to ridicule me, as he saw how earnestly I believed what I stated; but he, too, was amazed when later on I told them of a bright red line or *scratch* on the right-hand side of my sister's face, which I distinctly had seen.

When I mentioned this my mother rose trembling to her feet and nearly fainted away, and as soon as she sufficiently recovered her self-possession, with tears streaming down her face, she exclaimed that I had indeed seen my sister, as no living mortal but herself was aware of that scratch, which she had accidentally made while doing some little act of kindness after my sister's death. She said she well remembered how pained she was to think she should have, unintentionally, marred the features of her dead daughter, and that unknown to all, how she had carefully obliterated all traces of the slight scratch with the aid of powder, etc., and that she had never mentioned it to a human being from that day to this. In proof, neither my father nor any of our family had detected it, and positively were unaware of the incident, yet *I saw the scratch as bright as if just made.*[105] — HENRY ADDINGTON BRUCE

☛ CASE #91: I arose about the usual hour on the morning of [October 24th, 1889], probably about six o'clock. I had slept well throughout the night, had no dreams or sudden awakenings. I awoke feeling gloomy and depressed, which feeling I could not shake off.

After breakfast my husband went to his work, and, at the proper time, the children were gotten ready and sent to school, leaving me alone in the house. Soon after this I decided to steep and drink some tea, hoping it would relieve me of the gloomy feelings aforementioned. I went into the pantry, took down the tea canister, and as I turned around my brother Edmund—or his exact image—stood before me and only a few feet away. The apparition stood with back toward me, or, rather, partially so, and was in the act of falling forward—away from me—seemingly impelled by two ropes or a loop of rope drawing against his legs. The vision lasted but a moment, disappearing over a low railing or bulwark, but was very distinct.

I dropped the tea, clasped my hands to my face, and exclaimed, "My God! Ed is drowned."

At about half-past ten A.M. my husband received a telegram from Chicago, announcing the drowning of my brother [that same day]. When he arrived home he said to me, "Ed is sick in hospital at Chicago; I have just received a telegram." To which I replied, "Ed is drowned; I saw him go overboard."

I then gave him a minute description of what I had seen. I stated that my brother, as I saw him, was bareheaded, had on a heavy, blue sailor's shirt, no coat, and that he went over the rail or bulwark. I noticed that his pants legs were rolled up enough to show the white lining inside. I also described the appearance of the boat at the point where my brother went overboard. I am not nervous, and neither before nor since have I had any experience in the least degree similar to that above related. My brother was not subject to fainting or vertigo.

[A statement of the actual accident was later published:] On October 24th, 1889, Edmund Dunn, brother of Mrs. Agnes Paquet, was serving as fireman on the tug *Wolf*, a small steamer engaged in towing vessels in Chicago Harbour. At about 3 o'clock A.M., the tug fastened to a vessel, inside the piers, to tow her up the river. While adjusting the tow-line Mr. Dunn fell or was thrown overboard by the tow-line, and drowned. The body, though sought for, was not found until about three weeks after the accident, when it came to the surface near the place where Mr. Dunn disappeared.[106] — AGNES PAQUET

☛ CASE #92: I had known Mr. ____ as a medical man, under whose treatment I had been for some years, and at whose hands I had experienced great kindness. He had ceased to attend me for considerably more than a year at the time of his death. I was aware that he had given up practice, but beyond that I knew nothing of his proceedings, or of the state of his health. At the time I last saw him he appeared particularly well, and even made some remark himself as to the amount of vigour and work left in him.

On Thursday, the 16th day of December 1875, I had been for some little time on a visit at my brother-in-law's and sister's house near London. I was in good health, but from the morning and throughout the day I felt unaccountably depressed and out of spirits, which I attributed to the gloominess of the weather.

A short time after lunch, about two o'clock, I thought I would go up to the nursery to amuse myself with the children, and try to recover my spirits. The attempt failed, and I returned to the dining-room, where I sat by myself, my sister being engaged elsewhere.

The thought of Mr. came into my mind, and suddenly, with my eyes open, as I believe, for I was not feeling sleepy, I seemed to be in a room in which a man was lying dead in a small bed. I recognised the face at once as that of Mr. ____, and felt no doubt that he was dead, and not asleep only. The room appeared to be bare and without carpet or furniture. I cannot say how long the appearance lasted.

I did not mention the appearance to my sister or brother-in-law at the time. I tried to argue with myself that there could be nothing in what I had seen, chiefly on the ground that from what I knew of Mr. ____'s circumstances it was most improbable that, if dead, he would be in a room in so bare and unfurnished a state.

Two days afterwards, on December 18th, I left my sister's house for home. About a week after my arrival, another of my sisters read out of the daily papers the announcement of Mr. ____'s death, which had taken place abroad, and on December 16th, the day on which I had seen the appearance.

I have since been informed that Mr. had died in a small village hospital in a warm foreign climate, having been suddenly attacked with illness whilst on his travels.[107] — MR. J. BRADLEY DYNE

☛ CASE #93: An account of a circumstance which occurred to me when quartered at Templemore, Co. Tipperary, on 20th February 1847.

This afternoon, about 3 o'clock P.M., I was walking from my quarters towards the mess-room to put some letters into the

letter-box, when I distinctly saw Lieut.-Colonel Reed, 70th Regiment, walking from the corner of the range of buildings occupied by the officers towards the mess-room door; and I saw him go into the passage. He was dressed in a brown shooting-jacket, with grey summer regulation tweed trousers, and had a fishing-rod and a landing-net in his hand. Although at the time I saw him he was about 15 or 20 yards from me, and although anxious to speak to him at the moment, I did not do so, but followed him into the passage and turned into the anteroom on the left-hand side, where I expected to find him.

On opening the door, to my great surprise, he was not there; the only person in the room was Quartermaster Nolan, 70th Regiment, and I immediately asked him if he had seen the colonel, and he replied he had not; upon which I said, "I suppose he has gone upstairs," and I immediately left the room.

Thinking he might have gone upstairs to one of the officers' rooms, I listened at the bottom of the stairs and then went up to the first landing-place; but not hearing anything I went downstairs again and tried to open the bedroom door, which is opposite to the anteroom, thinking he might have gone there; but I found the door locked, as it usually is in the middle of the day. I was very much surprised at not finding the colonel, and I walked into the barrack-yard and joined Lieutenant Caulfield, 66th Regiment, who was walking there; and I told the story to him, and particularly described the dress in which I had seen the colonel.

We walked up and down the barrack-yard talking about it for about ten minutes, when, to my great surprise, never having kept my eye from the door leading to the mess-room (there is only one outlet from it), I saw the colonel walk into the barracks through the gate which is in the opposite direction—accompanied by Ensign Willington, 70th Regiment, in precisely the same dress in which I had seen him, and with a fishing-rod and a landing-net in his hand.

Lieutenant Caulfield and I immediately walked to them, and we were joined by Lieut.-Colonel Goldie, 66th Regiment, and Captain Hartford, and I asked Colonel Reed if he had not gone into the mess-room about ten minutes before. He replied that he certainly had not, for that he had been out fishing for more than two hours at some ponds about a mile from the barracks, and that he had not been near the mess-room at all since the morning.

At the time I saw Colonel Reed going into the mess-room, I was not aware that he had gone out fishing—a very unusual thing to do at this time of the year; neither had I seen him before in the dress I have described during that day. I had seen him in uniform in the morning at parade, but not afterwards at all until 3 o'clock—having been engaged in my room writing letters, and upon other business.

My eyesight being very good, and the colonel's figure and general appearance somewhat remarkable, it is morally impossible that I could have mistaken any other person in the world for him. That I did see him I shall continue to believe until the last day of my existence.[108] — WILLIAM MATTHEW BIGGE, MAJOR, 70TH REGIMENT

☛ CASE #94: I was playing the harmonium in the church of at about 4 P.M., August 1889, when I saw my eldest sister walk up the church towards the chancel with a roll of papers under her arm. When I looked up again she had disappeared, and I thought she had just come in for a few minutes and gone out again; but when I asked her afterwards what she wanted in the church, she was much surprised, and told me she had been in the rectory library all the afternoon, studying genealogical tables.

I am not sure of the exact date, but it was about the time I mention. I was practising on the harmonium; as far as I remember

I was quite well and not worried about anything. I was eighteen years old. A younger sister was the only other person in the church with me at the time. She was standing beside me on an old stone coffin, and also noticed my eldest sister walk up the church with papers under her arm, but thought it nothing unusual and looked away, and when she looked back again my sister had disappeared.

My eldest sister looked just as usual and wore her hat and jacket, as I and my younger sister both noticed. She walked rather briskly, looking straight before her. She assures us that she was sitting alone in the rectory library (the rectory is within a stone's throw of the church) all the afternoon. March 1892.[109] — MISS C. J. E.

☛ CASE #95: In the autumn of 1863, I was living with my husband and first baby, a child of eight months, in a lone house, called Sibberton, near Wansford, Northamptonshire, which in bygone days had been a church. As the weather became more wintry, a married cousin and her husband came on a visit.

One night, when we were having supper, an apparition [of me] stood at the end of the sideboard. We four sat at the dining-table; and yet, with great inconsistency, I stood as this ghostly visitor again, in a spotted, light muslin summer dress, and without any terrible peculiarities of air or manner. We all four saw it, my husband having attracted our attention to it, saying, "It is Sarah," in a tone of recognition, *meaning me*. It at once disappeared.

None of us felt any fear, it seemed too natural and familiar. The apparition [of me] seemed utterly apart from myself and my feelings, as a picture or statue. My three relatives, who, with me, saw the apparition, are all dead; they died in about the years 1868-69.[110] — SARAH JANE HALL

☛ CASE #96: Helen Alexander (maid to Lady Waldegrave) was lying here very ill with typhoid fever, and was attended by me. I was standing at the table by her bedside, pouring out her medicine, at about 4 o'clock in the morning of the 4th October 1880. I heard the call-bell ring (this had been heard twice before during the night in that same week), and was attracted by the door of the room opening, and by seeing a person entering the room whom I instantly felt to be the mother of the sick woman.

She had a brass candlestick in her hand, a red shawl over her shoulders, and a flannel petticoat on which had a hole in the front. I looked at her as much as to say, "I am glad you have come," but the woman looked at me sternly, as much as to say, "Why wasn't

I sent for before?" I gave the medicine to Helen Alexander, and then turned round to speak to the vision, but no one was there. She had gone. She was a short, dark person, and very stout.

At about 6 o'clock that morning Helen Alexander died. Two days after her parents and a sister came to Antony, and arrived between 1 and 2 o'clock in the morning; I and another maid let them in, and it gave me a great turn when I saw the living likeness of the vision I had seen two nights before. I told the sister about the vision, and she said that the description of the dress exactly answered to her mother's, and that they had brass candlesticks at home exactly like the one described. There was not the slightest resemblance between the mother and daughter.[111] — FRANCES REDDELL

☛ CASE #97: In the month of August 1864, about 3 or 4 o'clock in the afternoon, I was sitting reading in the verandah of our house in Barbadoes. My black nurse was driving my little girl, about eighteen months or so old, in her perambulator in the garden.

I got up after some time to go into the house, not having noticed anything at all—when this black woman said to me, "Missis, who was that gentleman that was talking to you just now?" "There was no one talking to me," I said. "Oh, yes, dere was, missis—a very pale gentleman, very tall, and he talked to you, and you was very rude, for you never answered him."

I repeated there was no one, and got rather cross with the woman, and she begged me to write down the day, for she knew she had seen some one. I did, and in a few days I heard of the death of my brother in Tobago. Now, the curious part is this, that I did not see him, but she—a stranger to him—did; and she said that he seemed very anxious for me to notice him.[112] — MAY CLERKE

☛ CASE #98: I remember in the June of 1889, I drove to Castleblaney [Castleblayney], a little town in the [Irish] county Monaghan, to meet my sister, who was coming by train from Longford. I expected her at three o'clock, but as she did not come with that train, I got the horse put up, and went for a walk in the demesne.

The day was very warm and bright, and I wandered on under the shade of the trees to the side of a lake, which is in the demesne. Being at length tired, I sat down to rest upon a rock, at the edge of the water. My attention was quite taken up with the extreme beauty of the scene before me. There was not a sound or movement, except the soft ripple of the water on the sand at my feet.

Presently I felt a cold chill creep through me, and a curious stiffness of my limbs, as if I could not move, though wishing to do so. I felt frightened, yet chained to the spot, and as if impelled to stare at the water straight in front of me. Gradually a black cloud seemed to rise, and in the midst of it I saw a tall man, in a suit of tweed, jump into the water and sink.

In a moment the darkness was gone, and I again became sensible of the heat and sunshine, but I was awed and felt "eerie"—it was then about four o'clock or so I cannot remember either the exact time or date.

On my sister's arrival I told her of the occurrence; she was surprised, but inclined to laugh at it. When we got home I told my brother; he treated the subject much in the same manner. However, about a week afterwards, a Mr. Espie, a bank clerk (unknown to me), committed suicide by drowning in that very spot. He left a letter for his wife, indicating that he had for some time contemplated his death. My sister's memory of the event is the only evidence I can give. I did not see the account of the inquest at the time, and did not mention my strange experience to any one, saving my sister and brother.[113] — F. C. McALPINE

☛ CASE #99: In the autumn of 1877, while at Sholebrook Lodge, Towcester, Northamptonshire, one night, at a little after ten o'clock, I remember I was about to move a lamp in my room to a position where I usually sat a little while before retiring to bed, when I suddenly saw a vision of my brother. It seemed to affect me like a mild shock of electricity. It surprised me so that I hesitated to carry out what I had intended, my eyes remaining fixed on the apparition of my brother. It gradually disappeared, leaving me wondering what it meant.

I am positive no light or reflection deceived me. I had not been sleeping or rubbing my eyes. I was again in the act of moving my lamp when I heard taps along the window. I looked towards it—the window was on the ground-floor—and heard a [real] voice, my brother's, say, "It's I, don't be frightened." I let him in; he remarked, "How cool you are! I thought I should have frightened you."

The fact was, that the distinct vision of my brother had quite prepared me for his call. He found the window by accident, as he had never been to the house before; to use his own words, "I thought it was your window, and that I should find you." He had unexpectedly left London to pay me a visit, and when near the house lost his way, and had found his way in the dark to the back of the place.[114] — JAMES CARROLL

☛ CASE #100: I was a student at St. Edward's School, Oxford, from autumn 1881 to Easter 1890, and during that long period Miss S. (the well-known philanthropist) was constantly at the school, being a great friend of the then Warden (the Rev. A. B. Simeon, well known in Oxford High Church circles). Of course I saw Miss S. constantly, often several times in one week. She was for many years perhaps the best-known figure in Oxford.

I was abroad from 1890 to Christmas 1894. In July, 1899, I came to live here, and in November of that year bicycled from here to Oxford to visit my old school, not having entered Oxford since Easter 1890. As I approached the Martyrs' Memorial I saw Miss S. She passed a very little way ahead of me, across the road, towards the Ashmolean, with her usual brisk and active style, the inevitable basket upon her arm. I don't suppose I had given the good lady a thought during the past nine years or so, but I was very pleased to see her there, having seen no other familiar face during my ride through Oxford.

I know I was surprised to see her looking so well and strong and active despite her years, and I slowed up, feeling a strong desire to speak to her, but on reaching the pavement where Beaumont Street begins, I lost sight of her in the crowd.

That incident of meeting with Miss S. always stood out very strongly in my memory (which is an exceptionally powerful one), but I thought little of it until about a month ago her life [biography] came into my hands (published by John Murray, 1902). While turning over the pages something seemed to say to me, "It was her spirit you saw that day."

Immediately I looked up the date of her death and found she had passed over on Friday, the 5th (or perhaps it was the 6th—I have not got the book now) of October, 1899. It was at 3 p.m. on Wednesday, 15th November, that I saw her in Oxford, more than a month later.

I must own I took no particular interest in Miss S., and really had no wish to see her, incarnate or otherwise. I need scarcely add I did not at the time know she was dead, and I certainly was not thinking of her, even remotely. June 9th, 1903.[115] — ERNEST G. HENHAM

☛ CASE #101: A little friend of ours, Hughey G., had been ill a long time. His mother, who was my greatest friend, had nursed her boy with infinite care, and during her short last illness was full of solicitude for him.

After her death he seemed to become stronger for a time, but again grew very ill, and needed the most constant care, his eldest sister watching over him as the mother had done.

As I was on the most intimate terms with the family, I saw a great deal of the invalid. On Sunday evening, June 28th, 1903, about 9 o'clock, I and the sister were standing at the foot of the bed, watching the sick one, who was unconscious, when suddenly I saw the mother distinctly. She was in her ordinary dress as when with us, nothing supernatural in her appearance. She was bending over her boy with a look of infinite love and longing and did not seem to notice us. After a minute or two she quietly and suddenly was not there.

I was so struck that I turned to speak to the sister, but she seemed so engrossed that I did not think it wise to say anything.

The little patient grew gradually worse, until on Tuesday evening, June 30th, I was summoned to go at once. When I arrived at the house he had passed away. After rendering the last offices of love to the dear little body, the sister and I again stood, as on the Sunday, when I said, " M____, I had a strange experience on Sunday evening here. She quickly replied, "Yes, mother was here; I saw her." The young girl is not given to fancies at all, and must have been impressed as I was. November 29th, 1903.116 — REV. ALFRED HOLBORN

☛ CASE #102: I have just read in your issue of to-day a paper entitled "Not Quite Ghosts," and am forcibly reminded of a story told in my house a few weeks ago by a man of absolute integrity and truthfulness, whose name and address I could give. He is, I may say, a very  intelligent local preacher, and we entertained him while he conducted the services at our village chapel. He is by trade a painter and decorator.

He said, "I was staying in a certain place to carry out some work, viz., to put in a panel at the railway station to advertise a well-known proprietary article. I finished my work too late to return home that night, and had to get lodgings in the place. There was a heavy thunderstorm during the night, and while my breakfast was being prepared I walked to the station to see if the panel had been injured by the storm.

"It was a beautiful summer morning, and the sun was shining brightly. I found my work was all right, and was returning to my lodgings, when I suddenly heard the sound of horses' hoofs close behind me, and, turning round, I saw a man trying to control a restive horse he was riding, to which he was calling out in a loud voice. I stepped on the footpath to avoid it, and turned again to look, when it had as suddenly disappeared.

"When I got back to my lodgings my landlady said, 'Oh, Mr.____, what is the matter? I fear you are not well.'

"I related what I had seen, and she asked what dress the man had on; and I described it as a riding dress and a particular kind of hat. She then threw up her hands, and exclaimed, 'Good God, you have seen Mr. ____, who was killed there last week, and whose horse was shot in consequence.'"

I know of no explanation of this remarkable occurrence, and Mr. ____ was in the best of health at the time. Perhaps some of your readers may have met with similar cases, but I thought this the most remarkable story I had ever heard from any one's lips. I enclose my card, and am, yours, etc.[117] — FROM THE *DAILY NEWS* OF FEBRUARY 19TH, 1903

☛ CASE #103: Sennen Cove is just north of the Land's End, at the point where the massive granite and the never-ceasing swell of the ocean give place to the drifted shells and glassy waters of Whitesand Bay. At the foot of the down, which falls steeply to the north with rounded bosses and walls of granite, are a few cottages; and here in May, 1895, my wife and I were staying with a fisherman, William James Penrose.

His house, which has a studio attached, is a resort of artists—[such] as J. C. Hook—and he and his wife are well known in such circles. Their only sitting room was occupied at the time, so we lived with the family whence this tale.

Before proceeding, I should say that the scene of it lies on the rocky slope behind the house, where, about 55 yards to the east and a little above it, is a well which is used for drinking water. It is a cavity between some granite blocks, about a yard square and deep, into which water drips from the hillside. It is approached by a path about four feet wide ascending from the north. By the well on the east side of the path is a bit of slightly sloping green about three yards in diameter, bounded on the further side by a granite rock some 2 feet 6 inches in height and overhanging about a foot.

After we had been in the house some days, and the folks had got to know us, Grace, the youngest daughter, a bright and intelligent girl, aged 25, gave me the following account, which I wrote down in her own words and it embodies questions I asked her:

> One evening in August, I think it was in 1888, but am not sure to a year, we wanted some water from the well. It was late and Minnie [an elder sister] was afraid to go by herself, and I went with her to keep her company. It was a splendid night. The moon and stars were shining as bright as could be: the moon was overhead and one could see the sands and cliffs quite plain.
>
> Minnie had got down into the well—the bottom of which was dry on the near side and was bending down dipping up the water with a cup from the back of the well, which is deeper. I was standing by the side nearest the house with my back to the rock facing the little green of grass, but was looking to the right and watching Minnie in the well.
>
> She had been down a minute dipping up the water into the pitcher, when I heard a squeaking like mice. I looked round, and there on the grass and about five feet in front of me were three little things like dolls, about as high as a chair seat, dancing round and round with hands joined as fast as they could go; they were covering I should say as much ground as a big tray.
>
> They were dressed in very thin white stuff like muslin, drawn in at the waist, and thrown all over their heads like a bride's veil, so that I could not see their faces, and coming down over their arms. Their arms were stretched out rather drooping from the shoulder, and their hands were joined. I saw their hands very plainly, but did not distinguish fingers.
>
> They were as white as snow, hands and all. They were all alike; I didn't see any difference. They had very small waists, no larger than the neck of that jug [6½ inches]. Their dresses swelled out at the bottom from the dancing; they were very long, and I don't think I saw their feet, but they appeared to be dancing with a movement as though they were working their legs. They did not glide around. They went round pretty fast, as fast as real people. I've played [just] like it before now.
>
> I watched them a minute, not longer; and they went around two or three times at least, as they were going round as fast as they could. They went round in the direction of the hands of a watch; and as gently as possible, with no sound of footsteps or rustling of dresses, but the squeaking noise kept up all the time. It was too pretty a sound for mice, and louder—quite loud—one could have heard it I should think at a little distance.
>
> Minnie in the well said, "Oh! what's that? what's that?" (she told me afterwards she had heard the same noise as I had), and I said, "Look! Look!" and then as if they were frightened, they all ran together as quick as lightning up against the rock and were out of sight in a moment.

I was that frightened, and was as white as a ghost when I came in. We looked at the clock and it was twelve. I have never been there before or since at that time of night. Mr. Webber, a German, was in the house; and Mr. Carter, who told me they were pixies, fairies, you know. I had never heard or read of any such things before. Mother has since said that things were seen there [at the well] in times gone by, but I did not know of that then.

When I told the story to Dr. Ferrier, who was staying with us, he asked if I had had anything the matter with my head afterwards, but I had not, either then or at any other time. I was 17 or 18 years old, in good health, the same as I am now. I never had a doctor in my life, or have been laid up for a single day. [Her mother confirmed this; and the girl certainly looked strong and healthy enough.] I never saw anything else [like it] in my life. 1897.[118] — TOLD BY MR. E. WESTLAKE

☛ CASE #104: I do solemnly declare, that, whilst on guard at the Recruit house, on or about the 3rd instant, about half past one o'clock in the morning, I perceived the figure of a woman, without a head, rise from the earth, at the distance of about three feet before me. I was so alarmed at the circumstance, that I had not power to speak to it, which was my wish to have done; but I distinctly observed that the figure was dressed in a red striped gown with red spots between each stripe, and that part of the dress and figure appeared to me to be enveloped in a cloud. In about the space of two seconds, whilst my eyes were fixed on the object, it vanished from my sight.

I was perfectly sober and collected at the time, and, being in great trepidation, called to the next sentinel, who met me about half way, and to whom I communicated the strange sight I had seen. January 15, 1804.[119] — GEORGE JONES OF LIEUTENANT-COLONEL TAYLOR'S COMPANY OF COLDSTREAM GUARDS

☛ CASE #105: Mother, Mrs. C____, Aunt C____, another lady, and myself, were all seated in front of a large pier glass, Mrs. C (the medium) being slightly nearer the glass (say 3 inches) than the rest of us. The gas was turned down to about half its strength.

Presently, after sitting ten minutes or so, we saw what appeared to be a white mist rising up in front of the medium's reflection, and it finally resolved into a good and distinct likeness of Grandad. When we recognised it the figure smiled and nodded its head.

Then a likeness of Aunt S____ appeared, not so distinct, but perfectly easy of recognition, after which a lady appeared unknown to four of us, but recognised by the lady who was sitting with us.

For a time we saw nothing but mist again, but it gradually cleared, and a long corridor became visible with a door at the further end evidently opened inwards, and screened on the side nearest us by looped curtains, through which we saw into a brilliantly lighted room, whether bright sunlight or artificial light we could not tell. Figures too distant to be recognised came and went in the room, and once a girl in what appeared to be bridal dress stood just behind the opening of the curtain. Then the doors appeared to be shut for a time, but presently opened, and two figures pushed aside the curtains and came down the corridor towards us, talking. We recognised them as Mother and E.

Then the picture faded again, and we closed the sitting. This is to the best of my recollection, but as I took no notes at the time, I may easily have forgotten details. October 1904.[120] — MISS A.

☛ CASE #106: On the 18th of November, 1904, I was bicycling from a village a mile or two from my home, by a lane which follows the windings of a river. A steep bank, lightly wooded, divides the road from the river, and at intervals along the top where the bushes are sparse there are bits of rail painted white. It was broad daylight; it could not have been later than 3:30, but there was a light silvery fog.

As I came round a corner, I saw a little distance ahead of me a man sitting on the rail in a very dejected attitude; he seemed to have no hat on and to be looking down at the water. I was not near enough to distinguish his features, my sight not being very good. I had a misgiving he might be a starving tramp, as it was so cold nobody would sit on a rail for pleasure, and fearing he might stop me, I looked round to see whether some men who were mending the road some way back were still in sight. They were not, and when I turned my head again the man had vanished.

I had come quite close to the place, and the bushes being leafless I could see all down the bank to the water, and he was nowhere to be seen. Had he been in the lane I must have overtaken him; had he crossed I must have seen him, as the bank going up to the field the other side is too steep for him to have climbed while my head was turned.

I then remembered having been told of a ghost who had been seen at a spot in another lane about half a mile off, on the other side of the main high road, but still following the same river, and I said to myself, "I really should have thought this was the ghost B. L. talks of, only it is the wrong place." I was not the least frightened, though I had been dreadfully afraid to pass the other place in the dusk when I had just been told of it, and had crossed myself and prayed for his release that I might not see it. I only knew that it was a man who had drowned himself about forty years before. Just beyond where I saw him, round the next bend, stands a little farm and a slope goes down to the water.

Some ten days later I sat next Miss L. at a luncheon party, and said to her, "I think I must have seen the ghost you talked of the other day; only it was in I____ Lane, not W____ Lane."

She exclaimed, "Where? Tell me exactly where."

"Sitting on the white rail where the lane bends round."

"Why!" she cried, "that is the place where he did it."

"But you told me W____ Lane," I said.

"Yes, because that is the only place I ever heard of his being seen. He was attached to a nursery governess of ours who jilted him; he used to wait for her and walk with her there, and not long after his suicide my mother saw him there; but he lived at T____ Farm, in I____ Lane, and he threw himself into the river near his home." I was a good deal impressed with this.

Early in January I was visiting the same old couple from whom I had been returning when I saw the man, and they chanced to mention they had lived in the same cottage over fifty years, so I asked, did they remember a young farmer who put an end to himself in that lane some forty years ago.

"Oh yes," they said, "that would be Sammy D____; he throwed hisself into the water alongside the farm where he lived just where the cattle goes down to watering."

Then the old woman took up the word; "Crossed in love Sammy was: he was courtin' one o' the maids up to S____ (Miss L.'s old home) and she wouldn't have him; so he come in one day and throwed his hat down on to the kitchen table and went out and drowned hisself."

The one detail I had observed was that the man had no hat on. I then told them what I had seen, but they had never seen him nor knew any who had; neither have I since, though I have passed both places often. April 25th, 1905.[121] — MISS JESSIE BEDFORD

☛ CASE #107: Last evening, after service, a lady who is staying with us and I walked part way home with a friend who lives at Ruffside Hall, about two miles from Edmundbyers. It was very misty.

On our way back along the moorland road two cyclists passed us. Further on, at a point where there is a steep bank up to the right and a sloping bank and wall on the left, I saw what I thought was another cyclist coming towards us. At the same instant my friend said, "Here's another cyclist, keep to this side."

We saw indistinctly what seemed to be a man bending slightly forward on his machine, and the movement of the wheels was apparent to both of us. Suddenly he vanished, and my companion said, "Whatever is the man doing? He must be riding in the ditch!"

I laughed and said, "I think he has tumbled off."

To our astonishment there was no man or machine to be found, and it was impossible for him to have got off the road. Much perplexed, we walked on about a hundred yards, and young man from the village, we asked whether a cyclist had passed him. He said, no, and there was no road along which the cyclist could have turned from the high road.

On reaching home, we asked my father for an explanation of what we had seen, and he could not give one. Later in the evening we were told by one of the maids that on the previous Saturday evening, at about the same time, nine o'clock, a man was found unconscious on the road by the village blacksmith, having fallen from his cycle when drunk. The spot where the accident occurred is the point where we saw the appearance. May 15th, 1905.[122] —
MISS MILDRED VAUGHAN

☛ CASE #108: On the night of Wednesday, 17th of March, 1904 (as nearly as I can remember the date), I was sleeping in my own room at the top of this house, my sister Elizabeth being in the room next mine.

In the middle of the night at what hour I do not know—I was awakened by a curious sensation of pressure from above, as of a weight resting gently but firmly on me, and looking up saw my sister Elizabeth suspended in some way above me in the air. She was lying with her eyes shut, covered with a quilt as if in bed, and looked very pale and ill. I felt no surprise but only concern for her evident suffering, and a strong impulse to get up and minister to her. (She is subject to occasional attacks of severe pain, and I have nursed her through them very frequently.)

However, as soon as I tried to rise I found myself too heavy with sleep to do so. My eyes would not open, and my shoulders seemed as if held down by their own weight. Yet I had felt quite wide awake and fully conscious of where I was, of the furniture in the room, etc. It seemed as if I gave up the attempt to rise, partly because she made me understand that she did not need my help, but only wanted to be near me. So I put out my arm—half sitting up, and without effort—and guided her to a place beside me on the bed, falling asleep again as soon as she was comfortably settled. She seemed to float through the air much as a child's India-rubber balloon would do, and was quite easily moved when I touched her.

After a while I woke again with a start and a feeling of distress at my own laziness, and again made an effort to rise, thinking remorsefully that she had been in pain and I ought to have got up and made a poultice, but had done nothing for her. There was again a difficulty in rousing myself, and then came the recollection that she was beside me, so that I didn't need to rise. I sat up (once more with ease) and asked, "Are you all right now?" I heard her answer, "Yes, I am all right, thank you," and went to sleep again.

In the morning I was wakened by my youngest sister Hilda, who came into the room saying, "Betty sent me to tell you that you came to her in your astral body last night."

"No I didn't!" I exclaimed, "she came to me. Was she in pain?"

"Yes."

I went to my sister's room and found she had been suffering during the night, had thought of calling me, but decided she wasn't ill enough to need any treatment. After lying awake for about half an-hour she fell asleep, and was awakened by my voice asking "are you all right now?" and looking up saw me near the door of her room—rather a shadowy figure enveloped in bed-clothes, even the head being partially covered. She answered, "Yes, I am all right, thank you," and went to sleep again with the impression that I had somehow ministered to her.

As a matter of fact I was lying much muffled up, as I had felt cold and drawn the clothes well up over my ears. I am perfectly certain I did not get out of bed all night, and I have never done anything in the sleep-walking line. This is my only "psychic experience" worth recording. I once previously had the same strong impression of a friend having come to me in the night, but have no corroborative evidence.

. . . My attention was not directed to these subjects at the time, and I dismissed the incident as a curiously vivid dream; but though I dream a good deal, these two experiences stand out from other dreams as different. I feel that whatever the state of consciousness may have been, I was awake and alive to my physical surroundings in a way quite unusual in ordinary dreams. A cousin (Mrs. Young) came to live with us on the 15th March, and recalls that it was after she arrived that the incident took place. I left home on the 22nd, so the "vision" came to me between these two dates, I believe on the 17th. May 8th, 1905.[123] — ISABELLE M. PAGAN

☞ CASE #109: I had been staying at the house of Mr. Ward, a retired Master in the Mercantile Marine, who resides at Northwood House, Llanishen, near Cardiff, and on Tuesday, June 20th, 1905, he drove me over to Whitchurch (about two miles from Llanishen) where I was to spend a couple of days with friends, Mr. and Mrs. Berwick. He left me there at about eleven o'clock in the forenoon and returned to his home.

On the following afternoon at about half-past three I was sitting alone in the drawing-room, Mrs. Berwick being in her own room, and, on happening to look up, I saw Mr. Ward standing at the bay window and looking in at me as though he desired to speak to me. He was in his usual dress and is not a man to be easily mistaken for any one else.

Thinking he had brought some letters for me, I rose hastily and went towards the window calling to him and waving my hand to him, partly in greeting and partly as a sign for him to go to the hall door, but when I reached the window I was surprised not to see him. I concluded, however, that he must have gone to the door without my noticing and so I hurried to the door to let him in. I was exceedingly surprised and alarmed when I opened the hall-door to see nobody there, nor anywhere about the house.

Later when Mrs. Berwick came down I told her—and also Mr. Berwick—of my experience, and like myself they felt extremely anxious lest some harm had happened to Mr. Ward, for whom we all felt a strong regard.

Next morning, however, soon after eleven o'clock Mr. Ward arrived in his trap [a horse-drawn pleasure carriage] according to arrangement to take me to the railway station to join the train for Manchester. He was in a very weak state and suffering from severe injuries to his ankle, neck, and shoulders, and he remarked to us, "It is a wonder I have been able to come to you in the body." It seemed that whilst driving home on Tuesday the horse, which was a very nervous animal, upset the trap and caused him to be thrown out and badly bruised and shaken.

The next afternoon, whilst lying on a couch in his sitting-room, he was wondering what Mrs. Green would think if she knew of the occurrence, when he suddenly heard her voice outside the house. There being only an elderly woman in the house he managed with great difficulty to get to the hall-door to admit Mrs. Green, and was greatly amazed not to see her. The time was between three o'clock and four, just about the time when Mrs. Green saw his form at Whitchurch. We certify that this account of the hallucinations seen and heard by Mrs. Green and Captain Ward is correct. July 26th, 1905.^{124} — ELLEN GREEN, FREDERICK WARD, JOHN BERWICK, FANNY A. BERWICK

☛ CASE #110: On Friday I arrived at A. on a visit to my friends, Mr. and Mrs. Z., whom I had not visited since they came to reside in A. On the following Sunday I went to church with Mrs. Z. Just before the service began, i.e., about 10:55 a.m., as I was taking my seat I suddenly felt a curious sensation that something was going to happen, and this sensation was somehow connected with the chancel or east end of the church, which I faced from my seat. The sensation passed, and the service began.

Very shortly afterwards, I had a strong impression of the presence of a figure standing close to the south-east angle of the chancel. This impression persisted throughout the greater part of the service, but the figure had disappeared before the conclusion of the sermon.

I use the phrase "impression of a figure" advisedly, as I never for a moment took it for an actual person; in fact, my visual impression persisted when I shut my eyes. The details were extremely distinct, and I observed and noted as much as I could, with a view to subsequent identification, if possible. The figure was stationary. It did not disappear, but on one occasion, when I looked for it, so to speak, as I did from time to time, it was not there, and no effort on my part could bring it back.

On my return from church I related my impression to Mr. and Mrs. Z., and my husband. The note made by Mr. Z. from my description is appended. That description reminded him of a portrait of one of two brothers, Mr. C. D. and Mr. E. D., closely connected with the parish, and buried in the churchyard.

The D. family was wholly unknown to me, but on the following day, Monday, I was shown engravings of both brothers, and at once identified in the younger brother, Mr. E. D., the original of the figure which I had seen in the church. The impression of that figure was so vivid that I had felt from the first confident that I should recognise the person if I saw him or his likeness. The age which the figure appeared to be was 40-45, and the age of Mr. E. D. at the time of the engraving was 37.

I subsequently saw two paintings, representing Mr. E. D. at different periods, and these confirmed the identification, though the ruddy colouring of the face of the younger portrait was unlike the sallow skin of the figure seen by me. The latest portrait, however, represented the effect, noted by me, of a skin darker than the hair, and in all three pictures the cut of hair and beard, as well as the general cast of the features and the expression, were well represented. None of the portraits represented more than the head and shoulders, so that nothing could be learnt from them as to the habitual attitude of Mr. E. D., and in none of them was he shown as wearing the frock coat in which the figure appeared to me. I need only add that I have never experienced any similar impression.[125] — MARGARET DE G. VERRALL

☛ CASE #111: You may imagine with what delight we received your telegram [i.e., announcing the birth of your first baby]. You must know a very funny thing happened to me, and never again pooh pooh presentiments. I told C. and Miss and H. the very next day, so that they would not say it was my idea.

On Thursday last, after having gone to sleep, I awoke suddenly with a sensation of some one being in my room. I sat up in bed and I saw you distinctly on a rocking-chair in a flannel loose blue dressing-gown. You were sitting up on the chair: I mean not leaning back, but stooping and rocking yourself as if in pain. It was so distinct that I forgot I was not there, and being, I suppose, myself half-asleep, said, "Oh, J. has begun," and was not frightened. Then you got up and went to the sofa, lay down, and then again to the chair. I then got so nervous, I got out of bed, went and washed my face with cold water, and got to bed and went to sleep. But again I awoke and *da capo* the same thing.

That morning I told them that I was sure you had had the baby, and was disappointed at not having any news. I afterwards forgot all about it, but when I heard you had had labour pains on that identical night, I am sure everything happened just as I saw it, and that when I went to sleep, so did you. Is it so? Tell me exactly what you did if you were up, and if you sat on a rocking-chair and lay on the sofa, and if you slept at intervals.

Lately, too, I have been very very nervous, and that may account for it, but see you I did as distinctly as possible. I hope we shall soon have news about you, as I am very anxious to hear particulars. December 14th 1884.[126] — MRS. C. (IN LIVERPOOL, UK) TO HER SISTER MRS. D. (IN ATHENS, GREECE)

☛ CASE #112: On the night of Saturday, March 4th, or rather, early morning of March 5th, 1905, I awoke and sat up to reach for something on the table beside my bed. The room was not dark, as the curtains were drawn back, and the blinds were up, and there are some strong lights in the street outside.

As I sat up all seemed dark except that I saw a face for a second, and the same face a little further to the right and a little lower down, also for a second. I am not sure whether I saw the two faces (which were exactly the same) at the same moment or one just after the other, but I think the sight of them overlapped. The faces were of Mrs. J. W., who lives at the village at home. I only saw her head, all else being swallowed in darkness. I noticed her black cap, without any white, which she always wears. Her face was not strongly illuminated, and wore her usual expression. There was about it no appearance of life or action.

I was sufficiently struck by this to say to myself that I would write to you next morning about it, so that if there was any coincidence about it you would have evidence beforehand. I also turned over to the other side of my bed, took up the watch standing there and noticed the time by it was 4:19 a.m. As this watch was 5 minutes fast by "Big Ben," the real time must have been just 4:14 a.m.

Unluckily when I woke next morning the whole thing went clean out of my recollection, and I never thought of it again till this morning (March 7th), when I received a letter from Mrs. N. (wife of the clergyman staying at my country home), dated March 6th, who among other things wrote as follows:

"Poor old J. W. [husband of the woman I had seen in my bedroom] at the village died yesterday morning early. He has been ill for a long time."

When I got Mrs. N.'s letter this morning (7th), I could not remember whether the face I had seen was on the night of Saturday 4th (morning of 5th) or on the night of Sunday 5th (morning of Monday 6th). I am, however, now pretty confident it was the former, for this reason.

On Friday evening 3rd, I had a committee here, and they said my clocks were all wrong. I replied that I had never heard Big Ben strike all the time I had been ill, so did not know the time when I set the clocks going again. Next night I did hear Big Ben, and noticed this because of the conversation the night before. When I heard it I looked at the watch beside my bed and noticed that it was 5 minutes fast.

J. W. had been ill some time before I left home (I left on

February 8th), but for some time before I left he had been much better, and was I believe out of bed every day. I had heard nothing of the W.'s since leaving home, and had no idea that he had been ill again. The only moment that I am aware of when the W.'s were in my mind was several days ago, when I was putting away my 1904 bills and noticed Mrs. W.'s bill for sweets for the schoolchildren among them. March 7th, 1905.[127] — MISS R.

☛ CASE #113: On the night of January 10th, 1879, I had retired early to rest. I awoke out of my first sleep to find the moon shining into my room. As I awoke my eyes were directed towards the panels of a cupboard, or wardrobe, built into the east wall of my room, and situated in the north-east corner. I watched the moonlight on the panels. As I gazed I suddenly saw a face form on the panels of the cupboard or wardrobe. Indistinct at first, it gradually became clearer until it was perfectly distinct as in life, when I saw the face of my grandmother. What particularly struck me at the moment and burnt itself into my recollection was the fact that the face wore an old-fashioned frilled or goffered cap. I gazed at it for a few seconds, during which it was as plain as the living face, when it faded gradually into the moonlight and was gone.

I was not alarmed, but, thinking that I had been deceived by the moonlight and that it was an illusion, I turned over and went off to sleep again.

In the morning when at breakfast I began telling the experience of the night to my parents. I had got well into my story, when, to my surprise, my father suddenly sprang up from his seat at the table and leaving his food almost untouched hurriedly left the room. As he walked towards the door I gazed after him in amazement, saying to mother, "Whatever is the matter with father?"

She raised her hand to enjoin silence. When the door had closed I again repeated my question. She replied, "Well, Charles, it is the strangest thing I ever heard of, but when I awoke this morning your father informed me that he was awakened in the night and saw his mother standing by his bedside, and that when he raised himself to speak to her she glided away."

This scene and conversation took place at about 8:30 a.m. on the morning of January 11th. Before noon we received a telegram announcing the death of my father's mother during the night. We found that the matter did not end here, for my father was afterwards informed by his sister that she also had seen the apparition of her mother standing at the foot of her bed. Thus, this remarkable apparition was manifested to three persons independently.

My apartment, in which I saw the vision, was at the other side of the house to that occupied by my parents, and was entirely separate and apart from their room, while my father's sister was nearly 20 miles away at Heckmondwike.

My father noted the time as 2 a.m. but I did not take note of the time, but have since been able to ascertain it closely in the following way.

The house at Crawshawbooth, in which we lived at the time, faces due south and the window of the apartment faces also due south. On the night of January 10-11, 1879, the moon was on the meridian at 14 hours 19 minutes Greenwich Mean Time, i.e., 2 hours 19 minutes, a.m., on January 11th. When on the meridian the moon illuminates the back and the east and west walls of the apartment. I am certain that the east wall of the room was illuminated (for there I saw the face in the moonlight) and also the back of the room, or north wall. The moon was therefore approximately on the meridian and the time close on 2 a.m., thus confirming my father's observation in a remarkable and unexpected manner.

The death of my grandmother took place at 12:15 a.m., and it is certain from the above considerations that the apparition to myself and my father occurred nearly two hours after death.

My father died in 1885, but my mother is living and well remembers all the details.

In the case of the apparition to my aunt, this did not take place until upwards of eighteen hours after the death. . . In the apparition to me, what particularly struck me and burnt itself into my memory was the goffered cap around the face. I made no attempt to verify this at the time, but specially mentioned it to my parents.

Some weeks ago, when I set to work to verify these details, I wrote to my uncle sending him a sketch of what I saw. I may say that I have never previously communicated with my uncle upon this subject and I had not seen my grandmother for some years previous to her appearance to me. *It is absolutely certain that the apparition occurred to each of the three independent witnesses after the death and that this case is therefore an unmistakable instance of apparitions of the dead and proof that the personality survives* [my emphasis, L.S.]. I am prepared at any time to make this statement on oath.[128] — CHARLES L. TWEEDALE, VICAR OF WESTON

☛ CASE #114: A young English lady had been betrothed to an officer before his departure to the East. During her lover's absence she was taken abroad by her mother, and on their arrival late one evening at a French inn they found it necessary to occupy rooms on different floors.

As Miss C____ was in the act of getting into bed late at night, she suddenly beheld the form of her lover standing in a remote corner of her chamber. His countenance was extremely sad, and she observed that round his right arm he wore a band of crape. Indignant at the conduct of her betrothed in entering her sleeping apartment, she called on him loudly to depart; the form of her lover remained speechless, but as she lifted up her voice his brow grew yet sadder, and as he glided silently out of the room he seemed a prey to the gloomiest feelings.

After a time Miss C____ summoned up sufficient courage to descend to her mother and recite her adventure. They caused diligent search to be made for the returned officer, but without success. Nor could the smallest trace of him be afterwards discovered. Several weeks later the young lady received the news of her lover's death in a general action in India.[129] — THE SPIRITUAL MAGAZINE

☛ CASE #115: A person of honour, veracity, and good sense, once when dangerously ill of his wounds, as he lay awake with a candle lighted in his room, he saw the curtains drawn back, and his wife—then in England—presented herself to his view at the opening of the curtains, and then disappeared. He was amazed and deeply affected at the sudden sight.

Shortly afterwards he received from England news of her death at about the same time when he had seen the phenomenon. He continued ever afterwards convinced of the certainty of apparitions. This event occurred about the year 1780, and was much noticed at the time of its occurrence.[130] — STORY FROM GENERAL SABINE, GOVERNOR OF GIBRALTAR

☛ CASE #116: [Review of a review of the 1872 book, *Notre Dame de Lourdes*, by M. Henri Lasserre.]
Bernardette was the daughter of a poor labourer of Lourdes, and could neither read nor write; she was of a delicate constitution and subject to asthma. Her sole employment being to tend sheep, her mind was left free to follow its strong devotional bent, and the lonely hours of the young creature were spent in reciting prayers to the Virgin Mary—the object in the Pyrenees of especial adoration.

At the age of 14—while preparing for her first

communion—having gone on the 11th of February, 1858, to gather wood on the banks of the Gave, on reaching the rocks of Massabielle she had her first vision. She heard, she said, *the sound as of a storm*, and raising her head, beheld above a grotto, and in a recess of the rock, the figure of a woman of wondrous beauty, robed in white, a veil over her head, and holding in her hand a rosary; a resplendent halo surrounded her.

Three days after Bernadette returned with some other children to the grotto, and again she, but she only, beheld "the lady."

On the 18th there was another apparition, but this time in the interior of the grotto, and this time it spoke; audibly, however, to her alone, desiring her to return every morning during a fortnight. The child did not fail.

Her parents—at first at a loss what to think of it—now followed her, witnessed her ecstacy, and were convinced that she in reality beheld the Holy Virgin. The report of the visions of the young girl spread around, and on the following Sunday, the 29th February, several thousands assembled on the banks of the Gave, at the early hour at which Bernadette resorted to the grotto. One of the two witnesses, the *Receveur des Contributions indirectes* of the place, has thus described her aspect in her ecstasies, and the impression she produced upon him:

> "Before the transfiguration of the young girl, all my preconceived notions, all my philosophic doubts, fell at once to the ground and gave way to an extraordinary sentiment which took possession of me in spite of myself. I felt the certainty, the irresistible intuition, that a mysterious being was there. Suddenly and completely transfigured, Bernadette was no longer Bernadette, but an angel from heaven, plunged in ecstasies unspeakable. She had no longer the same face; another intelligence, another soul informed it."

Bernadette had now conversations with "the lady" whose communications became more and more important (in fairness to the sceptics, to whom, no doubt, it will be a great handle we must not omit to mention, that when asked her name, the apparition answered, she was "the Immaculate Conception") sometimes these communications were of a mysterious nature, and she was forbidden to reveal them, sometimes they were orders which she was to execute.

"My child," said the Virgin to her one day, "go and tell the priests that I desire that a chapel be raised to me, here."

The girl went straight with the message to the Curé, who, somewhat embarrassed, expressed a wish for a confirmation of the message.

"We are now," he answered, "in the month of February; tell the apparition, if it desires a chapel, to cause the wild rosebush, which is, you tell me, at its feet, to flower." The rosebush did not flower; but by that time the general enthusiasm had become too intense to be easily chilled.

Besides, another marvel has been witnessed—*Bernardette had one day, in her ecstacy, put her fingers into the flame of a candle which she held, without feeling any pain, and without any mark being left on her flesh.*

And now came the crowning miracle. On the 29th of February, the day after the request of the Curé, the Madonna desired the girl to scratch the ground at her feet in the grotto, and to drink the water which would issue from the hollow. Bernardette obeyed, and lo! water arose under her hands; at first, muddy and slowly trickling in the thinnest streamlet, but in the course of a few days becoming limpid and abundant. Diseased people hastened to make trial of its presumed supernatural virtues, and cures immediately ensued.

The first was that of a man, who, from an accident, had almost entirely lost the sight of his right eye, and who recovered it suddenly on application of the water. This, it must be remarked, was a case of organic vision; two physicians, of whom one was a fellow of the Faculty of Montpellier, attest alike the facts, and the supernatural character of the cure; other cures as marvellous followed.

Some sufferers at a distance, had the water sent to them, and recovered their health as fully as those who drank from the fountain. Analysis, by the professor of the Faculty of Toulouse, showed the water to possess no properties differing from those of ordinary mountain streams.

In the midst of the great popular excitement, attendant on such a manifestation of supernatural power, the attitude of the clergy remained for a while neutral and calmly observant. They withstood, indeed, the impolitic intolerance of the Prêfect, who, by brute force, sought to crush "the superstition" at its birth, and they obtained from imperial authority reversal of measures taken towards that end; but they pronounced no opinion as to the truth of the alleged miracles, and it was not till some months had elapsed, and cure after cure had been reported, that they appointed a commission—composed, it is true, of the faithful; but among whom were a professor of physics, and a professor of chemistry, to enquire into the matter.

The report confirmed the reality of the cures; but, even then, it was not till three years after that the Bishop proclaimed that the Holy Virgin had chosen Lourdes therein to appear, and to work miracles; and that the chapel, now almost finished, began to be built on the rocks of Massabielle.

But alas for poor Bernardette! she, the chosen instrument of the miraculous intervention, experienced no benefit from the waters of the fountain. She is now a sister of charity, and continues to suffer cruelly. Her visions ceased after July, 1858.

In 1862, M. Lasserre, whose sight till then had been excellent, began to feel a weakness in his eyes, which went on rapidly increasing, till in the course of a few months he was unable to read or write. While in this distressed state, a friend of his, a protestant, just returned from Lourdes, urged him to try the miraculous water. M. Lasserre yielded to his advice, and was cured. He has described the deep emotion with which he received the water, the solemn feeling with which, after fervent prayer, he applied it to his eyes, his rapture on the instantaneous cure it affected; from being unable to read three lines, without painful effort, his sight became at once, and has continued, as good as ever in his life.

Such are the chief features of a recital, which seems just now to have made some sensation in the lettered circles of sceptical and materialistic Paris, calling forth volleys of derisive shouts, and epigrams from the many; but perplexing and staggering, it would appear, to a few.

The [book] reviewer [distinguished French critic, Mr. Scherer] himself, it must be said, though a disbeliever in the supernatural, discusses the matter with seriousness and fairness, doing justice to the well-known character of M. Lasserre. His arguments are of the ordinary well-known stamp of the so-called rationalistic school. Trickery, indeed, as an explanation of the miracles, he does not suspect. He ascribes them vaguely "to the hankering after the marvelous—to the love of emotion—to all the passions of which superstition is composed."

His objections are based on the two radical errors, that intervention of the invisible world would be subversive of the laws of nature; and that its source must be divine. His ignorance of the view taken of the subject by enlightened Spiritualists is complete.

I have italicised the passages where Bernardette describes having heard, just before beholding the apparition, the sound as of a storm; and also that which relates how she held her fingers in the candle without injury; because your readers will remember having seen or heard of such things at séances. The sound of a great wind not unfrequently precedes spiritual phenomena, and I have myself seen [Scottish medium] Mr. [Daniel D.] Home hold red-hot coals in his hands many minutes unharmed.[131] — I. H. D.

☛ CASE #117: It is, as a believer in Spiritualism, that I address to your Magazine the following account of occurrences which came under my own personal observation, long before I had an opportunity of learning any of the great truths of the spirit world; and when, if I ever thought about Spiritualism at all, I dismissed it from my mind as the religion of knaves and dupes, and unworthy the serious attention of a reasonable man.

Within the last year only have I found cause to change all my preconceived opinions on the subject; having been led to investigate the matter by a friend, on whose integrity I could rely, who, being himself a medium, was enabled to shew me such manifestations that I could no longer doubt however unwilling, I resigned my deep-seated prejudices against what I had been taught to consider a vulgar superstition.

Looking at some remarkable incidents in my past life by the new light which Spiritualism throws on them, I fancy they may be interesting to many of your readers, vouched as they can be by the evidence of the persons concerned,—all of whom are still alive. I mean only to narrate those occurrences in which I was personally concerned, and for which I have the evidence of my own senses.

The earliest case I can remember occurred in Edinburgh, when I was a boy of about fifteen, living with some relations in that city. Business had called my uncle, Mr. W, to Leeds, in Yorkshire, and he was not expected back for some time. One day, about two o'clock in the afternoon, I was sitting with my aunt, Mrs. W____, in the drawing-room in Edinburgh we had been conversing on different subjects—my aunt being in the best of spirits, and in excellent health—when, without the slightest warning, she suddenly fell back in her chair, apparently in a faint; a thing which never occurred to her before. She remained unconscious for a few minutes, recovering as suddenly as she had gone off, and without the least ill effects from the attack.

We had scarcely recovered from the confusion, consequent on the occurrence, when a telegram arrived from my uncle announcing his return that night, and asking if anything was wrong with his wife.

When he returned he narrated the following extraordinary incident. He was writing at a table in the coffee-room of the hotel at Leeds; the room was full of people, and several waiters were bustling about. Suddenly he felt constrained to look towards the door, which was closed. He distinctly saw it open, and my aunt walk in and come straight to where he sat. He remained spell-bound while she approached and stood for a few moments by his side, gazing at him with an intensely sorrowful expression. All at once she disappeared.

My uncle, in alarm, questioned all the persons in the apartment, but no one had seen the figure, and all agreed in declaring the door had not opened at all.

He came back to Edinburgh by the next train, fearing something had happened, and on comparing notes, we found that the exact time my aunt was in the faint, in Edinburgh, was the time he saw her in the coffee room at Leeds. Just at this period, my uncle sustained a heavy pecuniary loss, which was, however, partly averted by his return to Edinburgh that night.

The next incident occurred in Dublin, a short time afterwards, when I was residing with my mother at the house of a Mr. B____. An only child of Mr. B____ being seriously ill, my mother slept in her room to assist in watching the invalid who was also lying there. On the night in question I had retired to my bed about twelve o'clock, and had slept, I should say, about an hour when I awoke, and looking round the room saw that it was a bright moonlight night. The shutters were not closed, and I had opened the window before going to bed, so everything was clear as daylight. Suddenly the door, which was close to the head of my bed, creaked, and I saw, as I thought, my mother slowly enter dressed in her nightgown. She advanced to the middle of the room and stood there wringing her hands and showing every sign of deep grief. I called to her to know what was the matter, never doubting for a moment but that it was actually herself who stood there. Receiving no answer I imagined she must be in a state of somnambulism, to which I knew her to be occasionally subject. I therefore kept quiet and watched her till she moved over to the open window, when, fearing the effect of the night air, I thought it best to awaken her. I therefore jumped out of bed; but had hardly advanced a yard when the figure disappeared.

At that moment every bell in the house rang furiously. Much alarmed, I hastily lit a candle, and ran to Mrs. B____'s room. Entering, I found my mother in a heavy sleep; with difficulty I roused her, and on looking at the child we found it a corpse.

In both these cases it is remarkable that the persons whose apparitions were seen at the same time were, and still are, actually alive.

Reasoning by the light which Spiritualism has thrown on many hitherto unaccountable occurrences, I am now convinced that though at the moment of the appearances the persons were not actually dead—in the ordinary acceptation of that term—yet that their spirits had temporarily left their unconscious bodies to convey a warning, in the one case of pecuniary disaster, in the other of final death itself.

As to the ringing of the bells in the latter instance, it is a fact, provable by many witnesses, that this phenomenon invariably accompanies the decease of any member of Mr. B____'s family; and it is but one of the many ways in which spirits manifest their disembodied presence to mortal beings.[132] — S. A. W.

☞ CASE #118: At a recent meeting of the committee of the Dialectical Society, [Victorian medium] Mr. Daniel D. Home, in giving evidence, related a fact which occurred some years ago in the presence of the Emperor Napoleon [III]. He said:

> We were in a large room in the Salonde Louis Quatorze. The Empress and Emperor were present. I am now telling the story as I heard the Emperor tell it.
>
> A table was moved—then a hand was seen to come; it was a very beautifully formed hand. There were pencils on the table. It lifted, not the one next it, but one on the far side. We heard the sound of writing, and saw it writing on fine note-paper.
>
> The hand passed before me and went to the Emperor, and he kissed the hand. It went to the Empress; she withdrew from its touch, and the hand followed her. The Emperor said, "do not be frightened"; and she kissed it too. It was disappearing.
>
> I said I would like to kiss it. The hand seemed to be like a person thinking, and as if it were saying, "why should I?"
>
> It came back to me. It had written the word "Napoleon," and it remains written now. It was as much a material hand seemingly as my hand is now. The writing was an autograph of the Emperor Napoleon I, who had an exceedingly beautiful hand.

Mr. Home said that the Emperor of Russia as well as the Emperor Napoleon, had seen hands, and had taken hold of them, "when they seemed to float away into thin air."[133] — THE SPIRITUAL MAGAZINE

☞ CASE #119: A lady, lately become interested in the subject of Spiritualism, but having witnessed none of the ordinary phases of the "manifestation," experienced on the night of December 6th, 1868, a little incident which must undoubtedly be referred to spiritual origin, and which leads to the supposition that the lady herself may be gifted with "spiritual sight."

This lady, whom I will call "L____" is staying in London with a friend, in a house where an old lady breathed her last on Saturday, December 5th. This old lady was a pious and a patient sufferer, through a tedious and painful illness. She expired peacefully. L____ and her friend had been in the habit of occasionally visiting the sick woman, to read to her and minister in various ways to her comfort.

L____ had seen her very shortly before her decease, and went immediately afterwards to look at her peaceful corpse. She felt herself greatly affected by the spectacle, this being the first corpse of a grown person ever seen by her. The remembrance of the waxlike and placid countenance haunted her; and at length became so oppressive a thought to L____, that she strove in every way to banish the recollection of it, and to shake off from herself the painful sense of the presence of death, which so entirely had taken possession of her. She slept in a room beneath the chamber in which the corpse lay.

Sunday night was a remarkably stormy and wild night with heavy showers and gusts of wind, and there was no moon. Nevertheless L____ was suddenly awakened by a light in the room, as though it were illumined by soft moonlight; indeed, at the time, she supposed that it was moonlight, and so clear was the illumination, that the objects in the room became distinctly visible to her.

Startled by the illumination, she sat up in bed, and gazed around her. In the middle of the mantel shelf, opposite to her bed, had stood a work box; this she saw distinctly, but to her astonishment, she also beheld, standing upon this work box, a perfectly white and graceful vase filled with lovely sprays of long leaves, such as grapes and ferns, and a variety of beautiful flowers, all equally snowy white with the vase, both leaves and flowers. She was much surprised by thus seeing this beautiful and strange object unlike anything which she knew to be in the room or in the house.

As she sat contemplating it in wonder, the room again became dark; she then lay down, and believes that she fell asleep.

But again came the sudden and mild illumination of the room, and she once more looked towards the mantelpiece. There she still beheld the vase and flowers; but this time the mysterious object was not standing upon the box, but beside it, to the right hand side. L____ wondered still more at thus seeing that the vase with the flowers had been moved, or had moved itself.

The room once more sank into gloom, and L____ lay in her bed pondering and no little puzzled—indeed somewhat agitated.

Then again, and again, for nine successive times in all, did the mysterious light appear and disappear; each time exhibiting the vase removed farther and farther to the right of the work-box, along the mantel shelf, until at the ninth and last time, it was beheld standing upon the floor, when it disappeared entirely.

L____ connected this beautiful vase and its graceful contents in some way with the corpse laid out in the chamber above.

Did this little vision perhaps symbolize the purity of the newly released spirit, filled with the freshness and fragrance of Heavenly Life? And did the nine times of its appearance typify completion? Who can say?

But unquestionably the vase and flowers, and their movements originated in spiritual presence; possibly were a sign of affection and gratitude from the emancipated spirit who thus endeavoured to shew her remembrance of L____ by this presentation of a graceful and fragrant object, seeking thereby, as if by a "vial of sweet odours," to banish the haunting thoughts of decay and motility; and to spread around odours of immortality in place of the odours of the grave.[134] — *THE SPIRITUAL MAGAZINE*

☛ CASE #120: 1868: I have finally concluded to gratify the request so often made for me to write out an account of the surprising spiritual manifestations that took place in the village of Putnam, Conn., where I reside. I am well aware that story-telling is not my forte. All I can do is to state the facts as they occurred, according to my own observation and the testimony of reliable witnesses. In doing this I shall give the real name of the medium and most of the parties, with the exception of the family in whose house the principal manifestations took place, as they were not Spiritualists, and might object to having their names made public.

I shall endeavour to make no statements that I am not prepared to substantiate.

The opening events of the story date back to the month of September, in the fall of 1866. At that time there was living in a substantial two-story dwelling house, not far from the railroad station at Putnam, a family whom we will call, for convenience sake, Lind. The members of the family were Mr. Lind and wife, both being somewhat advanced in years, and their son, Mark Lind, and his wife, Mattie, who had rooms in the house, boarding with the old people. The senior Mr. and Mrs. Lind were members of the Methodist church, and considered respectable and well-to-do people. Mark had been married some few years, had been in the army, and become somewhat unsteady in his habits. His wife, Mattie, was a fine looking young woman, something over twenty years of age, active and intelligent, yet possessed of an exceedingly passionate and violent disposition, which, when aroused, was manifested in uncontrollable storms of rage.

As is often the case when a husband takes his wife home, Mattie and the lady did not agree very well, nor did Mark always maintain that kindly bearing toward her which she considered was due from a husband. These facts gave rise to more or less disputes, which, before being ended, usually drew in the whole family, to some extent, and generally terminated by Mattie getting very angry and leaving the house, declaring that she would never darken the doors again. But time always cooled her temper, and after two or three days she would return, to remain until another storm would produce a similar result.

Thus things continued, until one day they had an uncommonly severe and violent altercation which ended, as usual in Mattie's departure. But little notice was taken of the matter, the rest of the folks supposing of course she would return as she had always done. Imagine the surprise and horror of the old gentleman when he arose the next morning and found Mattie lying on the piazza of the house, dead. A post mortem examination revealed the fact that she had taken arsenic sufficient to cause death, or in other words, she had committed suicide by poison.

Of course it created a great sensation in our village, and for a time nothing else was talked of but the tragic death of the young and beautiful Mattie Lind.

Even great excitements cannot always last, and so ere long, the people believing that Mattie's death had closed the scene, ceased to give the subject thought. But it seems there was an *afterpiece* to come, which was not laid down in the programme. To be sure,

Mattie Lind's body lay over in the burying ground, but it soon appeared that she was not there.

On the same street, and near Mr. Lind's house, is an eating saloon, kept by one Thomas Capwell, who had in his employ a young man by the name of James Philips. I would here state that I am personally acquainted with Philips, and I am willing to vouch for his truthfulness and honesty. He was not a Spiritualist, and up to this time had not seen any of the phenomena; in fact, knew nothing whatever about the subject. Some little time after the afore-mentioned facts took place, Mr. Capwell went away, leaving the saloon in charge of Philips.

One day during Mr. Capwell's absence, it was noticed by Mrs. Capwell and others that Philips appeared very strange. He had a peculiarly wild look, and when spoken to would respond only in monosyllables, if at all. His appearance and actions were such as to lead the people to suppose that he was suffering from a temporary attack of insanity.

Mrs. Capwell, knowing that there was two hundred dollars in the money drawer, thought she would secure that, and went to get it, but to her consternation found it gone. She inquired of Philips what had become of it? He affirmed that he did not know; and although his person and the premises were thoroughly searched, no trace of the money could be found. He continued in that peculiar state of mind all day, and at nine o'clock locked up the shop and started for home, as usual. But instead of going home, he went directly to Mr. Lind's, and entering the kitchen where the old gentleman and his wife were sitting, took a lamp and went up to the room formerly occupied by Mark and his wife. The old people, supposing that Mark had sent him on some errand, said nothing.

About ten o'clock Mark came home, and before entering the house he was surprised to see a light in his room. He inquired who was there. His father replied that Mr. Philips was, asking if he did not send him. Mark passed up stairs and opened the door into his room, and beheld, to his utter astonishment, James Philips dressed in his wife's—Mattie's—clothes. I will here state that Philips is a man somewhat below the medium size.

When Mark had sufficiently mastered his surprise to speak, he inquired of Philips what he was there for? The reply was, "I should like to know who has a better right in Mattie Lind's bedroom than herself? Why didn't you come home before? It's time we were in bed. Come, get ready, and let us go to bed."

But Mark being completely confounded, not understanding the case, having seen little or nothing of the trance before, did not readily assent to the proposed arrangement. This aroused the amiable disposition of his late spouse, and she insisted upon his immediate compliance, in terms precisely similar to those employed in former days. The old folks, hearing the familiar sounds, rushed up stairs. The sight of the old lady did not serve to allay the wrath of the already enraged Mattie (for it was she in full control of the medium Philips), and she expressed herself in strong language, much of which is not found in polite literature stating that she was not dead, as they had supposed, that they had not got rid of her so easily, and she had come back to have her revenge both on Mark and the old woman; it was her determination to kill Mark Lind if she could; and as if to verify the statement, she hurled a penknife at his head, which barely missed him, and struck half the length of it in the door panel.

This demonstration had the effect to make the whole party beat a hasty retreat. Mark brought up the rear, and shutting the door after him attempted to hold it; but although he had the handle of the latch and the medium the "catch," he was unable to do so. Mark is a man weighing nearly two hundred pounds. He called his father to bring a rope, which he did, and by passing it through the handle of the door and winding it round the banister of the stairs, he succeeded in keeping the door fast.

The senior Lind then called in a Mr. Lucian, who is a Justice of the Peace, and when people get into trouble they always send for him, no matter what it is. He also called in Mrs. Capwell. Happily, Mr. Lucian is a Spiritualist. He describes the scene as being somewhat ludicrous when he arrived. He asked the old lady what the trouble was? She replied, "I do not know; Jim Philips is upstairs, and he acts just like Mattie Lind for all the world."

There stood Mark by the stair banister, as white as a sheet, holding on to the rope with all his might. "What is the matter, Mark?" said Lucian.

"Jim Philips is in my room, and he acts like possessed."

"Why don't you let go the rope and go in and see what is wanted?"

"I have been in there once, and I would not go again for a thousand dollars."

"Unfasten the door, and I will go in."

So Mr. L. opened the door and went in. There lay the medium in bed. Mattie's clothes were taken off and laid exactly as she used to lay them. All her little keepsakes were taken from the drawers where they were carefully put away, and lain upon the table. The album was open at her picture, and many other tests given to prove her identity. She addressed Mr. Lucian, "What are you here for? This is no place for you, in a lady's bedroom!"

He, understanding the case, said in substance, "I thought, Mattie, you would like to see me. How do you do?"

This pleased her much; her desire was to be recognized, and he had done so. He continued to converse with her in a pleasant manner, and finally prevailed upon her to yield to the control of the medium.

About midnight Philips put on his own clothes and went home, and there were no more demonstrations that night.

The next morning, when the bed was examined, there was found among the clothes a dirk knife that Mark had when in the army, and which had been lost for more than a year.

The next morning Philips was oblivious of the night's and most of the day's proceedings. When he went to the shop, Mrs. Capwell asked him about the missing money. With much surprise he asked, "What money?"

"The money that was in the drawer."

"I suppose it is in my pocket-book, where I always put it at nights," taking it out; and there, sure enough, it was, all done up in a nice package, with a string tied round it.

"Ah!" said he, who has fixed it up like this? I certainly did not do it." He was evidently unconscious that the money had been missing. No one knows where it went to this day, only Mattie says that it was one of "her tricks."

After this Mattie often took control of Philips, and whenever she did she was always for going to Lind's. She said she was determined to have her revenge on them some way. They had caused her to suffer, and she was going to return the compliment. I had considerable talk with her and endeavoured to shew her how wrong it was for her to entertain such feelings, but all in vain; she was inexorable. I conversed with Philips about her. He told me that he could always see her before she controlled him, just as distinctly as he could any one. She looked the same as she did in the earth-life, only there was a dark shadow across her forehead, indicating her unhappy condition. He suffered a good deal from fear that while under her control he might be made to do some bad thing. The prospect was certainly not pleasant, and I did not blame him for being disturbed.

But he was not destined to continue in this uncertain state long.

One day he saw approaching him a spirit whom he describes as a large, noble and very pleasant-looking man. This spirit spoke very kindly to him, saying, "You are very much annoyed by this bad spirit that seeks to use you for an evil purpose. I have come to take charge of you, and to prevent her using you to any injury. You need fear her no more. Trust me, and I will guide you free of danger."

Since that time, whenever Mattie has come and expressed herself vindictively, she is immediately made to retire by this benign and good spirit. He gave his name as Moses Figenbaum, a German by birth, lived in New York when he entered spirit life, and did business on such a street, giving the number; told all about his family, etc. We of course knew nothing of such a person.

One day an old German pedlar came to our place, who lived in New York. He stopped at Mr. Capwell's and Mrs. C. asked him if he ever knew Moses Figenbaum? He said he did, and was well acquainted with him. On being questioned, he corroborated every statement that had been made through Philips. This to us was a very satisfactory test.

Philips tells me a very remarkable circumstance, the truth of which is testified to by Mr. Capwell and Mr. Lind, which took place about this time. He says, "I was waked up one night about two o'clock, and saw my bedroom door opened, and Mattie Lind entered with a pencil and paper in her hand. She approached the bedside and spoke to me, saying, 'Mark Lind agreed to meet me to-night. He has not done so. I am going to write him a letter.' She sat down at the stand and wrote. I noticed that the pencil and paper were unlike any that was in the house. After writing for a time she arose and went out."

The next day Mark Lind came into the shop, and while there Philips was entranced by Mattie, and she said to him "I wrote you a letter last night, and carried it and put it on my grave in the cemetery. You will find it there, under the evergreen wreath. I tore the wreath to pieces—I am sorry I did so. Under the remnants you will find the letter."

Mr. Capwell proposed to go with him to verify the truth of the statement, so they both went over to the cemetery, which is a mile from the village, and coming to Mattie's grave they found the evergreen wreath torn to pieces and under the remnants they found a letter directed to Mark Lind, in the handwriting of Mattie Lind.

Since the good spirit has controlled Philips, Mattie has been powerless to use him as an instrument to wreak her vengeance on the objects of her hatred. But it seems that her wrath is still unquenched, and it is more than whispered that she has commenced business on her own responsibility, and strange sounds are heard and sights seen at Lind's. True it is that Mark Lind is an unhappy if not a haunted man.

Such is the substance of the story, as near as I am able to express it. All the parties mentioned still live in Putnam, and can be consulted in reference to the truthfulness of the account. I presume that I have left out many important items, but enough is mentioned to prove this one of the most remarkable manifestations on record. It is interesting because the facts throw much light upon the condition of spirit existence, and are thus made very instructive.

It should be borne in mind that these manifestations came spontaneously, wholly unsought, into a family who were not Spiritualists, and through a medium who was neither a Spiritualist nor at all acquainted with the phenomena.

The dark and unhappy condition of Mattie is a warning to all those who raise their hands against their own life, thinking to escape misery by so doing. Her persistent attempts to be revenged upon those whom she conceived to be the cause of her sufferings, shews that death does not make us saints, but that for a time at least we may retain the same feelings that governed us here.

On the other hand a beautiful lesson is taught us by the mild yet firm interposition of the good spirit in answer to Philips' desire to be freed from the dangerous influence of Mattie. But I will leave people to draw their own inferences. Putnam, Conn., June, 1868.[135] — A. E. CARPENTER

☛ CASE #121: A very curious case of spectral visitation occurred a few days since to the occupant of a chamber in one of our city hotels—a hotel which certainly has never previously made any pretensions to being haunted, and none of whose guests, permanent or transient, have ever before been heard to complain of company from the other world.

The gentleman to whom the adventure occurred is a well-known resident of this city, whose word is fully entitled to credence. He has occupied the chamber in which he saw the spectre for some months. It is inaccessible save by one door, which he asserts was securely locked on the night in question. The window could not be reached, save by a winged being from the outside, and as he found the blinds inside fastened after the spectre disappeared, he feels entirely sure that he was the victim of no practical joke.

He arrived at midnight from a neighbouring city, where he had been engaged in business all day, and went straight to his room and to bed without turning out the gas, as he desired to read one or two letters which had arrived during his absence. Having finished these, he turned the gas flame almost out, leaving a tiny jet, like the ray of a star, athwart the darkness, and lost himself in sleep.

He awoke suddenly, just as the City Hall bell was striking two, and feeling cold, pulled the clothing more carefully around his person. As he half rose to do this he became conscious of a presence, and an indistinct feeling of fear overcame him. Near the foot of the bed was a tall, slender, indefinite form, like "a pillar of cloud," which advanced quietly toward him. It had no human shape, was noiseless, but as it advanced, the gentleman grew deathly cold, felt overpowered, and desired to cry out. He was broad awake—he knew that; but he could not stir. He thought of optical illusions and wondered if this was one; but the thing, whatever it was, advanced slowly to the head of the bed, and the chill around him became frightful. His blood was congealing; he felt that he must do something or die.

Summoning all his courage, he instantly rose, trembling in every limb and walked to the shape. It stood between him and the gas jet, distinct now—an outline gradually developing into human proportions. Each second added to its development. He walked directly through it, caught at the gas pipe, turned on the full flame, and saw nothing! But he is firmly convinced that had he remained in bed he would have been found dead there the next morning, as the approach of the spectre gradually absorbed his life.

He is a cold-blooded man and not a believer in Spiritualism; but he is most positively sure he has seen a ghost—and rejects all theories of nightmare, nervousness and illusion as ridiculous. There may be many ghost stories, but this one has the advantage of being true, if any human testimony is to be believed.[136] — THE REPUBLICAN, SPRINGFIELD, MASS., U.S.

☛ CASE #122: There is a bungalow in Kussowlie [India] called "The Abbey," and one year some friends of mine had taken this house for a season, and I went to stay with them for a short while. My friends told me the house was haunted by the ghost of a lady, who always appeared dressed in a white silk dress. This lady did really live, a great many years ago, and was a very wicked woman, as far as I remember the story. Whether she was murdered, or whether she put an end to herself, I cannot say, but she was not buried in consecrated ground, and for this reason, it was said, her spirit cannot rest. Her grave may be seen by anybody, for it is still at Kussowlie.

When my friends told me this I laughed, and said I did not believe in ghosts; so they showed me a small room divided from the drawing-room by a door, which they told me was an especial pet of the ghost's; and that after it got dark, they always had to keep it shut and they dared me to go into that room at 10 P.M. one night. I said I would; so at 10 P.M. I lighted a candle, and went into the room.

It was small, had no cupboards, and only one sofa, and one table in the centre. I looked under the table and under the sofa, then I shut the door, and blowing out my candle, sat down to await the appearance of the ghost.

In a little while I heard the rustle of a silk dress, though I could see nothing. I got up, and backed towards the door, and as I backed, I could feel something coming towards me. At last I got to the door and threw it wide open and rushed into the drawing-room, leaving the door wide open to see if the ghost would follow after me.

I sat down by the fire, and in a little while, my courage returning, I thought I would go again into the little room; but upon trying the door, I found it was fast shut, and I could not open it, so I went to bed.

Another evening, a lady friend and I were sitting at a small round table with a lamp, reading; all of a sudden the light was blown out, and we were left in the dark. As soon as lights could be procured, it was found that the globe of the lamp had disappeared, and from that day to this, it has never been found. The ghost walks over the whole house at night, and has been seen in different rooms by different people. Kussowlie is between 30 and 40 miles away from Simla, in the direction of the plains.[137] — *THE THEOSOPHIST MAGAZINE*

☛ **CASE #123:** The events I shall now relate occurred in a family of our acquaintance. A Mr. P_____ had lost by consumption a wife whom he devotedly loved, and, one after another, several children. At last but one daughter remained, and upon her, naturally enough, centered all his affections.

She was a delicate girl, and being threatened with the same fate which had so cruelly carried away her mother and sisters, her father took her to live in Italy for change of climate. This girl grew to be about 17 or 18 when the father had to go over to London on business; so he left her with friends, and many and strict were his injunctions to them as to how she was to be looked after, and taken care of.

Well, he went, and whilst he was away, a fancy ball was to take place, to which these friends were going, and which of course, the girl also wished to attend. So they all wrote over to the father and begged and entreated she should be allowed to go, promising that they would take great care of her, and see that she did not get a chill. Much against his will, the poor man consented, and she went to the ball.

Some little time after, the father was awakened one night, by the curtains at the foot of his bed being drawn aside, and there, to his astonishment, stood his daughter, in her fancy dress. He could not move, or say anything, but he looked at her attentively. She smiled, closed the curtains, and disappeared.

He jumped up in great agitation, put down the date and the hour, and then wrote to Italy, asking after his daughter's health, giving a description of her dress and ornaments. Poor man; the next thing he heard was that the young lady had caught cold and died the very night she appeared to him in London. The friends said that even had he seen the dress, he could not have described everything more minutely.[138] — *THE THEOSOPHIST MAGAZINE*

☞ CASE #124: [Let us discuss the topic of the famed] . . . "haunted house" near Peterborough [UK]. This story relates to a farm belonging to the Duke of Bedford, at Thorney. One of the rooms in the house has long had the reputation of being haunted.

A recent search among the beams of the roof above this room has led to the discovery of the will of a farmer named John Cave, who died there more than a century ago, leaving a fortune amounting to £10,000. After his death the farm had been in the occupation of the Fullards, a family well known in the locality. The discovery of the will, which is dated 1794, was made by the present tenant, who is regarded as a trustworthy and intelligent man.

Reporters sent to the place by incredulous newspapers, such as the *Daily Chronicle*, the *Daily Express*, etc., confirmed the facts, and added that there was no doubt that various persons asserted that they had seen the ghost which was reputed to haunt the farm.

Miss Morris, "a highly respected person," who lives in the village, told the reporter of the *Chronicle* that she often went to Mrs. Fullard's, and once slept in the haunted room. Just as it had struck midnight she felt that there was something by her bed-side, and by the light of the moon, which shone into the room, she saw "a thin, gray-haired woman of about seventy-six, with a full-bordered cap, red chintz garment, and crossover wrap of the same material. She had only one tooth. She seemed to glide over the floor." The apparition did not speak but pointed to the ceiling of the room. Miss Morris strongly denied that this was merely a dream. She told the Fullards the next morning what she had seen, and they were greatly impressed by it.

Mrs. Russell, a dressmaker of Thorney, told a similar tale. She had had to pass a night in the "haunted room," as the house was full of guests. She said that there was a slight noise when the ghost appeared, and  again when it went away. She buried her head in the bed-clothes, but that noise in the dead of night remained in her memory.

Now that the will has been found the inhabitants of the house hope that the spirit will henceforth leave them in peace.[139] — *THE ANNALS OF PSYCHICAL SCIENCE*

☛ CASE #125: What I shall now relate about my adventures at the Eddy Homestead in Vermont, America, will tax your indulgence more than all that has preceded. For some years, previous to 1874, I had taken no active interest in the mediumistic phenomena. Nothing surpassingly novel had been reported as occurring, and the intelligence communicated through mediums was not usually instructive enough to induce one to leave his books and the company of their great authors.

But in that year it was rumoured that at a remote village, in the valley of the Green Mountains, an illiterate farmer and his equally ignorant brother were being visited daily by the "materialized," souls of the departed, who could be seen, heard and, in cases, touched by any visitor. This tempting novelty I determined to witness, for it certainly transcended in interest and importance everything that had ever been heard of in any age.

Accordingly, in August of that year, I went to Chittender, the village in question, and, with a single brief intermission of ten days, remained there until the latter part of October. I hope you will believe that I adopted every possible precaution against being befooled by village trickery. The room of the ghosts was a large chamber occupying the whole upper floor of a two-story wing of the house. It was perhaps twenty feet wide by forty long—I speak from memory. Below were two rooms a kitchen and a pantry. The kitchen chimney was in the gable end, of course, and passed through the seance room to the roof. It projected into the room two feet, and at the right, between it and the side of the house, was a plastered closet with a door next to the chimney. A window, two feet square, had been out in the outer wall of the closet to admit air. Running across this end of the large room was a narrow platform, raised about 18 inches from the floor, with a step to mount by at the extreme left, and a hand rail or baluster along the front edge of the platform.

Every evening, after the last meal, William Eddy, a stout built, square shouldered, hard handed farmer, would go upstairs, hang a thick woollen shawl across the doorway, enter the closet and seat himself on a low chair that stood at the extreme end. The visitors, who sometimes numbered forty of an evening, were accommodated on benches placed within a few feet of the platform. Horatio Eddy sat on a chair in front, and discoursed doleful music on a fiddle and led the singing—if such it might be called—without causing Mozart to turn in his grave; a feeble light was given by a kerosine lamp placed on the floor at the end of the room farthest from the platform, in an old drum from which both heads had been removed. Though the light was certainly very dim yet it sufficed to enable us to see if any one left his seat, and to distinguish through the gloom the height and costumes of the visitors from the other world.

At a first sitting this was difficult, but practice soon accustomed one's eyes to the conditions. After an interval of singing and fiddle scraping, sometimes of five, sometimes of twenty or thirty, minutes, we would see the shawl stirred, it would be pushed aside, and out upon the platform would step some figure. It might be a man, woman or child, a decrepit veteran or a babe carried in a woman's arms. The figure would have nothing at all of the supernatural or ghostly about it. A stranger entering at the other end of the room would simply fancy that a living mortal was standing there ready to address an audience.

Its dress would be the one it wore in life, its face, hands, feet, gestures, perfectly natural. Sometimes, it would call the name of the living friend it had come to meet. If it were strong the voice would be of the natural tone; if weak, the words came in faint whispers; if still more feeble, there was no voice at all, but the figure would stand leaning against the chimney or hand rail while the audience asked in turn: "Is it for me?" and it either bowed its head or caused raps to sound in the wall when the right one asked the question. Then the anxious visitor would lean forward, and scan the figure's appearance in the dim light, and often we would hear the joyful cry, "Oh! Mother; Father, Sister, Brother, Son, Daughter," or what not, "I know you."

Then the weird visitor would be seen to bow, or stretch out its hands, and then seeming to gather the last strength that remained to it in its evanescent frame, glide into the closet again, and drop the shawl before the hungry gaze of the eyes that watched it.

But, sometimes, the form would last much longer. Several times I saw come out of the closet an aged lady clad in the Quaker costume, with lawn cap and kerchief pinned across her bosom, grey dress and long housewifely apron, and, calling her son to the platform, seat herself in a chair beside him, and, after kissing him fondly, talk for some minutes with him in low tones about family matters. All the while she would be absently folding the hem of her apron into tucks, and smoothing them out again, and so continuing the thing over and over just as—her son told me—she was in the habit of doing while alive. More than once, just as she was ready to disappear; this gentleman would take her arm in his, come to the baluster, and say that he was requested by his old mother, whom we saw there, although she had been dead many years, to certify that it was, indeed, she herself and no deception, and bid them realize that man lives beyond the grave, and so live here as to ensure their happiness then.[140] — COL. HENRY STEEL OLCOTT

☛ CASE #126: Miss Leopoldina Reichel consented to be taken one very dark night to the cemetery of Grinzing, near Vienna, no great distance from my own house. And as a matter of fact she saw (November, 1844) fiery phenomena on several of the graves.

Taken on a later occasion to the huge burial grounds of Vienna, she saw a number of the burial mounds beset by moving lights. They moved in uniformity to and fro, almost like rows of dancers, or soldiers at drill. Some were large, almost the size of men, and others small, creeping on the ground like dwarfish kobolds [haunting spirits from German mythology]. But they were only to be seen among the more recent grave-rows; the old burial mounds had no fiery guard on duty.

Miss Reichel went timidly and slowly up to them. As she approached, the human-like figures melted away; she recognized the fact that they were no more than luminous clouds, such as she had seen in my dark chamber a thousand times. She now had the courage to go up to them, but only encountered a shining vapour; she walked without fear right into one of them; it reached as high as her neck, and she was able to whisk it about with movements of her skirt. The dancing and drilling was explained by movements of the wind, which had played the same game with all the luminosities simultaneously.[141] — KARL LUDWIG FREIHERR VON REICHENBACH

☛ CASE #127: [Desiring to travel abroad, skeptic and non-believing Scotsman Lord Henry Peter] Brougham started for Norway [with his traveling companion Lord Stuart of Rothsay]. By this time the weather had turned so cold that the [two] travelers resolved to bring their tour to a sudden end, and to press on as rapidly as the bad roads would permit to some Norwegian port, where they hoped to find a ship that would carry them back to Scotland. Accordingly, leaving Goteborg early in the morning of December 19, they journeyed steadily until after midnight, when they came to an inn that seemed to promise comfortable sleeping accommodations.

Stuart lost no time in going to bed; but Brougham decided to wait until a hot bath could be prepared for him. Plunging into it, and forgetful of everything save the warmth that was doubly welcome after the cold of the long drive, he suddenly became aware that he was not alone in the room. No door had opened, not a footstep had been heard; but in the light of the flickering candles he plainly saw the figure of a man seated in the chair on which he had carelessly thrown his clothes. And this figure he instantly recognized as that of his early playmate, the forgotten chum who, as he well knew, had years before gone from the land of the heather to the land of the blazing sun. Yet here he sat, in the quaintly furnished sleeping chamber of a Swedish roadside inn, gazing composedly at his astounded friend.

At once there flashed into Brougham's mind remembrance of the death pact, and he leaped from the bath, only to lose all consciousness and fall headlong to the floor. When he revived, the apparition had disappeared.

There was little sleep for the hard headed Scotchman that night. The vision had been too definite, the shock too intense. But, dressing, he sat down and strove to debate the matter in the light of cold reason. He must, he argued, have dozed off in the bath and experienced a strange dream. To be sure, he had not been thinking of his old comrade, and for years had had no communication with him. Nor had anything taken place during the tour to bring to memory either him or any member of his family, or to turn Brougham's mind to thoughts of India. Still, he found it impossible to believe that he had seen a ghost.

At most, he reiterated to himself, it could have been nothing more than an exceptionally clear cut dream. And to this opinion he stubbornly adhered, notwithstanding the receipt, soon after his return to Edinburgh, of a letter from India announcing the death of the friend who had been so mysteriously recalled to his recollection, and giving December 19 as the date of death.

More than sixty years later we find him, in his autobiography commenting, on the experience anew, granting that it was a strange coincidence but refusing to admit that it was anything more than the coincidence of a dream.

It was in his autobiography, by the way, that he first referred to the confirmatory letter. This fact, taken in connection with his reputation for holding the truth in light esteem and with several vague and puzzling statements contained in the detailed account of the experience itself as set forth in his journal of the Scandinavian tour, has led some critics to make the suggestion that his narrative partakes of the nature of fiction rather than of a sober recital of facts.

Against this, however, must be set Brougham's complete and invincible repugnance to accept at face value anything bordering on the supernatural. He took no pleasure in the thought that he had possibly been the recipient of a visit from a departed spirit. On the contrary, it annoyed him, and he sought earnestly to find a natural explanation for an occurrence which remained unique throughout his long life. No one would have been readier to point out the futility of the apparition if the absent friend had really continued hale and hearty after December 19.

And it is therefore reasonable to assume that had he wished to falsify at all, he would have given an altogether different sequel to the story of his vision or dream, as he preferred to call it, though the evidence which he himself furnishes shows that he was not asleep.[142] — HENRY ADDINGTON BRUCE

☞ CASE #128: [Let us examine] an experience that befell Miss Goodrich-Freer, at the time a most active member of the Society for Psychical Research, in Hampton Court Palace.

This old building is unquestionably one of the most famous of all haunted houses. It dates back to the time of the first Tudors, and according to tradition is haunted by several ghosts, notably the ghosts of Jane Seymour, Henry VIII's third queen; Catharine Howard, whose spirit is said to go shrieking along the gallery where she vainly begged brutal King Henry to spare her life; and Sybil Penn, King Edward VI's foster-mother.

Twice of late years the Howard ghost—or something that

passed for it—has been heard, once by Lady Eastlake, and once by Mrs. Cavendish Boyle. The latter was sleeping in an apartment next to the haunted gallery—which has long been unoccupied and used only as a storeroom for old pictures—when she was suddenly awakened by a loud and most unearthly shriek proceeding from that quarter, followed immediately by perfect silence. Lady Eastlake's experience was exactly similar.

Both ladies, of course, may have heard a real shriek, possibly coming from some nightmare tormented occupant of the palace. But no explanation of this sort is adequate in the case of Miss Goodrich-Freer, who passed a night at Hampton Court for the sole purpose of ascertaining whether or not there was any foundation for its ghostly legends.

The room she selected for her vigil was one especially reputed to be haunted, and opened into a second room, the door between the two, however, being blocked by a heavy piece of furniture. Thus the only means of entrance into her room was by a door from the corridor, and this she locked and bolted. After which, feeling confident that nothing but a real ghost could get in to trouble her, she settled down to read an essay on "Shall We Degrade Our Standard of Value?" a subject manifestly free from matters likely to occasion nervousness. In fact, the essay was so dull that by half past one Miss Goodrich-Freer, not able to keep awake longer, undressed, dropped into bed, and was almost instantly asleep.

Several hours later she was aroused by a noise as of some one opening the furniture-barricaded door. At this she put out her hand to reach a match-box which she knew was lying on a table at the head of the bed.

"I did not reach the matches," she reports. "It seemed to me that a detaining hand was laid on mine. I withdrew it quickly and gazed around into the darkness. Some minutes passed in blackness and silence. I had the sensation of a presence in the room, and finally, mindful of the tradition that a ghost should be spoken to, I said gently: 'Is any one there? Can I do anything for you?' I remembered that the last person who entertained the ghost had said: 'Go away, I don't want you,' and I hoped that my visitor would admire my better manners and be responsive. However, there was no answer, no sound of any kind."

Now Miss Goodrich-Freer left the bed and felt all around the room in the dark, until satisfied that she was alone. The corridor door was still locked and bolted; the piece of furniture against the inner door was in place. So she returned to bed.

Almost at once a soft light began to glow with increasing

brightness. It seemed to radiate from a central point, which gradually took form and became a tall, slender woman, moving slowly across the room. At the foot of the bed she stopped, so that the amazed observer had time to examine her profile and general appearance.

"Her face," Miss Goodrich-Freer says, "was insipidly pretty, that of a woman from thirty to thirty-five years of age, her figure slight, her dress of a soft, dark material, having a full skirt and broad sash or soft waistband tied high up almost under her arms, a crossed or draped handkerchief over the shoulders and sleeves which I noticed fitted very tight below the elbow. In spite of all this definiteness I was conscious that the figure was unsubstantial, and felt quite guilty of absurdity in asking once more: 'Will you let me help you? Can I be of any use to you?' My voice sounded preternaturally loud, but I felt no surprise at noticing that it produced no effect upon my visitor. She stood still for perhaps two minutes, though it is very difficult to estimate time on such occasions. Then she raised her hands, which were long and white, and held them before her as she sank upon her knees and slowly buried her face in the palms in an attitude of prayer—when quite suddenly the light went out, and I was alone in the darkness.

"I felt that the scene was ended, the curtain drawn, and had no hesitation in lighting the candle at my side. . . . The clock struck four."

Again investigation showed that the corridor door was locked and bolted as she had left it, and the inner door still firmly barricaded. Consequently, skeptical though she had been when she arrived at Hampton Court Palace, Miss Goodrich-Freer in leaving it entertained no doubt that she had witnessed a genuine psychical manifestation.[143] — HENRY ADDINGTON BRUCE

☛ CASE #129: The same conclusion [as arrived at in the previous case] was forced upon two ladies.

Miss Elizabeth Morison and Miss Frances Lamont, in connection with a visit paid by them to another famous haunted house, the Petit Trianon at Versailles, [France,] the favorite summer home of that unfortunate queen Marie Antoinette, whose ghost, as well as the ghosts of her attendants, has long been alleged to be visible at times in and around it.

Miss Morison and Miss Lamont had been sightseeing in the royal palace, but tiring of this had set off, in the early afternoon, to walk to the Trianon. Neither of them knew just where it was located, but taking the general direction indicated on Baedeker's map, they finally came to a broad drive, which, had they only known it, would have led them directly to their destination. As it was, they crossed the drive and went up a narrow lane through a thick wood to a point where three paths diverged. Here they began to have a series of experiences which, comparatively insignificant in themselves, had a sequel so amazing that it would be incredible were it not that the veracity of both ladies has been established beyond question.[144]

Ahead of them, on the middle path, they saw two men clad in curious, old-fashioned costumes of long, greenish coats, knee breeches, and small, three-cornered hats. Taking them for gardeners, they asked to be shown the way, and were told to go straight ahead. This brought them to a little clearing that had in it a light garden kiosk, circular and like a bandstand, near which a man was seated. As they approached, he turned his head and stared at them, and his expression was so repellent that they felt greatly frightened.

The next instant, coming from they knew not where, and breathless as if from running, a second man appeared, and speaking in French of a peculiar accent, ordered them brusquely to turn to the right, saying that the Trianon lay in that direction. Just as they reached it, they were again intercepted, this time by a young man who stepped out of a rear door, banged it behind him, and with a somewhat insolent air guided them to the main entrance of the palace.

While they were hurrying thither, Miss Morison noticed a lady, seated below a terrace, holding out a paper as though reading at arm's length. She glanced up as they passed, and Miss Morison, observing with surprise the peculiar cut of her gown, saw that she had a pretty "though not young" face.

"I looked straight at her," she adds in the published statement she has made regarding their adventure, "but some indescribable feeling made me turn away, disturbed at her being there."

Afterwards this "indescribable feeling" was accounted for when

Miss Morison identified in a rare portrait of Marie Antoinette the lady she had seen seated below the terrace!

Still more remarkable, subsequent visits to the Trianon brought to both ladies the startling knowledge that the actual surroundings of the place and the place itself differ vastly from what they saw that summer afternoon. The woods they entered are not there, and have not been there in the memory of man; the paths they trod have long been effaced; there is no kiosk, nor does anybody living, except Miss Morison and Miss Lamont, remember having seen one in the Trianon grounds; on the very spot where Miss Morison saw the lady in the peculiar dress a large bush is growing; and the rear door, out of which stepped the young man who guided them around to the front, opens from an old chapel that has been in a ruinous condition for many years, the door itself being "bolted, barred, and cob-webbed," and unused since the time of Marie Antoinette.

On the other hand, their personal researches in the archives of France have brought to light so many confirmatory facts that both Miss Morison and Miss Lamont are firmly persuaded that the Trianon, its environment, and its people were once exactly as they appeared to them; and that in very truth they saw the place as it looked, not at the time they first visited it, but in the closing years of the French Monarchy, more than a century before.[145] —
HENRY ADDINGTON BRUCE

☛ CASE #130: [The giving of death warnings by ghosts and apparitions] is by no means confined to family ghosts, as may be sufficiently indicated by relating an incident that happened in Canada some years ago, and that has always impressed me as one of the best ghost stories I have ever heard. It was told me by an actor in the strange little drama, and knowing as I do the persons concerned, I have not the slightest hesitation in vouching for its authenticity, incredible though the reader may be inclined to regard it.

In this instance the ghost was seen by a clergyman, the Reverend John Langtry, who afterward became a prominent dignitary of the English Church in Canada. His home was in Toronto, but on the occasion of the ghostly visitation he was at the house of a Mr. and Mrs. Ruttan, who lived with their only child, a young girl, in a small town some fifty or sixty miles north of Toronto. Mr. Ruttan was another Church of England clergyman, and was a warm friend of Doctor Langtry's. This time, however, the latter had journeyed to see him simply on a matter of diocesan business, and was anxious to complete it and get back to Toronto.

To his disappointment he found that Mr. Ruttan had been called out of town, and would not be home until a late hour, possibly not until the following day. On the chance that he might return earlier than expected, Doctor Langtry accepted Mrs. Ruttan's invitation to spend the evening with her.

As they were chatting together—she being so seated that her back was toward the door leading from the parlor, whereas Doctor Langtry's position gave him a full view of the hall—she noticed that all at once he stopped in the middle of a sentence, leaned forward, and stared fixedly into the hall. She instantly turned her head, and followed the direction of his gaze, but could see nothing.

"What is the matter, Doctor Langtry?" she asked. "What are you looking at?"

"Nothing, nothing," he muttered, recovering himself with an effort. "I fancied for a moment—" He paused, then changed the conversation.

But Mrs. Ruttan—from whom I got the story—saw that from time to time he glanced furtively into the hall, and finally half rose from his seat, his face white, his limbs trembling.

"Doctor Langtry!" was her startled exclamation. "Are you ill? Whatever is the matter?"

"Oh," he said shortly, "it is only a momentary faintness. I shall be all right presently. The fatigue of the journey must have unstrung me. I will trouble you to get me a glass of water, and then I think I will return to the hotel."

He drank the water, and rose to go. But when near the front door, he turned to Mrs. Ruttan, and said:

"I don't believe I have asked after your daughter. I trust she is well."

"She is quite well, thank you. I put her to bed just before you came in."

With his hand on the knob of the door, Doctor Langtry again paused irresolutely. "If it's not too much trouble," he asked, "I wish you would go up-stairs and make sure she is all right now."

Wondering at his request and at his manner, Mrs. Ruttan complied, and presently returned to report that the child was sleeping peacefully. Doctor Langtry bowed with an air of obvious relief, bade her good night, and left the house.

But next day, after he had transacted his business, and was about to start for Toronto, he said to Mr. Ruttan, who had accompanied him to the train:

"Ruttan, if your little girl should happen to fall ill while away from home, go to her at once, and take Mrs. Ruttan with you, even if you have no reason to feel that the illness is serious."

Mr. Ruttan laughed. "Of course we would go to her. You may be sure of that. But why—"

"Ask me no questions," said Doctor Langtry, "but bear my request in mind if the occasion should arise."

Within a very short time the child, visiting an aunt in a near-by town, was taken ill, failed rapidly, and died almost before her parents, who had been hastily telegraphed for, could reach her bedside. Doctor Langtry's warning immediately recurred to them, and they wrote him, beseeching an explanation.

"The reason I was anxious about your little girl," he then told them, "was because the night I was sitting with Mrs. Ruttan I saw an angel enter the hall, pass up the stairs, and return, carrying the child in its arms."[146] — HENRY ADDINGTON BRUCE

☛ CASE #131: . . . the kind of ghost most frequently seen is that which appears not before but immediately after, or coincidental with, a death. Its purpose is not to give warning of impending tragedy, but to convey the news of a tragedy already consummated. There are thousands of instances of this sort, so well authenticated as to compel credence. Not long ago an interesting case was reported to me by a gentleman living in Burlington, Vermont, the nephew of the lady—a Mrs. Hazard of Newport, Rhode Island—who saw the ghost. She was ill at the time, and under the care of a trained nurse.

One afternoon, her physician having allowed her to sit up for a couple of hours, she was seated in a chair by the side of her bed, when the nurse noticed her open wide her eyes and turn her head as if following the movements of some one. Then she heard her say, in a tone of surprise: "Hello! Hello! There he goes! There he goes!"

As far as the nurse could see, nobody was in the room with them. But, not wishing to alarm her patient, she merely asked: "Who is it, Mrs. Hazard?"

"Chet Keech. But he doesn't see me. And now he's gone."

Later in the day the nurse mentioned the incident to Mrs. Hazard's daughter, asking her if she knew anybody by the name of Chet Keech.

"Why, certainly I do," was the reply. "He is my cousin, and lives in Danielson, Connecticut."

That day Chet Keech had died at Danielson, as a letter informed the Hazards next morning.[147] — HENRY ADDINGTON BRUCE

☛ CASE #132: Consider this statement by the Reverend C. C.

McKechnie, a Scotch clergyman:

"I was about ten years of age at the time, and had for several years been living with my grandfather, who was an elder in the Kirk of Scotland and in good circumstances. He was very much attached to me and often expressed his intention of having me educated for a minister in the Kirk. Suddenly, however, he was seized with an illness which in a couple of days proved mortal."

"At the time of his death, and without my having any apprehension of his end, I happened to be at my father's house, about a mile off. I was leaning in a listless sort of way against the kitchen table, looking upward at the ceiling and thinking of nothing in particular, when my grandfather's face appeared to grow out of the ceiling, at first dim and indistinct, but becoming more and more complete until it seemed in every respect as full and perfect as I had ever seen it.

"It looked down upon me, as I thought, with a wonderful expression of tenderness and affection. Then it disappeared, not suddenly but gradually, its features fading and becoming demand indistinct, until I saw nothing but the bare ceiling. I spoke at the time of what I saw to my mother, but she made no account of it, thinking, probably, it was nothing more than a boyish vagary. But in about fifteen or twenty minutes after seeing the vision, a boy came running breathless to my father's with the news that my grandfather had just died.[148] — HENRY ADDINGTON BRUCE

☛ CASE #133: Even more remarkable [than the previous case] was the experience of an Illinois physician, Doctor J. S. W. Entwistle, a resident of one of the Chicago suburbs.

Hurrying one morning to catch a train Doctor Entwistle saw approaching him an acquaintance, once well to-do, who had ruined himself by drink. Glancing at him as they met, the physician noticed that his clothing was torn and his face bruised, and that there was a cut under one eye. He noticed, too, that the other kept looking steadily at him with a "woe-begone, God-forsaken expression."

Had he not been in such a hurry, he would have stopped and spoken to him, but as it was he passed him with a nod.

At the station Doctor Entwistle met his brother-in-law, and said, while the train was drawing in:

"Oh, by the way, I just saw Charlie M., and he was a sight. He must have been on a terrible tear."

"I wonder what he's doing in town, anyway?" commented the brother-in-law. "I suppose he was going to see his wife."

"Not a bit of it. She won't have him around."

Then the subject was dropped, and nothing more was said about it until after they had reached Chicago.

Both men, as it happened, had business at the Grand Pacific Hotel and went directly there from the train. They were met by a mutual friend, who had a copy of the Chicago *Tribune* in his hand.

"Hello," he greeted them. "Did you know that Charlie M. is dead? Here is a notice in the paper, stating that his body is at the morgue. He was killed in a saloon fight. The paper hasn't got the name quite right, but from the description it's Charlie, sure enough."

"But he can't be dead," said Doctor Entwistle, aghast, "for it was only a few minutes ago that I met him on the street in Englewood."

Nevertheless, it turned out that Charlie M. was dead, and that his body had been taken to the morgue several hours before Doctor Entwistle thought he saw him in the Chicago suburb. Moreover, on inquiry it was learned that the clothes worn by him when he was killed and the marks on his face "tallied in every particular with the description given by the doctor."[149] — HENRY ADDINGTON BRUCE

☛ CASE #134: Quite a similar experience [to the previous account] occurred to Mr. Harry E. Reeves when he was choirmaster at St. Luke's Church in San Francisco.

On a Friday, about three in the afternoon, Mr. Reeves was in an up-stairs room at his home. He had been working on some music. Wishing to rest for a few minutes, he threw himself on a lounge, but almost immediately an unaccountable impulse led him to get up again and open the door of his room.

Standing at the head of the stairs he saw Edwin Russell, a member of his choir and a well-known San Francisco real estate broker. Mr. Russell had promised to call on him the following day to look over the music for Sunday, and Mr. Reeves's first thought was that he had come a day earlier than intended.

He advanced to greet him, when, to his amazement and horror, the figure on the stairs turned as though to descend, and then faded into nothingness.

"My God!" gasped Reeves, and fell forward.

A door below was hastily opened, and two women and a man ran to his aid. The women were his sister and niece, the man was a Mr. Sprague. They found Mr. Reeves seated on the stairs, his face white and covered with perspiration, his body trembling.

"Uncle Harry!" cried the niece. "What in the world is the

matter?"

Mr. Reeves was in such a panic that he could hardly speak, but he managed to reply: "I have seen a ghost!"

"Whose ghost?" inquired Mr. Sprague, with a skeptical smile.

"The ghost of Edwin Russell."

Instantly the smile left Mr. Sprague's face. "That's strange," said he, "that's very strange. For, as these ladies will tell you, I came to consult with you regarding the music for Mr. Russell's funeral. He had a stroke of apoplexy this morning, and died a few hours ago."[150]
— HENRY ADDINGTON BRUCE

☛ CASE #135: Mobile, Alabama, 12th May, 1884. I resided in Camden, New Jersey, at the time of my brother's death. He lived in Louisiana. His death was caused by the collision of two steamers on the Mississippi. Some part of the mast fell on him, splitting his head open, causing instantaneous death.

An apparition appeared to my mother at the foot of her bed. It stood there for some time gazing at her, and disappeared. The apparition was clothed in a long white garment, with its head bound in a white cloth. My mother was not a superstitious person, nor did she believe in Spiritualism. She was wide awake at the time. It was not a dream.

She remarked to me when I saw her in the morning, "I shall hear bad news from Joseph," and related to me what she had seen. Two or three days from that time we heard of the sad accident.

I had another brother who was there at the time, and when he returned home I inquired of him all particulars, and how he was laid out. His description answered to what my mother saw, much to our astonishment.[151] — MRS. A. E. COLLYER

☛ CASE #136: About 2 o'clock on the morning of October 21st, 1881, while I was perfectly wide awake, and looking at a lamp burning on my washhand-stand, a person, as I thought, came into my room by mistake, and stopped, looking into the looking-glass on the table. It soon occurred to me it represented Robinson Kelsey, by his dress and wearing his hair long behind. When I raised myself up in bed and called out, it instantly disappeared.

The next day I mentioned to some of my friends how strange it was. So thoroughly convinced was I, that I searched the local papers that day (Saturday) and the following Tuesday, believing his death would be in one of them.

On the following Wednesday, a man, who formerly was my drover, came and told me Robinson Kelsey was dead. Anxious to know at what time he died, I wrote to Mr. Wood, the family undertaker at Lingfield; he learnt from the brother-in-law of the deceased that he died at 2 a.m.

He was my first cousin, and was apprenticed formerly to me as a miller; afterwards he lived with me as journeyman; altogether, 8 years. I never saw anything approaching that before. I am 72 years old, and never feel nervous; I am not afraid of the dead or their spirits.[152] — MR. MARCHANT

☛ CASE #137: I was dressing one morning in December, 1881, when a certain conviction came upon me that someone was in my dressing-room. On looking round, I saw no one, but then, instantaneously (in my mind's eye, I suppose), every feature of the face and form of my old friend, X., arose. This, as you may imagine, made a great impression on me, and I went at once into my wife's room and told her what had occurred, at the same time stating that I feared Mr. X. must be dead. The subject was mentioned between us several times that day.

Next morning, I received a letter from X.'s brother, then Consul-General at Odessa, but who I did not know was in England, saying that his brother had died at a quarter before 9 o'clock that morning. This was the very time the occurrence happened in my dressing-room.

It is right to add that we had heard some two months previously that X. was suffering from cancer, but still we were in no immediate apprehension of his death. I never on any other occasion had any hallucination of the senses, and sincerely trust I never again shall.[153] — ROB. RAWLINSON

☛ CASE #138: N. J. S. and F. L. were employed together in an office, were brought into intimate relations with one another, which lasted for about eight years, and held one another in very great regard and esteem.

On Monday, March 19th, 1883, F. L., in coming to the office, complained of having suffered from indigestion; he went to a chemist, who told him that his liver was a little out of order, and gave him some medicine. He did not seem much better on Thursday. On Saturday he was absent, and N. J. S. has since heard he was examined by a medical man, who thought he wanted a day or two of rest, but expressed no opinion that anything was serious.

On Saturday evening, March 24th, N. J. S., who had a headache, was sitting at home. He said to his wife that he was what he had not been for months, rather too warm; after making the remark he leaned back on the couch, and the next minute saw his friend, F. L., standing before him, dressed in his usual manner. N. J. S. noticed the details of his dress, that is, his hat with a black band, his overcoat unbuttoned, and a stick in his hand; he looked with a fixed regard at N. J. S., and then passed away.

N. J. S. quoted to himself from Job, "And lo, a spirit passed before me, and the hair of my flesh stood up." At that moment an icy chill passed through him, and his hair bristled. He then turned to his wife and asked her the time; she said, "12 minutes to 9." He then said, "The reason I ask you is that F. L. is dead. I have just seen him." She tried to persuade him it was fancy, but he most positively assured her that no argument was of avail to alter his opinion.

The next day, Sunday, about 3 p.m., A. L., brother of F. L., came to the house of N. J. S., who let him in. A. L. said, "I suppose you know what I have come to tell you?"

N. J. S. replied, "Yes, your brother is dead."

A. L. said, "I thought you would know it."

N. J. S. replied, "Why?"

A. L. said, "Because you were in such sympathy with one another."

N. J. S. afterwards ascertained that A. L. called on Saturday to see his brother, and on leaving him noticed the clock on the stairs was 25 minutes to 9 p.m. F. L.'s sister, on going to him at 9 p.m., found him dead from rupture of the aorta.

This is a plain statement of facts, and the only theory N. J. S. has on the subject is that at the supreme moment of death, F. L. must have felt a great wish to communicate with him, and in some way by force of will impressed his image on N. J. S.'s senses.[154] — N. J. S. [WRITTEN IN THE THIRD PERSON]

☞ CASE #139: July 21st, 1885. I am a gardener in employment at Sawston. I always go through Hinxton churchyard on my return home from work.

On Friday, May 8th, 1885, I was walking back as usual. On entering the churchyard, I looked rather carefully at the ground, in order to see a cow and donkey which used to lie just inside the gate. In so doing, I looked straight at the square stone vault in which the late Mr. de Fréville was at one time buried. I then saw [his wife] Mrs. de Fréville leaning on the rails, dressed much as I had usually seen her, in a coal-scuttle bonnet, black jacket with deep crape, and black dress. She was looking full at me. Her face was very white, much whiter than usual. I knew her well, having at one time been in her employ. I at once supposed that she had come, as she sometimes did, to the mausoleum in her own park, in order to have it opened and go in.

I supposed that Mr. Wiles, the mason from Cambridge, was in the tomb doing something. I walked round the tomb looking carefully at it, in order to see if the gate was open, keeping my eye on her and never more than five or six yards from her. Her face turned and followed me.

I passed between the church and the tomb (there are about four yards between the two), and peered forward to see whether the tomb was open, as she hid the part of the tomb which opened. I slightly stumbled on a hassock of grass, and looked at my feet for a moment only. When I looked up she was gone.

She could not possibly have got out of the churchyard, as in order to reach any of the exits she must have passed me. So I took for granted that she had quickly gone into the tomb. I went up to the door, which I expected to find open, but to my surprise it was shut and had not been opened, as there was no key in the lock. I rather hoped to have a look into the tomb myself, so I went back again and shook the gate to make sure, but there was no sign of any one's having been there. I was then much startled and looked at the clock, which marked 9:20.

When I got home I half thought it must have been my fancy, but I told my wife that I had seen Mrs. de Fréville.

Next day, when my little boy told me that she was dead, I gave a start, which my companion noticed, I was so much taken aback. I have never had any other hallucination whatever.[155] — ALFRED BARD

☛ CASE #140: On December 18th, 1873, I left my house in Lincolnshire to visit my wife's parents, then and now residing in Lord Street, Southport. Both my parents were, to all appearance, in good health when I started.

The next day after my arrival was spent in leisurely observation of the manifold attractions of this fashionable seaside resort. I spent the evening in company with my wife in the bay-windowed drawing-room upstairs, which fronts the main street of the town.

I proposed a game at chess, and we got out the board and began to play.

Perhaps half-an-hour had been thus occupied by us, during which I had made several very foolish mistakes. A deep melancholy was oppressing me. At length I remarked: "It is no use my trying to play, I cannot for the life think about what I am doing. Shall we shut it up and resume our talk? I feel literally wretched."

"Just as you like," said my wife, and the board was at once put aside.

This was about half-past 7 o'clock; and after a few minutes' desultory conversation, my wife suddenly remarked: "I feel very dull to-night. I think I will go downstairs to mamma, for a few minutes."

Soon after my wife's departure, I rose from my chair, and walked in the direction of the drawing-room door. Here I paused for a moment, and then passed out to the landing of the stairs.

It was then exactly 10 minutes to 8 o'clock. I stood for a moment upon the landing, and a lady, dressed as if she were going on a business errand, came out, apparently, from an adjoining bedroom, and passed close by me. I did not distinctly see her features, nor do I remember what it was that I said to her.

The form passed down the narrow winding stairs, and at the same instant my wife came up again, so that she must have passed close to the stranger, in fact, to all appearance, brushed against her.

I exclaimed, almost immediately, "Who is the lady, Polly, that you passed just now, coming up?"

Never can I forget, or account for, my wife's answer. "I passed nobody," she said.

"Nonsense," I replied; "You met a lady just now, dressed for a walk. She came out of the little bedroom. I spoke to her. She must be a visitor staying with your mother. She has gone out, no doubt, at the front door."

"It is impossible," said my wife. "There is not any company in the house. They all left nearly a week ago. There is no one in fact at all indoors, but ourselves and mamma."

"Strange," I said; I am certain that I saw and spoke to a lady, just before you came upstairs, and I saw her distinctly pass you; so that it seems incredible that you did not perceive her."

My wife positively asserted that the thing was impossible.

We went downstairs together, and I related the story to my wife's mother, who was busy with her household duties. She confirmed her daughter's previous statement. There was no one in the house but ourselves.

The next morning, early, a telegram reached me from Lincolnshire; it was from my elder sister, Julia (Mrs T. W. Bowman, of Prospect House, Stechford, Birmingham), and announced the afflicting intelligence that our dear mother had passed suddenly away the night before; and that we (i.e., myself and wife) were to return home to Gainsborough by the next train. The doctor said it was heart-disease, which in a few minutes had caused her death.

When all was over and Christmas Day had arrived, I ventured to ask my brother the exact moment of our mother's death.

"Well, father was out," he said, "at the school-room, and I did not see her alive. Julia was just in time to see her breathe her last. It was, as nearly as I can recollect, 10 minutes to 8 o'clock."

I looked at my wife for a moment, and then said: "Then I saw her in Southport, and can now account, unaccountably, for my impressions."

Before the said 19th of December I was utterly careless of these things; I had given little or no attention to spiritual apparitions or impressions.[156] — ROBT. BEE

☛ CASE #141: In 1888 a gentleman, whom I will call Mr. A., who has occupied a high public position in India, and whom I have known a long time, informed me verbally that he had had a remarkable experience.

He awoke one morning, in India, very early, and in the dawning light saw a lady, whom I will call Mrs. B., standing at the foot of his bed. At the same time he received an impression that she needed him. This was his sole experience of a hallucination; and it so much impressed him that he wrote to the lady, who was in England at the time, and mentioned the circumstance.

He afterwards heard from her that she had been in a trance-condition at the time, and had endeavoured to appear to him by way of an experiment.

Mr. A. did not give me the lady's name, supposing that she did not desire the incident to be spoken of; nor did he find an opportunity of himself inquiring as to her willingness to mention the matter.[157] — MR. F. W. H. MYERS

☛ CASE #142: Of the many spirits whom I have seen, only two have been those of persons known to me in my present life; one of these I have seen once, the other I have seen eight times.

One evening, on nearing the door of my dressing-room, I suddenly saw, just before me, a little to my left, what looked like a dark-haired man, in ordinary dress, in the act of passing through the wall in front of me. His head was slightly thrown back, his eyes were raised, and his face wore a sad, dreamy, and fixed expression.

On another occasion I saw in the same room, standing in the air like the "saints and angels" in old pictures, a group of eighteen or twenty handsome young men, in white tunics, with red belts and buskins, and curious red hats, with "cream-bowl" crowns and very broad brims, embroidered with gold, and set on so slantingly that the thin line of gold on the edge of the brims produced, round each head, something like the effect of a nimbus. The right hand of each grasped a stout crook, taller than himself, and resting on the ground. They looked as though they had halted on the march; and the eyes of all were fixed upon me with grave, earnest, and rather friendly gaze.

After looking at them for a few seconds, I put my hands to my eyes; and then, looking up again to see if they were still there, I saw the same group, but much higher up, at a height, apparently, far above the ceiling and proportionally fainter. This second glimpse was only instantaneous; and though I looked up several times during the evening in the hope of seeing them again, I saw nothing more of my white-vestured visitants.[158] — MISS ANNA BLACKWELL

☛ CASE #143: When the celebrated Miss Anna Maria Porter was residing at Esher, in Surrey, an aged gentleman of her acquaintance, who lived in the same village, was in the habit of frequenting her house, usually making his appearance every evening, reading the newspaper, and taking his cup of tea.

One evening Miss Porter saw him enter as usual, and seat himself at the table, but without speaking. She addressed some remark to him, to which he made no reply; and, after a few seconds, she saw him rise, and leave the room without uttering a word.

Astonished, and fearing that he might have been suddenly taken ill, she instantly sent her servant to his house to make inquiries. The reply was, that the old gentleman had died suddenly about an hour before.[159] — ROBERT DALE OWEN

CASE #144: In the year 1785, Sir John Sherbroke and General George Wynyard, then young men, were officers, the former Captain and the latter Lieutenant, in the same regiment, namely the 33rd, at that time commanded by Lieutenant-Colonel Forke, and stationed at Sydney, in the island of Cape Breton, off Nova Scotia.

On the 15th of October of that year, between eight and nine o'clock P.M., these two officers were seated before the fire at coffee, in Wynyard's parlour. It was a room in the new barracks, which had been erected the preceding summer, and had two doors—the one opening on an outer passage, the other into that officer's bedroom, from which bedroom there was no exit except by returning through the parlour.

Sherbroke, happening to look up, saw beside the door which opened on the passage the figure of a tall youth, apparently about twenty years of age, but pale and much emaciated.

Astonished at the presence of a stranger, Sherbroke called the attention of his brother officer, sitting near him, to the visitor. "I have heard," he said, in afterwards relating the incident, "of a man being as pale as death; but I never saw a living face assume the appearance of a corpse, except Wynyard's at that moment."

Both remained silently gazing on the figure as it passed slowly through the room and entered the bedchamber, casting on young Wynyard, as it passed, a look, as his friend thought, of melancholy affection.

The oppression of its presence was no sooner removed, than Wynyard, grasping his friend's arm, exclaimed, in scarcely articulate tones, "Great God! my brother!"

"Your brother! What can you mean?" replied Sherbroke; "there must be some deception in this."

And with that he instantly proceeded into the bedroom, followed by Wynyard. No one to be seen there!

They searched in every part, and convinced themselves that it was entirely untenanted. A brother officer, Lieutenant Ralph Gore, coming in soon after, joined in the search, but equally without avail.

Wynyard persisted in declaring that he had seen his brother's spirit; but, for a time, Sherbroke inclined to the belief that they might have been, in some way or other, deluded, possibly by a trick of some brother officer.

Nevertheless, at the suggestion of Lieutenant Gore, the next day Captain Sherbroke made a memorandum of the date; and all waited with the greatest anxiety for letters from England. This anxiety at last became so apparent on Wynyard's part, that his brother officers, in spite of his resolution to the contrary, finally won from him the confession of what he had seen.

The story was soon bruited abroad, and produced great excitement throughout the regiment.

When the expected vessel with letters arrived, there were none for Wynyard, but one for Sherbroke. As soon as that officer had opened it, he beckoned Wynyard from the room. Expectation was at its climax, especially as the two friends remained closeted for an hour.

On Sherbroke's return the mystery was solved. It was a letter from a brother officer, begging Sherbroke to break to his friend Wynyard the news of the death of his favourite brother, who had expired on the 15th of October, and at the same hour at which the friends saw the apparition in the block-house.[160] — ROBERT DALE OWEN

☛ CASE #145: — [Not a Victorian account, but narrated by a Victorian. L.S.] Pliny tells us that Athenodorus the philosopher arriving in Athens, noticed a large and fair house shut up and deserted, having a notice posted upon it that it was for sale. The terms required were so low that Athenodorus felt that there must be some mystery about it; he enquired and found that a spectre, drawing a chain along with him, had driven everyone from the house who had lived in it. He bought it, and sat up waiting to see the apparition.

At midnight the ghost appeared, clanking its irons, and beckoned to him; he made a motion that it might wait, and went on with his writing. This was several times repeated, till at length Athenodorus rose and followed it into an inner court, where it vanished. He laid some weeds and leaves on the spot, went to bed, and the next day waited on the magistrates, and desired them to send men to search the spot.

This was done, and a skeleton, bound up and entangled with chains, was discovered, and duly interred; and the house was free from the apparition ever afterwards.[161] — WILLIAM HOWITT

☛ CASE #146: The minister of a small village in Germany had been six weeks in possession of his new parsonage. He had duly visited his new neighbours; the domestic arrangements were completed; and his accounts with the widow of his predecessor were finally adjusted. Pleased at the termination of this important business, which, owing to the integrity of both parties, had been transacted without the intervention of lawyers, the pastor left his study, delivered the parcel containing the balance which he had yet to pay, to be forwarded to the widow, and then seated himself under the lime-trees which overhung the entrance of his habitation.

Here he was soon joined by his affectionate wife; they entered into conversation on the cheering prospect which promised them a decent provision, and the approach of those parental joys which they had not yet tasted.

A country blooming as a garden was extended before them. After a long succession of sultry days, a storm about noon had cooled the atmosphere. All nature had assumed a fresher appearance; the flowers were attired in gayer colours, and exhaled more fragrant perfumes; the soft breeze wantoned about the glowing cheek of the husbandman, who, summoned by the evening bell, slowly returned with his implements to the peaceful cots of his village.

"Dear Dorothy," said the pastor, when his wife rose to make preparations for supper, "the heat from the past sultry weather is still very perceptible in the house. Suppose we take our supper this evening here under the lime-trees? We shall thus have an opportunity of airing the house thoroughly, and shall enjoy the beauty of the evening an hour longer in the open air."

"You take the word out of my mouth," replied his wife. "The evening, indeed, is too fine, and we shall certainly relish the pigeons, which are at the fire, and a nice salad, as well again here as in the close rooms." No sooner said than done.

With cheerful industry Dorothy hastened to the kitchen; the pastor fetched the table and the chairs, laid the cloth, and even brought a bottle of wine out of the cellar. According to his general custom, this indulgence was reserved for Sundays or particular occasions; but this day, when, as the reader has been informed, he had so happily terminated the business of settling his accounts, seemed to him worthy of being made an exception: it was an important day for him, as it was not till now that he felt himself completely installed in his office and habitation.

Dorothy soon made her appearance with the pigeons, and she, with her husband and his sister, who had followed them to lend her assistance in removing, and in their new domestic arrangements, sat down to the rural repast. It was seasoned by cheerful conversation and innocent mirth, whilst a late nightingale charmed their ears with his strains, and the worthy pastor quaffed the generous beverage out of a goblet on which, as an heir-loom of his grandfather's, he set a particular value, till the joyous tone of his mind was plainly expressed in his countenance.

Thus the night stole upon them almost without their perceiving its approach.

Dorothy was going to fetch a candle, but her husband detained her. "The evening, to be sure, is still fine," said he, "but the air grows cooler. You know, Dorothy, that you must take care of yourself. As soon as I have finished this glass, we will all go in together."

Scarcely had the pastor finished speaking—scarcely had Dorothy taken her seat again, when all at once both the females started up with shrieks of terror. The pastor looked about, and to his utter astonishment an apparition stood beside him. It was a tall, elegant figure. The face, of exquisite beauty, seemed tinged with the roseate glow of evening; a rose-bud decorated its hair, which flowed in charming ringlets over a neck of snowy whiteness; a robe of azure blue, studded with stars of gold, covered its form; an effulgence resembling sunbeams encircled the angelic vision, which, with a look of inexpressible sweetness, seemed to invite the pastor to follow it.

The two ladies, as the reader has been already informed, had flown from their seats. The divine, attracted by the enchanting appearance of the phantom, rose and followed it. His wife and sister would have detained him, but he disengaged himself. When, however, the figure, moving on before him, directed its course towards the churchyard, his wife once more went up to him, clasped him in her arms, and intreated him with such earnestness and alarm to proceed no farther, that, in consideration of her state, he desisted from his intention.

He turned back with her, promising not to follow the apparition; but he could not help asking, over and over again, how she could be afraid of a being, which, so far from having any thing terrifying about it, rather looked like an angel from heaven, whose invitations could only be designed for some good purpose. Both stopped before the house-door, and watched the spirit, which proceeded to the wall of the churchyard, rose to the top of it, and disappeared. . . .[162]— ANONYMOUS

Chapter Two

TELEPATHIC ACCOUNTS

Cases of Thought Transference, Automatic Writing, and ESP

☞ CASE #147: The Bishop [Wilberforce] was in his library at Cuddesdon with three or four of his clergy writing with him at the same table. The Bishop suddenly raised his hand to his head, and exclaimed, "I am certain that something has happened to one of my sons." It afterwards transpired that just at that time his eldest son's foot (who was at sea) was badly crushed by an accident on board his ship.

The Bishop himself records the circumstance in a letter to Miss Noel, dated March 4th, 1847; he writes: "It is curious that at the time of his accident I was so possessed with the depressing consciousness of some evil having befallen my son Herbert, that at last on the third day after, the 13th, I wrote down that I was quite unable to shake off the impression that something had happened to him, and noted this down for remembrance."[163] — CANON ASHWELL

☞ CASE #148: One August morning at breakfast the well-known feeling stole over me. Waiting till all had left the table excepting my second daughter, I remarked to her, "I am feeling so restless about one of my absent boys! It is _____; and I feel as if I was looking at blood!"

The son in question, in a letter received a few days later, inquired of Mrs. Gates as follows: "Write in your next if you had any presentiments during last week. We were going to canal, fishing, and I got up at the first sound of the bell, and, taking my razor to shave, began to sharpen it on my hand, and being, I suppose, only half awake, failed to turn the razor, and cut a piece clean out of my left hand. An artery was cut in two places, and bled dreadfully." (Further details are given which shew that the pain and bleeding were probably at their maximum at the hour of Mrs. Gates's breakfast that same morning.)[164] — MRS. GATES

☛ CASE #149: A strange experience occurred in the autumn of the year 1879. A brother of mine had been from home for three or four days, when, one afternoon, at half-past five (as nearly as possible), I was astonished to hear my name called out very distinctly. I so clearly recognised my brother's voice that I looked all over the house for him, but not finding him and, indeed, knowing that he must be distant some forty miles, I ended by attributing the incident to a fancied delusion, and thought no more about the matter.

On my brother's arrival home, however, on the sixth day, he remarked amongst other things that he had narrowly escaped an ugly accident. It appeared that whilst getting out from a railway carriage he missed his footing, and fell along the platform; by putting out his hands quickly he broke the fall and only suffered a severe shaking. "Curiously enough," he said, "when I found myself falling I called out your name." This did not strike me for a moment, but on my asking him during what part of the day this happened, he gave me the time, which I found corresponded exactly with the moment I heard myself called.[165] — MR. R. FRYER

☛ CASE #150: Two years ago my son was ill in Durban, Natal. I was told by his medical attendant, who is also my son-in-law, that the illness was serious, but I had no reason to suppose it was expected to end fatally. Of course I, his mother, was anxious; but there came better accounts, and at last a letter from my son himself. He spoke of being really stronger, expressed regret at his enforced long silence, and added he hoped now to write regularly again.

The load was lifted from my mind, and I remarked I felt happier than I had done for months. At this time I too was ill, and had a trained nurse with me. A few nights after the receipt of the letter, I thought I had been lying awake, and requiring to call my nurse who was in my room, I sat up in bed and called loudly "Edward, Edward." I was roused by nurse answering, "I fear, ma'am, your son will not be able to come to you." I tried to laugh it off, but a chill struck to my heart. I noted the hour, 3:40 on Sunday morning.

Without mentioning my fears, I recounted the incident to my daughters, but I looked for the bad news to come, and on Monday received the cable message "Edward died last night." Subsequent letters named the hour as being identical with that in which I had involuntarily sent forth my cry for my loved one. His sister, Mrs. C., in writing to me, said, "Oh! mother, his one crave was for you, and to the last moment the yearning he had for you seemed to dwell in his eyes."

I may add we were more than even mother and son usually are to one another. I believe in that one moment our souls were permitted to meet, and I thank God for the memory of that hour.[166] — MRS. X.

☛ CASE #151: On the morning of February 7th, 1855, at Mount Pleasant, Co. Dublin, where I lived, I awakened from a troubled sleep and dream, exclaiming, "John is dead." My husband said, "Go asleep, you are dreaming." I did sleep and again awoke, repeating the same words, and asking him to look at the watch and tell me what o'clock it was then; he did so and said it was 2 o'clock.

I was much impressed by this dream, and next day went to the city to inquire at the house of business; Mr. John C. being at Danehum for the previous month. When I got to the house I saw the place closed up, and the man who answered the door told me the reason.

"Oh! ma'am, Mr. John C. is dead." "When did he die?" I said. "At two this morning," he said.

I was so much shocked he had to assist me to the waiting room and give me water. I had not heard of his illness and was speaking to him a fortnight previously, when he was complaining of a slight cold and expected the change to Danehum would benefit him so that he should return to town immediately. I never saw or heard of him after until I dreamt the foregoing.[167] — EMILY LINCOLN

☛ CASE #152: Dear sir,—Your favour of April 15th was received here on my return from Georgia, the 24th inst., and in reply I will state to you something of the cause of my investigations of the interesting and important phenomena before us.

The year 1850 found me exploring the Island of Sumatra. And at one time, with a Malay Rajah and a small company of native guards, after a long tramp in the blazing sun, I was stricken down exhausted with symptoms of sunstroke and fever. The Rajah called his doctor, and a wild, savage, naked, native Malay appeared, directed my clothes to be removed, then commenced manipulating and making passes from my head to feet, during which I felt his great magnetic [mesmeric] power, was put to sleep and within an hour awoke free from pain and refreshed. It astonished me and set me to investigating "animal magnetism."

From 1852 to the present my business as mining engineer has sent me all over the country, and much in the saddle, from which

I acquired perfect health, and in a short time realised that I had strong magnetic power, which, to cure disease, must emanate from a pure source.

To comply with the necessary conditions, I gave up the use of tobacco and all stimulating food and drink, and commenced a diet of plain nourishing food, with plenty of exercise on horseback, and sleep. I soon found my magnetism sought for by invalids for headache, rheumatism, neuralgia, and other diseases. And I performed most wonderful cures, and in many cases, after the patient had been given up by physicians to die, I have brought them up to health and they live to-day.

I write of this to show you my condition, the experimenting instrument.

I soon had quite a list of sensitives as patients. I found some more susceptible than others; several were relieved of all pain at once, by my taking their hands or placing my hand on their heads or part afflicted, or breathing upon them. For 18 years I experimented in California, then moved to Nevada, 600 miles east, then to New York, 3,000 miles east.

During these years I had visited the Atlantic States many times, and had patients (sensitives) in Massachusetts and New York, and as I have practised and relieved pain gratuitously, I secured the gratitude and intimate friendship of my patients, which I consider an important auxiliary to my experiments, or the phenomena.

In 1869 I crossed the great Humboldt (40 mile) desert, in the State of Nevada, for the sixth time, alone, in the saddle; by an accident my horse, a wild mustang, escaped, leaving me at 10 a.m. on foot in that ankle deep alkali sand, under the blazing July sun, and twenty miles from a drop of water, except that in my saddle bags on the horse. Hours were spent in the chase for my horse.

Then I tried to shoot him, but he escaped, leaving me exhausted, sunstruck, dizzy, and finally helplessly dying on the hot, shadeless alkali about noon.

I passed the agony of death by thirst, heat, and exhaustion, and became insensible. It was rare a traveller passed that way at that season, the track marked only by the bones of dead animals. A chance traveller came, saw my horse, and found me insensible, laid me in the shade of his waggon, and bathed me with water and vinegar until I came back to life. He lassoed my horse, and at sundown I mounted and rode to the settlements.

Between half-past two and three o'clock that afternoon one of my sensitive lady friends in Boston, Massachusetts (2,600 miles distant), while talking with her husband, suddenly threw up her hands and said, "Mr. Blake is dead," and could not be reconciled to the contrary. She persuaded her husband to visit my father in the same city and learn where I was, etc.

Two years after (in 1871) I visited the friends, and was immediately asked, "Where were you two years ago, the last week in July?" On comparing notes, and allowing for the difference in time, we concluded that at the time I became insensible on the desert my lady friend received the intelligence. I know I thought of the lady and her husband while lying on the sand, as we were long dear friends. Afterwards, during my residence in New York, 200 miles distant from Boston, this sensitive had positive mental communication with me. She knew when I was unwell, or disturbed by vexatious business, and I found I could by concentrating my thoughts on her make her think of me. Generally, the experiments were most satisfactory about twilight or early morning. I will say I never attempted to mesmerise a patient. I imparted magnetism by simply holding the hands or head, and not consciously exercising my will over their mind.

In the year 1866, I resided in Tuolumne County, California, interested in gold mining. I also had large gold mining property in Placer County, California, over 100 miles distant. My partner was a dear friend who resided at the mine in Placer County, while my home was then in Tuolumne County. Our correspondence was frequent, and soon after the establishment of the conditions, we noticed that questions asked in letters by either, about business and other matters, were answered, often the same day that the letter in which the question was asked was written, the letters passing each other on the road. This occurred dozens of times. And often we wrote our letters the same day and hour without previous arrangement.

In conversation we could often turn each other's thoughts to different subjects, and very often on meeting him at his house, after an absence, he would say "I've been thinking of you for an hour," or "I knew you were coming," while I had tried before arriving to impress upon his mind that I was approaching. And sometimes he would feel that I was coming when at a distance of 40 miles.

This gentleman was so sceptical about magnetism and kindred subjects that I refrained from talking with him about it, and he was not aware that I was experimenting, which made the tests more satisfactory to me.

In 1882 and 1883 I came to San Francisco from New York, 3,000 miles, and visited some of my old friends and patients, and selected one lady for experiment. I magnetised her often, and when I returned to New York opened a tri-weekly correspondence with her; by this I proved that mental communication is possible at that distance. She, very sensitive, not only knew of my mental state but physical surroundings, and I became aware of any mental agitation with her, such as sickness or sorrow. If I visit her house I can mentally call her to the door at once. I have views in explanation of some of these phenomena, but would be pleased to learn any explanation or views on the subject that you can give. Of course 34 years' investigation in this and kindred subjects has given me thousands of tests and incidents, some of which I may publish at some future time. I remain, very respectfully yours, San Francisco, California, May 30th, 1884.[168] — GORHAM BLAKE

☛ CASE #153: A good many years ago I was in Paris, and one Sunday afternoon I was taking coffee in the courtyard of the hotel, when all at once I seemed to hear a voice say, "Etta has fallen into the pond." The pond was an ornamental piece of water in our grounds, large enough for a boat, and deep, and surrounded by a grass path and shrubbery, and was my horror for the children. They were never allowed to go near it, unless with one of the family.

At once I seemed to see the whole thing, and I got so agitated that I could not rest, and walked about till nearly midnight in Paris, to get fatigued and sleepy.

The next day I felt just the same, and left for Brussels to get my letters, and as all seemed well I dismissed the subject. It was kept a profound secret, but it came out while I was at a dinner party.

On my return home I asked for the particulars, and was told that this little girl fell into the pond one Sunday afternoon while I was abroad, and was rescued by the hair of her head, by the governess, and was carried into the house in a very exhausted state;

but received no injury.

I found that it happened on the very afternoon, and at the same hour, 4:30, that I had that impression in Paris. It was a remarkable circumstance, and beyond my comprehension. January 23rd, 1884.[169] — R. H. KILLICK

☛ CASE #154: On October the 9th, 1874, at two or three minutes to 5 in the morning, I woke with the strange feeling that my cousin was dead and that he was in the room. I then saw a vision of him; it was quite momentary.

The boy died at that time, calling for me, and saying that he must see me. I knew that my cousin would not recover from the illness he was suffering from, but his death was not expected so soon.[170] — MISS THERESA THORNYCROFT

☛ CASE #155: Some years since my brother paid a visit, one Saturday evening, to a family residing in one of the London suburbs. He was on the point of returning to town, when the lady of the house (who had been unusually vivacious during the evening) suddenly broke a blood-vessel in her head. A rupture had taken place once before in the same part, so a fatal termination was momentarily expected.

This impression was shared by my brother; but he does not seem to have felt it acutely until the following Sunday evening, when, under the gentle stimulus of an apparently tedious discourse, his thoughts reverted, for a short time, to the lady. Conversation, and a short walk with a friend, however, directed his attention elsewhere; but after reading at his lodgings and partaking of a meal, he was attacked, precisely at 10 o'clock, by an extreme feeling of uneasiness. Again he thought of the sick lady, and discussed the subject of her illness with a younger brother, his anxiety now increasing.

He retired to rest at 11 o'clock, and had scarcely laid down, when, being still wide awake, he thought he saw the lady in bed, with her servants and two men by her side. One of the men said: "She is dead"; but the other, whom he took for a physician, gave her some medicine. Hereupon the lady struggled, the vision vanished, and my brother felt impressed with the notion that she was perfectly well again.

A letter of inquiry having been sent the following Monday to his friends, my brother was informed that, as the local doctor feared the worst, a City physician was telegraphed for at 11 p.m., and that until midnight, when recovery took place, hope had been resigned.

My brother had, therefore, been affected at first by only a simultaneous impulse; but he had anticipated the result of the crisis by three-quarters of an hour.[171] — DR. EDMUND J. MILLS

☛ CASE #156: About 1868, when at the Pen-y-graig Collieries, I had come from the works to my house, about dinner-time, 1 p.m., and having been up all night had got into bed, when, just as I was dropping off to sleep, and still between sleeping and waking, I saw the roof of the stall belonging to a man named William Thomas moving, and the timbers which supported it bending and breaking.

I got up at once and ran off to the colliery, just in time to meet William Thomas coming out of the works, the roof of his stall having fallen in, just as I had seen it. My vision must have taken place at the very moment of the accident.[172] — MR. ROWLAND ROWLANDS

☛ CASE #157: At a period during the formation of the Thames Tunnel, the date of which I cannot recall without reference to the daily papers, my brother, Cyrus Read Edmonds, was head-master of the Leicestershire Proprietary Grammar School, at Leicester, and lived almost close to the school buildings.

On one occasion, when he was in bed, his wife was awoke (I think, at somewhere about 5 or 6 in the morning) by a loud exclamation of terror from my brother. She inquired the cause, and he in a state of horror, said that he had seen the Thames Tunnel break through. That the workmen rushed to the staircases or ladders, the means of exit, but one poor fellow (less active than the others, who escaped) was overtaken by the rush of water and perished.

My brother was in a state of tremor and distress, such as a humane man might be supposed to suffer as a witness of such a scene. He begged his wife not to sleep, but to converse until it should be time to rise. She urged that it was but a dream, and that the effect would pass off if he could get a little sleep. "A dream," he said, "it is no dream. I distinctly saw all that I have described."

My brother was a man of intensely sensitive temperament, with an unusual shrinking from witnessing pain, whether inflicted for good or evil results. He was a most accomplished scholar, a great wit, and the finest conversationalist it has ever been my lot to meet, and this statement is not a piece of brotherly partiality, but many well-known men would endorse the statement, and others would—but some are fallen asleep.

At the same time I never considered him a superstitious man, but he was a great thinker, and was not deterred from investigating subjects because they were unpopular.

On the day in the early morning of which this vision occurred, my brother and his wife were engaged to a dinner party at the house of a gentleman, whose name, I believe, was Whetstone. I was not acquainted with him myself. Before they left the drawing-room for the dining-room, his host said to my brother, "Have you heard the sad news from London?" He said, "No, what is it?" He replied, "The Thames Tunnel has broken in. All the people in the works escaped, except, one poor fellow who was overwhelmed."

My brother thought that his wife might have told their host, and that they would rally him out of his depression. But on looking at her the look of astonishment quite precluded this notion. He asked his host if he were joking, at which he was much surprised, and asked how a joke could possibly be elicited from such an occurrence.

My brother then said, "I saw it happen, just as you have related it, so my wife will assure you, and I am yet suffering from the exhaustion and depression produced." He then told the company what I have related above. I heard the whole relation both from him and his wife, and many of our friends were acquainted with the history.

My brother has been dead some years, and his wife also some years later. I don't know that I can get any further confirmation in the case. My brother's eldest daughter and her husband are living in Norfolk, but I doubt if they could add anything of importance to the above relation. Certainly, if it were a dream, it must be considered a most remarkable one. I attempt no sort of solution of the occurrence, but submit the bare facts for your consideration.[173]

— J. AUGUSTUS EDMONDS

☛ CASE #158: About two years ago an elderly woman in this parish, named Elizabeth Cubitt, was drawing near her end with faculties and memory impaired by along illness, one feature of which was the nervous ailment called St. Vitus' dance. A grandson, aged 18, was at sea in a fishing boat.

One morning she declared that she knew he was drowned for she had seen him in the water, and she strongly persisted in the statement.

About three days afterwards the lad came home and related in explanation of the wet clothes he brought back how, in a storm, he had been washed overboard by a wave and washed back by the next wave into the boat. The date of the event coincided with that of the grandmother's dream or vision.[174] — HENRY W. HARDEN

☛ CASE #159: Dr. Notter (a friend of Dr. Perty's) describes a clairvoyant cousin of his as one of the most sober-minded, prosaic, thoroughly unimaginative men he knew, for which reason he did not care to say much about his clairvoyant experiences.

When in 1869 his eldest son was accompanying the expedition in Mexico as army surgeon, the father was, on one occasion in the forenoon, suddenly overcome with an irresistible inclination to sleep. He was a man extremely exact in his work, was never accustomed to sleep in the forenoon, and was then engaged on official accounts.

During this sleep, which, according to the testimony of attendants who were present, could not have lasted more than a minute and a-half, the father saw the son, pale, and leaning against the side of a narrow pass; his horse, which was a grey one, was close by, and also several military officers. He was greatly terrified at what he had seen, but in order not to alarm his family, said nothing to anyone, but satisfied himself with noting the day and hour.

After three or four weeks a letter came from the son in which he described how at that very time he had been thrown from his horse, and as he was again attempting to mount he received a kick which broke one of the bones in his foot. The pain had made him almost faint away, so that he was obliged to lean against the side of the roadway, but he soon recovered from the accident without any permanent ill effects. A later letter confirmed all particulars and mentioned that the doctor was actually riding a grey horse. 1877.[175] — PROF. DR. MAXIMILIAN PERTY

☛ CASE #160: Some time ago my brother joined the Loch Rannoch, and sailed from the tail of the bank for Melbourne. A few weeks after he left, my mother saw him clairvoyantly, or in a vision, swimming, astern of the ship and apparently naked. To increase her anxiety it looked as if the ship was leaving him. She saw him exerting every nerve to make up on her; at length he was successful and got safely on board.

On the ship's arrival in Melbourne, it so happened that my brother and I met in Melbourne on this occasion, and I remember he mentioned this incident at the time, and neither of us then knew that mother knew anything about it. My brother wrote home as usual, but did not in his letter mention about being overboard on the passage out. Mother did not, however, forget about it; for, on his return, she told him what she had seen (in vision) and asked him if anything of that nature had happened to him going out.

"Yes, mother," he said, one good day, when the ship was in the tropics, I went overboard to bathe. While swimming near the ship, a breeze of wind sprang up, and I dropped astern; for some minutes I felt very anxious. However, I at last succeeded in getting upon the ship; got on board," and he added, "I don't think I will ever do the same thing again." January 8th, 1883.[176] — J. COWIE

☛ CASE #161: Dr. Arndt, an eminent German physician, relates that, being one day seated near the bed of one of his somnambulists, on a sudden she became agitated, uttered sighs, as if tormented by some vision, exclaimed, "O heavens, my father! he is dying!" A few moments afterwards she awoke, seemed quite cheerful, and recollected nothing of the anxiety she had so recently manifested.

She again relapsed twice into the same state of magnetic sleep, and each time she was tormented by the same vision. Being asked what had happened to her father, she answered, "He is bathed in blood; he is dying." Soon afterwards she awoke, became composed, and the scene finished.

Some weeks afterwards, Dr. Arndt found this lady pensive and sorrowful. She had just received from her father, who was at a distance of some hundred miles, an account of a serious accident which had befallen him. In ascending the stair of his cellar, the door had fallen upon his breast considerable hemorrhage ensued, and the physician despaired of his life. Dr. Arndt, who had marked the precise time of the preceding scene of the somnambulism of this lady, found that it was exactly on the day and at the hour when the accident happened to her father. "This," observes the doctor, "could not have been the mere effect of chance; and assuredly, there was no conceit nor deceit on the part of the observer."[177] — DR. COLQUHOUN

☛ CASE #162: Two years ago I awoke, one night, with a curious sensation of being in a sick room, and of the presence of people who were anxiously watching by the bedside of some person, who was dangerously ill. It was not till some time after that we heard that one of my sisters, then living in Florida, had been very ill of a fever, and was at the time of the incident in a most critical state.

[Before this] I have never had any other experience of an

impression of sickness or death. The impression of sickness was not the continuation of a dream and hardly a distinct waking impression. I woke from a heavy sleep with a great sense of oppression, which gradually seemed to assume a distinct impression. It lasted about half an hour, that is, the actual impression, but I had a great feeling of uneasiness for several days. I have never had any hallucinations or dreams of death.[178] — MAGGIE E. PRITCHARD

☛ CASE #163: My uncle, the late A____ S____ Esq., of Thornbury, near Bristol, was living at his villa in that little town in the year 1842, and on the evening of a certain day in November had retired to bed in his usual health, at his customary hour. Contrary to his habit, however, he could not sleep, but lay awake counting the hours until three o'clock in the morning, when suddenly he found himself in a country whose features were quite strange to him. He became aware that he was in the Neilgherrie hill country of India, where his brother S____ was on invalid furlough. It appeared to him that he remained three months there with S____, that he attended him during his illness, and that finally S____ died, when the vision faded, and he found himself again in his bed. He was now satisfied that this vision had revealed a certainty to him, turned round and fell asleep, and in the morning he told my aunt all about it.

He has mentioned this matter to me several times, and always expressed his belief that he was broad awake while he saw the vision, which he thought must have passed with the rapidity of "thought," and was quite sure it was no dream.

In the next spring my uncle and aunt were at Cheltenham, whither they had gone for the benefit of Mrs. S____'s health; in due course my uncle received from his brother's agents at Madras a letter containing information of S____'s death at such and such a place in the Neilgherrie Hills, at the precise day and hour that my uncle saw the vision in his bed at Thornbury.

"It was no news to me," said my uncle to me when telling me of the circumstance; "I knew poor S____ was gone several months before."[179] — A. S.

☛ CASE #164: I had known Mr. H____ as a medical man, under whose treatment I had been for some years, and at whose hands I had experienced great kindness. He had ceased to attend me for considerably more than a year at the time of his death. I was aware that he had given up practice, but beyond that I knew nothing of his proceedings, or of the state of his health. At the time I last saw him, he appeared particularly well, and even made some remark himself as to the amount of vigour and work left in him.

On Thursday, the 16th day of December, 1875, I had been for some little time on a visit at my brother-in-law's and sister's house near London. I was in good health, but from the morning and throughout the day I felt unaccountably depressed and out of spirits, which I attributed to the gloominess of the weather. A short time after lunch, about two o'clock, I thought I would go up to the nursery to amuse myself with the children and try to recover my spirits. The attempt failed, and I returned to the dining-room where I sat by myself, my sister being engaged elsewhere.

The thought of Mr.____ came into my mind, and suddenly, with my eyes open, as I believe, for I was not feeling sleepy, I seemed to be in a room in which a man was lying dead in a small bed. I recognised the face at once as that of Mr.____ and felt, no doubt, that he was dead and not asleep only. The room appeared to be bare and without carpet or furniture. I cannot say how long the appearance lasted. I did not mention the appearance to my sister or brother-in-law at the time.

I tried to argue with myself that there could be nothing in what I had seen, chiefly on the ground that from what I knew of Mr.____'s circumstances, it was most improbable that, if dead, he would be in a room in so bare and unfurnished a state.

Two days afterwards, on December 18th, I left my sister's house for home. About a week after my arrival, another of my sisters read out of the daily papers the announcement of Mr.____'s death, which had taken place abroad, and on December 16th, the day on which I had seen the appearance. I have since been informed that Mr.____ had died in a small village hospital in a warm foreign climate, having been suddenly attacked with illness whilst on his travels.[180] — NAME WITHHELD BY THE S.P.R.

☞ CASE #165: Mary Campbell, a woman of acknowledged probity and candour, relates that when she was a young girl, living in her father's house upon the island of Scalpa, there was a notable old seer, one Evander Mac Mhaoldonich, a domestic in the family, who by the second sight, foretold several events which punctually came to pass; and in particular, that Kenneth Campbell, her brother, being on a jaunt in the Lewes, and as he was returning home, accompanied by his servant whom he had sent upon an errand to a village at some distance, as the said Kenneth was solitarily on his way, he found himself seized with a faintishness, which so gained upon him that he was obliged to crawl on all fours, through mires and puddles, to a desolate cottage, where he remained that night, and after a sound sleep, recovered of his ailment.

The old seer that night seemed frettish, and being asked the reason of his being so much out of humour, told that the said Kenneth Campbell was not at his ease, and that he observed him, by the second sight, in a very different condition, his clothes being fuddled, and all bespattered with filth and mud; which, upon his return to the family next day, he himself declared to have been literally true, according to the above prediction.[181] — DONALD MACLEOD

☛ CASE #166: The following experience took place nearly 25 years ago, but there is no doubt of its correctness in every detail.

I became acquainted with a young lady in London, who, I may say without vanity, fell violently in love with me. There was a strange fascination about her which attracted me to her, but although very young, I was far from reciprocating her affection. By degrees I discovered that she had the power of influencing me when I was away from her, making me seem to realise her presence about me when I knew that she was some distance away; and then that she was able, when I saw her, to tell me where I had been and what I had been doing at certain times. At first I thought that this was merely the result of accident—that some one had seen me and reported to her—until one day she told me that at a certain hour of the day I had been in a drawing-room, which she described, when I knew there had been no chance of collusion, and that no one could have told her of my visit to the house.

She then told me that when she began intently to fix her mind on me, she seemed to be able to see me and all my surroundings. At first she fancied it was only imagination, until she saw by my manner that what she described had really taken place.

I had several opportunities afterwards of testing this power, and found she was correct in every instance. I need scarcely say that when I had satisfied myself of this I kept out of the way of such a dangerous acquaintance.

We did not meet for about 10 years, and had drifted so widely apart as to lose sight of each other.

One day I was walking with my wife on the West Cliff at Ramsgate, when a strange feeling of oppression came over me, and I was compelled to sit down. A few minutes afterwards my old acquaintance stood before me, introducing me to her husband and asking to be introduced to my wife. We met several times while they stayed at Ramsgate, and I learned that she had been married for some years, and had several children; but I have seen nothing of them since, and have no wish, even if I had the opportunity, of renewing the acquaintance. No reference whatever was made to the past, and I did not learn whether she had still the strange power she formerly possessed.[182] — CLERGYMAN, YORKSHIRE, NAME WITHHELD

☛ CASE #167: —In reply to your note, the occurrence [of automatic writing by Mr. Nelson, which is narrated below] was related to me by Mr. Nelson himself, since dead. He told me, as nearly as I can remember, in the year 1868, but the event itself must have taken place four or five years before.

At the time he told me he was frequently in the habit of thus writing under some external influences, some of which he describes as agreeable and others very much the reverse. He showed me a book in which these writings were made, and I was much surprised at the singular differences in the apparently various handwritings. I also remember his saying that he could recognise the identity of some of these influences.

I never had any reason to do otherwise than believe what he said, particularly as he was always very reticent on the subject, which he said concerned nobody but himself.

I should note that the handwriting in this [Mr. Nelson's] book was as varied as possible—sometimes in a light, delicate, pointed hand, and at other times big, black, blurred, and heavy. He said that at times he became conscious of the presence of this external influence, which he could never get rid of without providing writing materials.

On one occasion this feeling seized him in the train when travelling from Raneegunge to Calcutta, and he tore a leaf out of a book and laid it on the seat of the carriage, his hand grasping a pencil resting upon it. Ordinarily, to write under such conditions would be impossible in a train rushing along; the motion would effectually prevent it. Nevertheless, a long communication was made purporting to be from his daughter, who was at school in England.

It contained a simple account of her illness and death, described the circumstances under which it occurred, and the persons who were present, adding that she wished to say good-bye to her father before leaving. This threw Mr. N. into a state of great excitement, for he did not even know of his daughter's illness.

He went home and said he was very uneasy about Bessie in England. Finally, he gave this note to his married daughter, Mrs. R., to keep till they could hear by the ordinary post.

The child had in reality died that very day, and under the very circumstances thus mysteriously communicated to Mr. N. I have subsequently received some corroborative evidence regarding this young lady's death from an entire stranger to the family. March 24th, 1884.[183] — SAMUEL JENNINGS

☛ CASE #168: You have probably received many reports of what may be called, "*apparitions in transitu.*" The following was told to me by three maiden ladies, my aunts, women of unimpeachable veracity, who were all present at the time.

Their uncle, a clergyman in London, had been obliged to give up his profession through failing health, and to return to his native town, Newcastle-under-Lyme. He was engaged to a cousin, who was herself very delicate, and when he was on his death-bed he expressed a strong desire to see the lady to whom he was attached.

On receiving the message (there were no railways or telegrams in those days) she instantly started from home, but was taken ill on the way. Meanwhile the dying man and his three nurses were anxiously expecting her arrival.

Suddenly he half-rose in bed, and exclaimed: "She is dead—at the Hop-pole, in Worcester." These were his last words.

The next post informed his friends that it was even so!

I believe the event occurred in 1783, when he was in his 37th year. This gentleman and his three nurses all bore the name of yours faithfully. Villa Carli, San Remo, Italy, February, 1885.[184] — REV. G. L. FENTON

☛ CASE #169: [On January 2nd, 1867, a young boy, Davie Adams, fell through some ice and drowned while attempting to ice skate on a frozen lake in Cayuga County, NY.] There is an incident connected with this terrible calamity which is as mysterious as it is touching.

A little cousin of Davie, residing in Cayuga County, aged 4 years, and who was tenderly attached to him, on Wednesday last, at about 4 o'clock, was playing with her doll, when she suddenly said, "Auntie, Davie is drowned." Astonished and terrified, as no allusion had been made to the little boy, the aunt inquired what she meant; and the same childish and simple answer was returned: "Auntie, Davie is drowned!"

At eight o'clock a telegram was received announcing the sad

event, and the ever singular words of little "Gussy" were remembered. We offer no explanation of this, but simply record the fact, leaving it for the revelations of the Great Day, when those separated ones shall be united, and all shall be told to solve the mystery and to acquaint us whether these little ones, in their guileless innocence, do indeed hear the whispering of the angels.[185] — FROM THE *PENN YANN EXPRESS*, JANUARY 9TH, 1867

☞ CASE #170: When your brother E. was at Winchester College (about 1856 or 1857) on going to bed one Saturday night, I could not sleep. When your mother came into the room, she found me restless and uneasy. I told her that a strong impression had seized me that something had happened to your brother.

The next day, your mother, on writing to E., asked me if I had any message for him, when I replied: "Tell him I particularly want to know if anything happened to him yesterday." Your mother laughed, and made the remark that I should be frightened if a letter in Dr. Moberly's handwriting reached us on Monday. I replied, "I should be afraid to open it."

On the Monday morning a letter did come from Dr. Moberly to tell me that E. had met with an accident, that one of his schoolfellows had thrown a piece of cheese at him which had struck one of his eyes; and that the medical man, Mr. Wickham, thought I had better come down immediately and take your brother to a London oculist.[186] — A CLERGYMAN WRITING TO HIS DAUGHTER [NAME WITHHELD BY THE SPR]

☞ CASE #171: On July 8, 1882, my wife went to London to have an operation (which we both believed to be a slight one) performed on her eyes by the late Mr. Critchett. The appointment was for 1:30, and, knowing from long previous experience the close sympathy of our minds, about that time I, at Brighton, got rather fidgety, and was much relieved—and perhaps a little surprised and disappointed—at not feeling any decided sensation which I could construe as sympathetic.

Taking it therefore for granted that all was well, I went out at 2:45 to conduct my concert at the Aquarium, expecting to find there a telegram, as had been arranged, to say that all was well. On my way I stopped, as usual, to compare my watch with the big clock outside Lawson's, the clockmaker's. At that instant I felt my eyes flooded with water, just as when a chill wind gives one a sudden cold in the eyes, though it was a hot, still summer's day. The affection was so unusual and startling that my attention could not but be strongly directed to it; yet, the time being then eleven minutes to three, I was sure it could have nothing to do with my wife's operation, and, as it continued for some little time, thought I must have taken cold. However, it passed off, and the concert immediately afterwards put it out of my mind.

At 4:00 I received a telegram from my wife: "All well over. A great success," and this quite took away all anxiety. But on going to town in the evening, I found her in a terrible state of nervous prostration; and it appeared that the operation, though marvellously successful, had been of a very severe character. Quite accidentally it came out that it was not till 2:30 that Mrs. Corder entered the operating-room, and that the operation commenced, after the due administration of an anesthetic, at about ten minutes to three, as near as we could calculate.[187] — MR. F. CORDER

☞ CASE #172: November 13th, 1851. Being exhausted in body and unhinged in mind by many nights' unremitting attendance on a relative who had been dangerously ill, my doctor insisted on my relinquishing my post to another and going elsewhere for change of scene and air. As my invalid was convalescent I went to Brighton to pass a few days with my father, who was then residing in the Old Steyne.

I arrived at his door on Tuesday, 11th, in the evening, and retired early to bed, sanguine that after so many sleepless vigils, I should enjoy a night of unbroken rest. I have always been blessed with a remarkable talent for sleep. I was therefore the more surprised on this occasion to find myself, within a couple of hours after I had retired, wide awake. I fancy this must have been about half-past 11, because half-an-hour after I heard the clock on the stairs strike 12.

I ought to mention that at night, in certain conditions of health, I have sometimes suffered from a morbid activity of memory utterly destructive of sleep or even tranquillity. At such times I have been governed by one prevailing idea, which I have been unable to shake off, or been haunted by snatches of old airs, or harassed by the reiteration of one text of Scripture, and one only. It was not long ago that after having drunk some very strong coffee, I lay awake for three hours repeating, in spite of myself, over and over again, the following words from St. Peter's First Epistle, "Whom having not seen, ye love; in Whom, though now ye see Him not, yet believing, ye rejoice with joy unspeakable and full of glory." By no exercise of ingenuity could I get rid of these words.

Well, it was under some such mental impression that, on

waking on Monday night last, I was possessed, as it were, by four mystic words, each of one syllable, conveying no more idea to my mind than if they were gibberish, and yet delivered with as much solemnity of tone, deliberation of manner, and pertinacity of sequence, as if they were meant to convey to me some momentous intimation. They were all the more exciting that they were unintelligible and apparently could not serve any ostensible purpose. They were accompanied by no vision. They were an audition and nothing more.

I could not exclude them by putting cotton wool in my ears, for they came from within and not from without. To try to supplant them by encouraging a fresh train of ideas was hopeless; my will and my reason were alike subservient to some irresistible occult force.

The words which beset me were "dowd," "swell," "pull," "court," and they were separated as I have written them into monosyllables, and were repeated with an incisive distinctness and monotonous precision which was quite maddening. I sat up in my bed and struck a light to make sure that I was awake, and not dreaming. All the while were reiterated, as if in a circle, the same wild words. "Dowd," "swell," "pull," "court." I lay down again and put out my candle: "dowd," "swell," "pull," "court." I turned on my left side, "dowd," "swell," "pull," "court." I turned on my right, "dowd," "swell," "pull," "court." I endeavoured as a means of dispersing these evil spirits—for they began to assume the importance of spirits in my heated brain—to count sheep over a stile, but still "dowd," "swell," "pull," "court," rang in my ears and reverberated through my mind.

I counted my respirations; I had recourse to every imaginable conceit by which to woo sleep. I tried to call to mind all the people I cared for, then all the people I disliked. I tried to conjure up the recollection of all the murders or sensational incidents I had ever read or heard of in the hope of diverting my thoughts—but in vain. I then began to analyse the meaning of the words themselves. "What," said I to myself, "can be the meaning of 'dowd'? Ah, I begin to discern the truth; I am trying to make sense out of nonsense. The painful scenes I have lately witnessed have upset the balance of my brain, and I am going mad."

 I had not pursued this melancholy train of reflections long, when I fell into a profound slumber, from which I was only aroused by my father's voice summoning me to breakfast. On his asking me how I had slept, I told him how curiously I had been disturbed in the night. My narrative inspired him with more of ridicule than of pity.

 About mid-day I paid a visit to the Misses Smith, daughters of the late Horace Smith. I found Frederick Robertson, then in the zenith of his well-deserved fame, sitting with them.

 After a while the conversation turned to Herr von Reichenbach's book, and his theory on the subject of Odic Force, and then to the philosophy of dreams. I repeated to them with avidity my nocturnal experience; but instead of its producing the effect I had expected on my auditors it only provoked an interchange of significant looks between them, which convinced me that, in Oriental phrase, I had been eating dirt.

 I soon rose and took my leave. Robertson . . . followed me, and when we reached the doorstep . . . perceiving that my vanity had been mortified, said, "My dear Young, I hope you will forgive me if I say that I never before heard you tell anything so pointless as what you have just repeated to the Miss Smiths and myself." "Ah," said I, "I perceived you thought so, but it does not alter my opinion. To me the whole thing is fraught with interest and mystery. I am sure that thereby hangs a tale indeed. I only wish I knew it."

 It was on Wednesday, the 12th, that these words passed between my friend, Frederick Robertson, and myself on Thursday, the 13th, I walked into Folthorp's Library to read the papers; and, as usual, ran my eye down the births, marriages, and deaths in the *Times*. As I came to the obituary the following notice caught my sight:—"On Tuesday night, November 11th, John E. Dowdswell, of Pull Court, Tewkesbury." So that probably, on the self-same night, at the very time when this gentleman's name and residence were so unaccountably and painfully present to my mind, he was actually dying.[188] — REV. JULIAN C. YOUNG

☛ CASE #173: On the morning of December 6th, 1879, I suddenly awoke, and sat up in the bed, as if startled. To my great surprise I found myself uttering the words, "Portland," "Portland."

The next day I read in the papers of the death of the Duke of Portland, which I believe took place about the time when I was involuntarily uttering his name.

I cannot account for this experience at all. No conversation respecting the Duke of Portland had taken place the evening previously; I did not know he was ill; never saw him in my life; had never been at any of his residences; and, in fact, neither knew nor cared anything about him. I was not dreaming just before I awoke, but believe I was sleeping, as is my wont, quite soundly.[189] — MR. GERVASE MARSON

☛ CASE #174: On the night of January 10, 1882, I was sleeping in one of the suburbs of Manchester in the house of a friend, into which house several rats had been driven by the excessive cold. I knew nothing about these rats, but during the night I was waked by feeling an unpleasantly cold something slithering down my right leg. I immediately struck a light and flung off the bed-clothes, and saw a rat run out of my bed under the fire-place. I told my friend the next morning, but he tried to persuade me I had been dreaming. However, a few days afterwards a rat was caught in my room.

On the morning of January 11, a [female] cousin of mine, who happened to be staying in my own home on the south coast, and to be occupying my room, came down to breakfast, and recounted a marvellous dream, in which a rat appeared to be eating off the extremities of my unfortunate self. My family laughed the matter off.

However, on the 13th, a letter was received from me giving an account of my unpleasant meeting with the rat and its subsequent capture. Then every one present remembered the dream my cousin had told certainly fifty-eight hours before, as having occurred on the night of January 10. My mother wrote me an account of the dream, ending up with the remark, "We always said _____ was a witch; she always knew about everything almost before it took place."[190] — MR. A. B. MCDOUGALL

☛ CASE #175: On September 9th, 1848, at the siege of Mooltan, Major-General R_____, C.B., then adjutant of his regiment, was most severely and dangerously wounded, and supposing himself dying, asked one of the officers with him to take the ring off his finger and send it to his wife, who, at the time, was fully 150 miles distant, at Ferozepore.

On the night of September 9th, 1848, I was lying on my bed, between sleeping and waking, when I distinctly saw my husband being carried off the field, seriously wounded, and heard his voice saying, "Take this ring off my finger, and send it to my wife." All the next day I could not get the sight or the voice out of my mind.

In due time I heard of General R_____ having been severely wounded in the assault on Mooltan. He survived, however, and is still living.

It was not for some time after the siege that I heard from Colonel L_____ the officer who helped to carry General R_____ off the field, that the request as to the ring was actually made to him, just as I had heard it at Ferozepore at that very time.[191] — M. A. R_____, WIFE OF GENERAL R_____.

☛ CASE #176: Dear Sir, The circumstance about which you inquire is as follows: I had left my house, ten miles from London, in the morning as usual, and in the course of the day was on my way to Victoria Street, Westminster, having reached Buckingham Palace, when in attempting to cross the road, recently made muddy and slippery by the water cart, I fell, and was nearly run over by a carriage coming in an opposite direction. The fall and the fright shook me considerably, but beyond that I was uninjured.

On reaching home I found my wife waiting anxiously, and this is what she related to me: She was occupied wiping a cup in the kitchen, which she suddenly dropped, exclaiming, "My God! he's hurt." Mrs. S., who was near her, heard the cry, and both agreed as to the details of time and so forth. I have often asked my wife why she cried out, but she is unable to explain the state of her feelings beyond saying, "I don't know why; I felt some great danger was near you."

These are simple facts, but other things more puzzling have happened in connection with the singular intuitions of my wife. Yours truly.[192] — T. W. SMITH

☛ CASE #177: Lady G. and her sister had been spending the evening with their mother, who was in her usual health and spirits when they left her. In the middle of the night the sister awoke in a fright, and said to her husband, "I must go to my mother at once; do order the carriage. I am sure she is taken ill." The husband, after trying in vain to convince his wife that it was only a fancy, ordered the carriage.

As she was approaching her mother's house, where two roads meet, she saw [her sister] Lady G.'s carriage. When they met, each asked the other why she was there. The same reply was made by both. "I could not sleep, feeling sure my mother was ill, and so I came to see." As they came in sight of the house, they saw their mother's confidential maid at the door, who told them when they arrived, that their mother had been taken suddenly ill, and was dying, and had expressed an earnest wish to see her daughters.[193]
— DR. CHARLES EDE

☛ CASE #178: There is a house about half-a-mile from my own, inhabited by some ladies, friends of our family. They have a large alarm bell outside their house. One night I awoke suddenly and said to my wife, "I am sure I hear Mrs. F.'s alarm bell ringing." After listening for sometime we heard nothing, and I went to sleep again.

The next day Mrs. F. called upon my wife, and said to her, "We were wishing for your husband last night, for we were alarmed by thieves. We were all up, and I was about to pull the alarm bell, hoping he would hear it, saying to my daughters, I am sure it will soon bring your husband, but we did not ring it." I asked what time it was; Mrs. F. said it was about half-past one, the time I awoke thinking I heard the bell.[194] — DR. CHARLES EDE

☛ CASE #179: I had one day been spending the morning in shopping, and returned by train just in time to sit down with my children to our early family dinner. My youngest child—a sensitive, quick-witted, little maiden of two years and six weeks old—was one of the circle.

Dinner had just commenced, when I suddenly recollected an incident in my morning's experience which I had intended to tell her, and I looked at the child with the full intention of saying, "Mother saw a big, black dog in a shop, with curly hair," catching her eyes in mine, as I paused an instant before speaking. Just then something called off my attention, and the sentence was not uttered.

What was my amazement, about two minutes afterwards, to hear my little lady announce, "Mother saw a big dog in a shop." I gasped. "Yes, I did!" I answered; "but how did you know?" "With funny hair?" she added, quite calmly, and ignoring my question. "What colour was it, Evelyn?" said one of her elder brothers; "was it black?" She said, "Yes."

Now, it was simply impossible that she could have received any hint of the incident verbally. I had had no friend with me when I had seen the dog. All the children had been at home, in our house in the country, four miles from the town; I had returned, as I said, just in time for the children's dinner, and I had not even remembered the circumstance until the moment when I fixed my eyes upon my little daughter's.

We have had in our family circle numerous examples of spiritual or mental insight or foresight; but this, I think, is decidedly the most remarkable that has ever come under my notice.[195] — CAROLINE BARBER

☛ CASE #180: A connection of mine was staying with a friend whose husband was engaged in making a line of railway in Spain. My friend was roused one night by her hostess, who was in a terrible fright, and said she was certain her husband was killed in a railway accident. She had been wakened with a start, and then had either seen the occurrence or been told in some way, but how, she could not remember.

My friend reminded her that the railway he was engaged on did not open till the next day, so that the accident was unlikely. It turned out, however, that her husband had been doubtful of the safety of one part of the line, and had insisted on running an engine over it in the night, to try it for the next day's opening, and he had been killed.[196] — MRS. G. BIDDER

☛ CASE #181: The following narrative was told to me by my aunt, Mrs. B.; the son to whom it relates is F. G. B., who fell at Inkerman on Sunday, November 5th, 1854. The narrative was told to me on Sunday afternoon, September 2nd, 1883, and written down at the time. She had told me substantially the same narrative many years before, though she did not like talking of it. My son, who was also present when the story was told, read over my account, and pronounced it correct. I do not believe that my aunt ever experienced any similar impression. I have known her intimately all my life, and stayed with her for months together, and never heard her mention anything of the kind. — E. E. G.

She had always prayed that she might know at the moment if he [her son F. G. B.] were killed or badly wounded. The 5th November was a Sunday; she was at R. Church, and early in the service (while kneeling in the Confession) she had a sudden sensation; she saw nothing, but felt sure something was by her, and that it was her son. Her husband asked her what was the matter, but she kept up, and did not leave the church. On returning home she said she was sure they would hear bad news. When the news did arrive, some days later, they found he was shot at the very hour when she felt his presence in R. Church.[197] — MR. S. B.

☛ CASE #182: A patient of mine, Mr. J. T_____, a solicitor, about sixty years of age, lived a short distance out of London, with his family, consisting of a wife and step-daughter, Miss W_____. One December he was asked to go to Edinburgh, to arbitrate in some matter of business. Accordingly he left London, expecting to be away nearly a week.

In the early morning of the third day after his departure, Mrs. T_____ awoke, and was surprised to find her husband, as she thought, standing by her bedside. She exclaimed, "How did you get in without my hearing you? Wait while I light the candle." She struck a match, and was very astonished at not seeing her husband in the room. While she was thinking over this singularly vivid delusion, her step-daughter, who occupied an adjoining room, knocked at the door, and on being admitted, said, "Oh! mother, I have had a horrible dream about father, and cannot sleep; I am afraid something has happened to him."

In the morning they both told their stories to their maid, and subsequently to a gentleman who called while they were at breakfast. In the course of the forenoon a telegram arrived from Mr. T_____ saying there had been an accident to the train in which he had been a passenger, that he was not hurt, and would be home in the course of the day.

It appears that he had arranged his business much quicker than he had expected, and was able to leave Edinburgh by the night train; a collision took place a few miles from London, owing to a thick fog, and about the time when the two ladies were disturbed by their dreams.

There was no doubt whatever of the truth of this strange coincidence, the ladies having told their dreams long before the arrival of the telegram. I attended the family many years, and although Mr. T_____ did not appear to have sustained injury at the time, he never recovered from the nervous shock.[198] — DR. WILTON

☛ CASE #183: My eldest brother went to New Zealand. One morning my sister Emily came down to breakfast, looking very white and queer, and directly she entered the room, said, "Ben has met with an accident." Disregarding our incredulous amusement, she declared she had seen him with his arm bandaged up, lying in a room where there were other beds.

We were longer than usual in hearing from my brother; he explained the delay, saying his arm had been broken, and that he had been for some time in the hospital. Comparing dates, we found he was injured the day my sister had her vision.[199] — ANTHONY ASHLEY.

☛ CASE #184: [During a gathering of myself and a group of friends, it] was proposed that we should attempt an experiment [on the subject of thought-reading]. Accordingly I was blindfolded and left the room. Whilst I was absent a reel of black cotton was secreted in a flower-pot near the window. On pressing the hand of the gentleman who had secreted it against my forehead, and requesting him to think of the object he had hidden, I saw plainly with my blindfolded eyes, as though in a dream, the figure of a reel of black cotton floating before me. I then told him to think of where he had hidden it, and I saw and led him to a bureau at the opposite end of the room to the window. This he said was wrong, but on inquiry I found that he had originally intended to have placed it there, but had altered his mind.

We then tried the question of localising a pain. Being blindfolded, and holding my friend's left hand against my forehead, I told him to imagine a pain. Almost immediately I felt a peculiar, indescribable sensation on the right side of my face, and told him that he was thinking of a pain there. He was, in fact, imagining a violent attack of neuralgia in the right upper jaw.

Other experiments were tried and have been tried since, some successful, some unsuccessful, but I have seen quite enough to convince me that there is truth in it. I don't pretend to offer a reason, but I would say to those who disbelieve it, "Try it for ourselves." All do not possess the power. I was the only one of a party of six or seven who was thus affected, but, doubtless, there are very many who could perform precisely the same experiments, and by continued inquiry it may be that the mystery will be solved.[200] — HENRY EDMONDS

☛ CASE #185: The way Mr. Smith conducts his experiment is this: He places himself *en rapport* with myself by taking my hands; and a strong concentration of will and mental vision on my part has enabled him to read my thoughts with an accuracy that approaches the miraculous. Not only can he, with slight hesitation, read numbers, words, and even whole sentences which I alone have seen, but the sympathy between us has been developed to such a degree that he rarely fails to experience the taste of any liquid or solid I choose to imagine. He has named, described, or discovered small articles he has never seen when they have been concealed by me in the most unusual places, and on two occasions he has successfully described portions of a scene which I either imagined or actually saw.[201] — DOUGLAS BLACKBURN

☛ CASE #186: One morning, not long ago, while engaged with some very easy work, I saw in my mind's eye a little wicker basket, containing five eggs, two very clean, of a more than usually elongated oval and of a yellowish hue, one very round, plain white, but smudged all over with dirt; the remaining two bore no peculiar marks. I asked myself what that insignificant but sudden image could mean. I never think of similar objects. But that basket remained fixed in my mind, and occupied it for some moments.

About two hours later I went into another room for lunch. I was at once struck with the remarkable similarity between the eggs standing in the egg-cups on the breakfast table and those two very long ones I had in my imagination previously seen. "Why do you keep looking at those eggs so carefully?" asked my wife; and it caused her great astonishment to learn from me how many eggs had been sent by her mother half an hour before. She then brought up the remaining three; there was the one with the dirt on it, and the basket, the same I had seen.

On further inquiry, I found that the eggs had been kept together by my mother-in-law, that she had placed them in the basket and thought of sending them to me; and, to use her own words, "I did of course think of you at that moment." She did this at ten in the morning, which (as I know from my regular habits) must have been just the time of my impression.[202] — MR. J. G. KEULEMANS

☛ CASE #187: One Sunday night last winter, at 1 A.M., I wished strongly to communicate the idea of my presence to two friends, who resided about three miles from the house where I was staying. When I next saw them, a few days afterwards, I expressly refrained from mentioning my experiment; but in the course of conversation, one of them said, "You would not believe what a strange night we spent last Sunday"; and then recounted that both the friends had believed themselves to see my figure standing in their room. The experience was vivid enough to wake them completely, and they both looked at their watches, and found it to be exactly one o'clock.[203] — NAMES WITHHELD BY THE SPR

☞ CASE #188: A mesmerist, well known to us, was requested by a lady to mesmerise her, in order to enable her to visit in spirit certain places of which he himself had no knowledge. He failed to produce this effect; but found that he could lead her to describe places unknown to her but familiar to him. Thus on one occasion he enabled her to describe a particular room which she had never entered, but which she described in perfect conformity with his recollection of it. It then occurred to him to imagine a large open umbrella as lying on a table in this room, whereupon the lady immediately exclaimed, "I see a large open umbrella on the table."[204] — NAMES WITHHELD BY THE SPR

☞ CASE #189: On June 10th, I had the following dream. Some one told me that [my friend] Miss E. [who was staying in the same house that night] was dead. I instantly, in my dream, rushed to her room, entered it, went to her bedside and pulled the clothes from off her face. She was quite cold; her eyes were wide open and staring at the ceiling. This so frightened me that I dropped at the foot of her bed, and knew no more until I was half out of bed in my own room and wide awake. The time was 5 o'clock a.m. Before leaving my room I told this dream to my sister, as it had been such an unpleasant one. February 18th, 1884. — C.S.B.

[In verifying the account above, the following account is from the woman thought to be "dead," named "Miss E."]

I awoke on the morning of June 10th, and was lying on my back with my eyes fixed on the ceiling, when I heard the door open and felt some one come in and bend over me, but not far enough to come between my eyes and the ceiling. Knowing it was only C., I did not move, but, instead of kissing me, she suddenly drew back and going towards the foot of the bed, crouched down there.

Thinking this very strange, I closed and opened my eyes several times, to convince myself that I was really awake, and then turned my head to see if she had left the door open, but found it still shut. Upon this a sort of horror came over me and I dared not look towards the figure which was crouching in the same position, gently moving the bedclothes from my feet.

I tried to call to the occupant of the next room, but my voice failed. At this moment she touched my bare foot, a cold chill ran all over me and I knew nothing more till I found myself out of bed looking for C., who must, I felt, be still in the room. I never doubted that she had really been there until I saw both doors fastened on the inside. On looking at my watch it was a few minutes past 5.

Although I am accustomed to have very vivid dreams, I have never had one of this kind before. When I found my friend was not in the room, and that the doors were securely fastened on the inside, I looked at my watch; [and as noted] it was a few minutes past 5.

I have never, I believe, walked in my sleep. There are two doors to my bedroom. One was locked on the inside; the handle was broken off the other on the outside. Thus it was impossible for anyone to open it except from the inside.[205] — K.E.

☛ CASE #190: About three months ago as I was sitting, quietly thinking, between 5 and 7 p.m., I experienced a very curious sensation. I can only describe it as like a cloud of calamity gradually wrapping me round. It was almost a physical feeling, so strong was it; and I seemed to be certain, in some inexplicable way, of disaster to some one of my relations or friends, though I could not in the least fix upon anybody in particular, and there was no one about whom I was anxious at the time. I do not remember ever experiencing such a thing before. I should say it lasted about half-an-hour.

This happened on a Saturday, and on Monday I got a letter from my sister, written on the Saturday evening to go by the post which leaves at 7 p.m., in which she told me she had received a telegram, an hour or so ago, informing her of the dangerous illness of her brother-in-law, at which she was greatly upset. This appeared to be a very probable explanation of my extraordinary presentiment, and I wrote and told her all about it at once.[206] — HON. MRS. A. C. POWYS

☛ CASE #191: In May, 1871, I was away from home for a change, leaving a sick sister behind, who had been ill for many months from mesenteric decline. I was to go to a ball at Willis' Rooms on May 11th, and left some friends in Kensington to stay with an old schoolfellow at Denmark Hill. I heard that my sister was worse, but concluded it was one of the usual spasmodic attacks of sickness that accompany the disease—how could I ever have been so blind!

It was a Thursday; my new dress had come, and dinner time came—a large family circle, and I the only stranger, as I had never stayed in the house before. I could hardly swallow my dinner, and felt a chillness all over me. When the time came to dress I went upstairs and slowly began. As I bent down to pick my dress up I stopped. I felt an unseen presence, and a terrible chillness, which, even as I write, returns only too vividly.

I rang the bell. When the servant came, I could only say faintly, "Ask Miss Emily to come to me." When my friend came, I could explain nothing; I merely said I could not go to the ball. I have often wondered how I looked at the time, for I know how I felt, even to my lips.

The next morning came the news that my sister had died on the previous morning, longing and calling for me to the last.[207] — MISS AGNES M.A.S.

☛ CASE #192: Sir A. B.'s father, in the year 1802, when returning from a tiger hunt in India, had a strong impression, or rather conviction, that his father (Sir A. B.'s grandfather), who was then in Ireland, was dead. He told one of the friends who accompanied him, of his impression.

The next mail from England brought the news of the death on the very day referred to. Sir A. B. had heard this story from his father's lips, and had also read it in his father's journal.

On the occasion of his father's and also of his sister's death, Sir A. B. himself was oppressed with a vague, but heavy sense of calamity, shortly before the receipt of the messenger, or telegram, which summoned him to the death-bed. So strong was his impression of calamity, that on the second occasion he even told his servant that he was sure some misfortune was about to happen to him.[208] — SIR A. B.

☛ CASE #193: It was in August, a few years ago—my husband was at the moors. I drove to a nursery garden to procure some flowers. I waited outside the gate under the shelter of some trees, sending the groom in for the flowers.

It was one of the hottest afternoons I ever experienced. My ponies, usually restive, stood perfectly still. Before I had waited there many minutes an unaccountable feeling took possession of me as though I foresaw and recognised the shadow of a coming sorrow. I immediately associated it with my husband—that some accident had befallen him. With this miserable apprehension upon me I got through the rest of the day and evening as best I could, but weighed down by the shadow, though I spoke of it that night to no one.

Nothing had happened to my husband. But a little child—a relation, who had lived with us and been almost as our own—had died that day rather suddenly in Kent, where she was then visiting her parents. I had thought a good deal of little Ada as I sat waiting in the phaeton that summer afternoon—had pictured her reaching out her hands to me—but the great apprehension I felt was for my husband—not for the child.[209] — MRS. HERBERT DAVY

☛ CASE #194: A very old gentleman, living at Hurworth, a friend of my husband's and with whom I was but slightly acquainted, had been ill many months. My sister-in-law, who resides also at H., often mentioned him in her letters, saying he was better or worse as the case might be.

Late last autumn my husband and I were staying at the Tynedale Hydropathic Establishment. One evening I suddenly laid down the book I was reading, with this thought so strong upon me I could scarcely refrain from putting it into words: "I believe that Mr. C. is at this moment dying." So strangely was I imbued with this belief—there had been nothing whatever said to lead to it—that I asked my husband to note the time particularly, and to remember it for a reason I would rather not state just then. "It is exactly 7 o'clock," he said, and that being our dinner hour, we went downstairs to dine.

The entire evening, however, I was haunted by the same strange feeling, and looked for a letter from my sister-in-law next morning. None came. But the following day there was one for her brother. In it she said: "Poor old Mr. C. died last night at 7 o'clock. It was past post-time, so I could not let you know before."[210] — MRS. HERBERT DAVY

☛ CASE #195: My dear Augusta,—I have had three different intimations of death—on Uncle William's death, on Henry H.'s death, and on Baker's [a beloved family servant]. The first two first were more sensations than anything else. It is a thing hardly to be described. It is like nothing else. Not alarming; rather like one's idea of the severance of nerves; of something cut off, that is, and lost to yourself, of a want, a something gone from you.

On the occasion of Henry' death, I did not know who was gone. I was away in Germany; but I awoke with the sensation, and I told my children, "I have had that feeling that I have had before on the loss of a relation. I do not know who is gone; but someone seems gone; perhaps it is Aunt Edward." Then in a day or so came the news of Henry's death.

The last occasion (i.e., of Baker's death) it was the most distinct of all. It was in 1880, in the autumn. I was in Germany. I had gone to lie down after the early dinner on Sunday, to rest before the long walk to church; and I fell asleep. I had the most calm and delightful awaking—no actual words, but a happy feeling that Baker was passing away to Heaven peacefully, and that I was intended to know it. If I put into words what my impression was, it was this—"As if some spirit had gently touched me and said, 'Baker is passing away, rise up and pray.'"

I at once rose up and went into the next room, and told my boys "I have had an intimation that Baker is dying, remember it. I shall hear."

I then went back to my bedside to kneel in prayer. The happiness and peace of the few minutes was intense. I had longed to see him once again before he died, and had feared I should not be in England in time, though I was going in a few days, as I knew his end was near: but being led to know the day and hour was to me like a leave-taking and a good-bye from himself, and I felt it was permitted to assure and comfort me.

Two or three days later I heard it was that very day he died; and when I got to England and saw his wife, Cath, I found it was the same time, allowing for my being nearly 40 minutes to the eastward on the globe.

The two first intimations, though not alarming, were not of the comforting, reassuring and happy feeling of the last. My boys were much impressed at the time, at the idea of the spiritual world being so near.[211] — MRS. POCHIN

☛ CASE #196: Mr. James Elliot (for many years Professor of Science at the Institute, at Liverpool) told me that when he was living in London (I forget the year), employed on some electrical experiments, he one day felt drawn to go and see the lady he was engaged to, then living at Dunkeld. The Professor was a cool-headed Scotchman, and, as he said, he at first put the thing aside altogether, for it was a time when he could only leave his work at a great sacrifice, and a coach journey was very fatiguing, and very exhausting to a slender purse.

However, when a second day he was possessed with the feeling that some misfortune was happening to the lady, and she urgently required his presence, he did yield to his feelings, and started for a journey to Dunkeld on the outside of the night coach. He had not heard that anything was wrong, but when he reached her home he found that a cold had the day before turned to serious illness, and she died very soon after his arrival.

He told me this story *apropos* of a small silver clasped Bible he always used, which she had then given him, and when, two years ago, he died, very suddenly, it was found he had left this Bible to me. I fear I can give you no further witnesses to this. The sister in whose hands he left the Bible for me died this year; but that *he* believed he was called, as I state, I can most confidently affirm.[212] — MRS. BIDDER

☛ CASE #197: On the evening of January 28th, 1863, I had met several old friends at dinner at a friend's house near Manchester, in which neighbourhood I had been paying visits. My return home to my father's house was fixed for the next afternoon. I ought to say that between that father and me, his first-born child, a more than common bond of affection and sympathy existed, arising from circumstances I need not mention, and I was looking forward to my return with earnest longing.

The evening had been bright and happy, surrounded by friends I valued. When I was about to leave, my hostess pressed me to play for her a very favourite old march. I declined, on account of the lateness of the hour, and keeping horses standing. She said, "It is not yet 12, and I have sent the carriage away for a quarter of an hour."

I sat down laughing, and before I played many bars, such an indescribable feeling came over me, intense sadness heralded a complete break down, and I was led away from the piano in hysterics.

By 10 o'clock the next morning I got a telegram, to say my father had gone to bed in his usual health, and at a quarter to 12 the night before had passed away in an epileptic fit, having previously said to my sister how glad he was to think of seeing me so soon, and when she bid him good night, praying God to give them both a quiet night and sleep.

. . . I never experienced a similar feeling. I am not at all naturally inclined to depression, and am perfectly free from what is commonly understood by superstition.[213] — MRS. A. M. BULL

☛ CASE #198: On March 16th, 1884, I was sitting alone in the drawing-room, reading an interesting book, and feeling perfectly well, when suddenly I experienced an undefined feeling of dread and horror; I looked at the clock and saw it was just 7 p.m. I was utterly unable to read so I got up, and walked about the room trying to throw off the feeling, but I could not; I became quite cold, and had a firm presentiment that I was dying.

This feeling lasted about half-an-hour, and then passed off, leaving me a good deal shaken all the evening; I went to bed feeling very weak, as if I had been seriously ill.

The next morning I received a telegram telling me of the death of a near and very dear cousin, Mrs. K., in Shropshire, with whom I had been most intimately associated all my life, but for the last two years had seen very little of her.

I did not associate this feeling of death with her or with any one else, but I had a most distinct impression that something terrible was happening. This feeling came over me, I afterwards found, just at the time when my cousin died (7 p.m.). The connection with her death may have been simply an accident. I have never experienced anything of the sort before. I was not aware that Mrs. K. was ill, and her death was peculiarly sad and sudden. September 4th, 1884.[214] — MISS K. MARTIN

☛ CASE #199: To the Editor of the *Journal of the Society for Psychical Research*. Sir—In an article in Part VII of the Proceedings of the Society for Psychical Research (p. 219) reference is made to an observation of M. Tagueton a patient under his care in the *Asile des Aliénées*, in Bordeaux, by name Noélie X., which is recorded in the *Annales Médico-psychologiques*, 1884, p. 325.

She is about 24 years of age, and has been treated as insane for some time, but her symptoms are variable, and every now and then in an *accès* she has shown some remarkable capacities, and among them what is termed by M. Taguet a "hyperæsthesia of sight." She will sit at such times facing a dull, blank wall with her eyes shut and her eyeballs apparently upturned in the fashion that often obtains in hysterical, mesmeric and other neurotic states; and in this condition, according to M. Taguet's description, can read apparently on the blank wall or on a sheet of blank cardboard held in front of her face the print, both small and large, of a newspaper held up behind the back of her head, which one could only expect her to see if the blank wall or cardboard were a mirror, or if her eyes were in the back of her head.

"Now, Dr. Taguet," says Mr. Frederic William Henry Myers, in the above-mentioned article, "does not attempt to explain this, further than by calling it hyperæsthesia of vision. But he can hardly mean that she really saw the words reflected in the cardboard. Perhaps the only other solution which suggested itself to him was that she saw the words clairvoyantly, and this solution he did not like to adopt. And there is, in fact, no reason, as the facts are reported, for assuming clairvoyance. Thought-transference would amply suffice to explain the phenomena."

Of course, to render an explanation by thought-transference possible, it must first be ascertained that the words read by Noélie

were previously known to some one present. Whether this was so or not is not mentioned in M. Taguet's article.

I wrote to him, and he very kindly sent me a reprint of his article, but I could learn nothing further on this particular point. I ventured to propose a visit, but unfortunately when I reached the *Asile des Aliénées* I found he was not in Bordeaux for that day. His assistant most courteously introduced me to the patient, Noélie X., with whom I talked a little. She was in fairly good health and good spirits, and her symptoms of mental derangement quite in abeyance. There was no sign of the abnormal capacities peculiar to the *accès*, and no attempt at an experiment was therefore made. M. Taguet's assistant had been present on some previous occasions when the "hyperæsthesia of sight" had been noticed, and did not seem confident of any explanation.

I believe I may say that I made the thought-reading hypothesis intelligible to him, but he was able at once to assure me that no one in the room could have been aware what were the words in the newspaper that was presented to the back of Noélie's head until they were looked at to confirm Noélie's reading; so that, in fact, he negatived the necessary foundation for a theory of thought-transference.

I do not think such a theory had occurred to the experimenters, and I am not sure that their attention had been closely given to the point in question. I wrote again later to M. Taguet, asking him to remark it in any future experiments. I am, yours faithfully."[215] — A. T. MYERS, M.D.

☛ CASE #200: In the year 1849 I was staying in Edinburgh. One Sunday as I was dressing my second boy (aged five years) for church at about 10:30 a.m., he looked up at me and said, "Mother, Cousin Janie is dead." I asked him which Cousin Janie he meant, and he answered, "Cousin Janie at the Cape, she's dead." I then tried to make him explain why he thought so, but he only kept repeating the statement.

This "Cousin Janie" was a girl of about 16 who had been staying in Edinburgh, and had gone out to the Cape with her parents some months before. She had been very fond of my boys and had often played with them. I was rather struck by the way the child kept repeating what he had said, and wrote down the day and the hour, and told my mother and sisters.

Some time afterwards the Cape mail brought the news that the girl had died on that very Sunday. She had been badly burnt the night before, and had lingered on till a little after mid day. April 7th, 1885.[216] — ALICE MUIR

☛ CASE #201: The gentleman [J. J. Hoare] who teaches music in my house tells me that if anything sad or terrible happens to any one he loves, he always has an intimation of it. He does not know what it is, but he says that he writes off to his own or his sisters' homes: "What is the matter? there is something wrong,"—and the return post brings him the history of either dangerous illness or accident.

He is a young man of a very highly strung organisation. Possibly, his education in music, for which he has a passion, put him out of ordinary spheres. He reads books on art, music, drawing, poetry, and he is deeply interested in all religious studies. About young men's pursuits, games, athletic sports, and his own affairs, money matters, etc., he seems indifferent. So much for the medium. Now for my story, peculiar, because though a fact, I see no good in it.

I am very fond of Mr. Hoare and I know he looks on me as a very true old friend, and one of my sons, now in India, is the dearest friend he has.

I went out one morning about 9 o'clock, carrying books for the library, and being very busy, took the short way to town. On some flags [stepping stones] in a very steep part of the road, some boys had made a slide. Both my feet flew away at the same moment that the back of my head resounded on the flags. A policeman picked me up, saw I was hurt, and rang at the Nurses' Home close by, to get me looked to. My head was cut, and while they were washing the blood away, I was worrying myself that I should be ill, and how should I manage my school till the end of the term.

I told no one in my house but my daughter, and no one but the policeman had seen me fall. I asked my daughter to tell no one. I had a miserably nervous feeling, but I pretended to her it was nothing.

The next morning, after a sleepless night, I could not get up. It was my habit to sit in the drawing-room while the music lessons were given, so my daughter went in to tell Mr. Hoare that I had had a bad night, and was not yet up.

He said, "I had a wretched night, too, and all through a most vivid dream."

"What was it?" she asked.

"I dreamed I was walking by the Nurses' Home, and I came on a slide, both my feet slipped, and I fell on the back of my head. I was helped to the Home, and while my head was being bathed I was worrying myself how I should manage my lessons till the end of the term, and the worrying feeling would not go. February 1884.[217] — MRS. WALSH

☛ CASE #202: The following account of a séance with [automatic-writer] Mr. Eglinton is sent by a gentleman whom we have reason to regard as an acute and careful observer:

I bought a three-leaf book slate on the way, one that had three loops and could be fastened with a stick of pencil, as small pocket-books are often made. The first trials Mr. Eglinton made were with his own slate, which I had previously cleaned, and marked with my name to avoid changing. With this nothing occurred.

He then took my slate, I having inserted a crumb of pencil and seen that it was all secure. It was then placed on the corner of the table, and we both rested our hands upon it. Shortly, in answer to my question, "Are the conditions favourable?" the pencil could distinctly be heard writing inside the slate, and when the three taps indicated that the message was finished, I unfastened the slate, and on one of the leaves found, "Yes, the conditions are very good."

Then followed a few trials, for which Mr. Eglinton held a slate under the table, with one hand, and writing was thus obtained, in answer to casual inquiries. The slate was always cleaned by me; it had my name on it; the writing was always on the surface next [to] the table; it was always found on the extreme edge of the slate farthest from the medium; always upside down with regard to him; and the pencil could always be heard writing. Moreover, a great part of his hand, and all his wrist was in view, and the slightest attempt at movement could not, I believe, have passed undetected.

However, the most satisfactory experiments were these. Mr. Eglinton has a strong mahogany book slate with a Brahma lock. On this I was requested to write the name of a deceased relation, mentioning the relationship, and asking a question. To make the thing as conclusive as possible I took the slate into the adjoining room, stood away from all mirrors, windows, etc., and wrote, "Mrs. D____, grandmother, are you present, and able to communicate?" I then quickly locked the slate, put the key into my pocket, and went back to Mr. Eglinton, never once letting the slate leave my hand. He then placed another slate half under the table, closely pressed against the under-surface; in a few seconds writing commenced, and the following was found: "Your grandmother, Mrs. D____, is not able to write, but she sends her love." I then, for the first time, unlocked the slate, and showed him what I had written.

At this point Mr. Eglinton was called away to two ladies, and I seized the opportunity to write on the Brahma slate: "Frank G____, cousin, are you present, and able to write to me?" Then I locked it, and waited for Mr. Eglinton to return. Upon hearing what I had done, he took a slate—the one marked with my name—thoroughly cleaned it, with my help, threw a crumb of pencil upon it, covered it with another clean one, and gave me the two to hold with him.

We were then sitting opposite to each other, each holding the two slates, and right away from the table. In a second or two I could not only hear the pencil, but could feel it writing, and could localise the sound and vibration as undoubtedly issuing from between the two slates. In one minute at the most, the signal of completion was given, and the underneath slate was found filled with writing, in three directions, and signed "Frank." I have the slate now, with the writing on it.

I forgot to mention that I always made a point of engaging Mr. Eglinton in conversation during the time the writing was taking place. I may also add that the communication purporting to come from "Frank" does not strike me at all as being the sort of thing he would write.[218] — FROM THE *JOURNAL* OF THE S.P.R.

☛ CASE #203: In March, 1861, I was living at Houghton, Hants. My wife was at the time confined to the house, by delicacy of the lungs. One day, walking through a lane, I found the first wild violets of the spring, and took them home to her.

Early in April I was attacked with a dangerous illness; and in June left the place. I never told my wife exactly where I found the violets, nor, for the reasons explained, did I ever walk with her past the place where they grew, for many years.

In November, 1873, we were staying with friends at Houghton; and myself and wife took a walk up the lane in question. As we passed by the place the recollection of those early violets of 12 years ago flashed upon my mind.

At the usual interval of some 20 or 30 seconds my wife remarked, "It's very curious, but if it were not impossible, I should declare that I could smell violets in the hedge."

I had not spoken, or made any gesture or movement of any kind, to indicate what I was thinking of. Neither had my memory called up the perfume. All that I thought of was the exact locality on the hedge bank; my memory being exceedingly minute for locality. January 26th, 1885.[219] — REV. P. H. NEWNHAM

☛ CASE #204: On Saturday, May 5th, 1884, I drove into Oxford in an open landau with my little boy and his nurse. On reaching the covered Market I got out, leaving the nurse and child in the carriage, which remained in the High Street.

It was my intention to go to a shop in the middle of the market, but before I reached it I became suddenly convinced that something had happened to the child, and that the carriage was being closed. The feeling was so strong that I stopped walking, and was about to turn round to go and see what had happened, when I felt I was foolishly fanciful, and for discipline's sake I decided to walk through the Market down a short street to Exeter College, where I had to leave a note, instead of driving there after my visit to the Market, as I had previously intended to do.

I did this, and then called at the shop, walking very fast all the time. I was nervously anxious to see the carriage again.

When I reached the High Street I saw a crowd looking at the carriage, which was closed, and on reaching it found that my little boy had fallen out of it, on to the street, about 2 minutes after I had left him. The child had been much frightened, and a crowd having assembled the coachman closed the carriage.[220] — HENRIETTA WILLERT

☛ CASE #205: When I was in Liverpool, in 1872, I heard from my friend, the late Rev. W. W. Stamp, D.D., a remarkable story of the faculty of second sight possessed by the Rev. John Drake, of Arbroath, in Scotland. I visited Arbroath in 1874, and recounted to Mr. Drake the story of Dr. Stamp, which Mr. Drake assented to as correct, and he called his faculty "clairvoyance." Subsequently, in 1881, I had the facts particularly verified by Mrs. Hutcheon, who was herself the subject of this clairvoyance of Mr. Drake.

When the Rev. John Drake was minister of the Wesleyan Church at Aberdeen, Miss Jessie Wilson, the daughter of one of the principal lay office bearers in that church, sailed for India, to join the Rev. John Hutcheon, M.A., then stationed as a missionary at Bangalore, to whom she was under engagement to be married. Mr. Drake, one morning, came down to Mr. Wilson's place of business and said, "Mr. Wilson, I am happy to be able to inform you that Jessie has had a pleasant voyage, and is now safely arrived in India."

Mr. Wilson said, "How do you know that, Mr. Drake?" to which Mr. Drake replied. "I saw it."

"But," said Mr. Wilson, "it cannot be, for it is a fortnight too soon. The vessel has never made the voyage within a fortnight of the time it is now since Jessie sailed."

To this Mr. Drake replied: "Now you jot it down in your book that John Drake called this morning and told you that Jessie has arrived in India this morning after a pleasant voyage."

Mr. Wilson accordingly made the entry, which Mrs. Hutcheon assured me she saw, when she returned home, and that it ran thus: "Mr. Drake, Jessie arrived India morning of June 5th, 1860."

This turned out to have been literally the case. The ship had fair winds all the way. and made a quicker passage by a fortnight than ever she had made before.[221] — REV. J. A. MACDONALD

☞ CASE #206: . . . all other mediums have been outshone by a New England woman, the celebrated Mrs. Leonora F. Piper, of Arlington, Mass., whose history may advantageously be reviewed as representing psychical mediumship at its zenith.

hat makes the case of Mrs. Piper doubly interesting is the circumstance that for fully twenty years she has been under the close observation of members of the Society for Psychical Research and has not once been detected in fraudulent practices. She was brought to the notice of the society in 1885 by Professor [William] James, who wrote that he was "persuaded of the medium's honesty and of the genuineness of her trance, and although at first disposed to think that the 'hits' she made were either lucky coincidences, or the result of knowledge on her part of who the sitter was and of his or her family affairs, I now believe her to be in possession of a power as yet unexplained."

At that time Mrs. Piper was supposed to be "controlled" by the spirit of a French physician with the peculiar name of "Phinuit," through whose instrumentality various sitters, including men prominent in the scientific life of the United States, received more or less intimate messages purporting to come from deceased friends.

Such was the impression made on the society by Professor James's report that in 1887 Dr. [Richard] Hodgson was commissioned to go to America and conduct an inquiry. His first step was to employ detectives to shadow both Mr. and Mrs. Piper, but nothing suspicious was discovered in the conduct of either, and, satisfied that, whatever their source, the phenomena manifested through her were not to be explained on the basis of fraud, Dr. Hodgson recommended that she be invited to England for further investigation.

Upon her arrival elaborate precautions were taken to prevent her securing any information concerning prospective sitters. She was met at Liverpool by Sir Oliver Lodge and conducted to a hotel, whence Mr. [Frederic W. H.] Myers took her to his home at Cambridge. There she was attended by a servant—a young woman from a country village selected by Mr. Myers—and quite ignorant of his and his friends' affairs. Her baggage was carefully overhauled for any data she might have brought with her, and her daily mail was closely examined. But no evidence was forthcoming to show that she secured her trance information by normal means.

Numerous sittings were held, not all of which were successful and some of which were marked by distinctly suspicious failures. But when success was achieved it was conspicuous and startling. To give an instance, Sir Oliver Lodge handed to the entranced Mrs. Piper a watch he had procured from an uncle who in turn had inherited it from a twin brother, then dead for some twenty years. Immediately "Phinuit," claiming to speak in behalf of the deceased uncle, recited several incidents of the latter's youth, and these were subsequently corroborated by the living uncle.

. . . Puzzled, but not wholly persuaded that the messages delivered through Mrs. Piper actually came from the dead, the society directed Dr. Hodgson to continue investigation in the United States. This mission, it may be added in passing, occupied him to the day of his death and was ultimately the means of converting him to the spiritistic hypothesis.[222] — HENRY ADDINGTON BRUCE

☛ CASE #207: One of the best [mediumistic] sitters was my next-door neighbor, Isaac C. Thompson, F.L.S., to whose name indeed, before he had been in any way introduced, "Phinuit" [see previous case] sent a message purporting to come from his father. Three generations of his and of his wife's family, living and dead (small and compact Quaker families), were, in the course of two or three sittings, conspicuously mentioned, with identifying detail; the main informant representing himself as his deceased brother, a young Edinburgh doctor, whose loss had been mourned some twenty years ago. The familiarity and touchingness of the messages communicated in this particular instance were very remarkable, and can by no means be reproduced in any printed report of the sitting. Their case is one in which very few mistakes were made, the details standing out vividly correct, so that in fact they found it impossible not to believe that their relatives were actually speaking to them.[223] — SIR OLIVER LODGE

☛ CASE #208: The following case of apparent telepathy from an animal was first published in *The Times* for July 21st, 1904, from which we [the S.P.R.] quote Mr. Rider Haggard's account of it:

Perhaps you will think with me that the following circumstances are worthy of record, if only for their scientific interest. It is principally because of this interest that, as such stories should not be told anonymously, after some hesitation I have made up my mind to publish them over my own name, although I am well aware that by so doing I may expose myself to a certain amount of ridicule and disbelief.

On the night of Saturday, July 9, I went to bed about 12:30, and suffered from what I took to be a nightmare. I was awakened by my wife's voice calling to me from her own bed upon the other side of the room. As I awoke, the nightmare itself, which had been long and vivid, faded from my brain. All I could remember of it was a sense of awful oppression and of desperate and terrified struggling for life such as the act of drowning would probably involve. But between the time that I heard my wife's voice and the time that my consciousness answered to it, or so it seemed to me, I had another dream.

I dreamed that a black retriever dog, a most amiable and intelligent beast named Bob, which was the property of my eldest daughter, was lying on its side among brushwood, or rough growth of some sort, by water. My own personality in some mysterious way seemed to me to be arising from the body of the dog, which I knew quite surely to be Bob and no other, so much so that my head was against its head, which was lifted up at an unnatural angle. In my vision the dog was trying to speak to me in words, and, failing, transmitted to my mind in an undefined fashion the knowledge that it was dying. Then everything vanished, and I woke to hear my wife asking me why on earth I was making those horrible and weird noises. I replied that I had had a nightmare about a fearful struggle, and that I had dreamed that old Bob was in a dreadful way, and was trying to talk to me and to tell me about it. Finally, seeing that it was still quite dark, I asked what the time was. She said she did not know, and shortly afterwards I went to sleep again and was disturbed no more.

On the Sunday morning Mrs. Rider Haggard told the tale at breakfast, and I repeated my story in a few words. This I need not do here, as the annexed statements set out what occurred quite clearly. Thinking that the whole thing was nothing more than a disagreeable dream, I made no enquiries about the dog and never learned even that it was missing until that Sunday night, when my little girl, who was in the habit of feeding it, told me so. At breakfast time, I may add, nobody knew that it was gone, as it had been seen late on the previous evening. Then I remembered my dream, and the following day enquiries were set on foot.

To be brief, on the morning of Thursday, the 14th, my servant, Charles Bedingfield, and I discovered the body of the dog floating in the [River] Waveney against a weir about a mile and a quarter away. The two certificates of the veterinary surgeon, Mr. Mullane, are enclosed herewith. They sufficiently describe its condition.

On Friday, the 15th, I was going into Bungay to offer a reward for the discovery of the persons who were supposed to have destroyed the dog in the fashion suggested in Mr. Mullane's first certificate, when at the level crossing on the Bungay road I was hailed by two platelayers, who are named respectively George Arterton and Harry Alger. These men informed me that the dog had been killed by a train, and took me on a trolly down to a certain open-work bridge which crosses the water between Ditchingham and Bungay, where they showed me evidences of its death. This is the sum of their evidence:

It appears that about 7 o'clock upon the Monday morning, very shortly after the first train had passed, in the course of his duties Harry Alger was on the bridge, where he found a dog's collar torn off and broken by the engine (since produced and positively identified as that worn by Bob), coagulated blood, and bits of flesh, of which remnants he cleaned the rails. On search also I personally found portions of black hair from the coat of a dog. On the Monday afternoon and subsequently his mate saw the body of the dog floating in the water beneath the bridge, whence it drifted down to the weir, it having risen with the natural expansion of gases, such as, in this hot weather, might be expected to occur within about 40 hours of death.

It would seem that the animal must have been killed by an

excursion train that left Ditchingham at 10:25 on Saturday night, returning empty from Harleston a little after 11. This was the last train which ran that night. No trains run on Sunday, and it is practically certain that it cannot have been killed on the Monday morning, for then the blood would have been still fluid.

Also men who were working around when the 6:30 train passed must have seen the dog on the line (they were questioned by Alger at the time and had seen nothing), and the engine-driver in broad daylight would also have witnessed and made a report

of the accident, of which in a dark night he would probably know nothing. Further, if it was living, the dog would almost certainly have come home during Sunday, and its body would not have risen so quickly from the bottom of the river, or presented the appearance it did on Thursday morning. From traces left upon the piers of the bridge it appears that the animal was knocked or carried along some yards by the train and fell into the brink of the water where reeds grow. Here, if it were still living,—and, although the veterinary thinks that death was practically instantaneous, its life may perhaps have lingered for a few minutes,—it must have suffocated and sunk, undergoing, I imagine, much the same sensations as I did in my dream, and in very similar surroundings to those that I saw therein,—namely, amongst a scrubby growth at the edge of water.

Both in a judicial and a private capacity I have been accustomed all my life to the investigation of evidence, and, if we may put aside our familiar friend "the long arm of coincidence," which in this case would surely be strained to dislocation, I confess that that [material] available upon this matter forces me to the following conclusions:

The dog Bob, between whom and myself there existed a mutual attachment, either at the moment of his death, if his existence can conceivably have been prolonged till after 1 in the morning, or, as seems more probable, about three hours after that event, did succeed in calling my attention to its actual or recent plight by placing whatever portion of my being is capable of receiving such impulses when enchained by sleep, into its own terrible position. That subsequently, as that chain of sleep was being broken by the voice of my wife calling me back to a normal condition of our human existence, with some last despairing effort, while that indefinable part of me was being slowly withdrawn from it (it will be remembered that in my dream I seemed to rise from the dog), it spoke to me, first trying to make use of my own tongue, and, failing therein, by some subtle means of communication whereof I have no knowledge telling me that it was dying, for I saw no blood or wounds which would suggest this to my mind. I recognise, further, that, if its dissolution took place at the moment when I dreamt, this communication must have been a form of that telepathy which is now very generally acknowledged to occur between human beings from time to time and under special circumstances, but which I have never heard of as occurring between a human being and one of the lower animals.

If, on the other hand, that dissolution happened, as I believe, over three hours previously what am I to say? Then it would seem that it must have been some non-bodily but surviving part of the life or of the spirit of the dog which, so soon as my deep sleep gave it an opportunity, reproduced those things in my mind, as they had already occurred, I presume, to advise me of the manner of its end or to bid me farewell.

There is a third possibility which I will quote, although the evidence seems to me to be overwhelmingly against it, and, for the reasons already given, it is inherently most improbable—namely, that the dog was really killed about half-past 6 on the Monday morning, in which case my dream was nothing but a shadow of its forthcoming fate.

Personally, however, I do not for a moment believe this to have been the case, especially as the veterinary's certificate states that the animal's body must have been "over three days" in the water at the time of its discovery.

On the remarkable issues opened up by this occurrence I cannot venture to speak further than to say that, although it is dangerous to generalise from a particular instance, however striking and well supported by evidence, which is so rarely obtainable in such obscure cases, it does seem to suggest that there is a more intimate ghostly connection between all members of the animal world, including man, than has hitherto been believed, at any rate by Western peoples; that they may be, in short, all of them different manifestations of some central, informing life, though inhabiting the universe in such various shapes.

The matter, however, is one for the consideration of learned people who have made a study of these mysterious questions. I will only add that I ask you to publish the annexed documents with this letter, as they constitute the written testimony at present available to the accuracy of what I state. Further, I may say that I shall welcome any investigation by competent persons.[224] — H. RIDER HAGGARD

☛ CASE #209: I own a rough terrier, about 5 years old, which I have brought up from a pup. I have always been a great lover of animals, dogs especially. This dog returns my affection so much that I never go anywhere, not even leave the room, but he must follow me. He is death on rats, and the scullery being visited occasionally by these rodents, I have a comfortable bed for Fido to sleep on. In this room there is a fire-place with an oven suitable for baking, and a boiler for washing, with a flue running back into the chimney. It was my custom to take him to his bed the last thing before retiring for the night.

I had undressed and was about getting into bed, when an unaccountable feeling came over me of impending danger. I could think of nothing possible but *Fire*, and the impression was so strong that I yielded to it and actually dressed again, and went downstairs and examined each room to satisfy myself that all was right. When I got to the scullery I missed Fido, and thinking he had slipped by me unobserved to go upstairs, I immediately began to call him, but getting no response, I called to my sister-in-law to know if she had heard him, and getting an answer in the negative, I began to feel excited, and rushed back to the scullery again, and called repeatedly, but not a sound could be heard.

What to do I did not know.

It then occurred to me that if anything will get him to respond it will be the sentence, "Come for a walk, Fido," which always gave him delight. As soon as I had repeated this sentence, I heard a faint cry, muffled as if distant; calling again, the cry of a dog in distress came plainly. I eventually traced it to the flue, where the flue uniting the boiler with chimney runs.

For the moment I could not think how I could get him out; moments were precious, life was in danger. I took a pickaxe and soon tore down a portion of the wall, when with some difficulty I drew him out half dead, panting, vomiting, tongue and body black with soot; my pet would soon have been dead, and as the boiler is only used occasionally, I should never have known what had become of him.

Hearing the noise my sister-in-law came to the scene. We found a rat-hole in the fireplace which led to the flue. Fido had evidently chased the rat into the flue and could not turn or retreat. This occurred a few months ago and was reported at the time in our local paper, but I never thought of sending it to you until I read the Rider Haggard story [see previous case]. November 13th, 1904.[225]
— J. F. YOUNG

☛ CASE #210: Lady Carbery presents her compliments to Mr. Rider Haggard, and thinks he may be interested in the enclosed account of how she was summoned to the help of a favourite mare. The statement could be confirmed by the coachman and others. "Kitty" [the mare] is still alive, ending her days in the fields among her foals, and doing no work. The account enclosed was as follows: On one hot Sunday afternoon in the summer of 1900, I went after luncheon to pay my customary visit to the stables, to give sugar and carrots to the horses, among the number being a favourite mare named Kitty. She was a shy, nervous, well-bred animal, and there existed between us a great and unusual sympathy. I used to ride her every morning before breakfast, whatever the weather might be—quiet solitary rides on the cliffs which overhang the sea at Castle Freke—and it always seemed to me that Kitty enjoyed that hour in the freshness of the day as much as I did.

On this particular afternoon I left the stables and walked alone to the garden, a distance of a quarter of a mile, and established myself under a tree with an interesting book, fully intending to remain there for a couple of hours. After about twenty minutes an uncomfortable sensation came between me and my reading, and at once I felt sure that there was something the matter with Kitty. I tried to put the feeling from me and to go on with my book, but the impression grew stronger, and I felt compelled to hasten back to the stables.

I went straight to Kitty's box, and found her "cast" [laying in a position—perhaps too close to a wall—where she could not roll onto her belly, unfold her legs, and stand up] and in urgent need of help. The stablemen were in a distant part of the stables, whence I fetched them to help the mare up. Their surprise was great to find me in the stables for the second time that afternoon.[226] — LADY CARBERY

☛ CASE #211: I reside with my husband at 15 Lupton Street, N.W. This afternoon I was lying on the sofa, sound asleep, when I suddenly awoke, thinking I heard my husband sigh as if in pain. I arose immediately, expecting to find him in the room. He was not there, and looking at my watch I found it was half-past three.

At six o'clock my husband came in. He called my attention to a bruise on his forehead, which was caused by his having knocked it against the stone steps in a Turkish bath.

I said to him, "I know when it happened—it was at half-past three, for I heard you sigh as if in pain at that time."

He replied, "Yes, that was the exact time, for I remember noticing the clock directly after."

The gentleman who appends his name as witness was present when this conversation took place. February 7th, 1891.[227] — LOUISA E. HARRISON

Chapter Three

ONEIROLOGICAL ACCOUNTS

CASES OF PERCIPIENT DREAMS

☞ CASE #212: In the early spring of 1881, Mrs. Barnes, of Brixham, Devonshire, whose husband was at sea, dreamt that his fishing-vessel was run into by a steamer. Their boy was with him, and she called out in her dream, "Save the boy!" At this moment another son sleeping in the next room rushed into hers, crying out, "Where's father?" She asked what he meant, when he said he had distinctly heard his father come upstairs and kick with his heavy boots against the door, as he was in the habit of doing when he returned from sea.

The boy's statement and her own dream so alarmed the woman that early next morning she told Mrs. Strong and other neighbours of her fears. News afterwards came that her husband's vessel had been run into by a steamer, and that he and the boy were drowned.[228] — VOUCHSAFED BY REV. R. B. F. ELRINGTON

☞ CASE #213: I am in a position to vouch for a very curious dream which my late husband, Mr. William Holden, dreamt about a brother of his, Dr. Ralph Holden, who was at that time travelling in the interior of Africa.

One morning in June or July, 1861, my husband woke me with the announcement, "Ralph is dead." I said, "You must be dreaming." "No, I am not dreaming now, but I dreamt twice over that I saw Ralph lying on the ground, supported by a man. He was lying under a large tree, and he was either dead or dying."

In December, came the news that Dr. Holden was dead; and from a Mr. Green, who had been exploring in the same region, they learnt that he must have died about the time when his brother dreamt about him, and that he died in the arms of his faithful native servant, lying under a large tree, where he was afterwards buried. The Holden family have a sketch which Mr. Green took on the spot of the tree and its surroundings, and on seeing it my husband said, "Yes, that is exactly the place where I saw Ralph in my dream, dying or dead."[229] — MRS. POWLES

☛ CASE #214: On the evening of Wednesday, the 7th of May, 1902, I went to the Schiller Theater at Kiel [Germany], and saw the *première* of Karl Bleibtreu's historical drama, *Zorndorf*. The action takes place in a house in the village during the battle, and an almost incessant cannonade is heard. The red glare of burning houses is visible through the window. A messenger describes an explosion which took place during the battle.

Afterwards I went to a bodega with K____ and H____ and drank a glass of sherry, another of vermouth, and another of port, which made me rather talkative, but I was perfectly sober.

I went to bed about 1:30, and soon fell asleep. I dreamt I was in my bedroom at home at Redhill. It was night. I looked out of the window and saw a red glare, accompanied by a terrific noise, as of a stupendous explosion. I had a very vivid impression that an appalling disaster had occurred, and that a whole town, or perhaps several, had been annihilated. I imagined that a piece of the earth's crust had been blown out, or in, and that in some way it was due to human carelessness. Almost immediately after the explosion I saw newspaper boys running up the road with special editions. I woke, and found myself trembling, and very excited. It was either dawn or daylight, I forget which. I dozed off, and saw an open newspaper with enormous headlines, but do not remember what the words were.

My idea now was that Brighton (where I spent a day in the Easter vacation) was destroyed. I also thought I was in the garden at home with a box full of loose dynamite, and that my brother placed it in the cellar, where at I protested. I don't think in the first dream there was any thought of dynamite, and certainly not of a battle, though, no doubt, the impression made by the glare of the burning houses in the play suggested part of the dream. The dynamite in the cellar was also due to the passage in the play, where some one blames the Russians for their recklessness in blowing up the ammunition which was stored in a cellar. (I didn't quite catch the drift of this story, which was spoken very fast.) I think I was half awake when I imagined Brighton to be the scene of the disaster.

It was nearly 11 a.m. before I rose, but I had been more or less awake for about an hour. I was rather sleepy in the morning, but had no headache. The eruption of Mt. Pelée, which overwhelmed St. Pierre, took place between 7 and 8 a.m. on the 8th, which would be about 12-1 mid-day by Berlin time, i.e., at least 3 or 4 hours after the dream. — P.S. Magnetic disturbances were noted at the Kiel Observatory both on Wednesday and Thursday. It is thought these may be connected with the eruption. The dream was one of the most vivid I have ever had. May 11th, 1902.²³⁰ — MR. A. B. GOUGH

☛ CASE #215: One Monday night in December, 1836, A. had the following dream, or, as he would prefer to call it, revelation. He found himself suddenly at the gate of Major N. M.'s avenue, many miles from his home. Close to him were a group of persons, one of them a woman with a basket on her arm, the rest men, four of whom were tenants of his own, while the others were unknown to him. Some of the strangers seemed to be murderously assaulting H. W., one of his tenants, and he interfered.

> "I struck violently at the man on my left, and then with greater violence at the man's face to my right. Finding to my surprise that I did not knock him down either, I struck again and again, with all the violence of a man frenzied at the sight of my poor friend's murder. To my great amazement I saw that my arms, although visible to my eye, were without substance; and the bodies of the men I struck at and my own came close together after each blow through the shadowy arms I struck with. My blows were delivered with more extreme violence than I think I ever exerted; but I became painfully convinced of my incompetency. I have no consciousness of what happened, after this feeling of unsubstantiality came upon me."

Next morning A. experienced the stiffness and soreness of violent bodily exercise, and was informed by his wife that in the course of the night he had much alarmed her by striking out again and again with his arms in a terrific manner, "as if fighting for his life." He in turn informed her of his dream, and begged her to remember the names of those actors in it who were known to him.

On the morning of the following day, Wednesday, A. received a letter from his agent, who resided in the town close to the scene of the dream, informing him that his tenant, H. W., had been found on Tuesday morning at Major N. M.'s gate, speechless and apparently dying from a fracture of the skull, and that there was no trace of the murderers.

That night A. started for the town, and arrived there on Thursday morning. On his way to a meeting of magistrates he met the senior magistrate of that part of the country, and requested him to give orders for the arrest of the three men whom, besides H. W., he had recognised in his dream, and to have them examined separately. This was at once done. The three men gave identical accounts of the occurrence, and all named the woman who was with them; she was then arrested, and gave precisely similar testimony.

They said that between eleven and twelve on the Monday night they had been walking homewards all together along the road, when they were overtaken by three strangers, two of whom savagely assaulted H. W., while the other prevented his friends from interfering. H. W. did not die, but was never the same man afterwards; he subsequently emigrated. Of the other parties concerned, the only survivor (except A. himself) gave an account of the occurrence to the archdeacon of the district in November, 1881, but varied from the true facts in stating that he had taken the wounded man home in his cart. Had this been the case he would, of course, have been called on for his testimony at once.[231] — NAME WITHHELD BY THE S.P.R.

☛ CASE #216: About 1871, Miss Phillips, of Church Street, Welshpool, had a deaf and dumb maid. This girl fell ill and needed a change of air, and Miss Phillips proposed to send her to her brother for three weeks. The girl was very unwilling to go, and on the appointed morning, a Tuesday, she handed over a tray which she was carrying upstairs to another servant, and was not seen afterwards. Miss Phillips and her friends in great alarm searched the house all over, including the cellar in which the girl was afterwards found.

On the following Friday (or possibly the Wednesday) morning, the superintendent of police, Strefford, called and said that he had an impression on his mind that she was concealed in the house, and begged to be allowed to make search. Miss Phillips consented, and Strefford, who had never been in the house before, walked straight to the door of the cellar stairs and went down. In the cellar they found the girl jammed fast in an open flue directly beneath the fire-place in the room above, the ashes of which it was meant to receive. The opening from the flue to the cellar was not above eighteen inches high, and the girl had drawn some carpeting after her so as to conceal her legs. They had to get bricklayer's tools and dig down the bricks before they could get her out.

Now as to the cause of Strefford's assurance that he would find her there."My father," says Mr. John C. Strefford, "awoke my mother in the middle of the night and said, 'I know where that poor girl is. She is up a chimney in the cellar belonging to the house in which she lives.'" He could not rest after this; got up at five o'clock, went to the house, and found the girl, as above narrated.[232]
— REV. J. E. HILL

☛ CASE #217: I dreamt one night (in London) that I was in the Carnival in Naples, and among other projectiles that were being used along with the confetti were squibs and [fire] crackers; some of these struck a very fine palm-tree; in fact, the people in one balcony were making it their butt.

I was indignant at the injury to the beautiful tree, and called to them to desist. A friend with me seconded these endeavours of mine, but what seemed to strike me most was that he kept urging on me confidentially not to say palm-tree, that no one ever now-a-days used the word, that the accepted name in good society was "stem-tree."

The next morning the *Times* contained an account of a quantity of "*stems of palm-trees*" having been washed ashore somewhere on the east coast of England.[233] — MISS R. H. BUSK

☛ CASE #218: One night, in Rome, I dreamt that in some shop, where I went, with one of my sisters, the assistants were all deaf and dumb, to whom we could only explain our meaning by signs; nevertheless they were talking together glibly enough. I thought I pointed this out with some indignation, and that my sister answered, "Of course, deaf and dumb people can always talk to each other; it is only with us that they can't communicate."

The comicality of this fancy led me to tell her of the dream the next morning.

Later in the day we went to a shop in the Via San Romualdo, where we often dealt, but through there being a new shopman who did not know the location of the goods, we were led to observe for the first time that the mistress of the shop, who sat at the desk, was deaf and dumb, as she had to direct him by signs how to find what we required.[234] — MISS R. H. BUSK

☛ CASE #219: Another time my dream was all about a brown retriever, it seemed to me I had never seen any but black retrievers before, and wondered how this *lusus naturæ* had arrived.

The next morning, walking near Portman Square, a brown retriever ran up against me. Of course, brown retrievers are not very rare, and my unaccountable surprise at seeing one in a dream, in conjunction with meeting one, not in a game country, but in Portman Square, was another "useless coincidence."[235] — MISS R. H. BUSK

☛ CASE #220: Another time I dreamt that a friend was about to be married to a gentleman of my acquaintance; but as the said friend was already married I was greatly puzzled, for, with the usual certainty with which the knowledge of an event presents itself in a dream, I had no doubt on the head that the said marriage was to take place; I was only bothered by the contradictory fact I have named.

By the next morning's post I received a letter from this very friend announcing the sudden death of her husband. (She did not marry the other man, however.)[236] — MISS R. H. BUSK

☛ CASE #221: In another dream I found myself, without surprise, seated in a Protestant church, notwithstanding that I had some years before become a Catholic, but I thought I was greatly concerned in keeping the place next me for a friend who was to join me there. To my dismay, a gentleman came, "without with your leave, or by your leave," and established himself in this place in a peremptory manner. I turned round with the intention of evicting the intruder, though my hints had no effect upon him, but in doing so I observed that he was Canon Kingsley.

The next morning the first event that caught my eye in the newspaper was the announcement of Canon Kingsley's death.

Now, I knew no more of Canon Kingsley than of the Shah of Persia; I had seen both in public, and I had read a book by each, and there my acquaintance ended. I had not been thinking or talking about him. It could only have been a kaleidoscope mixing up of images in the brain—yet, had it been some particularly dear friend whom I had thought I felt placing himself so unexpectedly by my side, and had that friend also died unknown to me the day before, it would have been said by all ghost-believing people that it was the actual spirit of the dear departed. As this was certainly no apparition of the sort, I argue that in the cases where the condition of affection enters into the details of the case, they are yet nothing more than fortuitous coincidences either.[237] — MISS R. H. BUSK

☛ CASE #222: I had an uncle who, after spending thirty-three years on board ship, left the sea, got married, and settled down near London. His only son and myself were constant playmates, and for a short time schoolfellows also.

My cousin's one great wish was to go to sea, but this, so far from being encouraged, always provoked a stern rebuke, if even the topic only was mentioned. At last Cousin Jack seemed to have got over his yearning for the naval service; he quietly bore with a good grace what to him was a bitter disappointment. As he was now a big lad it was necessary to find him something to do.

A post was found for him under my father in a house of business in the City. Here he did well, and soon won golden opinions from all about him.

One day—it was Lord Mayor's Day, and the City was too excited to settle down to sober business—Jack asked my father for half a day's holiday and an advance of five shillings. The holiday was granted and he was told he could take the money and enter it in the proper book. After that he went, as was thought, for a few hours' pleasure.

He never returned.

Inquiries were made at every likely place, but to no purpose. His parents were utterly disconsolate at his disappearance. We all guessed that he had gone off to sea, but none dared give utterance in the father's presence to the thought, knowing how unwelcome such an explanation would be.

Months passed by and no news came.

At length-perhaps it was twelve or eighteen months afterwards—my thoughts were again directed to my missing cousin. It was in this way.

One Sunday morning my father invited me to go with him to see my uncle and aunt. On the road he told me that during the night he had had a most remarkable dream, and he wished to test it as far as he could, for he was strongly persuaded that it would be fulfilled. At the same time he urged me to notice the date and preserve in my memory the details as far as possible. I may just say, in parenthesis, that we continued our journey, paid the visit, but found that nothing had been heard of my cousin. The dream, so far as I can recollect it at this distance of time, was somewhat as follows:

The scene is in a foreign port (guessed at the time to be Spanish). On board a British man-of-war that is anchored there a young man (my cousin Jack) is giving instructions to some men at work in the rigging. He is apparently dissatisfied with what they are doing, for he hurries up, makes some slight alteration, and then descends. A rung of the rope ladder gives way as his foot touches it, he falls backward, head first, and dies instantly. The surgeon hurries to the spot, examines the body, but leaves it as he can do nothing there.

Then arrangements are made for the burial. The coffin is taken on shore, some of the officers and men accompany it, and it is solemnly lowered into the grave. There the dream ended.

Some time after my father (he had already ascertained the time it would take for a letter to come from the Spanish coast to England) asked me one morning if I still remembered his strange dream. He then made me repeat it to him. After that he said: "Well, if there is anything in it, your uncle will have heard something about it by this time, let us go and see him."

When we reached the house we could see at a glance that something had happened. My father at once asked if there was any news yet of Jack. Yes, that morning's post had brought a large envelope bearing the Lisbon post-mark. It was written by one of the officers of a man-of-war that was then anchored at Lisbon, and its purpose was to make known the death of my cousin. After a very kind and favourable notice of Jack's general conduct and abilities, it gave full details of his death and burial. Those details tallied exactly with the details given in my father's dream, and it occurred the very date of the dream. I was perfectly amazed.

I inspected the letter and could not see any point in which there was the slightest contradiction or even divergence. Of course my uncle was then informed of the dream, and I feel sure the talk we then had about the matter helped my uncle to bear his bitter trial with more serenity than he would have done if we had not been there with our visions from dreamland.[238] — MR. F. TEESDALE REED

☛ CASE #223: When my daughter returned from Switzerland she was accompanied by a schoolfellow who was going to a situation at London as governess. On reaching England they parted and never met again. Once only my daughter heard of her that she was married.

Now, my daughter who lives in Birmingham still, struck up a very warm friendship with another schoolfellow and they correspond regularly. Towards the end of last year [1902] she dreamt that she saw the girl who came to England with her and her husband. They appeared well and in very good circumstances.

By the next post came a letter from her Swiss friend saying that Alice Birman (now Mrs. Smith) and her husband had called on her without any warning. They were very well off and had a sudden whim to go on the Continent, followed by another to call on her old friend.

My daughter at once wrote for a description of Mr. Smith, and it corresponded singularly with the visionary gentleman. In the dream he was fair, with a gentle air, and shorter than his wife, and had a slight, fair moustache, and also told my daughter they were going to an exhibition. In reality he was the same, only clean shaven, and they were going that day to show a dog at an exhibition.

I may add that my daughter sent me the description of the dream of Mr. Smith before she received that of the real one, and before she opened [the] first letter was convinced it would say something about [the incidents of her dream]. January 1903.[239] — MR. A. H. ATKINS

☛ CASE #224: It was in 1863 that I took charge of the Unitarian Church in Exeter, New Hampshire [USA]. Five miles away, Rev. A. M. Bridge was preaching at Hampton Falls,—with whom I sometimes exchanged pulpits. After a year or so he gave up the work in this little parish, and somewhat later entered upon an engagement in the town of East Marshfield, Mass., as the railroad runs, nearly 80 miles from Exeter.

On Wednesday, December 13th, 1865, on waking in the morning, I remarked to my wife upon the very vivid and singular dream which I had had, and related it fully.

I had seen Mr. Bridge taken suddenly and violently ill. He seemed to be in a school-room. He sank down helpless, but was borne away by friendly hands and laid upon a couch or lounge. I was by him, and assisted others in whatever way I could. But he grew worse; even the open-air did not revive him; a leaden pallor soon spread over his features; peculiar spots, which I had never noticed before, like moles or discolourations of the skin, appeared upon his face, and after much suffering he died.

Immediately after breakfast, and while we were again speaking of the dream, a ring at the door admitted to my house Mr. Wells Healey, an old parishioner of Mr. Bridge's, at Hampton Falls. I guessed the nature of his message. He had come to ask me to attend the funeral services of his former minister, who had suddenly died two days before (Monday), at East Marshfield. Mr. Bridge's family had not removed there, but he would be buried among the people he had so recently left.

I attended the funeral as requested. I learned from the family and friends the particulars of his death, which coincided remarkably in several points with the dream already repeated to my wife; and when I looked at the face of the dead man as he lay in his coffin, my attention was arrested and fixed by the peculiar spots upon the face to which I have alluded, and which were stereotyped upon memory by the dream. September 4th, 1884.[240] — REV. J. C. LEARNED

☛ CASE #225: When I was in the South of France, in 1878, I had a dream that a sister, who is especially dear to me, was in a carriage accident, and my dream I saw her killed, but on reaching her I found her unhurt; and as she smiled at me I dreamed I was dying of the agony of mind I had gone through.

I never can forget the dream, the suffering was so intense. I awoke with pain in my heart and faintness, and woke my husband and told him. (I think my cries in my sleep awoke him.) I wrote to my sister, and when her answer arrived she gave me in it the account of the danger she had passed through.[241] — MRS. C. M. W.

☛ CASE #226: [This entry is by the sister mentioned by Mrs. C. M. W. in the previous case.] On one occasion I received an anxious letter from my sister inquiring if anything had happened to me, as she had dreamed of a serious carriage accident in which I was in danger. This letter was received by me before I had informed her of the danger in which I had been placed, and the serious consequences which mercifully were averted by the presence of mind of my coachman.[242] — BESSIE S.

☛ CASE #227: I received your letter yesterday, and in compliance with your request shall relate my dream. Long years have passed since the Easter morning when I awoke from it, but so vivid it was and so greatly it impressed me, I have no difficulty in recalling it.

My cousin, Mr. Wright, knew of my brother's emigration, and also knew who the gentleman was (Mr. R.) at whose house he died. This gentleman had gone out to Australia three years before my brother, and having ample means, had established himself there comfortably. We had all been on intimate terms with him except my brother Stephen, who was one of a shy, reserved nature, never caring to make friends. We were unaware of the fact of Mr. R. having gone to Australia till nearly a year after my brother's departure, but upon hearing of it my mother wrote to my brother telling him to make his way to Mr. R.'s settlement, as she would feel so happy to think he was near a friend whose advice, etc., would be beneficial.

His reply to this letter was that the great distance, nearly 300 miles, precluded any possibility of their meeting, as the journey should nearly altogether be accomplished on foot, and that he preferred staying in the neighbourhood of Sydney, etc., etc. He wrote very seldom, and the subject was not renewed, and we lost all thought of their ever coming together.

On the Easter morning I dreamt that I was looking out of my bedroom window, and that I saw Mr. R. walking up the avenue, and that knowing him to be in Australia, I felt so surprised and pleased that I ran down to meet him at the glass portico. When I put out my hand I said, "Oh how glad I am to see you again." He looked so sad and said, "You will not be glad, as I bring you sad news. Your brother Stephen is dead."

I awoke at the moment, and it seemed as though the words were sounding in my ears. When the servant came to assist me to dress I told her my dream, and to comfort me she said that dreams always went by contraries, "and that he was most likely being married," but said I must not tell this dream to my mother or to any one who might do so, as my brother writing so seldom always made her so anxious and unhappy; and so acting upon her advice I did not speak of it, but the thought of it constantly recurred during the four months that intervened between the Easter and a visit to Bangor, in Wales, where a letter from Mr. R. was forwarded to me.

He wrote to me for the reason that he thought I could more gently break the sad news to my dear mother, and his letter commenced almost with the same words that I had heard in the dream. He told how that a fortnight before his death my brother had reached his home sadly out of health, and worn with the toilsome journey. At once he became too ill to write, and continued so till he died on Easter Sunday morning. Yours very truly.[243] — OLIVIA A. DENROCHE

☛ CASE #228: My aunt has asked me to try and recall a dream that I dreamt many years ago about an old man, the road-mender in our village, whom I had known and loved from my earliest childhood. He was naturally a bright cheerful old man, but was at the time I am speaking of in extremely low spirits on account, as we supposed, of his wife, who was very ill and wretched, lying on what proved to be her death bed.

On the morning of my dream my sister and myself had both been awake at 6 o'clock, and I had fallen asleep again before the servant came in as usual about 7 o'clock. On my waking from this sleep, I told my sister that I had had a very painful dream about old

William Thompson, whom I had seen in my dream running down the lane towards the Church fields, in his grey stockings, looking very miserable, and I turned to her and said, I fear old William is going to make away with himself.

I had hardly finished telling my sister the dream, when our servant came in to call us, and said that our father (the rector of the parish) had been sent for in a great hurry to old William Thompson, who had just been found in the Church fields with his throat cut. He was without his shoes, and when my father got to him, he was still alive. These are the circumstances as accurately related as I can recall them.[244] — S. S. P.

☛ CASE #229: Towards morning of the 10th January, 1885, I was conscious of a young woman standing by my bedside clad in a grey dressing-gown, holding in her arms, towards me, a child. The woman was weeping bitterly, and said, "Oh! Mrs. Saunders, I am in such trouble." I instantly recognised her as Mrs. C. R. Seymour, and was about to interrogate her as to her trouble, when I was awakened by my husband asking me what was the matter, as I seemed so distressed.

I told him I had had such a sad dream about poor Fanny Goodall (maiden name of Mrs. C. R. S.), but it really was to me more than a dream, so much so, that after rising I communicated it to the governess, Miss Monkman, also to the nurse and servant.

I decided to send to her mother, Mrs. Goodall, to inquire if she had received any tidings of her daughter, who was resident in New Zealand with her husband and two children, but, as on after consideration I felt it might cause her alarm, I altered my intention.

This dream or vision made so deep and lasting an impression that I constantly alluded to it to members of our household, until circumstances occasioned my calling on Mrs. Goodall about the beginning of this month, March, 1885, when I made particular inquiries for her daughter; and on being assured that she was well, according to letters by the most recent mail, I ventured to express my gratification, giving, as my reason for such, a narration of the "vision" that had not even then ceased to haunt me; which elicited from Mrs. Goodall and both of her daughters, who were present, fervent hopes that all was well with Mrs. Seymour.

On the 12th of March, 1885, I again called on Mrs. Goodall, who on receiving me, with much emotion said, "Oh, have you heard the bad news from Fanny? I have thought so much of what you told me; her dear little Dottie has gone. I will read you her letters," both of which, although coming by different mails, had only been received within the past 24 hours.

I have since written to Miss Monkman to ask her what she recollects of the incident, and her remarks are also given, with my husband's corroboration. That of my servant and nurse could also be obtained, but the latter is very ill in the hospital at present.

I should mention that although I have felt very interested in and thought much of Mrs. C. R. S. before and since her departure from this country, yet I have never corresponded with her, but I now learn that she invariably mentioned me in her home correspondence, and felt much indebted to me for some trifling kindness I had been able to show her in the past. I am able to fix the date of my vision from circumstances which I need not here relate. Recorded March 18th, 1885.[245] — BESSIE SAUNDERS

☛ CASE #230: [From the same writer in the previous account.] In October, 1878, while residing at St. Helen's, five miles from Ryde, I had a vivid dream as follows:

I saw a hearse and pair of horses drive up to the house, from which alighted a lady, Mrs. B., of Ryde, who, having knocked at the door, was duly announced by the housemaid, who also handed me her visiting-card. I then saw that Mrs. B. was in deep mourning.

As this lady was in the habit of using her carriage and pair when visiting me, it struck me as remarkable that, with the exception of the "hearse" and the "deep mourning," the dream was very life-like. I, therefore, on awaking repeated it to my husband and thought much of it throughout the day; indeed, it made so great an impression on me that, we being in Newport that afternoon, I asked my husband to pass the house of Mr. M. (Mrs. B.'s brother) as I should like to be reassured that the family had sustained no loss by noticing that the blinds were not drawn.

We did so, but found that the blinds were all down, so I then asked him to inquire at the house the cause of the mourning. He then learnt that Mrs. M., the mother of Mrs. B., had died at Ryde during the night.

From subsequent inquiries, I learnt that Mrs. B. was in attendance. I knew that Mrs. M. had been ailing, but had no idea she was seriously ill, or I should certainly have gone to see her as she was an old friend from my childhood and was much attached to me. And as far as I know I had not been thinking nor speaking of her or hers for some time previously.[246] — BESSIE SAUNDERS

☛ CASE #231: I will as far as I can, give particulars relative to my dream. It was in June, 1869, when I was residing in Paris; my son was at the Imperial College de Vanves, near Paris. I saw him in my dream with his eyes so red and inflamed that I thought to apply a bandage over them. I was much troubled, so much so that it left a great impression all the next day on my mind.

In the afternoon of that day I received intimation that my son was ill, and went to the college, and found him exactly as I had seen him in my dream, but did not remember seeing the surroundings in the room.

I spoke of it to my family the next morning. The only surviving member now is a brother who resides in Paris, who well remembers my dream. I will forward your letter to him, and ask him to write to you.

As you asked if this was the most vivid dream I had had, I must mention one I had many years before my marriage (I unfortunately cannot give you the date) relative to a very dear lady friend I had not seen for several months.

I was residing in Paris, and I knew her to be in England, but I had not heard of her for a long time. I told my family my dream (as I was much impressed by it), that I saw her dressed in a peculiar fur tippet, with muff, white, with black spots (I had never seen her with it), and that she would look in upon us all while at dinner, and to surprise us the more, would enter quietly by a back door.

It came to pass as I had said; all my relations were so startled at the time that for a few moments they had not a word for this dear friend, who, in return, was rather surprised, as you may imagine—they all so well remembered my statement that I had given that day in the morning.[247] — MRS. E. ALLIBERT

☞ CASE #232: The Rev. A. B. having communicated to me the fact that since January 1st, 1884, he had had an exceptionally vivid dream—which haunted him for a portion of two days—of the death of an acquaintance, and that the dream had corresponded with the fact, the usual questions were asked. He replied as follows:

The Vicarage, December 9th, 1884. In reference to the subject of your note, I am able to say that I had no means of knowing that the lady in question was ailing or even in delicate health. She was the wife of a cousin from whom or of whom I do not think I had heard for some months. I have so much to do in my parish that I have little time for correspondence, but in consequence of what I dreamed I at once wrote to the son of the lady referred to, having previously, on awaking, mentioned the matter to my own wife.

My remark to her was, "We shall hear some bad news, I fear,

from R____" (the residence of my cousin), and I then repeated the dream.

Within another [mail] post I heard that Mrs. B. had died on that night. I had, some years afterwards, another very troubled dream about the same household, but not such as to lead me to think that a death had taken place. I immediately wrote, and learned that there was a very serious anxiety there about a contemplated marriage of an undesirable nature, and had reason to know that the dream had an important influence in averting the step. I mentioned that in my family I was not the only member who had these premonitions.

A very near relative by whom, in my early boyhood, I was reared, knew for a certainty of the death of her own father, and subsequently of that of a much-loved niece, and this under circumstances which she had no other means of knowing than by dream or vision, and did not know until a special messenger arrived to communicate the news. This was in the days when postal communications in Ireland were both intricate and tedious, and a distance of some 25 miles might occupy a good part of a week, but of the fact I am able to vouch.

Many years afterwards, when I was a student in the university, the same favoured relative wrote to me that she feared I would hear some bad news of my father, and I did immediately, that he was dead. There was no communication at the time between her and my father's house. These matters are communicated in confidence for the purposes of the Society, for they are not much spoken of in the family. I am, dear sir, very faithfully yours. December 11th, 1884.[248] — REV. A. B.

☞ CASE #233: In the year 1857, I had a brother in the very centre of the Indian Mutiny. I had been ill in the spring, and taken from my lessons in the school-room. Consequently I heard more of what was going on from the newspapers than a girl of 13 ordinarily would in those days. We were in the habit of hearing regularly from my brother, but in the June and July of that year no letters came, and what arrived in August proved to have been written quite early in the spring, and were full of the disturbances around his station. He was in the service of the East India Company—an officer in the 8th Native Infantry.

I had always been devoted to him, and I grieved and fretted far more than any of my elders knew at his danger. I cannot say I dreamt constantly of him, but when I did the impressions were vivid and abiding.

On one occasion his personal appearance was being discussed, and I remarked, "He is not like that now, he has no beard nor whiskers," and when asked why I said such a thing I replied, "I knew it, for I had seen him in my dreams," and this brought a severe reprimand from my governess, who never allowed "such nonsense" to be talked of.

On the morning of the 25th September, quite early, I awoke from a dream to find my sister holding me, and much alarmed. I had screamed out, struggled, crying out, "Is he really dead?" When I fully awoke I felt a burning sensation in my head. I could not speak for a moment or two; I knew my sister was there, but I neither felt nor saw her. In about a minute, during which she said my eyes were staring beyond her, I ceased struggling, cried out, "Harry's dead, they have shot him," and fainted.

When I recovered I found my sister had been sent away, and an aunt who had always (on account of my mother's health) looked after me, sitting by my bed. In order to soothe my excitement she allowed me to tell her my dream, trying all the time to persuade me to regard it as a natural consequence of my anxiety. When in the narration I said he was riding with another officer, and mounted soldiers behind them, she exclaimed, "My dear, that shows you it is only a dream, for you know dear Harry is in an infantry, not a cavalry, regiment."

Nothing, however, shook my feelings that I had seen a reality, and she was so much struck by my persistence, that she privately made notes of the date, and of the incidents, even to the minutest details of my dream, and then for a few days the matter dropped, but I felt the truth was coming nearer and nearer to all.

In a short time the news came in the papers—shot down on the morning of the 25th when on his way to Lucknow. A few days later came one of his missing letters, telling how his own regiment had mutinied, and that he had been transferred to a command in the 12th Irregular Cavalry, bound to join Havelock's force in the relief of Lucknow.

Some eight years after the officer who was riding by him when he fell, visited us, and when, in compliance, with my aunt's request, he detailed the incidents of that sad hour his narration tallied (even to the description of the buildings on their left) with the notes she had taken the morning of my dream.

I should also add that we heard he had made an alteration in his beard and whiskers just about the time that I had spoken of him as wearing them differently.

. . . I have always been a dreamer. My mother says that as a baby and very young child I was unlike any of her other 13 children; that I often lay with my eyes open, pointing at nothing she could see, and smiling. And as I grew old enough to talk, the nurses told her I was always talking aloud in my sleep. I never had the same sort of dream of death. January 31st, 1885.[249] — MISS L. A. W.

☛ CASE #234: When I was about 19 and 20, I was in very indifferent health; and yet, as my father remarked, no one seemed to know what was the matter with me. The doctors said I had studied too much at school, and that this was the reaction. My mother thought I was too much at my books and writing, and I was ordered tonics, horse exercise, and to go out visiting whenever I was asked. All this time only one of my sisters knew that I had disturbed nights, and dreams so peculiar that I hesitated sometimes to tell them even to her; but in a private note-book I had put down from time to time dates of certain dreams, and more particularly notes of the appearance and conduct of the individual who literally haunted my waking and sleeping hours. It would take too long were I to give the whole of my experiences. I will, as briefly as I can, give an epitome of them.

The dreams commenced in March one year, and continued, at intervals, till the June in the next. Sometimes I went a week without one of these peculiar visitations; sometimes they came night after night; and on one occasion I was nearly four months free from them. I could neither attribute them to any one particular course of study, nor to indigestion, nor to any special diet, for I tried change in every way for my own comfort's sake.

I was not in love, nor indeed had I been; and certainly no feeling but that of a mysterious repugnance (and at the same time an inability to avoid or escape from the influence of the person of whom I dreamt) actuated me. He was someone I had never in all my life wittingly seen, though I had reason to think afterwards that he had seen me at a Birmingham musical festival. On that occasion I had apparently fainted, and it was attributed to the heat and the excitement of the music. I hardly knew if it were or not. I only knew I felt all my pulses stop, and a burning and singing in my head, and that I was perfectly conscious of those around me, but unable to speak and tell them so.

To return to my dreams.

I always knew as I slept when the influence was coming over me, and often in my dream I commenced it by thinking, "Here it is, or here he comes again." They were not always disagreeable dreams in themselves, but the fascination was always dreadful to me, and a kind of struggle between two natures within me seemed to drag my powers of mind and body two ways. I used to awake as cold as a stone in the hottest nights, my head having the queer feeling of a hot iron pressing somewhere in its inside. I would shiver and my teeth chatter with a terror which seemed unreasonable, for there was, even in the subjects of my dreams, seldom anything wicked or terrifying.

As to any idea of love between me and this mysterious stranger, there never was any approach to it in my impressions. There was an interval when a gentleman was paying me some little attention in my day life, that the irritability of my tormentor seemed in my dreams to be extreme. I can remember some of them perfectly; and I have notes of others, but they can, I think, be scarcely needed.

Suffice it to say that I became so thin and so nervous that bad nights were suspected, and I underwent a course of sedatives and opiates, which induced or rather compelled sleep, and when under this treatment I found a difficulty in dreaming, an inability to follow dim visions of dreams, a stupor upon my senses, and after some three or four months I was pronounced well; and it certainly proved true that all exciting circumstances had passed from my sleep.

In the early months of the next year but one, I went with a sister to visit in Liverpool, where we had much gaiety, and were out nearly every night. I can truly say I had forgotten for the time my dreams of a year and a-half ago, not that they ever ceased to be mysterious, and perfectly vivid when I thought of them, but I never did this if I could help it.

One night we went with our friends to a large private ball. The rooms for dancing were two, curtains of lace being half across the opening between them, and these were looped back against pillars. I had enjoyed two or three good dances, and was sitting out one, by the lady of the house, when, not suddenly, but by degrees, I felt myself turning cold and stony, and the peculiar burning in my head. If I could have spoken I would have said, "My dreams! my dreams!" but I only shivered, which attracted the notice of my companion, who exclaimed, "You are ill, my dear. Come for some wine, or hot coffee."

I rose, knowing what I was going to see, and as I turned, I looked straight into the eyes of the fac-simile of the being who had been present to my sleeping thoughts for so long, and the next instant he stepped forward from the pillar against which he was leaning behind the lace curtain and shook hands with my companion. He accompanied us to the refreshment room, attended to my wants, and was introduced to me. I declined dancing, but could not avoid conversation. His first remark was, "We are not strangers to each other. Where have we met?" I fear I shall scarcely be believed when I say, that (setting my teeth and nerving myself to meet what I felt would conquer me, if I once submitted in even the slightest degree) I answered that I never remembered meeting him before, and to all his questionings returned the most reserved answers. He seemed much annoyed and puzzled, but on that occasion did not mention dreams.

I took an opportunity of asking my sister if she remembered my description of the man of my dreams, and upon her answering "Yes," asked her to look round the rooms and see if any one there resembled him, and half-an-hour later she came up, saying, "There is the man, he has even the mole on the left side of his mouth."

We made inquiries cautiously as to who the gentleman was, and heard that he came from the United States, had letters of recommendation to some of the first families in Liverpool society, was supposed to be half English, half German, very peculiar in his notions, very studious, very fascinating when he chose to be so. I met him at almost every party I went to, and it seemed a matter of course that he should sit and converse with me when he could get the opportunity. He was sometimes so gloomy and fierce at my determined avoidance of any but the most ordinary conversation, that I felt quite a terror of meeting him. He frequently asked if I believed in dreams; if I could relate any to him; if I had never seen him before; and would say, after my persistent avoidance of the subject, "I can do nothing, so long as you will not trust me."

Our friends thought there was a flirtation going on, but on neither side was there anything approaching it. I found, however, that his repeated questions became more and more difficult to parry, that his conversations were deeply interesting, though I always felt a dread of what they might lead me into, and I wrote home, saying, I found my nerves were not standing well the gaiety and late hours, and asked to be recalled on some home pretext. I did not even tell my sister what I had done, but the very day the letter went I met Mr.____ at a concert, and he said, "You have written to be sent for home," and then spoke most bitterly of what we had both lost through my obstinacy and want of faith, and a great deal more, which made my brain reel at the pictures he painted.

I have never met him again; but seven years ago I had a short return of dreaming of him, but it only lasted three months, and everything was always indistinct and as if through a mist. I have heard of him, or of some one of the same name, once or twice as lecturing in different places, but my friends left Liverpool, and whether he has or has not been in England lately I cannot say.

No one can tell how much strength was taken out of me by the continual struggle of will which I maintained through those ever-memorable three weeks in Liverpool. I used to feel bruised and shaken all over when I had met him—the tension of my nerves seemed to react upon my senses of feeling and touch, and now, when I think of it, I can only wonder at the physical, moral and mental struggle which seemed to possess me through what were indeed hard battles to fight.

Some have said to me, "Oh! why did you not tell him you had dreamt of him, and see what he would say?" My answer was and is, that I felt always that as I completely lost my own will and my own identity in those dreams, so should I have given myself up to do his will had I given way in our personal interviews, and either acknowledged or accepted his power.

. . . It would take me more time than I can spare just now to examine, weed out, and note down any details from my "Dream Note-Book," or entries from my diaries, which I should choose to send, to be made public. At that time, I had never been in Italy, nor Switzerland, though I had always longed to go, and one set of dreams I have down, describing how in the first place the companion of my dreams suggested showing me the world, how we seemed to fly through space—no wings, but passing through crowds of people unseen, just a few feet from the ground, hearing and seeing everything, floating through rooms invisible to all. I have several pages of this set of dreams; they were enthralling, but there was always the feeling—and I have it noted down—that I was not a free agent, that I could not help myself, that I had to go, and that all this would end in my being the slave, the agent, the victim of my mysterious guide.

When conversing with him in the flesh, he asked me if I had "ever travelled." I said "No." He showed surprise, and began to dilate on the wonders of such and such a place or scene, all of which I felt sure I had seen with him, and entered in my note-book. It was deeply interesting, and I was totally absorbed in his recitals, time after time, when he abruptly stopped, saying, "But have you never had scenes such as these before you?" and I replied, "Yes, in my dreams I have."

Such, or similar remarks, I know I have noted down, and his

eagerness to make me admit similar experiences was at times almost fierce. I had a great longing at times to tell him everything, but an innate sense that by so doing I should be as completely his slave, and tool as I had been in dreams, always stopped me.

My sister has no hesitation in saying she remembers all the circumstances of those years, my dreams, and their frequency, many of which I recounted to her; also the description of the man as tallying with the reality we both met. I have not now mentioned the matter to her, as none of my home people know I am writing on this subject to you, but it is not a year ago since we were talking of the matter to some friends.

You are right in your conjecture that he inferred he had seen me in dreams. He often talked as if I were perfectly aware that I knew it, but that I would not go beyond a certain limit in admitting anything. He frequently talked of electro-biology, second sight, and similar subjects leading to these.

Now, as to your last remark. "Names"! I am quite sure it would be highly distasteful to my family to have my name published in reference to these dreams. I should not like it, but were I alone I would have consented to it, were there any good to be derived from it, and I can understand that cases of this kind furnish more aid if names and addresses can be given. January 1885.[250] — MISS L. A. W.

☛ CASE #235: When a boy, about 14 years of age, I was in school in Edinburgh, my home being in the West of Scotland. A thoughtless boy, free from all care or anxiety, in the " Eleven" of my school, and popular with my companions, I had nothing to worry or annoy me. I boarded with two old ladies, now both dead.

One afternoon on the day previous to a most important cricket match in which I was to take part—I was overwhelmed with a most unusual sense of depression and melancholy. I shunned my friends and got "chaffed" for my most unusual dulness and sulkiness. I felt utterly miserable, and even to this day I have a most vivid recollection of my misery that afternoon.

I knew that my father suffered from a most dangerous disease in the stomach a gastric ulcer—and that he was always more or less in danger, but I knew that he was in his usual bad health, and that nothing exceptional ailed him.

That same night I had a dream. [In the dream] I was engaged in the cricket match. I saw a telegram being brought to me while batting, and it told me that my father was dying, and telling me to come home at once. I told the ladies with whom I boarded what my dream had been, and told them how real the impression was. I went to the ground and was engaged in the game, batting, and making a score. I saw a telegram being brought out, read it, and fainted.

I at once left for home, and found my father had just died when I reached the house. The ulcer in the stomach had suddenly burst about 4 o'clock on the previous day, and it was about that hour that I had experienced the most unusual depression I have described.

The sensations I had on that afternoon have left a most clear and distinct impression on my mind, and now, after the lapse of 15 years, I well remember my miserable feelings.[251] — DR. J. D.

☛ CASE #236: In compliance with thy request, I give thee the particulars of my dream.

[In the dream] I saw two respectably-dressed females driving alone in a vehicle like a mineral water cart. Their horse stopped at a water to drink; but as there was no footing, he lost his balance, and in trying to recover it he plunged right in. With the shock, the women stood up and shouted for help, and their hats rose off their heads, and as all were going down I turned away crying, and saying, "Was there no one at all to help them?" upon which I awoke, and my husband asked me what was the matter.

I related the above dream to him, and he asked me if I knew them. I said I did not, and thought I had never seen either of them. The impression of the dream and the trouble it brought was over me all day. I remarked to my son it was the anniversary of his birthday and my own also—the 10th of First Month, and this is why I remember the date.

The following Third Month I got a letter and newspaper from my brother in Australia, named Allen, letting me know the sad trouble which had befallen him in the loss, by drowning, of one of his daughters and her companion. Thou will see by the description given of it in the paper how the event corresponded with my dream. My niece was born in Australia, and I never saw her.

Please return the paper at thy convenience. Considering that our night [in the UK] is their day [in Australia], I must have been in sympathy with the sufferers at the time of the accident, on the Tenth of First Month, 1878. It is referred to in two separate places in the newspaper [see clipping below]. January 21st, 1885. — MRS. GREEN

From the *Inglewood Advertiser*.
Friday evening, January 11th, 1878.

A dreadful accident occurred in the neighbourhood of Wedderburn, on Wednesday last, resulting in the death of two women, named Lehey and Allen. It appears that the deceased were driving into Wedderburn in a spring cart from the direction of Kinypanial, when they attempted to water their horse at a dam on the boundary of Torpichen Station. The dam was 10 or 12 feet deep in one spot, and into this deep hole they must have inadvertently driven, for Mr. W. McKechnie, manager of Torpichen Station, upon going to the dam some hours afterwards, discovered the spring cart and horse under the water, and two women's hats floating on the surface. The dam was searched, and the bodies of the two women, clasped in each other's arms, recovered.[252]

☛ CASE #237: My father [Mr. Thomas Pickerden] was an architect and builder, which obliged him to be about very early of mornings; and on Monday, the 19th January, 1857, at 7 a.m., whilst on his way to see some of his men, he fell, in a fit of some kind.

That same morning I perfectly well remember not falling asleep until after 2 a.m., having counted the clock up to that hour, and wondering why I could not sleep, as I always slept well at that time. As we breakfasted at 10 a.m. in those days, we were not early risers, so probably it might have been 8 or 9 o'clock before I woke.

I cannot make a nearer statement, as I am not positive as to the time; but my dream was between the hours mentioned. It was that my father had been taken suddenly ill in the streets of Hastings, that he was put into a fly by two men, and taken home—when I woke.

The dream seemed to impress me very much. I tried not to think seriously of it; having dressed and breakfasted, still the dream haunted me. I could not shake it off.

When I spoke to my sisters-in-law, with whom I was staying (my then husband was their brother) they advised me to tell him, which I did, and he at once granted my request of going on to Hastings. He left me at Etchingham Station, and going direct to our home, Hawkhurst, he found a telegram there to the effect that my father was ill, and that I was to go at once. I had by this time reached Hastings and found my dream verified.

The event occurring so many years back, not one witness is living. November 22nd, 1884.[253] — MRS. ANNIE SMITHERS

☛ CASE #238: Two friends of ours, Mr. X. and Mr. Y., lived together till the marriage of Mr. X., and were, therefore, intimately associated in our minds. It happened that though Mrs. X. and I had exchanged cards we had not met, and I merely knew her by sight at the time when Mr. Y. also married. But as I had found Mrs. Y. at home I was slightly acquainted with her.

It was a few months after Mr. Y.'s marriage, on the night of May 14th, 1879, when my dream occurred. I was staying at Bristol at the time. [In my dream it] seemed to me that I was making my first call on Mrs. Y., and that she proceeded to show me her trousseau—a thing that would never have occurred to her in actual life, or to any but very intimate friends. A variety of dresses were displayed, and as I was looking at a black-net evening dress, with crimson trimmings, thinking it was very like one of my own, a sudden transformation took place. Mrs. Y. had changed into Mrs. X., and the dress was a widow's dress complete.

I woke very strongly impressed with the dream, and mentioned it to my father the next morning. It haunted me till, on May 15th or 16th, I saw the *Times* announcement of Mr. X.'s death. Afterwards I learnt that, on the afternoon preceding my dream, Mr. X. had returned home, apparently in his usual good health, only rather tired, but within half-an-hour had died of quite unsuspected heart disease. My father was ill at the time of my dream, and does not remember the circumstance. But my sister remembers it clearly and testifies to the fact.[254] — MISS A. E. R.

☛ CASE #239: Whilst staying at Mrs. M.'s in June, 1867, on the night either of June 3rd or 4th, I had a vivid dream that I saw an old friend [name given in confidence] lying dead with a wound in his head, noting the colour of his hair and other particulars.

I told Mrs. M. of this dream, and later in the day we heard that the friend I had seen in my dream had actually been killed by a blow on the head, in a fall from a conveyance, on the night before the dream. The wound was on the opposite side of the head from that seen in my dream. The scene of the accident was some miles from the house where I was staying.[255] — J. R.

☛ CASE #240: I dreamed that I was at Hastings, on the shore. I saw my friend, Miss Adams, running towards me. She passed me by, and then took off her hat and bent her head down into the sea. I tried to grasp her by her clothes, but she cried out, "Don't stop me, for my mother is dying."

In the morning I jumped out of bed on hearing the post [mail], and said to Marianne Varah, "Have you had a letter from Miss Adams? There must be something the matter with her mother."

Miss Varah answered: "I have a letter, but have not opened it. I have had a very strange dream, but I thought nothing of it, because Mr. Adams is so ill."

Miss Varah then opened her letter, and called out, "You are right." There were a few lines, "My mother is dangerously ill; doctors say no hope. We will send a telegram."

The telegram came during the morning of February 24th, 1876, saying she was dead. She had been in perfect health the day before. Neither Miss Varah nor myself are at all given to dreams, and had not till then believed in them at all. January 1885.[256] — EMILY E. MULLER

☛ CASE #241: Some 40 years ago my father was house-surgeon at the City of Dublin Hospital, and one day a young man, a sailor, was brought in who had fallen from one of the yards of the vessel on which he served. He was badly injured, and in about three days he died.

Late in the afternoon of the day on which the man died, an old woman, very poor and fagged, came up to the hospital and asked to see the surgeon. My father saw her and inquired what he could do for her; when she inquired whether a young sailor had been brought to that institution, and if so, could she see him. My father told her of the man above mentioned, and that he had died that morning.

It turned out that the old woman was the young man's mother, that she lived in the Co. Carlow, and that three nights previously she had dreamt that her son had fallen from the rigging of the vessel and had been taken to an hospital. So vivid was the dream that she could not rest till she got to Dublin (where she had never been before), and the moment she saw the hospital she recognised it as the building she had seen in her dream.

Her dream was only too true, for she found that her son had died from the effects of injuries occasioned by a fall just as appeared in her dream. The old woman had walked a distance of over 60 miles, and entered the city by the road which passed the front of the hospital. January 2nd, 1884.²⁵⁷ — A. W. ORR

☛ CASE #242: Some years ago I had young children who were allowed, when in the drawing-room, to amuse themselves with playing with a set of red and white ivory chessmen. They were not allowed to take the chessmen into their nursery. It was their mother's constant habit to visit her nursery almost immediately on rising in the morning.

One morning she dreamed that she had received a letter from a brother in a distant part of the world, in which he enclosed the upper half of the head and neck of a red ivory chess-knight, saying that he thought it must belong to her. On waking, and going as usual into the nursery, her eldest little boy ran up to her, saying, "Oh, mamma, see what I have found," and holding up the head of an ivory chessman—a knight.

A good instance of the sympathy on which all true thought-reading must depend. Probably, into a dream about a letter from her brother intruded the idea of the red knight's head, and was blended with it. January 28th, 1885.²⁵⁸ — REGINALD COURTENAY

☛ CASE #243: On the morning of the 18th July, 1874, at 2 o'clock I woke up with a loud sigh from the following dream or vision. It seemed like a succession of dissolving views.

First I saw in a glimmer of light, a railway train and the puff of its engine, as it were, in the corner of the room; I thought "What's going on up there? Travelling? I wonder if any of us are travelling, and I dreaming of it."

Then a voice of some one, unseen, seemed to me to answer "No! something quite different." I felt unwilling to see it.

Then I saw, behind my head, my twin-brother William, the upper half of him, lying as it were half up, leaning back; eyes and mouth half open. His chest moved for a moment convulsively; he raised his right arm; then bent forward; muttering "I suppose I should move out of this."

I felt somehow glad that he moved. Then I saw him lying flat on the ground at my side, the chimney of an engine behind him. I called out "Oh that will strike him." He seemed then leaning up on his elbow, startled, and saying "Is it the train, the train?" His right shoulder then shaking, and reverberating as if struck rapidly from behind. He fell back; his eyes rolled, an arm was thrown up.

Then something like panelling of wood passed by, and the whole went off with a swish, leaving what seemed a faint gleam of moonlight in the distance.

Next, there appeared before me in very bright light a compartment of a railway carriage, and in the window of this a young clergyman I had only seen once, the minister of the district where my brother had been residing. A porter went up to him and seemed to ask, "Have you seen anything of ____?" Mr. J. seemed to answer "No!" And the porter ran off.

After all this I saw the full figure of my brother at my side, standing. He put his hand over his face and began slowly to move away. I seemed to call out "Is he going?" The voice that seemed to speak always from over my head answered "Yes"; and then seemed to moved along over my brother's head. I saw then a pale face as of one figure and the back of another ushering him, as it were, along.

I then woke, as I have said, with a loud sigh; and my husband, waking up with the start, asked me what was the matter. I felt very unwilling at the time to repeat what I had seen, and only saying I had been dreaming about a railway and asking him "what was that light?" though there was none in the room. I fell asleep at once, tired out.

At this time I had no anxiety about my brother; but a few days after this dream my husband received a letter from that same clergyman, and telling of my brother being killed by a railway train on the night of the 18th July, and that the fatal accident must have occurred about half-past 9 or 10 o'clock. This clergyman was in the train that killed my brother! It would seem that my brother had started in the cool of the evening from the village where he had been residing, with the intention of walking to a town about 15 miles off; that he had chosen, possibly as the nearest road, the railway line; that he had felt tired and heated, taken off his boots, lain down on the sloping bank, very likely dozed off; and, startled and confused by the rapid rush of the approaching train, tried, by a convulsive effort, to get up, and was struck while rising by some projecting part of the train. It was on the head and the right shoulder that it struck him.

I may add that I retired that evening in a strongly nervous state, and while undressing had the sensation as if something or some presence was in the room! Perhaps I should add that the scene of the fatal accident to my brother was some 400 miles distant from my own home at the time.[259] — MRS. S.

☛ CASE #244: In 1874, when reading for college, I frequently visited a man named William Edwards (of Llanrhidian, near Swansea), who was then seriously ill; he often professed pleasure at, and benefit from, my ministrations. He at length recovered so far as to resume work. I left the neighbourhood, and amid new scenes and hard work, I cannot say that I ever thought of him.

I had been at college some 12 months, when one night, or rather early morning, between 12 at midnight and 3 in the morning, I had a most vivid dream. I seemed to hear the voice of the above-named William Edwards calling me in earnest tones. In my dream I seemed to go to him and saw him quite distinctly. I prayed with him and saw him die. When I awoke the dream seemed intensely real, so much that I remarked the time, 3 a.m. in the morning. I could not forget it and told some college friends all particulars.

The next day I received a letter from my mother, with this P.S.: "The bell is tolling; I fear poor William Edwards is dead."

On inquiry I found that he did die between 12 and 3; that he frequently expressed the wish that I were with him. I had no idea that he was ill.

[To reconfirm:] My dream took place between midnight and 3 in the morning. William Edwards died within that time. My mother wrote her letter just after breakfast, when the death-bell was tolling for him. Just at the time I mentioned my dream to some friends. I received the letter either the next night or the morning after. It was generally a two-days' post.

I was particular to inquire if the death took place the night of my dream; it did. I have not the date of the occurrence, but can get it, no doubt, from inquiring the date of the man's death. I had no object in making any note of it then.

The friends, I believe, were Rev. G. L. Rees, Howden, Rev. J. W. Roberts (dead), and, I think, the Rev. T. S. Cunningham; I will ask him.

I have on other occasions dreamt of deaths, but have not taken any trouble to investigate them. I have sometimes dreamt I saw a person dying, and then heard they were ill. The vividness and reality of the case I mention caused me to take such notice of it. May 1885.[260] — REV. W. D. WOOD REES

☛ CASE #245: On Palm Sunday morning, 15 years ago, I awoke with a start about 4 o'clock, having dreamed that some one had been on the lawn in front of my house and taken away about 50 roots of wall flowers which I had in bloom, and that the only thing left was a portion of blossom which had dropped near the entrance gate.

I at once related my dream to my wife, and afterwards slept

until about 8 o'clock in the morning, when I awoke through the servant girl rapping at my bedroom-door and shouting in an excited state, "A donkey has been on the lawn and eaten up all the flowers."

I immediately got out of bed and looked out of the window, and the first object I saw was the bit of blossom by the gate where I had previously seen it in my dream, and I found the border relieved of every root as I had dreamed.

I have, ever since, felt satisfied that if I had got out of bed and looked out of the window at the time I first awoke, I would have found the thief in the act of taking away the flowers. I should say that the gate was locked, so that it was impossible for any animal to have done the mischief. May 7th, 1885.[261] — MR. R. EVANS

☛ CASE #246: I received your letter on the 24th inst., and would have answered before now, but that I have been ill and depressed in spirits. I have no objection in telling you what I dreamt on two occasions, namely, the 2nd of November last, and the 5th of January, the date of husband's death.

My husband was at home with me from the 26th to the 30th of October last, when he left me to join his steamer *Alfonso* at Garston, some miles further up than where we live. I went to the station with him. He had wished the children and myself good-bye in the house, but, as he was turning from me to enter the train, I drew him back and kissed him, and he left me, smiling as he entered the train; and that was the last I saw of him, as they were sent to Scotland next voyage.

But two nights after he left I dreamt that one man came to me and told me there had been a collision with another steamer, and that the Alfonso had sunk with all hands except himself. I thought I knelt at his feet and said the words: "For the love of heaven, don't tell me that!" and I awoke with a scream.

The next day, Saturday, I spent very depressed, and decided upon going to Newport, where they were bound for. Then again I thought I'd wait until Sunday for a letter from him, which came all right, telling me they had arrived safely with the exception of a slight collision on their way round to Holyhead on the Thursday morning; so I naturally thought that dispelled my dream. But I told it to my husband in my letter that I wrote on the same Sunday to him, and before sealing it I said to myself three times, "Shall I ask him to come home?" but I didn't, as I thought he would think me silly.

So they went away on that voyage and were away nearly seven weeks, letters being exchanged between us in the meantime. I told that dream to a lady living two doors from me, and also about getting my letter mentioning the slight collision; but it was this last collision that I dreamt of. If I had only gone to Newport then, I might have saved all their lives, but I suppose it is the will of God, and that was the death destined for them.

Well, my second dream was on the very morning of their death, as Captain Burnett tells me it happened between 1 and 2 o'clock on Sunday, the 5th January. I dreamt I was in the field fronting our house and overlooking the river, when they passed on their way to sea. All my five little children were with me, ranging from ten years to my baby six months old. I thought we saw a small white boat coming in from sea with six men in her; all were rowing, but as they came nearer to us they rested on their oars, and just as they came in front of us I said to the children: "There is your father and Mr. O'Neil on the seat in front"; but I did not see the other men's faces, but as they were drifting past me my husband turned his face to me, and smiled. I said to the children, "Wave your hands in good-bye to your father," doing the same myself, and as we did so every man's oar went up in salute to us. I watched them as far as I could see, and said to myself, "What a strange way to come home."

I awoke with a happy restful feeling, holding my baby's hand. I lit a match and looked at my watch, and it was between a quarter and twenty minutes to two o'clock. I was awake nearly until seven, when I got up to prepare for church at eight, and when coming home I went as far as the river, and thought of my husband and the other men.

There was a letter waiting for me when I came home from him, which he had written on New Year's Eve, telling me they were leaving Carthagena that evening for Maryport, and that all was well with them in every way. So I thanked God for His mercy in watching over them, little thinking what had happened that same Sunday morning.

So I heard nothing further until Monday evening, [January] 6th, when the news was called out in the streets, as we had no intimation from the owners in any form. But the shock to me of the sudden news has been terrible, especially as I was nursing my little baby at the time. I have not realised it yet, nor [ever] will—with never seeing his face in death.

We were married just thirteen years on the 11th December last, and we never had one word of dispute in that time. He was just as happy to get home to us as we were to see him, and our thoughts always seemed to be [the] same, no matter on what subject. . . . I have not seen my friend who lives at 23 in the same block, but I don't think she would object to make a statement if you wished it. I may add that I've had other warnings, and can recall them quite distinctly, relating to death. I have written the truth, word for word, and you are at liberty to make what use you like of it.

[Note:] I mentioned the first dream of the collision before I heard anything, but the second one of seeing my husband and the men in a boat, I spoke of to no one, except to my eldest boy, aged 10 years, until after the disaster. I spoke of it to some people, and I had hope that they [might] have been saved until I saw the captain. The cargo was iron, so they must have sunk almost immediately. January 31st, 1902.^{262} — MRS. SULLIVAN

☛ CASE #247: I was staying from the 20th of last March until Tuesday the 1st of April, at a place where I have been frequently and for many years, called by my official inspections, and with which, therefore, I am well acquainted. My recent stay there included two Sundays, Palm Sunday, the 23rd, and Easter Sunday, the 30th of March, on both of which days I went to services at the Parish Church as usual.

On the night of Monday, the 31st, I had a ridiculous dream. I thought I was standing among a row of others in a front pew, next to a lady who was my governess when a child, and whom I have not seen for some years, nor has anything recalled her specially to my mind. My governess was behaving in a very unsuitable manner, for she continued to talk and laugh aloud, in spite of my efforts to stop her. Thereupon, the Vicar, who was standing in the reading desk immediately in front of us, stepped out of it in a very angry and rude manner, and came up to me, apparently with the intention of pushing or striking me; but I looked him up and down with such severity that he contented himself with touching me with one finger. He then turned his attentions to my governess, and slapped her vigorously with a black glove which he held in his hand.

Next day, Tuesday, the 1st of April, I was discussing the Easter services with a lady who has been for many years a resident in the place, and I told her of my absurd dream. She then said how curious it was that the Vicar should persist in wearing gloves in church, and told me that he always, at every service without exception, wore a glove on one hand, carrying the other; it had been a subject of annoyance to his congregation ever since he had been there.

Now, it may seem strange that I had never myself noticed this, often as I have been to the church. But I am not in the habit of looking at the clergyman in church, and at this place I generally sit quite at the further end. I cannot remember, even now, ever having seen the gloves, or heard any one speaking of them, and I was altogether surprised at hearing that the clergyman wore them. I suppose I must have seen them unconsciously, and that my sub-conscious knowledge came out in my dream. May 12th, 1902.[263] — MISS M.

☛ CASE #248: I send you an account of an incident which has just taken place in my household.

I have a silver cream jug which I value very much, as it belonged to my great-grandmother; on Christmas Day it was missing. It had been used the Sunday before, and the housemaid in whose charge it was thought she had put it away as usual in a closet at the top of the house. She and her fellow-servant hunted for it without success. I have had one servant five years, the other more than one; they are both perfectly honest and respectable.

This morning the housemaid came in excited to my friend, Fräulein Müller, saying she had found the jug. She told me afterwards the same story which she told Fräulein Müller, that she dreamed in the night some one told her it was on a certain box. This box, a black portmanteau, stands on the landing with others, near the closet where the silver is kept. The dream made such an impression on her that she went to look, and on moving the boxes found the jug fallen down by this special black portmanteau. I enclose Fräulein Müller's account and the servant's as it was taken down from her dictation.[264] — A. R. MARTEN

☛ CASE #249: Two men lost their lives in the Severn at Bewdley on March 22, and it was not until Wednesday that the first body—that of Stephen Price—was found. At the inquest yesterday afternoon at Stourport, Thomas Butler, who found the body, said it was owing to a dream the night before that he visited the spot where he found the body. It was six miles from the scene of the fatality. A verdict of "Accidentally drowned" was returned, the coroner remarking on the curious circumstance of the dream. April 18th, 1903.[265] — FROM A NEWSPAPER

☛ CASE #250: In December, 1870, Mr. Pickernell received a letter from Lord Poulett in which the nobleman asked him to ride "The Lamb" in the Grand National [Hunt Horse Race]. His lordship informed him that the previous night he twice dreamed that he saw the race run. The first time "The Lamb" was last, and the second time had won by four lengths. Mr. Pickernell rode him . . . at Liverpool, and the horse won by four lengths.[266] — *PALL MALL GAZETTE*, APRIL 7TH, 1903

☛ CASE #251: In answer to your request with reference to my wife's dream, I hereby state that my wife had gone to the theatre with a friend. On going to the front door I looked behind as I sometimes do, to see if there were any letters. I found one from my wife's sister, Julia. As we had received one from her only a day or two before, I thought something must be the matter, so I opened it and found it was a request from her for particulars of her birth entry in a family Bible. I hunted about and found it in a box of old books that had come from the old home.

When my wife came in she saw the Bible, and said as soon as she got inside the door, "What have you got that old Bible for? I was dreaming about it last night. I dreamed that Julia wanted it to get her birth entry from it."

I had not had even a chance to speak to her before she got that out, nor had she seen the letter, because I had put it behind the tea-box on the mantel-shelf where we usually put our letters after reading them. I was so much struck with the remarkable coincidence that I told my fellow-workmen about it in the morning. April 6th, 1903.[267] — R. H. HOPE

☛ CASE #252: In the year 1891 or 1892, I cannot say which, but it was the year in which [the famous racing horse] "Sir Hugo" won the Derby, I was stationed at Halifax Barracks; Captain Robert Marshall of my regiment was stationed there also.

A few days before the Derby was to be run, Captain Marshall came in to breakfast in the mess, and said he had dreamt the winner of the Derby, that he had seen the race run, and had heard the crowd shouting the horse's name. On being asked the horse's name, he said he could not remember, but would know it, if he heard it.

We accordingly read out the names of the horses mentioned in the betting [section] from a newspaper, but he said the name was not there.

The next day we looked in the paper again, and read out amongst other names of horses that of "Sir Hugo," which was not mentioned in the issue of the previous day. Immediately the name "Sir Hugo" was mentioned, Captain Marshall said, "That is the horse, that is the one I saw win in my dream, I shall back it. I heard the crowd shouting out, 'Hugo Victor, Hugo Victor.'"

Captain Marshall backed "Sir Hugo" to win, and persuaded me to do the same, so positive was he, though I was very sceptical.

It is a matter of history that "Sir Hugo" won. Captain Marshall informed me that before going to sleep on the night in which his dream occurred, he was reading a book by Victor Hugo.[268] — C. A. FEDDEN

☛ CASE #253: In the matter of P.C. Wheeler's dream, it appears that on August 3rd, 1903, Miss Eva Seabrook, of 6 Raglan Street, Forest Hill; Miss Lilly Dudley, of 11 Clyde Place, Forest Hill; and James Baldwin, address unknown, were in a boat with Mr. Risley on the lake in the south corner of the grounds of the Crystal Palace.

During the afternoon the boat overturned; Risley was drowned, and the others saved by a soldier and some bystanders.

On October 31st, I visited P.C. Wheeler at his house, No. 31 Barnfield Road, Gipsy Hill, and showed him the following report of his dream and its fulfilment. He acknowledged its substantial correctness . . . November 13th, 1903.[269] — LIEUT.-COLONEL TAYLOR

☛ CASE #254: A young lady lives with us who is a Kindergarten Teacher. She is the intimate friend and companion of her head-mistress, who was engaged to be married next Christmas. She often went for walks and outings with the affianced couple. Both were dear to her. He was Art Master at the Pupil Teachers' Centre.

One morning about three weeks ago our young lady came down to breakfast in a very excited and gloomy state, and said that she had been terribly upset by an awful but very vivid dream. She had dreamt that the Art Master had been suddenly taken ill, and that the Head-Mistress had gone to nurse him, but that in spite of every effort they had failed to save his life.

I said "Pooh, pooh, dreams go by the contrary, it refers to the wedding."

She said, "It has upset me very much; it seemed so real."

That day she asked her friend how her fiancé was, who answered that he was splendid. "Because," said she, "I dreamt last night he was very ill."

"Oh," replied her friend, "he was as strong as a lion last night anyhow."

During the day she remarked, "I shall be glad to see him to-night, your dream has made me somewhat anxious."

She met him and found that he had contracted a slight cold. The slight cold lasted a fortnight and then developed into pneumonia.

His fiancée went to nurse him. Every effort was made to save him, but he was buried at ____ churchyard yesterday. December 10th, 1903.[270] — REV. A. T. FRYER

☛ CASE #255: On Monday, September 28th, 1903, Miss Elliott casually said to me that she intended going to Sunderland on the following Saturday, to see a friend.

That night I had a vivid dream: Miss Elliot came to me to show a letter which she had received from her Sunderland friend, asking her to postpone her visit, as bad news—some family trouble—necessitated her immediate departure.

I was much surprised when on the next day I told this dream to [her to] hear that a letter in actually the same words had been that morning received by Miss Elliott. I may add I do not profess to attach any importance to dreams, and it is quite an unusual thing for me to relate one.[271] — MISS M. ROBSON

☛ CASE #256: The following two accounts [concerning simultaneous dreaming] were enclosed in a letter from Miss Raleigh, dated April 28th, 1904, and were, she says, written by the witnesses independently of each other. They gave their full names and addresses, but wished initials only to be printed. — S.P.R.

[First account from the first sister, Miss M. L. B.:] On the evening of November 18th, 1903, I, M. L. B., retired about half-past nine o'clock and fell asleep. I had a most peculiar vision or dream. I thought I was walking through streets in a strange place; it was artificially lighted; there were a number of people walking to and fro on either side of the streets.

I heard a peculiar noise, and turned partly round to see what was the cause of it. A vehicle was coming rushing across the top of the street; I was a few paces down; it looked something like a train, but not a train, it was running on metals; something was coming down where I had crossed; there was an awful crash as if my (so-called) train had run upon something, and in a moment something heavy fell with a sickening thud on the pavement, at my feet. I tried to cry out, but could not.

In a moment a crowd had collected, and several people picked up the body which had fallen at my feet. I could see it was a man. I could not see the face, only a large gash on the back of the head, and near the lips, from which the blood was flowing. As the drops fell they splashed into a puddle of blood on the ground and sprinkled on to me. Some one said, "Take him away."

I tried to cry out, "What shall I do?" and awoke trembling and perspiring, and crying bitterly. I could not think where I was, [but] found I was in bed, and had been dreaming, as I supposed.

I lay quite still for fear of disturbing my sister. In a short time my sister lit a match and looked at her watch, and said, "It is past eleven o'clock." I did not tell her of my dream, as I did not wish her to worry. I thought it strange for her to get a light and tell me the time.

I was fearfully worried for some days.

On the Monday morning following, I had another dream. I dreamed my brother, H. B., (I had not seen him since the previous January, or even heard from him) was lying ill in a strange room, and a man was putting him in an ambulance. I thought he said, "Take my sister away, I am not fit to be where she is." He looked so strange, I awoke again in great agitation.

On the same evening a young friend, Miss P., came to call, and my sister left us alone. After she had gone I said, "R., have you heard if my nephew, or any one belonging to me, has met with an accident, and they will not tell me, as I have had such strange dreams and feel I don't know what to do with myself. I feel haunted. I have not felt like this since just before Mother died."

I told my dreams and cried very much. She said, "Don't fret," and assured me she had heard nothing concerning any one belonging to me. I still felt miserable.

On the 26th of November we received the news that our brother, H., was lying ill in F_____ Infirmary, in a precarious condition; on the 27th we received the news that he was dead, died the previous day after the letter was posted to us. On the paper enclosed you will find all the main information we received regarding our brother's accident and death. If you compare the dates you will find the accident happened at the time I was dreaming about it. I had better state here I have never seen an electric tramcar. What I have written here is perfectly true. I have not seen my brother either living or dead since a year last January, as I was much too ill to go to his funeral.

[Second account from the second sister, Miss H. M.:] November 18th, 1903, I went to bed at 10 p.m. and was going to sleep when a loud crashing sound roused me, and the voice of my brother followed saying, "Oh Duck, I am done for." I covered my eyes and said, "Oh H., is it your face that is hurt?" He said "No."

The horror of it was extremely depressing. It was about 11:15 and I could get no sleep through the night, it worried me so.

I had not seen my brother since the previous January, and he had not written to me since. Duck was his pet name for me.

[3rd account by their mutual friend Miss P.:] On the 23rd of November, 1903, I. R. P., went to _____ to see my friend Miss M. B. On the 23rd of November my friend told me of her distressing dream that she had dreamed on the 18th of November, 1903; it seemed as if she could not forget it, she said that it seemed to worry her so. The time that my friend told me about her dream was between the hours of seven and eight o'clock in the evening, and my friend said it was some one had met with an accident, and the face was hurt, but [she] could not see who it was, and my friend said that it looked like a train, and yet not so, as it had no engine on, and my friend has never seen an electric car at all, and she could not forget her dream; and then on the 26th of November my friend had news about her brother's accident.[272] — R. P.

☛ CASE #257: On the night of Friday, January 22nd, 1904, I had a vivid dream. I saw my old friend, Dr. X., who left Cambridge about 10 years ago, and I had not seen him since, sitting by my side. He took hold of my hand saying, "Why have you not been to see me?"

I said, "Oh! I've been so busy that I've not been able to get away. You are so altered since I saw you last."

"Yes," he said, "but that is so long ago." He then disappeared.

The dream so impressed me that I told it to my husband at breakfast the next morning, Saturday 23rd, and also to a friend who knew the doctor on the 25th.

On Saturday morning, the 30th, my husband at breakfast said he had received a memorial notice of Dr. X.'s death, which took place on the 23rd instant, the day after my dream. February 11th, 1904.[273] — MRS. MANN

☛ CASE #258: In the summer of 1901 I went into camp with the Durham L. I. Volunteers. Whilst there I took some photographs which I developed at home when I came back. The negatives were roll films, and were neglected for some few days owing to stress of work. When a fellow Volunteer asked me for a photograph I could not find the films in my photograph cupboard, nor did a thorough search in all possible drawers and cupboards bring them to light. This was aggravating, for my friends would ask for prints very frequently.

At last they slowly began to give up asking, but about a month after I lost the negatives, another request reminded me of their mishap, but as they were given up for lost, I thought no more about it.

That night I had a vivid dream; in fact, I am not subject to dreaming, and I never remember having dreamt so "well" as to remember much about it next day. But I did remember this one in detail. I dreamt that I knew where the negatives were, that I went and found them there, and that I was not at all surprised at the occurrence.

Next morning I woke with the dream in my mind. I went immediately to my father's wardrobe, took down an old coat, which at times I wore indoors, and drew out the missing negatives. I felt certain they were there, but could not think how they came to be there. I felt I was merely repeating what I had done in my dream. As I never remember carrying negatives in my coat pockets at any time, or even putting them in any pocket, the circumstance that in the dream I "knew" that they were there is interesting.

No one in the house remembered placing them there, and consequently I had no previous suggestions from them concerning the coat. January 25th, 1905.[274] — MR. L. G. REED

☛ CASE #259: I have received your note of 20th inst. about a dream or experience of a mother regarding a fatal accident to her son,—some seventy or eighty miles away,—both undoubtedly occurring within a few minutes of each other.

The people concerned are all so respectable, and so far removed from any suspicion of creating a sensation either about themselves or others that I don't think the facts can be questioned. Even the small discrepancies, such as the dream bridge being the railway bridge visible from the parents' house, and not the one at Paisley Station where the accident occurred, the mother still insists upon.

I propose getting a statement from the mother and from all others who can confirm her story at first hand, signed by each. I shall also ask the Hospital Authorities at Paisley to let me have a full note of the time of admission to the hospital and nature of the injuries of the patient. (He died the morning after admission, but was conscious when found on the railway.) So soon as complete, I shall forward you the statements, and I shall be most careful to be as accurate as possible in every detail, and have independent confirmation where possible.

The dreamer is the least likely woman to have had such a strange experience a solid, matter-of-fact, practical, hard-working woman of the smaller farmer class, who "had had dreams like other people, but never paid the smallest attention to them, and never once thought or believed all her life that they might come true." [Mr. Clarke's subsequent report follows.]

Before replying to your letter of the 23rd ult. I waited till I could get a personal interview with the "dream" woman. The following is a clear statement got from her the other day. She is absolutely trustworthy.

Mrs. Kerr, Gateside, Holywood, Dumfriesshire, one night in June ten years ago, retired to bed at 10 o'clock. She fell asleep shortly after, and dreamt that she saw one of her sons—a fireman on a passenger train,—hanging on to the tender of an engine. As the engine passed through a bridge her son's head struck the masonry and he fell, the wheels seeming to "pass up along his body." She saw that his right arm was seriously injured and his right leg completely severed below the knee, the boot being on the foot. He raised his hand to the right side of his head, which she saw was seriously injured.

She woke with a scream, the hour being ten minutes to 11 o'clock. She woke her husband and told him, who tried to assure her it was only a dream. (This the husband has confirmed to me.) Unable to rest, she got up, lighted the fire, and went to a neighbour's house, Mrs. Dickson, now dead,—to whom she told the story. She also woke Mrs. Mundell, Holywood Kirkhouses, (still alive), and asked her to send her son, young Mundell, with a message to her own son who lived at a distance, begging him to come to her, as an accident had happened to his brother.

Before the arrival of the two young men, a telegram arrived at Holywood Station at 2 a.m. summoning Mr. and Mrs. Kerr to Paisley Infirmary, as their son had met with a serious accident at Paisley Station the night before.

Before starting for Paisley in the morning Mrs. Kerr told M'Ardle, the Station-Master at Holywood, (and still there), about her dream, asserting that her son's injuries were of such a nature that he must either be dead, or that he could not possibly recover.

On their arrival at Paisley the son was still alive, though

unconscious, and he died shortly after. His injuries were exactly as she had seen in her dream. At the coffining the same night she noticed the absence of the right leg, and on asking for it, it was produced with the boot still on the foot. The only discrepancy between the dream and the reality was that the bridge where the accident occurred, (which she visited and saw hair and blood on the stonework), was outside Paisley Station, while she insists that the bridge of her dream was one in view of her Dumfriesshire home.

Mrs. Kerr related to me two somewhat similar experiences. On December 27th, 1903, when walking along the road about 8 p.m., near her home, a light as if from a lantern shone in front of her feet. There was neither light nor person near. Her pallor was so marked when she got home that her relatives asked what had happened. She replied that she did not know, but that something had happened to one of the family. Next morning she received a letter stating that an aunt had died at that time the night before.

When 21 years of age, Mrs. Kerr had promised to sit up with a sick neighbour all night. When about to proceed to the house, the form of the sick woman appeared distinctly before her. Mrs. Kerr said to her friends that there was no need to go now, as the woman was dead. It was found that the woman died at the very time the apparition appeared. Mrs. Kerr says she knows quite well when those experiences signify more than mere dreams. Yours very truly.[275] — FRED. HUGH CLARKE

☛ CASE #260: [In the following case, four persons, all in different places, experience independently in the course of about twelve hours various impressions relating to a certain deceased person. S.P.R.]

April 1st, 1906. I write the following and appended statement of my dream, because of an apparent coincidence concerning it and what has been mentioned to me by Mrs. F. since my telling it to her on last Monday (March 26th).

Mrs. F. told me on 30th ult. that (a) her daughter, Mrs. A., had recently, while reclining on a sofa, seen her sister L., who passed away in November last, and that (b) she herself (Mrs. F.) had felt L. was with her on March 25th about 8:30 p.m. She also mentioned that (c) her sister, Miss P., had seen L. in a kind of vision when travelling. This would be on March 19th. Mrs. F. told me of (a), (b), (c) for the first time on 30th ult., and said that she had been impressed by the coincidences. I have asked her to obtain statements from Mrs. A. and Miss P., and to write a statement herself.

In reference to Miss P. seeing the vision, it is to be noted I have not heard clear details of this, and that I have experienced while in the train a remarkable vision of my friend L. Mrs. F. and I were on March 19th seeing Miss P. off to Scotland, and a little later I was hoping she would have a pleasant journey and that L. would be able to give her the experience I got, or that she might have it even as a corroboration of telepathy from (e.g.) me.

Statement about Dream: About a week or 10 days ago (I have every reason to believe that the night of my dream referred to was that of Sunday, March 25/06) I dreamt that I was in a sort of cellar with other people, Mrs. F. being near me on my right. At my right front was somewhat like the corner of a brick wall. There were bricks in the structure of the cellar. This wall ran directly into the background, but on the right there was space communicating with where I was. I seemed to be at a spiritualist séance.

A form appeared in front of me—I was facing to the background—but slightly to my right. As it became definite I said, "Why, it's L.!" She replied in a joyous lively way, "Of course it is." She seemed absolutely natural, and the picture of health. The complexion was of the pink of health.

I made an exclamation and my voice partly woke me up, and I knew that I was in bed. Then I made some remark asking her to show herself to her mother. (I think I said, "Tell your mother.") Then I thought her mother must see. (As I write now I *believe* L. said to this request, "No, you," but I am not certain.) I think there was pink about her dress. I noticed—or remember—the right shoulder specially: the dress was loose.

[The following report by the S.P.R. editor of her interview with Mr. M. was sent to him for revision and endorsement, and is printed here as amended by him:] April 26th, 1906. Mr. M. called on me on April 23rd and gave me verbally a somewhat fuller account of the incidents described above. The young lady of whom he dreamt, and whom he calls here "L.," had died last November, at the age of about 18; she and all her family were very intimate friends of his.

Not long after her death, while travelling and dozing with his eyes shut in the railway carriage, he saw her face in a sort of mind's-eye vision. It appeared perfectly distinct and life-like, and seemed to smile and look at him. The sight startled him into complete wakefulness, and the vision impressed him a good deal, because it seemed to him quite unique in his experience. He is normally not at all a good visualiser of faces; but has had many vivid dreams at different times—sometimes as vivid as reality. He mentioned this incident to Mrs. F., L.'s mother, but he believed that the rest of the family did not know of it.

On March 19th last, he and Mrs. F. were at the station, seeing her sister, Miss P., off for Scotland, and, remembering his own experience, he hoped that a similar one might occur to her on the journey. This wish was, of course, only expressed mentally; he said nothing about it either to Miss P. or to Mrs. F., and did not hear till some time later from Mrs. F. that it had been fulfilled.

It was on the night of Sunday, March 25th, 1906, that his dream took place. He himself has no doubt that this was the date, though, from a desire to be scrupulously accurate in his statement, he wrote on April 1st that it happened "about a week or ten days ago." He went the next day, Monday, to call on Mrs. F., and told her on that day of his dream.

Mrs. F. states that on the following morning (Tuesday), she heard from her sister of her experience on the Monday morning (March 26th) between 2 and 3 a.m. and on the same evening (Tuesday) heard from her daughter that she had seen L. on the Sunday afternoon. She also states that she herself had felt L.'s presence on the Sunday evening. It thus appears that, besides the less definite impression of Mrs. F., three persons had had a vision or dream of L. within twelve hours of one another, each having recorded or told it before knowing of the experience of the others.

In Mr. M.'s dream he appeared to be in a sort of cellar or underground room with a number of other persons, of whom Mrs. F. was one, at a séance. (He is accustomed to attend séances, but is not a spiritualist.) At his right front there was something like a corner of two walls at right angles to each other, the direction of one of them being straight away into the background, and the other away towards the right. It was immediately in front of him that the form of L. appeared. The form was extremely vivid and life-like. He spoke to it, and the sound of his voice woke him up sufficiently to realise that he was sitting up in bed. He lay back, however, and at once succeeded in going to sleep again and continuing the dream.

He saw L. again and again she seemed perfectly real and life-like. She smiled, and he heard her speak. She moved her hands about as if to indicate something he did not know what—but after hearing of the experiences of his friends he interpreted this movement to mean that she was trying to draw his attention to her dress—a topic on which he is habitually inobservant as a further mark of identity.

Mr. M. was at the time, before hearing of any coincidence with this dream, strongly impressed with its exceptional character. It seemed to carry with it, as to L., a clear sense of reality, involving the absolute conviction that it was L. herself that he saw.[276] — ALICE JOHNSON

☛ CASE #261: On the morning of January 24, my husband said to me on waking, "I have had a very vivid dream about your goldfinch. I saw him lying dead in the pond with the wings out." On going downstairs into the conservatory, as usual, I naturally looked anxiously at the pond, and was agreeably surprised to find that all was well.

Although relieved, I did not feel reassured; and so the next morning was not at all surprised, on going into the conservatory, to see the bird lying dead. The bird was lying dead in the little pond with his wings outstretched. Other birds of mine which have died have died with the wings closed; though others have fallen dead near the pond. I have ten or eleven in my aviary, but only one goldfinch. The goldfinch was a special favourite.

There had been no conversation nor incident which, so far as I can trace, could have suggested the dream. To the best of my belief the bird was in good health. He had made a complete recovery from his autumn moulting. February 11th, 1906.[277] — FLORINE BOWRING

☛ CASE #262: [The following is an interesting account published in the *English Mechanic and World of Science* for September 1st, 1905, of a premonitory—or possibly telepathic— dream of the discovery of the comet Barnard-Hartwig (1886). S.P.R.]

I awoke one morning about 4 a.m. from a very vivid dream of a comet in the morning sky, i.e., in the east, rising before the sun. I was so much impressed that I at once dressed and went out to a small platform upon which I used my 8 in. reflector [telescope]. I put this into position and prepared to sweep for the comet, nothing being visible to the naked eye.

I set the instrument at random, at an altitude of about 30°, and slowly swept it across the sky, using a low-power eye-piece, and during the first sweep the comet came into the field of view.

I intended to despatch a telegram announcing my discovery as soon as the post-office opened, but by the first post I received a paper in which was published the information that the comet had already been discovered by [Edward Emerson] Barnard and the night afterwards by [Carl Ernst Albrecht] Hartwig.[278] — CHARLES L. TWEEDALE, VICAR OF WESTON

☛ CASE #263: April 30th, 1906. A great friend of ours was taken ill on Sunday of this year. The illness developed into pneumonia, and naturally gave us much anxiety, but the complaint attacked only one lung, and there was always hope of recovery.

In the early morning of Tuesday (nine days later), just at grey dawn, I was wakened by hearing my wife wailing and moaning, and I started up, fearing that something was wrong. She was apparently sound asleep, but was calling out, very clearly and distinctly, "O-oh, on Thursday, at four o'clock. On Thursday, at four o'clock."

In the morning I said to her, "What was the matter last night? Were you dreaming a terrible dream? You were moaning and calling out about Thursday, at four o'clock."

She then told me the dream, which I enclose with this letter, and she said that she had dreamt that the doctor had told her that our friend (Mr. C.) would die on Thursday at four o'clock.

Thursday came, but Mr. C. was then easier, and in a few days was almost out of danger.

On the following Thursday, however, he suddenly collapsed, and died at four o'clock.

There can be no doubt as to the time, for my wife (to my knowledge) left our own house a little (perhaps 20 minutes) before that hour, and went with some of Mr. C.'s children direct to their home, which is not more than five minutes' walk from the house in which we live. In about a quarter of an hour after they entered the house Mr. C. died.

I cannot very well ask any of the relatives to verify the hour of death, nor do I care to ask the doctor to do so (he is a cousin of Mrs. C.), but from my knowledge of the time at which my wife left our house I can be certain within a very few minutes, and my wife is absolutely sure of the hour.[279] — MR. L.

☛ CASE #264: One night, in the Autumn or Winter of 1549, while Marguerite de la Valois, Queen of Valois, was asleep, a beautiful [angelic] female, clothed in white, and bearing in her hand a crown composed of every kind of flowers, appeared to her in a dream. The apparition approached her, and held up before her the crown, muttering at the same time the word "Quickly!"

The queen was deeply impressed by the vision, as being a supernatural intimation of her speedy removal [from life], and the crown as a symbol of eternal life. She made preparations for her death, which occurred December 21, 1549. It should be stated that her health had been for some time failing.[280] — *THE SPIRITUAL*

MAGAZINE

☞ **CASE #265:** The shadowy realm of dreams in which the external senses are locked in the repose of sleep, lies around us, weird, mysterious, unexplored, a border-land lying between the glorious realities of the purely spiritual life and this material sphere of existence.

In a recent interview with a patient, an English lady of culture and refinement, the conversation turned upon dreams, and she related several most remarkable dreams from her own experience, that cannot fail to interest our readers. We give them here as related to us, suppressing only the names of the parties.

While yet a girl at boarding school, she dreamed that her father sent for her to come home, and taking her into the library said to her, "Now, my dear, you have been long enough at school. I wish you to marry, and the gentleman I wish you to marry is here in the house, and I shall introduce you to him in the breakfast room." Presently her father rose, led her into the breakfast room, and there introduced to her a gentleman whose every feature she saw in her dream most vividly, and distinctly remembered on waking.

Three nights in succession this dream haunted her sleeping hours.

In about a week there came a letter from her father, summoning her home. She went, and on the morning after her arrival, her father took her into the library, and announced to her in the literal language of her dream, his wishes and intentions regarding her, and then leading her into the breakfast room, he introduced to her the identical stranger whose face she saw in her dreams, and so clearly did she recognize the same form and features, that she nearly swooned from the excess of her emotions.

This lady had an aunt living in the city of London, England. She had visited there when about five years old. In the meantime a cousin of her own age had grown to look marvellously like her. But she had not seen this cousin since the time of her visit there, and knew not of the striking resemblance that existed between them.

She dreamed that she was in her aunt's house in London standing at the foot of a staircase in the hall, and on looking up she saw her aunt stumble and fall down the stairs and lie as if dead, while some one that she thought was herself bent over her in an agony of grief.

She woke as she thought fully, and threw her hand out of the bed over one side, and to her horror it rested upon the cold face of a dead person, who seemed lying in a coffin by the side of her bed.

She screamed with terror, sprang from the bed and procured a light; all was serene and quiet around her.

The dream made such an impression upon her mind that with a pencil she wrote down upon the wall the date, April 25th, 18__.

In due time there came a letter from England informing her father that on the very date of her dream, his sister had fallen downstairs and died instantly from dislocation of the neck. In the letter was a picture of the cousin who in her dream she mistook for herself.

The same lady related an experience that can hardly be called a dream, and yet so full of interest is it, that we cannot forbear relating it in this connection.

She was in the habit of employing a young person in the capacity of seamstress. But she was taken very ill with consumption and obliged to give up her work. After the disease had progressed to that extent that she was confined to her room, this lady would often go in and read to her, and in many ways minister to her comfort. The disease culminated in death, and for several days previously Mrs. M____ herself had been quite ill and unable to get in to see her.

One evening she was lying in her bed looking out upon the Bay of Halifax. It was a glorious night. Her servant had just left her. The moon was very brilliant, but slightly obscured for the passing moment by a floating cloud, throwing a dark shadow upon the water, while in the background a distant flag-ship lying at anchor was bathed in the full radiance of the lustrous moonlight. She was thinking what a lovely picture the scene would make could it be transferred to canvas, when she heard the door of her room open.

Supposing it to be the servant who had returned for something, she spoke and said, "What is wanted?"

Hearing no answer, she turned in bed and to her astonishment beheld standing in her room, the sick girl as she last saw her. She exclaimed "Why, S____, what does this mean? Have those crazy people let you come out to-night?"

She made no reply to this exclamation but advancing towards her said, "Oh, Mrs. M____, I do want to kiss your hand," and reaching out she touched her, but the hand was icy cold, and startled her so that she screamed with fright. The servant came rushing in, but the apparition had vanished.

She told the servant what she had seen, and bade her put on her bonnet and go directly to the house of the sick girl and ascertain why she had been allowed to go out at night. Before the servant could leave the house, a messenger arrived with the intelligence that S____ was dead. She died a few minutes before she presented herself to Mrs. M____, and her last words in dying were, "Oh, Mrs. M____, I do want to kiss your hand."

By what power did the mind reach forward to events in the future, and listen to conversations that seemed dependent on circumstances and sudden mental emotions? How did this spirit recognize persons not known, and appear in scenes not yet transpired? To admit these facts admits almost the whole phenomena of Spiritualism, since we may not limit the capacity of the mind to our sphere, but must recognize its far-reaching power. The body does not intensify mental action, and the spirit far from the body must retain its faculties, and in its wider range must exhibit more perfectly their free action.[281] — THE PRESENT AGE

☛ CASE #266: Soon after her [famous] husband's death, Mrs. [Robert] Burns [Jean Armour] had a very remarkable dream. Her bedroom had been removed to the family parlour, when she imagined that her husband drew the curtains and said, "Are you asleep? I have been permitted to return and take one look of you and that child; but I have not time to stay." The dream was so vivid that Mrs. Burns started up, and even to this moment the scene seems to her a reality.[282] — THE SPIRITUAL MAGAZINE

☛ CASE #267: A few nights ago a lady, while taking a walk, lost a valuable diamond ring from her finger in some unaccountable way. Diligent and extensive search was made, without any clue to the ring, and the lady gave it up as gone "for good and all."

Before daylight the following morning the lady was surprised by the calls of her nurse, a small negro girl. On being admitted to her mistress, the girl, who had not heard of the ring being lost, said she had just had a dream, in which she was apprised when, where and how the jewel had been lost, and that, if allowed, she felt sure she could find it. She then described the place and manner in which the ring disappeared, and begged her mistress to go with her and test the dream.

This strange circumstance was made known to the household, but all treated it with the utmost incredulity.

It was afterwards concluded to humour the girl, however, and she and several white members of the family proceeded to the designated spot, more than one hundred yards from the house. Here the dreamer told her mistress that, as directed in her dream, she must drop another ring, and it would roll as a guide to the missing one. A plain gold ring was handed the girl; she let it fall, and sure enough, it rolled and stopped within two inches of the lost diamond ring, which had got into a crevice between two bricks of the pavement.

It may be imagined that the ring-hunters were somewhat astounded at the miracle. There is not the least fiction about this curious dream and its result.[283] — *LOUISVILLE COURIER JOURNAL*

☞ **CASE #268**: The other day an entry clerk employed in the machine printing room at the works of Messrs. Butterworth and Brooks, calico printers, Sunnyside, [UK], remarked to one of the machine printers that he was glad to see him at his work. The machine printer asked his reason for his congratulation, when the clerk observed that during the previous night he (the clerk) had dreamed that he (the printer) had, while at his work, dropped down dead. The printer replied in a jocular way, "You see you were mistaken, for I am alive yet."

The conversation took place in the presence of respectable witnesses, but as the printer was in his usual health and spirits, no further notice was taken of the matter.

But singular enough, at three o'clock in the afternoon of the same day, the printer, while attending to his duties at his machine, did, without the least warning, drop down dead.[284] — *MANCHESTER COURIER*

☞ **CASE #269**: I may . . . tell you of something that came under the observation of my mother, some twenty years ago.

An acquaintance of hers, a young Mr. W____, was on a ship which in a terrific gale was wrecked on an island off the coast of Africa. News of the disaster was brought to England by another ship and it was supposed that every soul on board had been lost. Mr. W____'s relatives went into mourning, but his mother would not, for she was convinced that he had escaped. And as a matter of record she put into writing an account of what she had seen in a dream.

The whole scene of the shipwreck had appeared to her as though she were an eyewitness. She had seen her son and another man dashed by the surf upon a rock whence they had managed to crawl up to a place of safety. For two whole days they sat there without food or water, not daring to move for fear of being carried off again by the surges. Finally they were picked up by a foreign vessel and carried to Portugal, whence they were just then taking ship to England.

The mother's vision was shortly corroborated to the very

letter; and the son, arriving at home, said that if his mother had been present in body she could not have more accurately described the circumstances.²⁸⁵ — *THE THEOSOPHIST MAGAZINE*

☛ CASE #270: In India, early on the morning of November 2nd, 1868 (which would be about 10 to 11 P.M. of November 1st in England), I had so clear and striking a dream or vision (repeated a second time after a short waking interval) that, on rising as usual between 6 and 7 o'clock, I felt impelled at once to write an entry in my diary, which is now before me.

At the time referred to my wife and I were in Simla, in the Himalayas, the summer seat of the Governor-General, and my father-in-law and mother-in-law were living in Brighton. We had not heard of or from either of them for weeks, nor had I been recently speaking or thinking of them, for there was no reason for anxiety regarding them. It is right, however, to say that my wife's father had gone to Brighton some months before on account of his health, though he was not more delicate than his elder brother, who is (1884) still living.

It seemed in my dream that I stood at the open door of a bedroom in a house in Brighton, and that before me, by candlelight, I saw my father-in-law lying pale upon his bed, while my mother-in-law passed silently across the room in attendance on him. The vision soon passed away, and I slept on for sometime.

On waking, however, the nature of the impression left upon me unmistakably was that my father-in-law was dead. I at once noted down the dream, after which I broke the news of what I felt to be a revelation to my wife, when we thought over again and again all that could bear upon the matter, without being able to assign any reason for my being so strongly and thoroughly impressed.

The telegraph from England to Simla had been open for some time, but now there was an interruption, which lasted for about a fortnight longer, and on the 17th (fifteen days after my dream) I was neither unprepared nor surprised to receive a telegram from England, saying that my father-in-law had died in Brighton on November 1st. Subsequent letters showed that the death occurred on the night of the 1st.

Dreams, as a rule, leave little impression on me, and the one above referred to is the only one I ever thought of making a note of, or of looking expectantly for its fulfilment.[286] — R. VICARY BOYLE

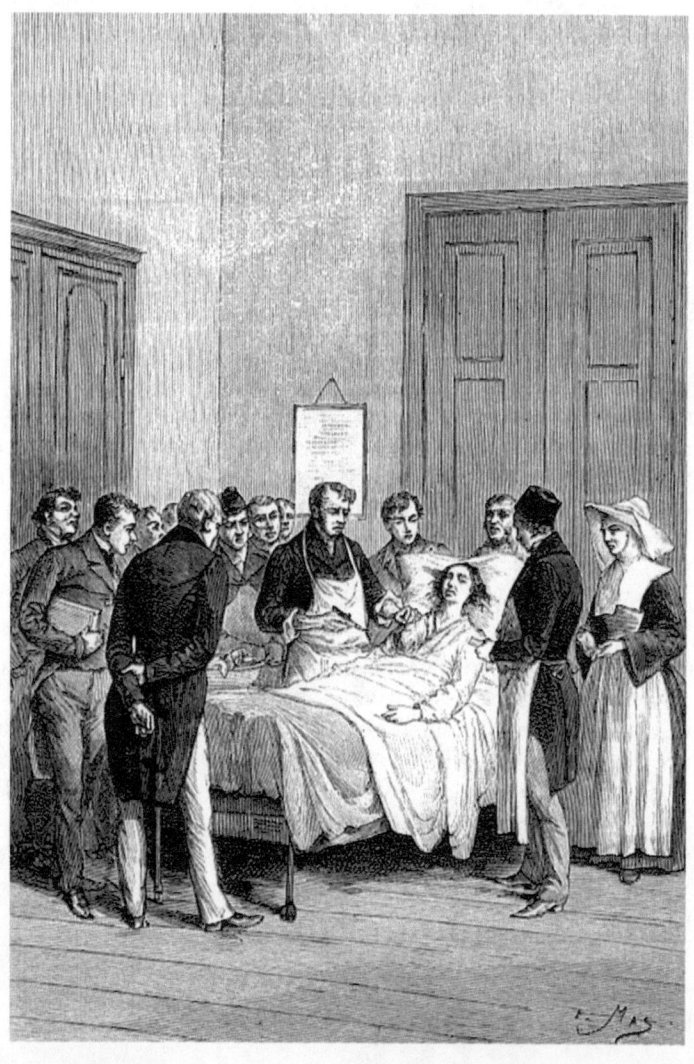

Chapter Four

AUDITORY ACCOUNTS

Cases of Spectral Voices and Sounds

☛ CASE #271: [From the same individual in the previous case.] Some six years after the above occurrence, in the September of 1870, my husband was at D. Hall for his holiday. His parents were then living at Dieppe. He was roused one night by a peculiar moaning, as if some person or animal was in pain. He got up, and went through the house and out into the gardens and shrubberies, but could see nothing. He heard the same noise at intervals all that day, but could not find out the cause.

He returned to London next day to find a telegram summoning him to Dieppe, as his mother was dying. When he got into the house at Dieppe, the first sound he heard was a repetition of the same noise that he heard at D. Hall, and he found it was his mother who was making it, and he learned she had been doing so for two days. She died a few hours after he arrived.

We had no knowledge of Mrs. B.'s illness at the time my husband heard the noise. My husband's parents had been obliged to leave D. Hall under painful circumstances, and possibly the thoughts of her loved home may have been paramount with Mrs. B., or it may have been that they flew to my husband, who was her youngest son.

At any rate, my husband always held that it was his mother's moaning he heard at D. Hall though she was in France. She was speechless when he reached her, so no solution could be arrived at.[287] — E. A. B.

☛ CASE #272: On October 24th, 1877, I was in London, and after preparing to go to bed, I had just extinguished the light when I heard the voice of my sister, who was then in Wolverhampton, call me by my name, "Joanna." I instantly answered, "Yes, Polly."

The voice was low, almost a whisper, but perfectly clear, and I was so sure that she spoke that I turned to the part of the room from which the voice came. Again I heard the voice, and after that, once more, making three times in all.

When I realised that it could not possibly be my sister I felt—not exactly frightened but awed, and I could not sleep till near morning for thinking of it.

The next day I heard from my family that they had had a telegram to say that she was dangerously ill, and some one was to go to her. Another sister went and found her dead, and the time of her death agreed exactly with the time when I heard the voice. She died very suddenly of mortification, and I had not the least idea she was ill; also, we had become estranged from each other, although we were exceedingly fond of each other, and I think that is the reason she spoke to me. May 6th, 1884.[288] — JOANNA WALSH

☛ CASE #273: During the months of May and June, 1881, my brother was staying with us. He went out one Sunday night, between 5 and 6 o'clock. He did not say what time he would return, but his time was generally about 10 p.m.

About 7 o'clock, while I was reading by the window, and Mrs. S. by the fire, all being quiet, I heard a voice say, "David is coming." I instantly turned to Mrs. S., asking what she said. She said, "I have not spoken a word." I told her that I heard some one say that "David is coming."

I then thought I had imagined it; but, lo and behold! in less than three minutes in he came, quite unexpected. I was surprised, but did not mention anything to him about it. The position of the house prevented us from seeing him until just about to enter the house. He was in good health, as we all were at the time.

This is a candid statement of the facts. I shall be glad to give any further information if required. April 20th, 1885.[289] — JOS. STEVENSON

☛ CASE #274: On the 26th of December 1830, about half-past four in the afternoon, Mrs. A. was standing near the fire in the hall and on the point of going up stairs to dress, when she heard, as she supposed, her husband's voice calling her by name, "____ ____ Come here! come to me!" She imagined that he was calling at the door to have it opened, but upon going there and opening the door she was surprised to find no person there. Upon returning to the fire, she again heard the same voice calling out very distinctly and loudly, "Come, come here!" She then opened two other doors of the same room, and upon seeing no person she returned to the fire-place.

After a few moments she heard the same voice still calling, "____ ____ Come to me, come! come away!" in a loud, plaintive, and somewhat impatient tone. She answered as loudly, "Where are you? I don't know where you are"; still imagining that he was somewhere in search of her; but receiving no answer she shortly went up stairs.

On Mr A.'s return to the house, about half an hour afterwards, she inquired why he called to her so often, and where he was; and she was of course greatly surprised to learn that he had not been near the house at the time.

A similar illusion, which excited no particular notice at the time, occurred to Mrs A. when residing at Florence about ten years before, and when she was in perfect health. When she was undressing after a ball, she heard a voice call her repeatedly by name, and she was at that time unable to account for it.[290] — DR. BREWSTER

☛ CASE #275: In the beginning of March, when Mr. A. had been about a fortnight from home, Mrs. A. [of the above entry] frequently heard him moving near her. Nearly every night as she lay awake, she distinctly heard sounds like his breathing hard on the pillow by her side, and other sounds such as he might make while turning in bed.

. . . On another occasion, during Mr. A.'s absence, while riding with a neighbour Mr. ____, she heard his voice frequently as if he were riding by his side. She heard also the tramp of his horse's feet, and was almost puzzled by hearing him address her at the same time with the person really in company. His voice made remarks on the scenery, improvements, etc., such as he probably should have done had he been present. On this occasion, however, there was no visible apparition.[291] — DR. BREWSTER

☛ CASE #276: In the autumn of 1874 my elder brother, W. M., resided in Edinburgh with his wife and family. Taking advantage of the temporary absence of his household on a visit to Glasgow, he went to stay for a few days with a married sister who lived in the country, 18 miles east from town. Previous to this time he had been subject, at irregular intervals, to attacks of illness of a severe character, but, at the date at which I write, was in fair health, and attending to business.

Two or three days after his arrival at our sister's house he was quite unexpectedly seized, late one evening, with serious illness, hematemesis supervened, and within two or three hours from the first seizure he was a corpse. The late hour, and distance from the railway station, prevented any communication during the night with our household in Edinburgh. My brother's wife being also expected to join him in the country next day, it was judged advisable to convey the intelligence to her *en route*, in case after receipt of it she might be unable to make the journey. I mention these latter facts to show that on the night when my brother's death actually occurred, no intelligence of it could possibly have reached our Edinburgh house, where my aged father and mother at that time were residing, and also, for the night, my brother's wife on her way from Glasgow.

Between 11 and 12 o'clock that night my mother, aged then 72, but active and vigorous in body and mind, as indeed she is still, was alone in her bedroom and in the act of undressing. She occupied this room alone, and it was the only sleeping apartment on the dining-room flat which was in use that night, the only other bedroom there being the adjoining room, then untenanted, owing to my own absence in the North. My father, eldest brother, and sister-in-law occupied rooms on the flat above. The servants' accommodation was in the under, or sunk flat beneath, shut off from the upper by a swing door at the foot of a flight of steps. A small dog, the only other inmate of the house, slept that night, and indeed always, in the kitchen.

My mother was in her usual good health, her faculties perfectly preserved, and her mind untroubled with any apprehensions of evil tidings. She had read, as usual, a portion of her Bible, and was in the act of undressing, when she was suddenly startled by a most extraordinary noise at the door of her room, which opened directly into the inner lobby. It was as if made by a person standing directly outside and close to the door, but it was utterly unlike any ordinary summons or alarm. In her own words it was like nothing so much as the noise of someone hastily and imperiously lashing the door with a heavy riding whip, demanding admittance. It was loud, and repeated three or four times, as if insisting on attention, with brief intervals between. Then it ceased.

My mother, though possessed of considerable coolness, was startled, but with a resolution which many might envy, she proceeded to light a candle, knowing the hall lights were extinguished, the whole of the inmates having before retired for the night, and went to the door. "I knew," she said, that it was no one in the house seeking admission. Such an imperative summons would never have been made at my door. On opening it nothing was visible, the various doors opening on the lobby were closed, and the fastening of the front door undisturbed. Much surprised, though retaining self-possession, my mother debated with herself as to rousing the other members of the family, but ultimately resolved not to do so unless the sound was repeated, which it was not. It was about midnight, but my mother did not note the precise hour and minute.

Early next forenoon, my father and sister-in-law having left, the news came that my brother had expired at midnight, 18 miles off by road from Edinburgh.

It may be noted that nothing near or in the door could possibly have occasioned the noise in question, the material being old, well-seasoned timber not liable to warp or crack. It afterwards appeared that the noise in question had not been heard by anyone in the house save by my mother, which no one will wonder at who knows how perfectly "deafened" old fashioned stone houses in Edinburgh invariably are.

Speaking for my own part, I would not have placed so much reliance on the narrative which I have from my mother's own lips, had it come from any other person in the house. The others might have been imaginative or nervous, or wise after the event, or possibly wholly mistaken. But with my mother's clear and balanced judgment, little affected by matters which powerfully sway others, I have no room for hesitation whatsoever. I believe, as firmly as I believe in the fact of my own existence, that the circumstances happened exactly as she narrated them, and also, in her instinctive feeling, at the time of their occurrence, that the sound in question was not accidental or caused by any agency of which we have present cognisance, I believe she was right.[292] — NAME WITHHELD BY THE S.P.R.

☛ CASE #277: I cannot, unfortunately, introduce you to a spectre, and it is difficult to convey an accurate impression of the mysterious annoyances at my old home, which appealed rather to touch and hearing than to sight. They were nonetheless real and distressing. It was difficult for my mother to keep her servants any length of time, and guests seldom renewed their visits to the rectory. Phantom feet trod the passages at night and were heard ascending the staircases, locks turned, doors opened and closed, furniture appeared to be dragged about in unoccupied rooms, viewless hands rustled the bed-curtains and moved across the pillows. Sometimes weird, unearthly screams echoed through the house; and these manifestations were not confined to the hours of night.

But these are generalities.

I will now state a particular incident which appeared to point to influences beyond the ken of our philosophy.

My father was not the incumbent; he was only the curate-in-charge. The rector, a wealthy country squire of old family, although he drew nearly £1,200 a-year from the living, resided on his own estate, never did any church duty, and left the parish entirely in my father's hands, merely paying him a friendly visit now and then.

On one of these visits, when he came accompanied by his wife, my mother eagerly invited the opinion of the latter about the noises which so often disturbed our rest, and proved a constant source of terror to the servants.

"I have no opinion to offer," she replied; "all I know is that the house has so long enjoyed the reputation of being haunted that, in the case of servants, one might suggest superstition, working on an already excited and expectant imagination; but this easy solution is, of course, inapplicable either to strong-minded persons like yourself and Mr. V or to those who had never heard the reports, like your visitors. One of the current legends you may some day have the opportunity of verifying, though I trust that that day is far distant. According to this tradition, no sooner does a rector of B____ die, than a strange, incomprehensible sound proceeds from the landing of the front staircase. This noise, I am told, has been compared to the slashes of a cart-whip falling on a metal tube."

This unromantic comparison excited more merriment than credulity, and the matter was soon forgotten.

A good many months had elapsed, when one autumnal evening, about 9 p.m., my mother was startled by a most unusual disturbance: the loud slashes of a whip on some metallic substance echoed through the passage and down the stairs. No one was to be seen anywhere, and the origin of the sound could not be traced.

Two days later, my father received the tidings of his rector's sudden death. The day and hour of this quite unexpected event coincided with the predicted supernatural warning.

At the time of the rector's sudden death he was on a visit to a countryseat at least 50 miles from the rectory. He was apparently in his usual health and spirits until the moment of the seizure, which in half-an-hour ended fatally. Railways and telegraphs were not, and the place was 16 miles from a coach-road.[293] — NAME WITHHELD BY THE S.P.R.

☛ CASE #278: My mother had been superintending the bathing of her children, and had sent them up to bed. She washed her hands in the bath they had and turned half way back, and was drying her hands when she heard a great splash as if someone had fallen into the bath. She looked round hastily, and was amazed to find not a ripple on the water. She noted the time and date, and afterwards learned that her brother had been drowned at that very time, in a storm at sea. This my mother related to me herself, when I was a girl.[294] — MRS. R. A.

☛ CASE #279: In the autumn of 1859 we were expecting my youngest brother home from Australia, after an absence of eight years. He was a passenger onboard the *Royal Charter*.

The night, or rather in the early dawn of the fatal morning of the wreck of that unhappy vessel, I suddenly started out of my sleep and found myself seizing hold of my husband's arm, horrified at the most awful wail of agony, which appeared to me to fill the house. Finding my husband still asleep—he was a medical man, and had been out the whole of the previous night, so was unusually tired—I slipped out of bed and went round to look at all the children and to the servants' room, but found all quietly sleeping, so thinking it must have been the wind only which so disturbed me, I lay down again, but could not sleep. I noticed that day was just breaking.

In the morning I asked different people if they had been disturbed by any unusual noise, but no one had heard it.

The post brought a letter from a cousin in Liverpool, telling us the *Royal Charter* was telegraphed as having arrived at Queenstown, and we might expect to see Frank very shortly.

We passed the day in most joyful anticipations of the meeting. My mother had his room prepared, a good fire burning, and his night-shirt and slippers laid out for use, and a nice supper ready.

Wheels were heard, but, instead of Frank, my cousin appeared. She, as soon as the awful news of the wreck reached Liverpool, started off herself to bring us the melancholy tidings. Even then I did not connect the fearful sounds I heard with the wreck, but when the newspapers came and I read the accounts of the eye witnesses of the wreck, and of the screams which rent the air as the ship broke her back and all on board were overwhelmed in the waves I could only shudder and exclaim, "*that* was what I heard."

It was months before I could forget the horror which thrilled my very soul at the remembrance of that awful night. A full month later my poor brother's body was recovered with several others, and was brought home to be laid in the dear little churchyard at Kinwarton. I never have had, at any other time than this one, a vivid dream of death, or an auditory hallucination of any kind.[295] —
FRANCES A. PURTON

☛ CASE #280: During a night in the year 1812, or thereabouts, somewhere about 1 or 2 o'clock, as my mother lay half awake, after her first sleep, as it is termed, she was suddenly startled and alarmed by a terrible crash on the window of the bedroom, by which the whole glass was apparently shivered to pieces in a moment; and immediately thereafter, as if in the distance, a low, melancholy wail, though quite distinct, of "O Vale, Vale."

My mother, in great trepidation, instantly awoke my father, and informed him that the whole window was smashed to pieces, so strongly was the circumstance impressed on her mind, begging him to procure a light instantly and ascertain what was wrong, for there was some one outside in terrible distress. My father immediately proceeded to make the necessary investigation and found as perhaps he somewhat expected, the window quite intact, nor was there any storm, the night being comparatively calm, to account for the delusion under which my mother was labouring. She was, however, terribly agitated and insisted that inquiry should be made in the morning of the wife of the captain of a little vessel in which they were all interested, and who lived in the town about a mile distant.

Now, to understand properly the full bearing of all the circumstances attending the singular phenomenon, it will be necessary to relate some previous circumstances and arrangements entered into betwixt my father and certain other parties.

My mother had a special school companion and friend of the name of "Vale" Fenwick (whatever, contraction the Christian name may indicate) who married a young sailor who had been employed as a ship captain, but he had fallen out of employment after their marriage, and, in order to get him a more lucrative appointment, my mother, at her friend's instigation, induced my father to join him in purchasing a nice little brig for £900, of which each paid the one-half. The speculation turned out a very satisfactory one till the time that the curious little incident recorded above happened.

In the morning following the little episode related above, after a sleepless night, my mother's nervous agitation and anxiety for the safety of her early friend's husband, were little allayed, and a messenger was at once despatched to inquire of the captain's wife if she had had recent intelligence from her husband. She replied that she had had a letter from her husband a few days previously, from a port in the Moray Firth, and that they were all well.

Some little time afterwards, on communicating with the authorities at the port, from which the captain's last letter had been sent, my father was informed that the vessel had sailed thence, about eleven o'clock, at the flood-tide, without having shipped any ballast, having only a short distance to sail to another port, where she was to load a cargo, and this was ascertained to be on the very night on which my mother's singular illusion took place; and it was added that there was a rumour that a vessel of her size had been sighted by some boats setting out for the fishing early in the morning on her beam ends or bottom up, somewhere about 3 or 4 o'clock in the morning, and that she had settled down before they had lost sight of her, and this was the last that ever was heard of the ill-fated vessel or her crew.

When the melancholy facts were fairly brought home to the poor wife, she lost her reason for a time, and was ever after so nervous that she could never be trusted alone. There was no previous circumstance, whatever, that could form an association of ideas, or other connecting link, to account for the apparition, or rather, telepathic (?) influence. Of course, my evidence is, in a manner, second-hand, but as young people have always a hankering after the supernatural or ghost stories, we induced my mother to relate the circumstances to us over and over again, and all the minutia seemed quite indelible from her mind, as naturally the loss of the money was a serious consideration for the family, even without the vexation for an early friend, suddenly left in ruin and despair.

As these narrations generally took place in my father's presence, we had his acquiescence in all the circumstances; and as to my mother's veracity, no one could possibly stand higher in the opinion of her family as a lover of the truth.[296] — F. W. H.

MYERS

☞ CASE #281: One night I was awakened out of my sound sleep by a voice close to my ear, saying, "Rise, you have no time to lose"; and words to the effect that the child of this very dear sister was dying, and that she needed my prayers. I cannot remember the exact words, but I felt it was conveyed to me that I had to help her with all the earnestness I could, and there was an awe about it I cannot describe.

Afterwards I found that at this very time on that night her most beloved child had passed through the crisis in diphtheria. Nothing of importance ever happened to any one very dear to me without my feeling it, though I may be far from them.[297] — MRS. C. M. W.

☞ CASE #282: About 30 years ago Miss Mildred Nash, my mother's aunt, died in my mother's house, at the advanced age of 82 years. She had been blind for some years, and an orphan cousin of mine had been much in attendance on her. My aunt lived and died in a room on the ground floor in the front of our house, which was situated in a retired street of Tralee.

A few days after her death my cousin and I were sitting, on a summer evening, at the window of the room over the room in which my aunt had died. I heard distinctly the words "Rosy, Rosy" (my cousin's name) apparently from the room beneath, and in my aunt's voice; then I heard my cousin answer to the call, she also heard the voice.

I, struck with the strangeness of the circumstance, at once threw up the window to see if it were a voice from the street, but there was no one visible, and there could be no one there without being seen. I then searched the house all around, but there was nobody near except ourselves—my cousin and myself. The tale ends there; nothing afterwards happened in connection;—merely the unaccountable fact that two persons did independently hear such a voice as I have mentioned. I heard both the name called, and the answer. January 9th, 1885.[298] — WM. RAYMOND, RECTOR OF BALLYHEIGNE

☞ CASE #283: —I can furnish you with an instance of my name being called by my mother, who was 18 miles off, and dying at the time. I was not aware she was ill, nor was I thinking about her at the time. No one here knew my name, and it was her voice calling, as I was always addressed at home "Lizzy." I can give you more exact information if you require it. Yours truly, E. B. [See letter attached below.]

> The Poplars, Normans Place, Altrincham. March 18th, 1885. In regard to voice which I heard call my name on the 19th February, 1882, I recognised it instantly as being that of my mother. It was very loud, sharp, and impetuous as if frightened at something.
> Our house is detached, very quiet, and the only inmates of the house beside myself were two gentlemen, aged respectively 58 and 37, and a widowed daughter-in-law [of the elder gentleman] who had lived with them five years; and not one of them knew my Christian name. I was thunderstruck, and ran out of my room to see if I could account for the voice. I told the lady the same morning.
> I never saw anything I thought supernatural, and only once before had anything like a similar hallucination. My father and mother were not superstitious people, and a healthier family could not possibly be than ours.[299] — MISS ELIZABETH BURROWS

☛ CASE #284: When I lived at Penketh, about 40 years ago, I was sitting one evening reading, and a voice came to me, saying, "Send a loaf to James Gandy's." I continued reading, and the voice came to me again, "Send a loaf to James Gandy's." Still I continued reading, when a third time the voice came to me with greater emphasis, "Send a loaf to James Gandy's"; and this time it was accompanied by an almost irresistible impulse to get up.

I obeyed this impulse and went into the village, bought a large loaf, and seeing a lad at the shop door, I asked him if he knew James Gandy's. He said he did; so I gave him a trifle and asked him to take the loaf there, and to say a gentleman had sent it.

Mrs. Gandy was a member of my class, and I went down next morning to see what had come of it, when she told me that a strange thing had happened to her last night. She said she wanted to put the children to bed, and they began to cry for food, and she had not any to give them; for her husband had been for four or five days out of work. She then went to prayer, to ask God to send them something; soon after which a lad came to the door with a loaf, which he said a gentleman gave him to bring to her.

I calculated upon inquiry made of her that her prayer and the voice which I heard exactly coincided in point of time. November 24th, 1884.[300] — DR. JOSEPH SMITH, METHODIST

☛ CASE #285: I have received the following account direct from Mrs. Robinson, an elderly lady, now living in Reading.

One evening in the year 1871 she was sitting alone at needlework when she heard the voice of an absent son, Stamford

Robinson (supposed to be abroad, but he had not been heard of for some considerable time), in the passage outside, calling loudly three times, "Nar, Nar, Nar." This was the pet name of an old family nurse, who had stood to all the children almost in a mother's place, owing to Mrs. Robinson's constant attendance on an invalid husband.

She rose and opened the door, fully expecting to find her son in the hall, but seeing no one, resumed her work, and concluded the sound was due to her own imagination.

No sooner had she done so than the same cry was repeated three times as before. This time Mrs. Robinson felt that it was due to some exceptional cause, and a strong conviction that her son was in some trouble, which conviction she expressed to more than one person in the house.

The next day her son arrived home, suddenly and most unexpectedly, in an almost dying condition, and after a three weeks' illness died at a very early age about 25, if I remember rightly. August 19th, 1884.[301] — JESSIE LEETE

☛ CASE #286: On December 29th, or 30th, 1881, about 1 a.m., I awoke hearing my name called. Nobody was in the house, the servants being away for a holiday. I recognised the voice of my father.

Next afternoon I received a telegram saying he was unwell, and on arriving I learnt from the doctor that my father had been unconscious, and had repeatedly called for me during the night in question.

I had no idea of his illness at the time, and believed him to be perfectly well. The attack was very short and severe. He was in Dumfries, and I at Tynemouth, Northumberland. December 1884.[302] — ANONYMOUS

☛ CASE #287: I was deeply interested in the account of our mother's last illness, and was particularly struck by the circumstance of my name being called, because I heard it. I am not accustomed to dream, and am sure I speak far within the mark when I say that I have not dreamed a dozen times since my marriage, 23 years since.

Dreams, too, are supposed to arise from something affecting one's mind, and producing some temporary strong impression, and in this case there was nothing which could affect me in that direction, but some quite the reverse.

Our first horticultural show of the season took place on

November 27th. I won several prizes; and after the show closed at 10 p.m., I had to take home some of my smaller exhibits, and arrange for getting the others home next morning. It was thus near midnight when I reached home, and the only things talked about by ____ and myself afterwards were the show and matters of local interest. If anything, therefore, were likely to be on my mind when I fell asleep, it would probably be one or other of the above matters.

 I do not know how long I slept, but my first sleep was over and I was lying in a sort of half-awake, half-asleep state, when I distinctly heard our mother's voice say faintly, "Harry, Harry!" and when daylight came and I thought the matter over, I wondered what could have possessed me to fancy such a thing.

 Our Uncle C. and his family called me Harry, and Uncle B. sometimes did so, and the D.'s also called me Harry, but with these exceptions I was called Henry by all our relations. It is possible our mother may have called me "Harry" during my very early childhood, but so long as I can remember she always called our father "Papa" and me "Henry."

 It seemed to me, therefore, so utterly absurd that I should fancy her calling me by a name that I never recollected to have heard her use, that I mentally laughed at the idea and wondered how such a thing should have entered my head. Still the circumstance struck me as so strange that I underlined the date on the margin of my working diary in order that if anything should occur to corroborate it, I might be certain as to the time.

 Directly, therefore, after I reached home with S.'s and your letters, I turned to the diary and found the underlined date was November 28th. It was evidently during the afternoon of November 27th that our mother uttered my name (this would have been so, A. F.); and allowing for the difference of longitude, the time would be early morning of the 28th with us, so that I don't think there can be any question that the call actually reached my ear. I am only sorry that I was not sufficiently awake to note the exact time, but should fancy it to have been between 2 and 3 o'clock in the morning, which would represent a few minutes later on the previous afternoon with you.

 The whole circumstance, however, only adds another to the numberless ones which prove that our minds or souls possess powers of which we have, as yet, a most imperfect knowledge, and means of communication with each other which are beyond our finite comprehension. They are, in fact, the strongest evidence, in my opinion, which we have of the existence of the soul; and I believe it is this feeling which leads the class of people who arrogate to themselves the title of "free-thinkers," to try to explain them away or cast doubt upon them, since it is perfectly certain that they cannot be accounted for by the action of any materialistic portion of our being. March 7th, 1874.[303] — VICAR AUGUSTUS FIELD [BROTHER OF THE WRITER, QUOTING A LETTER]

☛ CASE #288: In March, 187_, I went to the curacy of A., and had been, as well as I remember, about a month there, when the following happened.

I am a native of a town in the North of England, and in my childhood had a friend of my own age whom I will call C. Our friendship lasted till manhood, though our circumstances and walks of life were very different, and I had always a great deal of influence over him, insomuch that he would allow himself to be restrained by me when he would not by others. He became, towards his 20th year or so, rather addicted to drink, but I always had the same friendship for him, and would have done anything to serve or help him.

In 187_ his family were living at X [near Z.], and as all my other old friends had long left the neighbourhood of Z, my native town, I always used to go to them whenever I visited that part, as I was and am still on sufficiently friendly terms with them to go at any time without notice.

On the day in question I had been visiting some of the parishioners, and having made an end of this, came to a cross-road of two of the lanes near the church, and not only was I not thinking of my friend, whom I had not heard of for some years, but I distinctly remember what I was thinking of, which was whether to go home to my lodgings for my tea, turning to the left, or whether to trespass on the hospitality of a lady who lived to the right of the crossing.

When thus standing in doubt, a kind of shudder passed through me, accompanied by a most extraordinary feeling, which I can only compare to that of a jug of cold water poured on the nape of the neck and running down the spine; and as this passed off, though I cannot say I *heard* a voice, I was distinctly conscious of the words, "Go to Z by this evening's train" being said in my ear. There was no one at the time within 100 yards of me.

I was not very flush of money just then, and could not well afford the expense, besides not wishing to absent myself from duty so soon after taking it up. But it seemed so distinct that I almost made up my mind to obey it, but on announcing the fact to my landlady, to whom, of course, I could not tell my true reason, she remonstrated so earnestly that, coupling this with the affairs of my duty, etc., I did conclude to disregard it.

I could not, however, settle to anything, read, write, or sit in comfort, till the time was elapsed when I could have caught the train, when the uneasy, restless feeling gradually went off, and in a few hours I was ready to laugh at myself.

Three or four days after I received the sad news that my friend had, on that day, gone down home from London, had been taken ill, and two days afterwards had, in a fit of temporary insanity, put an end to his life. I have no doubt in my own mind that had I obeyed the intimation I might have saved his life, for I must have gone to their house, no other in the neighbourhood being available, and had I found him in the condition in which he was you may be very sure he would never have got out of arm's length of me until all danger was over.

I have ever since reproached myself with it, and have made up my mind that should I ever have such another experience I will do what is directed, seem it never so absurd or difficult.[304] — CLERGYMAN, NAME WITHHELD

☛ CASE #289: Miss Craigie has written to me to ask me to send you the account of Elizabeth calling for Mr. Reggy and me. She called him and I was not dreaming, for she called "Reggy" and "Cook" so plainly I could not rest in bed; and I told the housemaid, E. Morris, and we wondered what it meant. I could not go that day, but I went the next, and the porter told me she died the morning before at 20 minutes to 4.

I went to the Infirmary the day she was buried, and the old dame in the bed next to hers told me she called for Reggy and Cook with her last breath. It troubled me much, for we had been friends for years, and I went to see her as often as I could. I never had anything of the kind happen to me before, and she called us so plain. I have often wondered what it could mean, and I shall never forget it. June 1st, 1885.[305] — MRS. E. STENT

☛ CASE #290: I would very gladly write the short statement you ask for, but though to my own mind it is pretty conclusive, still I feel that to outsiders it is wanting in two important details. (1) I mentioned the fact of hearing the voice to no one at the time, and (2) I could not tell whose voice it was.

It was on Thursday evening, January 10th, 1884, that I was sitting alone in the house reading, and it seemed strange, and still not strange, to hear my name called with a sort of eager entreaty.

Shortly after the others came in. I was leaving for Ellesmere next day, and in the bustle of departure I thought no more of the circumstance. It was only when coming down to breakfast on the Saturday morning and finding the letter telling of E.'s death that I instantly recalled the circumstances, and saw that the time and day corresponded with when they knew she must have slipped out and down to the river.

I wonder I did not associate it with her, for she had written me some very pitiable letters beforehand.

For the sake of my dead friend's relations, I should hardly like to give very identifying details (if for publication), as her death was a particularly sad one. We were school-fellows together for nearly three years and great friends; and she had written to me previous to her death in a terribly depressed state, but I had not the least idea her mind was affected. I never have had a hallucination of the senses at any other time.

It was about 8 o'clock in the evening, I fancy, when I heard the voice. She was not found till 2 o'clock the next morning when the tide turned on the river; she then had been dead several hours, having slipped out, I fancy, between 7 and 9 the previous evening.[306] — MARY WYLD

☛ CASE #291: Mr. W. Colman, of 44, Finsbury Circus, E.C., writing to us on May 10th, 1885, enclosed the following account. He had heard the particulars about a fortnight before, when staying in apartments which Mrs. Longley lets. Mrs. Longley, of 4, Liverpool Lawn, Ramsgate, a respectable married woman, wife of a small tradesman, both resident upwards of 35 years in the town, states:

My eldest son, Pilcher, in February, 1884, was one of the crew of the *Young Eliza*, cutter, of Grimsby, employed in collecting fish from the fishing fleet, and was then 28 years old. On the 10th of that month, at 3:10 a.m., he was washed overboard in a storm, and drowned.

On that morning I was restless, and being unable to sleep, determined to watch how long the moon would take to cross a certain pane of glass in the window, and while so doing heard a voice three times distinctly call "Mother." Supposing my [other] son George was at the door, I called out several times, "Is that you, George? What do you want?" waking my husband, to whom I told what had occurred.

Having no reply, I got up, lit a candle, and went upstairs to George's bedroom, and found him sleeping soundly, without any signs of having recently been awake or moving. Looking at the clock on the stairs I noticed it was 3:15 a.m.

Nine days after a telegram arrived, stating my eldest son had been drowned on the morning referred to.

My husband went to Grimsby, saw the captain of the vessel, and ascertained that Pilcher was washed overboard at the time stated, on a moonlight night, and that his first cry was, "Mother! mother! mother! save me for my mother's sake!"

He swam for 15 minutes, calling out occasionally, much as at first, but rescue was impossible. The distance from Ramsgate to where he was drowned was over 200 miles. He was a most affectionate son, and before going this voyage, had promised me it should be his last.[307] — SARAH LONGLEY

☛ CASE #292: After mentioning that he married while abroad, and was staying with his wife at Berlin, Mr. Jaffé continues:

As soon as my parents had learned of my arrival at Berlin, where I had engaged furnished apartments, my mother immediately came to see me and my foreign wife. She remained with us for three days, and two days after her departure my father and sister came to see us, staying also three days, and then returned home.

My wife and I, both young, in good health, and happy, were thoroughly enjoying ourselves, and were free from all serious thought.

About a week after my father's departure, we (my wife and I), having been to a concert, arrived at our rooms about 11 o'clock at night, and went to bed at once, being tired. My wife fell asleep almost immediately, and after a little while I also was in the arms of Morpheus.

Soon after, however, I awoke suddenly, with all my senses alive, as if I had slept for hours instead of only about 20 minutes, and heard what is commonly called the death-watch ticking. I knew that it could not be my gold repeater [watch], for its spring was broken, and it did not go therefore. I was well aware then that such ticking was caused by some insects in the woodwork, and was not alarmed in the very least degree. The noise continuing, however, for a long time, curiosity got the better of me, and I lit the candle, got softly out of bed, and tried to find out in what part of the room the ticking was. But the noise was like a will-o'-the-wisp; when I went to one part of the room, it went to another.

I got at last tired of the hunt, and crept softly into bed.

Nevertheless, I must have disturbed my wife, for she said to me, in a half-conscious state, "Alfy, your watch is going!" I did not answer her, for I saw she was asleep again as soon as the words were spoken and I also slept soundly till the morning.

At breakfast my wife said, "Alfy, I had such a funny dream. I saw your mother with a handkerchief tied under the chin, making such faces to me, and moving her jaws in a most extraordinary manner. We both laughed, and went to dress for a drive to Charlottenburg. I was the first dressed, and went into the sitting-room, waiting for my wife.

A knock at the door. It is the servant, handing me a telegram. It was from my father and ran: "Mother died last night. Letter to follow."

In the evening I received the letter, which stated among others: "Mother was paralysed, and had lost, for 6 hours before death, though no consciousness, but the power of speech. All this time she struggled fearfully to articulate, and the doctor tied, at last, her jaw with a cloth, to prevent her opening it. She died at 4 o'clock this morning." May 28th, 1885.[308] — ALFRED JAFFÉ

☛ CASE #293: An acquaintance of Mrs. Davies had changed her abode unexpectedly, and it was arranged that Mrs. Davies should receive her mail until she could communicate her new address to her friends, and particularly to her husband, who was in India.

One evening a letter arrived bearing the India postmark, and Mrs. Davies placed it on the chimney-piece intending to ask her brother to hand it next day to the addressee. Suddenly she became aware of a strange ticking sound that seemed to proceed from the letter itself. Her brother, too, heard it and, yielding to superstition, they imagined that the sound meant, "Important. To be delivered at once."

The brother thereupon put on his hat and carried the letter to their friend, who found it to be a communication from an unknown correspondent, some servant, or companion, notifying her of her husband's death.[309] — HENRY ADDINGTON BRUCE

☛ CASE #294: Before moving to Villa Isabel, I was the neighbour of my friend Senr. Francisco Coelho Lage at Capão do Bispo. Our families were intimate and there was a certain sympathy between my son Edgardo and Deolinda, one of the daughters of Senr. Lage.

In the middle of 1901 I was away travelling and stopped at Campinas in São Paulo, whence I intended to proceed still farther into the interior. But in that town I experienced a phenomenon which, although it is of frequent occurrence in my case, produced such an impression on me that I resolved to return at once to Rio de Janeiro. I heard my name called twice: "Joppert, Joppert!" There was no one near me I opened the street door, but saw not a living soul. Suspecting that something had happened at home, I did not sleep for the rest of the night.

My son had an intuitive feeling that I was coming, and declared that I should return on a Wednesday, which was in fact the day of my arrival home. I found Edgardo complaining of a headache. It was the beginning of a malady that sometimes assumed the character of a pernicious fever, sometimes that of a typhoid, but which really presented all the symptoms of the bubonic plague and terminated fatally after nine days of suffering.

Up to the last moments my son was conscious. He took leave of his mother and me [that is, said goodbye] about an hour before he expired, and he again embraced us a few minutes before the end. The death agony had not yet ceased when Senr. Franklin, a neighbour of ours, with whom, however, we were not on very intimate terms, rushed into our house exclaiming, "I am not a spiritist, Senr. Joppert, but your son [in spirit form] came to take leave of me!"

Senr. Franklin remained with us and was present at the death of my son, which took place at 7 o'clock in the morning of August 10th, 1901. Edgardo had not yet completed his twentieth year.

We afterwards heard that at the hour of his death Senr. Lage's daughter Deolinda also received a warning. She was yet in her room, and having to attend to a child, lighted a candle. The candle, however, went out of its own accord and [she then heard footsteps and] . . . felt both her hands grasped.

I have never paid any attention to subjects connected with spiritism, but in witness of the truth I sign this deposition, which I believe to be an exact narration of the facts. 36, RUA LUIZ BARBOZA, VILLA ISABEL, RIO DE JANEIRO, September 30th, 1902.[310] — HENRIQUE SUCKOW JOPPERT

☛ CASE #295: February 21st, 1902. On the evening of February 25th, 1897, I was sitting alone, as I almost invariably did, and reading, when I suddenly thought of the Beethoven Trio Op. 1 No.

1 so vividly that I got up to look for the music, which I had not touched for nearly 20 years. It was just as if I could hear the cello and violin parts, and the bowing and expression seemed to be that of two gentlemen who had played with me often in C____ so many years before.

One of them, Kammermusiker L____, first cellist of the Residence Theatre in C____ had been my eldest son's master, but had been called to H____ in 1878. The other, who was employed by my husband at that time as clerk of the works, had subsequently quitted C also, and removed in the middle of the nineties to H____. I had often seen him since he left C____, and had also played duets with him, but never again in a trio.

I got out the piano part and began to play; I must here admit that I had played with Z____ and L____ principally the Op. 97, and the one in C flat, Op. 1 No. 3, and was myself surprised that this Op. 1 No. 1, which we had hardly ever played, was ringing in my ears. At any rate I heard with my mental ear this melody so exactly that I played the piece right through to the end.

About 10 o'clock the bell rang and my house mate, the daughter of Lieutenant-Col. G____ who lived over me, came in. She apologised for her late visit and assured me that she could not sleep until she had found out what I had been playing. I supplied the information, and she remarked, "Well, what brought that into your head?"

"I don't know, I haven't opened the book for twenty years, but before I began I heard Z____ and L____ playing and I felt I must recall the full harmony."

The next day the enclosed [post] card [attached below] came; it had been written, as we established by subsequent correspondence, on the same evening and at the same hour, and as the post-mark shows, delivered (in Kiel, Germany) the following morning:

"February 25th, 1897. After playing Beethoven Op. 1 No. 1 we send you hearty greetings in remembrance of happy hours spent together in the past. Z____, R____, L____."[311] — MRS. M. U.

☛ CASE #296: I do hereby declare, that, whilst on guard behind the Armoury house (to the best of my recollection about three weeks ago), I heard, at twelve o'clock at night, a tremendous noise, which proceeded from the window of an uninhabited house, near to the spot where I was upon duty. At the same time, I heard a voice cry out, "Bring me a light! bring me a light!" The last sentence was uttered in so feeble and so changeable tone of voice, that I concluded some person was ill, and consequently offered them my assistance to procure a light. I could, however, obtain no answer to my proposal, although I repeated it several times, and as often heard the voice use the same terms. I endeavoured to see the person who called out, but in vain.

On a sudden the violent noise was renewed, which appeared to me to resemble sashes of windows lifted hastily up and down, but then they were moved in such quick succession, and at different parts of the house nearly at the same time, that it seemed impossible to me that one person could accomplish the whole business. I heard several of the regiment say they have heard similar noises and proceedings, but I have never heard the cause accounted for. Whitehall, January 15, 1804.[312] — RICHARD DONKIN 12TH COMPANY OF COLDSTREAM GUARDS

☛ CASE #297: The following narrative was communicated to me by Mrs. Page of Caerphilly, a lady whose intelligence and high character render the account, I venture to think, of special value.

Mrs. Page is the inventor of a valuable ointment. A young man living in the district had been in the habit of using this ointment for his chest. He, however, was consumptive, and though he had great faith in the efficacy of the ointment, it was evident it could be of no material use, and, indeed, despite his doctor's care, he grew worse and worse.

On the early morning of the 21st December, 1903, about 3 o'clock a.m., Mrs. Page was in bed, when she was awakened by steps coming up the stairs, followed by sharp knocking [three knocks] at her bedroom door. This was also heard by relatives sleeping in an adjoining room. She jumped up, went to the door and out into the passage, but there was no one there.

In the course of the day she learnt that the young man had died at the very time she heard the above. He was most eager to see Mrs. Page, and had implicit faith in her remedy up to the last.

This is the real statement of fact, but Mrs. Page will gladly answer any question that may be put to her on the subject. I may add that she is a strong woman mentally and physically, possessed of abundance of common- sense, and not in the least superstitious.[313] — ARTHUR MEE, ASSISTANT EDITOR *WESTERN MAIL*

☛ CASE #298: On Saturday, September 10th, I was in my daughter's garden pruning some trees. I had just completed my work about 7 p.m. when I distinctly heard my daughter's voice calling me, "When are you coming down?" using a familiar name by which no one but she addresses me. I looked all round me and could see no one, so I called to her several times, but receiving no answer supposed that she had called me and then gone home.

However, when I got to the bottom of the garden, a distance of about 40 yards from where I was pruning, I found her at work among her flowers, and on asking her why she had called me, she said "I never called you at all, but I was thinking of you very much a short time ago and thought I must call you, but I did not."

It is perfectly certain that I heard her voice distinctly, and it is equally certain that my daughter did not call me. I write this simple account as it may be possible that other people may have met with occurrences of a similar nature. Is it within the bounds of probability that thought can, under certain conditions, be transferred into audible sound? September 14th, 1904.[314] — MR. E. M. CLISSOLD

☛ CASE #299: A few years ago my wife and I, who had been for our summer holiday in Wales, determined to spend a few days at Malvern on our way home.

The journey from Aberystwyth was somewhat long, and it was past nine on a lovely moonlight night when we arrived at that favourite health resort beside the sheltering hills. Many years had elapsed since our last visit, and that had not extended over more than two or three days. The only other time that I had been there was as a child of six years old, so that my knowledge of the locality was very hazy.

The lateness of the hour made it impossible for me to recognise any landmarks, even supposing that I had any recollection of the place.

Next morning I announced my intention of going to the top of the Beacon after breakfast, and asked my wife, who knew the place well, how I should find my way. She gave me the needful directions, and following her advice I soon discovered an opening that at once brought me to the foot of the Beacon, and, looking up, I could see two or three groups of donkeys following the winding path that led to the top. I knew therefore that I was all right, and, having set my aneroid, I took a "bee line" for the summit. Purposely I avoided looking about, for I was interested in watching the fall of the needle in the aneroid which was in my hand, and moreover I wished to have the grand view as a surprise at the end. It was a bright sunny morning, with a fresh breeze, and the contrast between twelve hours in the train on the previous day and the exhilarating freedom of present circumstances made me step upward gaily.

Climbing is to me an inspiring exercise. Many a time have I raced uphill whistling in challenged competition with young nephews and nieces, but even without their pleasant companionship the bracing air and delightful surroundings were an invigorating tonic. With eyes fixed on the aneroid, and an occasional glance upward to see that I was going straight, I rapidly ascended, crossing the winding pathway from time to time, and being just conscious of the strings of donkeys, with their living freight, making in a leisurely way for the same goal.

Much sooner than I expected the summit was reached, and, having glanced round to see that I was really there, I hastily adjusted the aneroid and calculated the height of the ascent. All this is ordinary experience; nothing that I have narrated is contrary to the sensations of men who have walked to the top of the Beacon a hundred times, and, like the King of France in ancient story, "then walked down again."

Now, however, comes the marvellous part of my tale.

To be quite sure that there was no higher point to reach, I looked well around and took in everything. I was alone, quite alone, but for the presence—about fifty yards away—of an old applewoman, who, in a sort of bastion of fruit baskets and ginger-beer bottles, was hopefully prepared for the friendly assaults to be made upon her position during the day. Between me and the aged female aforesaid was a long low stone, and, as my eye fell upon it, I heard distinctly a well-known voice saying to me: "*Well, this is the longest walk that I have taken since I was laid up, and I never could have done it but for your arm.*"

I almost leaped into the air! It was the voice of a favourite sister, whom I had not seen for years, and whom at that moment I believed to be in her pretty vicarage home some three hundred miles away. I looked hastily all round. There was no one near but the old applewoman aforesaid, knitting peacefully in her fortification, and down below me, at a little distance, the first contingent of donkeys and children could be seen gradually approaching.

In utter amazement my eyes stared at everything—donkeys, applewoman—and then again they fell upon the long low stone just in front of me. Wonder of wonders! Again the Voice spoke, but this time in lower tones: "Well, this is the longest walk that I have taken since I was laid up, and I never could have done it but for your arm."

What did it all mean? Whence came those well-known accents? I stood rooted to the ground in blank wonderment. Again I looked for explanation all around. From below the ripple of childish laughter was coming nearer, but I was surely in another world than theirs. They could not explain my mystery, neither could the placid being guarding the refreshments.

Once more I looked involuntarily on the old grey stone, and—wonderful to relate once more the mysterious Voice uttered the familiar sentence, but this time in minute and fairy tones:

> "Well, this is the longest walk that I have taken since I was laid up, and I never could have done it but for your arm."

There was no standing it. The mystery must be solved; so, without sitting down to rest, without thinking of the splendid prospect which I had anticipated so eagerly, I turned and strode down the steep way that I had come, making with the greatest speed for the house and the room in which I had left my wife.

Having told my story faithfully, I begged her if possible to throw some light upon the dark enigma.

After a pause she replied: "Fourteen years ago we all were staying at a house on the other side, nearer the Beacon than this one, and you came for a visit of two or three days. I remember that Mary had sprained her knee, but that is all that I can tell."

This information made things more interesting, so without delay I sat down and wrote to my far-away sister, requesting her to set to work at once and help me to fathom the mystery.

By return post I received a letter from which I extract the following: "Your marvellous experience fills us with astonishment. Yes, it is quite true, when you came to us at 'The Ruby' fourteen years ago I was beginning to recover from a sprain that had laid me up for a long time, and had made me very nervous about trying to walk. I recollect perfectly how you coaxed me out for a little turn, leaning on your arm; how you told me ever so many funny stories, so that I quite forgot myself and did not perceive that you were craftily leading me on until at last you astonished me by saying, 'Now, you who cannot walk are at the top of the Beacon!' Then, I have no doubt—although I have no recollection of it—I must have said the words which you have just heard, somehow, in such an extraordinary way."

This letter supplied a clue to the mystery up to a certain point, but there still remained the question: whence came this Voice, or what seemed like one? What power called this spirit from the vast deep of Memory?

Turning my mind back upon the events of this strange incident it seemed to me as if *that long low stone* had something to say in the matter. I remembered clearly that as I looked at it again the sentence came back both the second and third time.

[It is probable], therefore, [that] I had placed my companion on this the only seat at hand; that as I did so, exulting in the success of my device, she uttered the sentence above mentioned; and that when I next saw that stone, fourteen years afterwards, the law of association of ideas produced in my brain what seemed like a sound in my ears. Whether there was any audible sound is another question, but to me it seemed like an actual voice, as recognisable as if my sister stood before me; wholly unexpected, because I was not thinking of her; and not "evolved from inner consciousness," because I had so entirely forgotten the incident that I needed to be reminded of it before the meaning of the words could be explained.

I have never in the course of my life met with, nor have I heard of, a similar experience, but I venture to submit that it throws a side-light on some of those narratives which from time to time astonish the world, of "voices speaking distinctly" to individuals in visions by night or even in the daylight.

I would go further and say that it may account for some of the "appearances" of which we have occasionally heard. If those cells of the brain which are connected with the ear may be acted upon by association, or some similar power, so as to produce the effect of sound, why could not those which command the eye be influenced in the same or a kindred way?[315] — REV. J. H. TOWNSEND

☛ CASE #300: In the autumn of 1902 I was recovering from a long illness, in consequence of which I wore a spinal jacket by day, and had turned my downstairs study into my bedroom. It was also my custom to go to bed about 8 p.m. I have a boarding-house at a public school with the care of about 30 boys; the majority of these live in a part of the house shut off from our private rooms, but five or six boys sleep in two rooms on the first floor near the bedroom used at the time by my wife.

On Sunday, December 7th, 1902, about 7:30 or 8 p.m., I was sitting alone in my room and thought I heard a knock on the door. I said "Come in," but no one appeared, and I concluded the noise was due to the wind, as there was a breeze that evening. I still think it may have been the effect of wind. A second time I heard a knock and there was no one, but still I was not much surprised. Shortly afterwards I took off my jacket and went to bed. At that time when I had taken off the jacket I was not allowed to raise my shoulders until I had it on again. My wife was in the room.

Suddenly we heard a tremendous bang upon the door, as if some one had struck it full with the fist. I said to my wife, "Go and see what it is." She replied, "I dare not." If I had been able to rise, I think I should have gone at once, but I wish to note that I felt seriously alarmed, in a way that I could hardly explain. My wife's remark shows that she felt the same, and this feeling of unreasonable fright is what remains with us both as the strongest impression.

We listened intently, and are quite sure that no one could have left the neighbourhood of the door without being heard, and in four or five seconds my wife went to the door and found no one. I heard nothing more.

Next morning my wife at breakfast told me that in the night she woke up and felt sure she heard some one walking up the stairs. She went out of her room and while on the landing close to the door of a room in which three boys were sleeping, she heard distinctly one or two deep sighs. Beyond this she heard nothing and returned to her room. We thought a great deal about the occurrence and told several friends.

About Christmas we received a letter from India to say that Mr. W_____, father of one of the boys who slept in the room mentioned above, had died on December 6th after a short illness. It is worth mentioning that I had only once seen Mr. W_____, on the sole occasion when he came to my house and had an interview with me in the room where the knock was heard. It seems to me probable that there is some connection between the death and the noise. I should further say that I have never had any experience of the kind or other hallucination, but that my wife on several occasions has heard unaccountable noises at the time of death of some of her relatives.

The boy W_____ left my house in April, 1903, and I did not see his mother, Mrs. W_____, until September, 1904, when she came to call upon me with a view to sending her son back. I then told her what had happened. She was not surprised, and told me of a strange occurrence that took place in India the same night.

Mr. W____ was attacked by typhoid fever. The doctor told Mrs. W____ that the only chance for him was to conceal from him the danger of his state, and he died after a very short illness without any farewell about 12 midnight, December 6. The following evening (I think somewhat late), Mrs. W____ was in the room alone with the body, and said, "O you never said good-bye, dear." Instantly she heard behind her a voice which said quite loudly, "Good-bye, dear." She left the room, crossed the verandah, and went into another room on the far side of the verandah where the children were sleeping.

There she asked the nurse, "Did you hear anything just now?"

The nurse said "Yes, Miss J____ rose straight up in her bed asleep and said quite loud, 'Good-bye, dear,' and then fell back again."

Mrs. W____ tells me that the girl could not possibly have heard what she (Mrs. W____) said in the other room, as the rooms were too far apart. January 13th, 1905.[316] — MR. C.

☛ CASE #301: [Second incident related to the previous case:] The incident is explained to me by my child being so devoted and so sympathetic—it was perfectly natural that she should feel what I was feeling. . . . There were two bedrooms side by side—not opening into each other—both opened on to a balcony which ran along the house. My little girl, about 3 years old, and her nurse were in one room asleep. It was about 2 a.m.

I was kneeling by my husband's coffin in the other room. I was greatly distressed that he had not said "good-bye" to me. We were most devoted and his death was a terribly sudden shock.

It may seem strange that in the midst of such desperate trouble such a small thing as his not actually having said the word "good-bye" should have affected me, but it did; and I said, "You never even said good-bye."

At the moment I heard a voice which seemed to come direct from the coffin say, "Good-bye, Mummy, good-bye." I went into the next room and asked the nurse if she had heard anything and she said "No."

I said, "Did no one speak?" and she said, "Now, do rest; Miss J____ is asleep. She just now rose straight to her feet and said, 'Good-bye, Mummy, good-bye,' but she is asleep now." He [my husband] often called me "Mummy" as the child did. February 4th,

1905.[317] — MRS. W.

☛ CASE #302: We had spent the winter 1896-7 in Egypt for C.'s [her husband's] health, and we went to Hyères about a fortnight before Easter. There I left him, being obliged to come to London, and I intended to stay over Easter in town, if he continued as well as when I had left him. He wrote cheerfully, describing his daily walks, and telling me that he felt very well. I was therefore not feeling anxious about him.

About 1 a.m. on Easter Monday I awoke thinking I heard him call me. I sprang up in great anxiety, feeling sure that he was ill. After a time I persuaded myself that I had only been dreaming, and fell asleep again, only to wake a second time in the early morning with the impression again that he was calling me. This time I got up, dressed and packed my things, and when my maid came in with a telegram she found me almost ready to start. The telegram was "Come at once." Hemorrhage had come on about midnight, and all that night C. had been thinking of me and wondering how quickly I could get to him.

I was able to catch the first train from London and arrived at Hyères several hours before the doctor, who had been telegraphed for at the same time. [Editor's note: Mr. Carmichael survived this illness, but passed away about a year later. L.S.] January 3rd, 1905.[318] — MARY CARMICHAEL

☛ CASE #303: I have been requested to write down a vision which I had on the night of February 19th, 1893, just before I had a serious illness.

My husband . . . had been reading his sermon to me by my bedside; it was his custom to read his sermons to me before he preached them and the subject of this one was that of Abraham offering up Isaac.

In the night, some time, I heard a voice calling me, saying, "M____ G____." I could not see any one, but I knew it was God.

I answered: "Yes, God."

Then God came and said, "Are you ready to die?"

I answered, "No; I am not."

"But you must die," said God.

"Really, God, I cannot die; it is impossible," I said.

Then God said, "But you must die and be willing to give up all."

Then I answered again, "It is quite impossible; what would my husband and my little baby do if I died? They could not get on without me; there would be no one to take care of and look after them (my babe was then 5 or 6 days old)."

God answered, "Yes, you must leave them; I can take care of them without you; My care is sufficient for them; you must say, 'Thy will be done,' and die."

Then followed a long silence and a long fight with myself to conquer myself and reconcile myself to give up all and die. During this struggle many scenes of my life passed before me in which I saw how slack I had been in my life many times, and in my duties, and then I felt that in spite of these failures God had still taken care of me and my relatives without my help. All this time God was waiting near for an answer, and I had a feeling of surrender.

I felt it must be and I said, "Yes, God, I will say 'Thy will be done,' and die."

I said, "Thy will be done," and lay still.

God said, "That is right; as you have said that, you shall not die, but you must be very ill; but you shall not die," and so it was.

In the morning I told my husband the [auditory] vision, and I shall never forget it. After that I was very ill indeed; all thought I was dying. But no thought of death troubled me, because I had heard God say, "You shall not die." It happened 13 years ago, but it is still fresh in my memory. November 19th, 1905.[319] — MRS. X.

☛ CASE #304: I was lying awake in bed on the morning of October 30th when I heard a distinct knocking which I took to be at the outside door of the cottage. We knew that the woman in whom we were interested (a Mrs. C., who lives about mile from us) was in a dying state, and I immediately assumed that one of her children had come to fetch my wife. I therefore touched my wife to rouse her, and told her that I thought the C.'s had come to fetch her. I do not remember whether anything was said to show that my wife was awake or asleep at the time.

She went down immediately, but came back and said that nobody was there.

The knocks were not less than 5 and not more than 7: I think there were five in rapid succession, as of some one knocking sharply at the door.

Our bedroom is on the first floor, and the knocking sounded to be downstairs, was certainly not in our room. It did not occur to us to attach any particular significance to the sound at the time.

The above is all that I can state at first-hand, but the following at second-hand may be interesting. The servant, who sleeps in the adjoining room, and who says that she also heard the knocking, looked at her clock and found it to be 20 past 5 (her clock was known to be a few minutes fast).

At breakfast-time some neighbours came down to tell us that Mrs. C. had died at past 5 that morning. After breakfast my wife went to see the C.'s and they told her that Mrs. C. had died at past 5.[320] — HERBERT RIX

☛ CASE #305: Our usually quiet town [Columbia City, Indiana] has, during the last few days, been thrown into a state of feverish excitement by a strange and unusual spiritual phenomenon heard in and about a woollen factory and the neighbouring buildings, situated in the southwestern suburbs of the town.

For some time past, the employés who sleep in the factory have been disturbed by noises like that caused by opening and closing doors, persons walking about the rooms, rattling loose boards, etc., etc. At first the employés supposed these unusual sounds proceeded from some burglarious depredation on the premises, and accordingly thoroughly searched and guarded the premises, but without success. The closest examination revealed nothing, but the strange noise continued.

For some time, perhaps through fear of being laughed at, the employés kept the matter a secret, but at length the annoyance became so great that they refused to sleep in the building, and the strange affair was made public.

About this time the noises changed both in character and locality. The inmates of a neighbouring house were startled by noises under and about the building, similar to that produced by striking a muffled drum. While these continued all was quiet at the factory; but when they ceased, the noises at the factory were again heard.

On Sunday night the mysterious drumming was heard for several hours at the house, by a number of persons. An effort was made [using a drum] by those present to learn something of the mysterious affair by questions, which to some extent, was apparently successful.

The answers, given by a specified number of taps on the spirit drum, stated that the disquieted spirit was that of a man who had been murdered in that vicinity about eight years ago; that he was fifty-one years old when murdered; and that he was buried sixteen feet deep near the factory. His name and other particulars were not given. Other questions were answered in the same manner, by the number of taps on the drum required by the person asking the question. When no questions were asked, the drumming continued; sometimes slow and regular, and at other times quick and irregular.

At one time an old lady, somewhat deaf, requested the "spirit" to beat louder that she might hear it more distinctly. The "spirit" complied with her request by giving a succession of vigorous taps which were distinctly heard at a considerable distance from the house.

On Monday night crowds of people visited the place, and listened to the mysterious drumming, but owing to the crowd and confusion, no questions were asked or answered.

These mysterious manifestations have thrown the whole community into a state of intense excitement. Crowds of people visit the place, and the family living in the haunted house have been so annoyed by the visitors and strange manifestations going on about them, that they have been able to procure but little rest for several days, and will probably be compelled to move away from the seemingly accursed place.

By what agency these sounds are produced I cannot pretend to say; but that they are produced by some invisible agency, hundreds who have heard them can testify. The seeming impossibility that such an effect could be produced by any human agency envelopes the matter in a strange and inexplicable mystery. A thorough examination of the premises is being made, and, if there is any way to get at the bottom of the mysterious affair, the spirits will be unearthed and exposed. There is little hope however, that any additional light will be thrown on the matter.[321] — *CHICAGO TRIBUNE*

☛ CASE #306: [In my house] . . . manifestations [such] as tipping, rapping, writing, have been going on continuously. About a fortnight ago sounds began in my bed room and in other parts of the house as of a person ascending and descending the stairs. At times the room became half illuminated. Thinking that it might be some departed member of the family wishful to speak to me, I placed a slate and pencil on the table. The next morning I found a flourished circle, in which could fairly be traced the name of a very dear relative. Lights and sounds are nightly seen and heard by us between the hours of twelve and three, they are often most beautiful and pleasant. . . .[322] — W. BANKS

☛ CASE #307: Equally noteworthy [to the above mentioned] . . . spectral messenger of tragedy is the so-called Drummer of Cortachy Castle, a Scottish ghost that haunts the ancient stronghold of the Ogilvys, Earls of Airlie, but is in evidence only when an

Ogilvy is about to die.

The story goes that, hundreds of years ago, when the Scots were little better than barbarians, a Highland chieftain sent a drummer to Cortachy Castle with a message that was not at all to the liking of the Ogilvy of that time. As an appropriate token of his displeasure, he seized the luckless drummer, stuffed him into his drum—he must have been a very small drummer, and have carried a very big drum—and hurled him from the topmost battlements of the castle, breaking his neck. Just before he was tossed off, the drummer threatened to make a ghost of himself, and haunt the Ogilvys forevermore.

He has been, it would seem, as good as his word. Every once in a while ghostly drumming is heard at Cortachy Castle, and always the death of an Ogilvy follows.

An especially impressive account of one instance of this peculiar and most unpleasant haunting has been left by a Miss Dalrymple, who happened to be a guest at Cortachy during Christmas week of 1844. It was her first visit to the Castle, and she was entirely unaware of the existence of the family ghost.

On the evening of her arrival, while dressing for dinner, she was startled by hearing under her window music like the muffled beating of a drum. She looked out, but could see nothing, and presently the drumming died away. For the time she thought no more of it, but at dinner she turned to her host, the Earl of Airlie, and asked: "My lord, who is your drummer?" His lordship made no reply. Lady Airlie became exceedingly pale, and several of the company, all of whom had heard the question, looked embarrassed. Realizing that she had made a slip of some sort, Miss Dalrymple quickly changed the subject, but after dinner, naturally feeling somewhat curious, she brought it up with one of the younger members of the family, and was answered:

"What! Have you never heard of the Drummer of Cortachy?"

"No," said she. "Who in the world is he?"

"Why, he is a person who goes about playing his drum whenever there is a death impending in our family. The last time he was heard was shortly before the death of the late countess, the earl's first wife, and that is why Lady Airlie turned so pale when you mentioned it."

The next night Miss Dalrymple heard the drumming again, and, falling into a panic when she learned that nobody else had heard it, hurriedly left Cortachy Castle. But the drumming was not for her. True to tradition, the drummer was concerned only with announcing the death of an Ogilvy, one of whom, the Lady Airlie who had been so disturbed by Miss Dalrymple's question, died soon afterward while on a visit to Brighton.

Five years later the drumming was once more heard, this time by an Englishman who had been invited to spend a few days with the Earl of Airlie's oldest son. Lord Ogilvy, at a shooting box near Cortachy. Crossing a gloomy moor, in company with an old Highlander, the Englishman suddenly stopped, and, with a look of amazement, exclaimed:

"What can a band be doing in this lonely place? Has Lord Ogilvy brought a band with him?"

The Highlander glanced at him strangely. "I hear naething," he said.

"Why, yes, can't you hear it? A band playing in the distance—or at any rate, somebody playing a drum."

"An' is it a drum ye hear?" cried the Highlander. "Then 'tis something no canny."

In another moment the lighted windows of the shooting box came into view, and the Englishman hastened forward, fully expecting to have the mystery solved. But he found no musicians—only a scene of considerable confusion. Lord Ogilvy, it appeared, had just started for London, summoned by news that his father was dangerously ill. And the very next day, as the Englishman's Highlander guide was not at all surprised to learn, the Earl of Airlie died.[323] — HENRY ADDINGTON BRUCE

☛ CASE #308: On the morning of October 27th, 1879, being in perfect health and having been awake for some considerable time, I heard myself called by my Christian name by an anxious and suffering voice, several times in succession. I recognised the voice as that of an old friend, almost playfellow, but who had not been in my thoughts for many weeks, or even months. I knew he was with his regiment in India, but not that he had been ordered to the front, and nothing had recalled him to my recollection.

Within a few days I heard of his death from cholera on the morning I seemed to hear his call. The impression was so strong I noted the date and fact in my diary before breakfast.[324] — ANONYMOUS WOMAN

☛ CASE #309: In 1876, I was living in a small agricultural parish in the East of England, one of my neighbours at the time being a young man, S. B., who had recently come into the occupation of a large farm in the place.

Pending the alteration of his house, he lodged and boarded with his groom at the other end of the village, furthest removed from my own residence, which was half a mile distant and separated by many houses, gardens, a plantation, and farm buildings. He was fond of field sports, and spent much of his spare time during the season in hunting. He was not a personal friend of mine, only an acquaintance, and I felt no interest in him except as a tenant on the estate. I have asked him occasionally to my house, as a matter of civility, but to the best of my recollection was never inside his lodgings.

One afternoon in March, 1876, when leaving, along with my wife, our railway station to walk home, I was accosted by S. B.; he accompanied us as far as my front gate, where he kept us in conversation for sometime, but on no special subject. I may now state that the distance from this gate, going along the carriage drive, to the dining and breakfast room windows is about 60 yards; both the windows of these rooms face the north-east and are parallel with the carriage drive.

On S. B. taking leave of us my wife remarked [to me], "Young B. evidently wished to be asked in, but I thought you would not care to be troubled with him."

Subsequently—about half-an-hour later—I again met him, and, as I was then on my way to look at some work at a distant part of the estate, asked him to walk with me, which he did. His conversation was of the ordinary character; if anything, he seemed somewhat depressed at the bad times and the low prices of farming produce. I remember he asked me to give him some wire rope to make a fence on his farm, which I consented to do.

Returning from our walk, and on entering the village, I pulled up at the crossroads to say good evening, the road to his lodgings taking him at right angles to mine. I was surprised to hear him say, "Come and smoke a cigar with me to-night." To which I replied, "I cannot very well, I am engaged this evening."

"Do come," he said.

"No," I replied, I will look in another evening." And with this we parted.

We had separated about 40 yards when he turned around and exclaimed, "Then if you will not come, good-bye."

This was the last time I saw him alive.

I spent the evening in my dining-room in writing, and for some hours I may say that probably no thought of young B. passed through my mind. The night was bright and clear, full or nearly full moon, still, and without wind. Since I had come in slight snow had fallen, just sufficient to make the ground show white.

At about 5 minutes to 10 o'clock I got up and left the room, taking up a lamp from the hall table, and replacing it on a small table standing in a recess of the window in the breakfast-room. The curtains were not drawn across the window. I had just taken down from the nearest bookcase a volume of *Macgillivray's British Birds* for reference, and was in the act of reading the passage, the book held close to the lamp, and my shoulder touching the window shutter, and in a position in which almost the slightest outside sound would be heard, when I distinctly heard the front gate opened and shut again with a clap, and footsteps advancing at a run up the drive; when opposite the window the steps changed from sharp and distinct on gravel to dull and less clear on the grass slip below the window, and at the same time I was conscious that someone or something stood close to me outside, only the thin shutter and a sheet of glass dividing us.

I could hear the quick panting laboured breathing of the messenger, or whatever it was, as if trying to recover breath before speaking. Had he been attracted by the light through the shutter?

Suddenly, like a gunshot, inside, outside, and all around, there broke out the most appalling shriek—a prolonged wail of horror, which seemed to freeze the blood. It was not a single shriek, but more prolonged, commencing in a high key, and then less and less, wailing away towards the north, and becoming weaker and weaker as it receded in sobbing pulsations of intense agony.

Of my fright and horror I can say nothing—increased tenfold when I walked into the dining-room and found my wife sitting quietly at her work close to the window, in the same line and distant only 10 or 12 feet from the corresponding window in the breakfast-room. She had heard nothing. I could see that at once; and from the position in which she was sitting, I knew she could not have failed to hear any noise outside and any footstep on the gravel.

Perceiving I was alarmed about something, she asked, "What is the matter?"

"Only someone outside," I said.

"Then why do you not go out and see? You always do when you hear any unusual noise."

I said, "There is something so queer and dreadful about the noise. I dare not face it. It must have been the Banshee shrieking."

Young S. B., on leaving me, went home to his lodgings. He spent most of the evening on the sofa, reading one of Whyte Melville's novels. He saw his groom at 9 o'clock and gave him orders for the following day. The groom and his wife, who were the only people in the house besides S. B., then went to bed.

At the inquest the groom stated that when about falling asleep, he was suddenly aroused by a shriek, and on running into his master's room found him expiring on the floor. It appeared that young B. had undressed upstairs, and then came down to his sitting-room in trousers and nightshirt, had poured out half-a-glass of water, into which he emptied a small bottle of prussic acid (procured that morning under the plea of poisoning a dog, which he did not possess). He walked upstairs, and on entering his room drank off the glass, and with a scream fell dead on the floor. All this happened, as near as I can ascertain, at the exact time when I had been so much alarmed at my own house. It is utterly impossible that any sound short of a cannon shot could have reached me from B.'s lodgings, through closed windows and doors, and the many intervening obstacles of houses and gardens, farmsteads and plantations, etc.

Having to leave home by the early train, I was out very soon on the following morning, and on going to examine the ground beneath the window found no footsteps on grass or drive, still covered with the slight sprinkling of snow which had fallen on the previous evening.

The whole thing had been a dream of the moment—an imagination, call it what you will; I simply state these facts as they occurred, without attempting any explanation, which, indeed, I am totally unable to give. The entire incident is a mystery, and will ever remain a mystery to me. I did not hear the particulars of the tragedy till the following afternoon, having left home by an early train. The motive of suicide was said to be a love affair.[325] — MR. A. Z.

Chapter Five

OLFACTOROUS ACCOUNTS

CASES OF PARANORMAL SMELLS

☛ CASE #310: The following is the account of the two curious experiences I mentioned to you as having happened to me.

The first, which occurred some years ago, was at a visit I paid with several friends to a picture gallery in Bond Street. Among the paintings, which, I think, were all by French artists, was one representing a pyramid of human heads in various and advanced stages of decomposition. I walked towards it, looking at something which had taken my attention in my catalogue, when I became conscious of a most horrible and overpowering stench, such as would probably have been caused by remains of the kind in reality. I did not know anything about the picture, its subject, or its position in the gallery, and it was not until I was close to it that I perceived what it was at all. Sight had, therefore, nothing to do with suggesting the odour to the sense of smell.

I mentioned the fact to the friends who were with me, but they only laughed and said there was nothing of the kind, that it was merely imagination worked upon by the horrid subject of the painting.

This experience was brought back to me rather vividly by another and similar one, which occurred at the Academy, either of last year or the year before, I forget for the moment which.

I became suddenly aware of a delightful scent of wallflowers, stocks, etc., etc., such as one would expect in a lovely old-fashioned garden. People do not generally use a scent of that kind (wallflower), and I was wondering where it came from, when, on looking up, I saw a painting representing just such an old garden, and which I think I should have passed without seeing if the scent had not made me look round.

This was not all.

Before leaving the Academy, I usually go once through the galleries just as they are closing for one look round when the crowd has gone. I did so on this occasion, and, on passing the picture, the same thing happened again. I did not know I was near it until the scent of flowers made me look up. Without this, I should certainly have missed seeing it the second time, as I had quite forgotten in which gallery it was hanging. September 11th, 1905.[326] — MISS GODDARD

Chapter Six

CLAIRVOYANT ACCOUNTS

CASES OF VISIONS AND MIRAGES

☛ CASE #311: I very distinctly remember that one day, a few years ago, my father [William Deering] lay down for a few minutes, as at that time usual before going to his office in the afternoon. Seated on a stool beside him, and with my left hand enfolded in one of his, I read the book in which I was at the time interested, for five or possibly seven minutes. At the end of that time he turned his face toward me, and seeing that the room was shaded, remarked: "Anna, you will injure your eyes reading in this dim light." "And I do not particularly like this book," I responded.

I held in my hand a historical novel, the name of which I am sorry I cannot recollect, but I remember vividly that the passage I had just read purported to be one of the last scenes in the life of Marie Antoinette, and I remember as distinctly that in that scene a tall man carried a coffin from a room in which Marie Antoinette and some attendant ladies were at the time standing. I remember that in the story that tall man stood prominently in the foreground, and that my mind was strained under the part he took in that scene almost to the verge of repugnance.

In reply to my father's question why I did not like the book, I replied in substance as in the foregoing, and he immediately told me that he had just seen what I had described, and had opened his eyes and turned his face toward me to dissipate the scene, which for the moment he had looked upon as an isolated phantasm. Louisville, Kentucky, U.S., October 18th, 1884.[327] — ANNA M. DEERING

☛ CASE #312: [William Deering's account regarding the previous entry.] While I lay with my daughter's hand in mine, as she relates in the accompanying memoir, I fell into the semi-slumber usual with me on lying down to rest for a few minutes after my luncheon, early in the afternoon. At these times I very seldom fall asleep, but simply into a species of slumber, in which I frequently find myself in a kind of rayless or moonless moonlight, looking, and this usually with serene pleasure, at near-by gardens, slopes, rivulets, and various little vistas, which more times than otherwise vanish at my bidding, and, except I fall asleep, are immediately replaced by others. Sometimes these are peopled with apparently living figures, and frequently these also dissolve at my bidding, and are replaced by others.

There is, however, this difference, any control I exercise for the purpose of a change seems to be more immediate and more absolute over a change of figures than over a change of scenes.

I am quite sure that at these times I do not fall into any condition that fairly can be called pathological.

Under the slumber now under consideration, my attention became fixed on a tall thin man, with head uncovered, beardless, and dressed in black. He came toward the foot of the bed on which I lay from the left; and perhaps I should note that my daughter sat upon my left. Immediately I saw several other figures; and though these stood outside the lines or field of my direct vision, I remember distinctly that they made on me an impression of sympathy with powerlessness.

I might think that the sympathy touched me through the countenance of the man, were it not that he impressed me with also the opposite of powerlessness. His age seemed to be about 50, his face oblong, a little sallow, seriously thoughtful, and withal indicative of great but quiet firmness in action, whether from a sense of duty based on his own judgment, or duty under a sense of obedience, I cannot determine, though in the absence of any appearance of the vindictive, I think, or at least am inclined to think, that alike his presence and his action were based on simply an obedience to some rightful authority. This action was a reverent stepping forward, and a silent laying of his hands on a coffin that seemed to rest across the foot of the bed.

The moment I saw the coffin I thought: I do not like this scene; please go away and let something more agreeable come in. But the scene would not change, and again I thought: Please go away and let something more agreeable come in; and again the scene would not change.

He raised the coffin, it seemed as easily as though it had been that of an infant, and was in the act of stepping backward, as though withdrawing from a presence, when I thought: Then I will not prolong this slumber; I will open my eyes and arouse myself. And, on immediately doing so, I spoke to my daughter as she narrates, and then without anything like amazement, listened to her description from the book.

I have been minute, as in the foregoing, because I wish to put every feature of and every impression given me by the scene carefully on record, against a search which I purpose to keep up for the book out of which my daughter at the time sat reading. She did not then or ever read to me what she had read, but simply and in her own language drew the scene; and this in, perhaps, as few words as she has now written it, nor have we since that time in any particular way conversed about it.

My impression is that the book she read was an octavo in paper covers, but its name or author, or whose it was or what became of it, neither of us can recollect; nor do either of us at this time remember any of the scenes immediately preceding or attending the tragic death of Marie Antoinette as these are, or may be, recorded in history. Louisville, Kentucky, U.S., October 18th, 1884.[328] — WILLIAM DEERING

☞ CASE #313: Joseph Wilkins, while a young man, absent from home, dreamt, without any apparent reason, that he returned home, reached the house at night, found the front door locked, entered by the back door, visited his mother's room, found her awake, and said to her, "Mother, I am going on a long journey and am come to bid you good-bye."

A day or two afterwards this young man received a letter from his father, asking how he was, and alleging his mother's anxiety on account of a vision which had visited her on a night which was, in fact, that of the son's dream. The mother, lying awake in bed, had heard some one try the front door and enter by the back door, and had then seen the son enter her room, heard him say to her, "Mother, I am going on a long journey and am come to bid you good-bye," and had answered, "O dear son thou art dead!" words which the son also had heard her say in his dream.[329] — REV. JOSEPH WILKINS

☞ CASE #314: Three years ago, when staying at Ems for my health, one morning after having my bath I was resting on the sofa reading. A slight drowsiness came over me and I distinctly saw the following:—My husband, who was then in England, appeared to me riding down the lane leading from my father's house. Suddenly the horse grew restive, then plunged and kicked, and finally unseated his rider, throwing him violently to the ground.

I jumped up hastily, thinking I had been asleep, and on my going down to luncheon, I related to a lady who was seated next me what I had seen and made the remark, "I hope all is well at home."

My friend, seeing I was anxious, laughed and told me not to be superstitious, and so I forgot the incident, until two days afterwards I received a letter from home saying my husband had been thrown from his horse and had dislocated his shoulder. The time and place of the accident exactly agreed with my vision. October 17th, 1882.[330] — LAURA FLEMING

☞ CASE #315: On a summer's evening in the year 1743, when Daniel Stricket, servant to John Wren of Wilton Hall, was sitting at the door along with his master, they saw the figure of a man with a dog pursuing some horses along Souterfell side, a place so extremely steep that a horse could scarcely travel upon it at all. The figures appeared to run at an amazing pace, till they got out of sight at the lower end of the fell.

On the following morning Stricket and his master ascended the steep side of the mountain, in the full expectation of finding the man dead, and of picking up some of the shoes of the horses, which they thought must have been cast while galloping at such a furious rate. Their expectations, however, were disappointed. No traces either of man or horse could be found, and they could not even discover upon the turf the single mark of a horse's hoof.

These strange appearances, seen at the same time by two different persons in perfect health, could not fail to make a deep impression on their minds. They at first concealed what they had seen, but they at length disclosed it, and were laughed at for their credulity.[331] — DR. BREWSTER

☞ CASE #316: In the following year, on the 23rd June 1744, Daniel Stricket [of the above entry], who was then servant to Mr. Lancaster of Blakehills (a place near Wilton Hall, and both of which places are only about half a mile from Souterfell), was walking, about seven o'clock in the evening, a little above the house, when he saw a troop of horsemen riding on [the] Souterfell side in pretty close ranks, and at a brisk pace. Recollecting the ridicule that had been cast upon him the preceding year, he continued to observe the figures for some time in silence; but being at last convinced that there could be no deception in the matter, he went to the house and informed his master that he had something curious to show him.

They accordingly went out together; but before Stricket had pointed out the place Mr. Lancaster's son had discovered the aërial figures. The family was then summoned to the spot, and the phenomena were seen alike by them all. The equestrian figures seemed to come from the lowest parts of Souterfell, and became visible at a place called Knott. They then advanced in regular troops along the side of the Fell, till they came opposite to Blakehills, when they went over the mountain, after describing a kind of curvilineal path. The pace at which the figures moved was a regular swift walk, and they continued to be seen for upwards of two hours, the approach of darkness alone preventing them from being visible. Many troops were seen in succession; and frequently the last but one in a troop quitted his position, galloped to the front, and took up the same pace with the rest.

The changes in the figures were seen equally by all the spectators, and the view of them was not confined to the farm of Blakehills only, but they were seen by every person at every cottage within the distance of a mile, the number of persons who saw them amounting to about twenty-six. The attestation of these facts, signed by Lancaster and Stricket, bears the date of the 21st July 1785.^{332} — DR. BREWSTER

☛ CASE #317: [Similar extraordinary sights, similar to those described in the entry above, have] been frequently seen in the Straits of Messina between Sicily and the coast of Italy, and whenever it takes place, the people, in a state of exultation, as if it were not only a pleasing but a lucky phenomenon, hurry down to the sea, exclaiming *Morgana, Morgana.*

When the rays of the rising sun form an angle of 45° on the sea of Reggio, and when the surface of the water is perfectly unruffled either by the wind or the current, a spectator placed upon an eminence in the city, and having his back to the sun and his face to the sea, observes upon the surface of the water superb palaces with their balconies and windows, lofty towers, herds and flocks grazing in wooded valleys and fertile plains, armies of men on horseback and on foot, with multiplied fragments of buildings, such as columns, pilasters, and arches. These objects pass rapidly in succession along the surface of the sea during the brief period of their appearance. The various objects thus enumerated are pictures of palaces and buildings actually existing on shore, and the living objects are of course only seen when they happen to form a part of the general landscape.

If at the time that these phenomena are visible the atmosphere is charged with vapour or dense exhalations, the same objects which are depicted upon the sea will be seen also in the air occupying a space which extends from the surface to the height of twenty-five feet. These images, however, are less distinctly delineated than the former. If the air is in such a state as to deposit dew, and is capable of forming the rainbow, the objects will be seen only on the surface of the sea, but they all appear fringed with red, yellow, and blue light as if they were seen through a prism.[333] — DR. BREWSTER

☛ CASE #318: [In 19th-Century England spectral scenes] still more extraordinary [than those described in the previous entry] have been witnessed. From Hastings, on the coast of Sussex, the cliffs on the French coast are fifty miles distant, and they are actually hid by the convexity of the earth, that is, a strait line drawn from Hastings to the French coast would pass through the sea.

On Wednesday the 26th July 1798, about five o'clock in the afternoon, Mr. Latham, a Fellow of the Royal Society, then residing at Hastings, was surprised to see a crowd of people running to the sea side. Upon inquiry into the cause of this, he learned that the coast of France could be seen by the naked eye, and he immediately went down to witness so singular a sight. He distinctly saw the cliffs extending for some leagues along the French coast, and they appeared as if they were only a few miles off. They gradually appeared more and more elevated, and seemed to approach nearer to the eye.

The sailors with whom Mr. Latham walked along the water's edge were at first unwilling to believe in the reality of the appearance, but they soon became so thoroughly convinced of it, that they pointed out and named to him the different places which they had been accustomed to visit, and which they conceived to be as near as if they were sailing at a small distance into the harbour.

These appearances continued for nearly an hour, the cliffs sometimes appearing brighter and nearer, and at other times fainter and more remote. Mr. Latham then went upon the eastern cliff or hill, which is of considerable height, when, as he remarks, a most beautiful scene presented itself to his view. He beheld at once

Dungeness, Dover Cliffs, and the French coast all along from Calais, Boulogne, etc., to St. Vallery, and, as some of the fishermen affirmed, as far west as Dieppe. With the help of a telescope, the French fishing boats were plainly seen at anchor, and the different colours of the land upon the heights, together with the buildings, were perfectly discernible.

Mr. Latham likewise states that the cape of land called Dungeness, which extends nearly two miles into the sea, and is about sixteen miles in a straight line from Hastings, appeared as if quite close to it, and the vessels and fishing-boats which were sailing between the two places appeared equally near, and were magnified to a high degree. These curious phenomena continued "in the highest splendour" till past eight o'clock, although a black cloud had for some time totally obscured the face of the sun.[334] — DR. BREWSTER

☛ CASE #319: A phenomenon no less marvellous [as that described in the previous entry] was seen by Professor Vince of Cambridge and another gentleman on the 6th August 1806 at Ramsgate.

The summits *v w x y* of the four turrets of Dover Castle are usually seen over the hill A B, upon which it stands, lying between Ramsgate and Dover; but on the day above-mentioned, at seven o'clock in the evening, when the air was very still and a little hazy, not only were the tops *v w x y* of the four towers of Dover Castle seen over the adjacent hill A B, but the whole of the Castle *m n r s*, appeared as if it were situated on the side of the hill next [to] Ramsgate, and rising above the hill as much as usual.

This phenomenon was so very singular and unexpected, that at first sight Dr. Vince thought it an illusion; but upon continuing his observations, he became satisfied that it was a real image of the Castle. Upon this he gave a telescope to a person present, who, upon attentive examination, saw also a very clear image of the castle, as the Doctor had described it. He continued to observe it for about twenty minutes, during which time the appearance remained precisely the same, but rain coming on, they were prevented from making any farther observations. Between the observers and the land from which the hill rises, there was about six miles of sea, and from thence to the top of the hill there was about the same distance. Their own height above the surface of the water was about seventy feet.

This illusion derived great force from the remarkable circumstance, that the hill itself did not appear through the image, as it might have been expected to do. The image of the castle was very strong and well defined, and though the rays from the hill behind it must undoubtedly have come to the eye, yet the strength of the image of the castle so far obscured the back ground, that it made no sensible impression on the observers. Their attention was, of course, principally directed to the image of the castle; but if the hill behind had been at all visible, Dr. Vince conceives that it could not have escaped their observation, as they continued to look at it for a considerable time with a good telescope.[335] — DR. BREWSTER

☛ CASE #320: . . . of all the phenomena witnessed by [explorer] Mr. Scoresby, that of the *Enchanted Coast*, as it may be called, must have been the most remarkable.

This singular effect was seen on the 18th July, when the sky was clear, and a tremulous and perfectly transparent vapour was particularly sensible and profuse: At nine o'clock in the morning, when the phenomenon was first seen, the thermometer stood at 42° Fahr. but in the preceding evening it must have been greatly lower, as the sea was in many places covered with a considerable pellicle of new ice,—a circumstance which in the very warmest time of the year must be considered as quite extraordinary, especially when it is known that 10° farther to the north no freezing of the sea at this season had ever before been observed.

Having approached on this occasion so near the unexplored shore of Greenland that the land appeared distinct and bold, Mr. Scoresby was anxious to obtain a drawing of it, but on making the attempt he found that the outline was constantly changing, and he was induced to examine the coast with a telescope, and to sketch the various appearances which presented themselves. These are shown [see illustration below] without any regard to their proper order which we shall describe in Mr. Scoresby's own words:

The general telescopic appearance of the coast was that of an extensive ancient city abounding with the ruins of castles, obelisks, churches, and monuments, with other large and conspicuous buildings. Some of the hills seemed to be surmounted by turrets, battlements, spires, and pinnacles; while others, subjected to one or two reflexions, exhibited large masses of rock, apparently suspended in the air, at a considerable elevation above the actual termination of the mountains to which they referred. The whole exhibition was a grand phantasmagoria.

Scarcely was any particular portion sketched before it changed its appearance, and assumed the form of an object totally different. It was perhaps alternately a castle, a cathedral, or an obelisk; then expanding horizontally, and coalescing with the adjoining hills, united the intermediate valleys, though some miles in width, by a bridge of a single arch, of the most magnificent appearance and extent.

Notwithstanding these repeated changes, the various figures represented in the drawing had all the distinctness of reality; and not only the different strata, but also the veins of the rocks, with the wreaths of snow occupying ravines and fissures, formed sharp and distinct lines, and exhibited every appearance of the most perfect solidity.[336] — DR. BREWSTER

☛ CASE #321: One of the most remarkable facts respecting aërial images presented itself to Mr. Scoresby in a later voyage which he performed to the coast of Greenland in 1822.

Having seen an inverted image of a ship in the air he directed to it his telescope; he was able to discover it to be his father's ship, which was at the time below the horizon. "It was," says he, "so well defined, that I could distinguish by a telescope every sail, the general rig of the ship, and its particular character; insomuch, that I confidently pronounced it to be my father's ship, the *Fame*, which it afterwards proved to be; though, on comparing notes with my father, I found that our relative position, at the time, gave a distance from one another very nearly 30 miles, being about seventeen miles beyond the horizon, and some leagues beyond the limit of direct vision. I was so struck with the peculiarity of the circumstance, that I mentioned it to the officer of the watch, stating my full conviction that the *Fame* was then cruising in the neighbouring inlet."[337] — DR. BREWSTER

☛ CASE #322: Several curious effects of the mirage were observed by Baron [Alexander] Humboldt during his travels in South America. When he was residing at Cumana, he frequently saw the islands of Picuita and Boracha suspended in the air, and sometimes with an inverted image. On one occasion he observed small fishing boats swimming in the air, during more than three or four minutes, above the well defined horizon of the sea, and when they were viewed through a telescope, one of the boats had an inverted image accompanying it in its movements.

This distinguished traveller observed similar phenomena in the barren steppes of the Caraccas, and on the borders of the Orinoco, where the river is surrounded by sandy plains. Little hills and chains of hills appeared suspended in the air, when seen from the steppes, at three or four leagues distance. Palm trees standing single in the Llanos appeared to be cut off at bottom, as if a stratum of air separated them from the ground; and, as in the African desert, plains destitute of vegetation appeared to be rivers or lakes.

At the Mesa de Pavona M. Humboldt and M. Bonpland saw cows suspended in the air at the distance of 1000 toises, and having their feet elevated 3' 20" above the soil. In this case the images were erect, but the travellers learned from good authority that inverted images of horses had been seen suspended in the air near Calabozo.[338] — DR. BREWSTER

☛ CASE #323: Princess Schwartzenberg perished at Paris, at the great fire which took place at the Austrian Embassy. She had left her youngest children at Vienna.

The Cardinal, being then a baby of six months old, was in his cradle one night, when suddenly his nurse, an old and very respectable, but by no means either a clever or imaginative woman, fell down on her knees and exclaimed, "Jesu, Maria, Joseph! there is the figure of the Princess, standing over the baby's cradle."

Several nursery-maids, who were in the room, heard the exclamation, though they saw nothing, but to her dying day the nurse affirmed the truth of the vision, and, there being no telegraphs then, it was not for many days after that the news of the Princess Schwartzenberg's untimely fate reached Vienna.[339] — LADY BLOOMFIELD

☛ CASE #324: When I was a child I had many remarkable experiences of a psychical nature, which I remember to have looked upon as ordinary and natural at the time.

On one occasion (I am unable to fix the date, but I must have been about 10 years old) I was walking in a country lane at A., the place where my parents then resided. I was reading geometry as I walked along, a subject little likely to produce fancies or morbid phenomena of any kind, when in a moment, I saw a bedroom known as the White Room in my home, and upon the floor lay my mother, to all appearance dead.

The vision must have remained some minutes, during which time my real surroundings appeared to pale and die out; but as the vision faded, actual surroundings came back, at first dimly, and then clearly. I could not doubt that what I had seen was real, so, instead of going home, I went at once to the house of our medical man and found him at home. He at once set out with me for my home, on the way putting questions I could not answer, as my mother was to all appearance well when I left home.

I led the doctor straight to the White Room, where we found my mother actually lying as in my vision. This was true even to minute details. She had been seized suddenly by an attack at the heart, and would soon have breathed her last but for the doctor's timely advent. I shall get my father and mother to read this and sign it. "We certify that the above is correct. S. G. Gwynne, J. W. Gwynne." November 1884.[340] — JEANIE GWYNNE-BETTANY

☛ CASE #325: One afternoon, during the absence of my brother in Normandy, I was asked to look in a ring containing a semi-transparent Persian stone of dark green colour. I was to think of my brother and see if any picture in the stone would reveal his whereabouts. After a few moments of gazing with no result, I was going to hand the ring back, when quite suddenly I distinctly saw [in the ring] a lovely little sea-piece. A lighthouse stood at the end of a ridge of rocks which were shewing well above the blue water, it being clearly low tide. A little fishing vessel with dark reddish-brown sails was further out to sea to the left of the lighthouse.

I was astonished to see it all so plainly, but thinking my brother was at Rouen, could find no connexion with him.

However on his return two days later I told him of my experiment, when he said that he had, at that identical time, been looking at exactly the view I described from his hotel window at Cherbourg. It had struck him as being so pretty, that he called the friend with whom he was travelling to admire it with him. I thereupon made a rough sort of sketch of what I had seen and shewed it to this friend without telling him the reason. He at once recognised it also. This happened about August 18th, 1898, at Alton in Hampshire. I may add that I have never myself visited Cherbourg either before or after this incident. September 6th, 1903.[341] — ADELA F. SUMNER

☛ CASE #326: On the night of April 16th I retired to bed feeling unusually depressed, placing a glass of water on the table for drinking during the night. My husband was on night duty at the time on the L.N.W. line.

I awoke with a start about three o'clock in the morning, and feeling thirsty, reached out of bed for the water; when about to partake of it, I saw, to my surprise, a moving picture in the glass, comprising waggons, and in the rear a guard van; as I looked they all appeared to smash into each other, and I noticed the van in particular was the most damaged.

My husband came home about two hours later and told me that he passed the scene of the accident, and that the guard was seriously injured. I regard the above as something more than a mere coincidence. May 26th, 1902.[342] — MRS. H.

☛ CASE #327: Saturday, January 27th, 1900. This afternoon while I was sitting near the fire talking to L., I was holding a small photo. of Mrs. H. and describing her.

"Where is she now?" asked L.

"In Rome," I answered, "settled for the winter."

And as I spoke, suddenly I felt conscious of what she might be doing at the time.

"Do you know," I went on, "I think she must be just coming out of her room on to a high terrace such as we have here, only that there is green over it."

L. did not say "nonsense," but just asked quietly: "What is she wearing?"

"A black skirt," I answered, "and a mauve blouse—she is looking out over many roofs and spires—and now she has gone back into the room and a maid is closing the shutters."

"Can you see her room?" asked L.

"I think it is small," I said, "there is a cottage-piano and a writing-table near it. I think the large head of Hermes stands on it and something silver."

And then I felt nothing more and added, "What nonsense I have been talking."

L. thinks there may be some truth in the impression and wants me to write and ask Mrs. H. what she remembers of this afternoon. It was about six o'clock.

I cannot say I saw anything; somehow I seemed to *feel* her surroundings were just so. I have never been to Rome, nor has she told me anything of where she lives beyond the address. — MRS. D.

[What follows is Mrs. H. response to Mrs. D.'s letter above, corroborating he vision in every particular. L.S.]

Rome, Italy, February 5th, 1900. Two days ago, as I was dressing in the morning, I was *thinking of you*. You had been so much in my thoughts for some days that I had really worried, wondering if you were still ill, or E. again. That morning as I awoke, thoughts of you came, and I determined to write you as soon as I had had my coffee.

Imagine my surprise and delight, therefore, to receive your letter, a letter so full of interest to me, that I have had no rest since its arrival, in my great desire to answer it. I have really had no moment to call my own. The two days since it came seem like two weeks to me, for when one desires to do anything very much, the time seems long, doesn't it? [The writer then explains at length why she had been prevented from writing for two days.]

. . . You have certainly, however, filled much of my thoughts these days, and I have felt you in an extraordinary manner. You certainly have a power to visit your friends, and to see them, and to make them feel you. Your letter is absolutely startling and mysterious. And now I can answer it detail for detail, and item for item. [The writer then avows her belief in telepathy and clairvoyance.]

. . . That you have peeped at me in my small Roman house is certainly a fact. As you state the facts, every small detail is not altogether exact, but the facts as a whole are true and exact and perfect, as you shall see. Your vision (if I may call it so) is so true and marvellous that on Sunday last, the 4ᵗʰ, about 3 p.m. (that was yesterday) as I was looking from my window in the salon with Mr. S., watching a great funeral of one of Rome's best-loved Cardinals, I related your glimpse into my house, and I could not help exclaiming: "perhaps Madame D. sees us now . . . as we are standing here in our window."

Let me begin by answering bit by bit all you say. I have a dear little vine-covered terrace, looking out into the Piazza di Spagna, and looking also right up to the spires or rather towers of S. Trinita dei Monti, with the great obelisk in front. The afternoon of Jan. 27ᵗʰ I returned to my home, after a walk and [after] making a few purchases, at 5 p.m. I took off my fur jacquette, and went at once into my dining-room to see about the dinner-table, as three friends came at 7 p.m. to dine. I busied myself about the table for some time, then stepped on to the terrace (which is so pretty, but opens, unfortunately, from the kitchen). I went into the terrace at that time to see about our dessert for dinner, which I had put there to become cool. Then I went back into the dining-room, and as the hanging-lamp had just been lighted, I ordered the maid to drop the outside curtains. She did so.

I remember that I looked just then at the clock, and it was 5:35 p.m. I had on a black skirt, a black silk blouse, and a mauve tie, which twisted about my neck and hung in two ends to my waist. It looked to you like a mauve blouse. Then I went into our small salon and took something from the table. I remember it distinctly. Our salon is very small; there is an upright piano and a writing-table, on which are photos and books too, and a lot of little silver things. Hermes (your photo to me) stands very near, on another little table, quite near in fact. It is all quite mysterious. I believe you have really peeped into my house.

You fairly startled me when you tell me that our acquaintance was made in just five days! I had never counted it, and yet you are perfectly right, it was just five days, and made up of bits of time together and a few conversations. As I remember, you and I really never had one moment actually by ourselves. You say truly that our intellectual friendship will have gone far ahead of the personal. Then French-reading and my piano and zither I bring in when a rainy day or spare moments offer. Tell me of your day, do.[343] — MRS. H.

☞ CASE #328: A circle of fire was seen at Bethel [during the Welsh Christian Revival services] last Friday evening, and was seen by many. It appeared before the pulpit and above the big seat. It was about 3 feet in diameter, and moved upwards as high as the gallery, and then disappeared. I cannot say how many saw it. I can refer you to two young men who are candidates for the Ministry. Both saw it distinctly, and it has made a lasting impression on their minds. [One was] Mr. J. C. Jones, c/o Mr. Griffith Jones, Builder. The other one is T. M. Jones, who lives near to the former. Pontycymmer, Glamorgan, December 1st, 1905.[344] — MR. D. MARDY DAVIES

Chapter Seven

PARANORMAL ACCOUNTS

Cases of Haunted Houses and Poltergeists

☛ CASE #329: In the suburbs of a large manufacturing town, there is an old house with which I am well acquainted, as also with its inhabitants. It was built about 1790, and for the most part has been used as a gentleman's residence. It has, I know, been considered haunted for the last fifty years. Its first occupant was an eccentric doctor, and I think that it is in his history that we must look for the origin of the disturbances which undoubtedly take place. I can at present only speak as to the events of the last eighteen months, which are, however, merely samples of what is believed to have formerly taken place. They are as follows:

About Christmas, 1883, C. D. and W. G. D., the two little boys, came to their mother in the middle of the day, saying they had just seen "such a funny little old woman" come out of E.'s bedroom. On being questioned their statements tallied exactly, not differing in the slightest detail. A little old woman, dressed in brown, had come out of E.'s bedroom on to the landing where they were, and looked at them. They then came downstairs in a great hurry, and it was at once ascertained that no other person was upstairs, and that no one answering their description was in the house. This was not mentioned [to anyone else] by the mother, and the family generally were in ignorance of it.

A short time after, E. being at a dance was introduced to two ladies whom he had not previously known. On informing them where he lived, they at once told him that the house was haunted by a little old woman dressed in brown. He mentioned this to his mother as a good joke, who then told him that the boys had seen this old woman, and asked him not to say anything about it to the other members of the family. Prior to this they had lived there for six years without having been disturbed or annoyed in anyway.

Nothing further occurred until the end of August, 1884, when E., going to bed late one night, and without a light, on entering the inner landing which contains his bedroom door and three others, distinctly felt someone coming out of his room move past him. This "someone" turned to the right and went upstairs to the unused garret, E. hearing each footstep on the wooden stairs.

Getting a light from his room he at once followed, but the garret was empty; no one had come down the stairs, and there is no other exit. It afterwards transpired that none of the family had been up at that hour. He returned to his room and made a note of the circumstance in his diary, the exact time being five minutes to twelve.

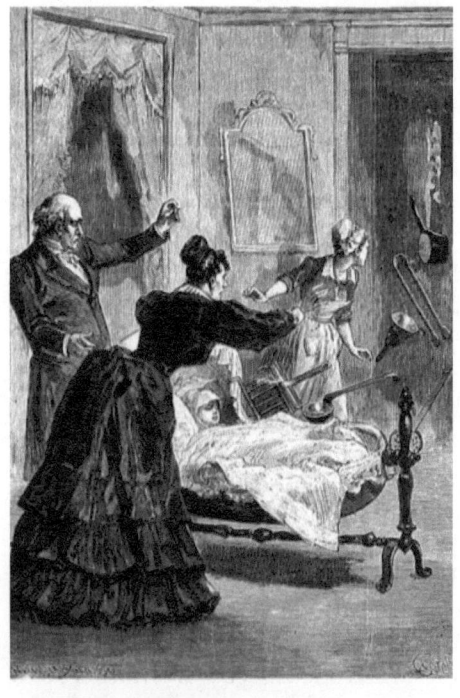

. . . Shortly after this a cousin on a visit slept in E.'s room alone, and complained next day of being disturbed in the night by someone who tried the handle of the door, and then delivered three loud knocks on the panel. Investigation proved that no bodily inmate of the house had caused these effects.

A friend of mind, of some experience in mesmerism, who knows the house and its inmates, was now consulted. He was acquainted with the foregoing particulars. He placed a lady of proved capacity as a clairvoyante on the track. The clairvoyante saw and described, shuddering, the apparitions of a man and woman; her description tallied with the foregoing particulars, and she added several minor details, also tallying, of which the mesmerist was not previously aware. The clairvoyante did not know the house or anything about the supposed supernatural phenomena.

. . . Prior to this, . . . E. [while] going up to bed about one o'clock in the morning heard, on reaching the first stone landing, his own name called three times. This calling came apparently from T.'s room, which at that time was occupied by one of his sisters. E.

did not answer, but ascertained the next morning that no member of the family had called him. On mentioning the matter he was told that a day or two before his sister M. [when] going upstairs in the course of the evening had had at the same place a precisely similar experience.

About a fortnight after this (November, 1884) Mr. D. [the father] and M. were sitting together in one of the rooms downstairs, E. and Mrs. D. [the mother] being upstairs, and the rest of the family out. Suddenly M.'s name was loudly called three times, being heard with equal distinctness by Mr. D. and his daughter. He, thinking that Mrs. D. was calling from upstairs, at once sent M. to see; but Mrs. D. certainly had not called, and E. states positively that M. had not been called by any one upstairs. At the time M. herself thought the sound came from another part of the house.

In every one of these instances it was clearly proved that no member of the family had caused these sounds: the matter has defied explanation, and the strictest enquiry has only served to demonstrate its unaccountable nature.

. . . Friday night last, 18th Sept. [1885], one of the girls, M. C. P., went upstairs to her bedroom, the rest of the family being in one room downstairs. The time was exactly twenty minutes past ten. On reaching the foot of the steps, she was very much startled to see a lady come rapidly out of her room, and, without the slightest noise, cross apparently into another room, at a distance of about six feet from herself. This apparition was of medium height, in build just like the girl to whom she appeared, head slightly bent on one side, and was dressed in white. She went half across the passage and then disappeared, having apparently crossed into the room I have indicated. I am not certain as to the precise style of dress she wore, whether or not it was a night-dress I cannot now positively say, but the most noticeable thing about her was the excessive whiteness of her dress.

It is absolutely certain that no one in the house was concerned or connected with this in any way, and I believe it to be a thoroughly genuine case of an apparition.

The lady who underwent this curious experience is thoroughly well known to me. She is possessed of very strong nerve, and she is one of the very last persons who would be likely to imagine such an occurrence.

Personally I have the most absolute trust in the truth of the foregoing statements. Granting that this is an apparition, I wish to draw your attention to two things. First, that nothing has led us to presuppose an apparition answering this description. The woman seen on a previous occasion by the two boys was old, and presented an entirely different appearance; and the experiments made in clairvoyance, while revealing the existence of two spirits and confirming our previous information, said nothing at all about a third.

Second, that while I have carefully avoided drawing attention to the fact, yet it is an undoubted fact that in every particular, so far as I know, the apparition of Friday last was the exact image of the girl by whom it was seen. The head bent a little on one side is a very marked and peculiar characteristic, and, owing to this fact of the head being bent, the face of the apparition was not visible. It does not appear to have for a moment occurred to the girl or to any of the family that this was her double, but it seems to me very much like a case of döppelganger.

. . . I have to-day had a long conversation with the young lady [i.e., M. C. P.] who saw the apparition I described in my last letter to you. I find that the landing was brilliantly lighted with gas, and that the gas was also lit in the bedroom from which the figure issued. The dress of the figure was minutely described to me as apparently consisting of very white, shiny satin, and was more of the nature of a night-dress than anything else. There is not the slightest doubt that the figure was a genuine apparition, as I have carefully ascertained that the investigation which this young lady at once carried out was most minute and thorough.

An interesting fact I have discovered is that the wall into which the figure appeared to vanish is, apparently without any reason, almost two feet thick. In this respect it differs from the other interior walls of the house.

This young lady has also informed me privately that she has seen this figure twice before: on each occasion she was coming downstairs, and saw the figure standing on the steps outside the front door (this opens into a large garden, not into a road or street). In neither instance did she see the face of the figure. Both these occurrences took place during the last winter [i.e., 1884], and she has carefully refrained from mentioning them hitherto. She has, however, promised now to keep me immediately informed of even the slightest incident which may take place, of even the most trivial importance. March 17th, 1885.[345] — MR. B.

☛ CASE #330: I returned home about 7 on the Friday night (March 12th). I had been absent from home on Monday and Tuesday nights: and it was during my absence that my wife took in the girl

Rose, who shared her bed in the front inner room. I slept at home on Wednesday, and the girl then slept on the squab in the kitchen. I left again on Thursday morning, and returned as mentioned on the Friday.

When told by my wife and Tom what had happened on Thursday night [extreme poltergeist activity] I said some one must have been tricking, and didn't think much more about it. But I chaffed the lass (Rose) a good deal, for she was much frightened.

About 11:30 on Friday evening, when my wife, the girl, and I were alone in the kitchen, just going up to bed, I heard a noise as if some one had come down the passage between the two houses, and were standing just outside our door. They didn't knock; but I said to Rose, "Go and see who's there." But she was frightened and didn't go.

Then presently, a lot of things came rattling down the stairs. I don't know what came first; but a lot of things came—a surcingle, bits of carpet, knives and forks, a corkscrew, etc. The girl went to pick them up, and put them on the table, and just as fast as she put them on more things came down. Then my wife said to me, "The salt-cellar came down last night, but you won't have it down to-night, for here it is on the table." She was using it at the time for salting Tom's dinner for next day.

She had hardly said this, when the salt-cellar flew off from the table, and into the corner near the outer door. Rose was in that corner, and not near the table; my wife was at the table but certainly didn't touch the cellar. I saw the thing go, though I couldn't believe my eyes. My wife didn't see it go, but we both saw it as it struck the wall in the corner. All the salt was spilled out of it.

I fairly couldn't believe my own eyes; but I couldn't help thinking it must be Tom. So I went upstairs to him, and told him to leave off. "Thou'lt frighten our Liz to death." He said, "It's not me, Joe. I'll take my oath it isn't. I've never thrown nowt down."

Whilst I was still talking to him, I heard a crash downstairs; and the women screamed; and my wife cried, "Come down, Joe." As I was just coming into the room the candle which I held in my hand went out—I don't know how at all—and we were left in darkness, except for the firelight.

Then something hit me on the forehead, and I cried out, "Who threw that?" Then there was a crash in the corner. I found out when we had a light again, that the salt-cellar had fallen again into the corner, and broken itself. Then I found out that the candle was not in the candlestick, and asked where it was. I told the girl to look for it, and then she felt among the things at the bottom of the stairs and picked up three candles, two of them quite new. We had only had two candles in the house which had been bought just before, and both had been partly burnt. I lit the old ones and left the new ones on the table; but they disappeared afterwards, and I have never seen them since.

When the candle was lit again, I saw the little [porcelain] china woman jump off from the mantelpiece, and go into the same corner. It fell on its side, and then righted itself, and stood upright, unbroken. I distinctly saw it go through the air; it passed near me as I stood about the middle of the room. None of us were near the mantelpiece. I picked it up, and presently it fell into the corner again, and broke itself. Then the tea-caddy and the candlestick, all from the mantelpiece, followed.

Then I went out and found George Ford ("Buck" Ford), and asked him to fetch Dr. Lloyd for the child—for they had told me that all this disturbance meant the death of the child, who was very ill with an abscess in its back. Then I got my wife to take the little lad out, and lay him next door, he lying on the squab in the kitchen at the time. Rose went with her, and they took all the children with them.

Before going, Rose had to go into the inner room, and then things began to fly about there and make a disturbance. All had been quiet there before.

I went after the others into the next house and stayed there some little time. When I came back, I found the Police-constable Higgs in the kitchen. He and I went alone there. (Rose all this time was next door.) We heard a crash in the inner room, and we went in—Solomon Wass and Tom, who had just entered with us, and Higgs with his lantern, and we found the chest of drawers turned up on end, and the lustres and looking-glass, and everything else that had been on it, in pieces on the floor.

Then we came back into the kitchen, and we saw the cupboard door open, and a big glass jar flew out, and flew into the yard and broke itself. Also some things flew off the bin at the side of the door, from the end near the fire; and they pitched in the corner, and then went out in the yard. Things often pitched on the floor by the door first, and then got up again and flew out into the yard.

Then Dr. Lloyd came in with my wife, and Higgs showed him what had happened in the inner room. Then when we had got into the kitchen again, and were all standing near the door of the inner room—Higgs, my wife, and Tom, and Wass, and Lloyd—who was about six feet from the bin, and the nearest to it of our party—we all saw a basin which was lying on the bin near the door, get up two or three times in the air, rising slowly a few inches or perhaps a foot, and then falling plump. Then it got up higher, and went slowly, wobbling as it went, up to the ceiling, and when it reached the ceiling, it fell down all at once, and broke itself.

Dr. Lloyd then looked in the bin, saying the devil must be in the house, and then left. All the others shortly afterwards left, Mrs. W., Rose and the children stopping in the next house.

Tom and I sat in the chair on either side of the fire until the next morning at 8 a.m. Things kept on moving every now and then until about 2 a.m., and then was all quiet, and we got to sleep a bit.

At about 8 a.m. I had to go out to see after a pig, which had been pigging, and then things began again; and a lot of folks came in to see about it, Currass came in, and I went with him into the inner room and showed him the chest of drawers, he and I alone; we came out leaving the door open—I am quite sure it was open—and I was sitting near the fire, and Currass was just inside the kitchen, not far from the open door, when Wass's little lad, who was sitting at the table, said, "There's the clock striking," meaning the big clock which hung over our bed. I couldn't hear it, and I said it was a lie. Just then we heard a crash, and I asked what it was, and Currass looked round, and said it was the American clock had fallen right across the bed, and lay on the floor at the foot, with its bottom knocked out. Then I took it into the yard. I don't think—indeed, I am sure that Coulter was not here when all this happened. The other clock fell and was broken, but whether before or after I cannot remember; and he may have seen that. I don't remember where the girl Rose was when the American clock fell. She may have been in the kitchen, but she certainly wasn't in the inner room; no one was in that room, I am sure. I don't remember saying just at that time, though I often did say, that wherever she went the things smashed.

After that, Currass and I and one or two others were standing near to the outer door talking, when the china dogs, or one of them, flew off the mantelpiece and smashed; and lot of things kept on flying into the corner and smashing. I saw one of the dogs leave the mantelpiece and go through the air. I don't remember exactly when Coulter came; he may have been here when the china dog was smashed, but I don't remember that he was. Then a cream jug fell off the table; it had done so four or five times without smashing. At last I filled it with milk, and had placed it on the bin, when it suddenly fell off and smashed, and the milk was all spilt.

Then I was tired, and lay down on the squab; but things kept moving. I was told some pictures on the wall began to move, but I didn't see them.

At about 2 p.m., a Salvation Army woman came in and was talking to me as I lay on the squab; she stood near the inner door; Rose was near the outer door having brought in some carpet. There were two candlesticks on the bin, at the end near the fireplace. Suddenly something dropped behind the Salvation Army woman. No one saw it going through the air; but we turned round and found that it was one of the brass candlesticks. It was half balanced on the small end where the candle goes, and was wobbling about on the end. Then the Salvation woman said, "I must go"; and she went.

Then a little after, when Rose was going to lay down the carpet, and no one else in the room, a medicine bottle, full, fell from the bin on to [a] roll of carpet, about three or four yards off, and was broken. A lamp glass had fallen several times without breaking; but at last that fell and broke. Then an empty bottle flew off from the mantelpiece. That was one of the last things that happened.

Well then, I couldn't stand it any longer. Wherever the lass seemed to go, things seemed to fly about. So I said to her, "You'll have to go." She began to roar. But my wife gave her some tea, and she went. That was between 4 and 5 p.m., very soon after the last disturbance. Nothing happened after she left. We sat up in the kitchen that evening, a lot of us, as the newspapers tell; but nothing happened at all.

I have been in the house three years. I think the house had been built four or five years before that. Nothing of the kind had ever happened in it before, as far as I know, except that once I thought I heard some one moving in the yard, and fancied it might be some one after the fowls; but there was no one there; and there was that strange tilting of the table when my wife was washing up the things about a week before. The Wasses and the Willises [Mrs. Willis is Wass's sister] had lived together in the next house; but since all these disturbances, the Willises have left the house; but Mr. and Mrs. Wass are still there. New Building Ground, Worksop. April 8th, 1884.[346] — JOSEPH "JOE" WHITE

☛ CASE #331: In accordance with your instructions [that is, of the S.P.R.] I have been to Norwich to gather all the available evidence in connection with the "hauntings" which you were informed occurred there. I called upon Mr. I. O. Howard Taylor (an Associate of the Society for Psychical Research), who first drew your attention to the matter, and ascertained from him the address of the person who was inhabiting the house at the time the disturbances were said to occur. He is a clerk, and we may call him Mr. X. He gave his evidence clearly and very emphatically; he is an exceedingly intelligent witness, but I consider him to be of a somewhat nervous and excitable temperament, although, of course, his occasional highly-strung manner may have been due to the nature of the circumstances which he was relating. His statements were to the following effect:

In September, 1883, he returned from his marriage trip and, with his wife, took possession of a house in ____ Road. He cannot say how soon disturbances were noticed with extra interest, for it was several months before the noises which were heard in the house were recognised as of an unusual character. However, when Mr. and Mrs. X. were in their bedroom at night, tramping sounds, like people occupying the sitting-room they had just left, were heard, the handle of a door at the foot of the stairs was once or twice unmistakably tried, and sounds of footsteps mounting the stairs were heard.

Instant investigation failed to discover a cause for these sounds, and their frequent repetition led to the conclusion that the house was "haunted by a haunt," to use Mr. X.'s own expression. The first unmistakable proof, however, of the correctness of this conclusion was presented to him one night in the form of an apparition.

He was in bed with his wife in the spare bedroom—a window having been broken in their own room. His wife was asleep; he could not sleep, but was lying quite still, and wide awake. Suddenly, on the first stroke of 12 from a clock in the city, there was an audible "swish," and the figure of a man stood before him, at the foot of the bed. The figure was that of a respectable old gentleman of about 60, with sharp, well-marked features. He was dressed in a black coat and waistcoat, and stood quite motionless, staring intently at him. Mr. X., without the ability to do otherwise, stared in return, until the last stroke of 12, when the apparition appeared to raise its arms and sink through the floor.

This experience had a very marked effect upon his nerves, and during the four months which elapsed between that date and the time they were compelled to vacate the premises, he was continually apprehensive and nervous, sometimes feeling utterly unable to go down from the dining-room to the kitchen alone. This arose from a sense of fear, which he could not overcome, even if by so doing he could have possessed himself of a handsome reward. He did not mention his experience to his wife, nor to *anyone*; she, however, did not fail to observe his changed behaviour and looks, and frequently remarked upon the facts, as did also their friends and neighbours.

The noises still continued, and formed the subject of much speculation between them; the servant frequently heard footsteps walking up and down the kitchen stairs, and at night they were frequently heard, very distinctly and unmistakably, in different parts of the house. The servant, too, says she sometimes heard subdued voices and other vocal sounds, but she seems hazy in separating these from those produced by the woman next door, who suffers from a chronic cough. But the one manifestation which brought about their retreat from the house occurred about 8:30 in the evening, in the last week of September, 1884.

Mrs. X., the servant, and a little girl who had been taking tea with them, were sitting in the back room of the two which form the ground floor. They were chatting unconcernedly, and Mrs. X. was assisting the little girl with some painting, standing with her back to the window, which overlooks the yard. Suddenly, apparently from a vacant chair which stood beneath the window, there came a loud *sigh*, which was quickly followed by five more low gasping sighs, as from a strongman in great bodily and mental anguish; then a pause of a few seconds, followed by another sigh, much louder than the preceding ones, and partaking more of the nature of a groan.

The three hearers were considerably frightened and upset: Mrs. X. was seized with a violent cramp in her side, the little girl was fearfully ill, and the servant had an attack of hysteria, and, as soon as they recovered the use of their limbs, they lost no time in leaving the house.

As they left the room, and were entering the front one, which opens into the street, they heard three raps on the wall of the staircase as they passed it.

Mr. X., meanwhile, was at his business; he returned home to find the house locked up, and a neighbour explained to him what had occurred, and told him where to find his wife.

He found her, with the servant, at the house of a friend. Both of them were very ill and hysterical, and it was only after considerable discussion and persuasion that they could be induced to return to the house for one more night.

Ultimately they did return, and Mr. X. went upstairs to wash his hands. Then came his turn to be again startled.

As he was passing the spare room he declares that he distinctly heard a woman's whisper, saying, "Hark! the master of the house has returned; we must depart." A sound of footsteps followed, apparently crossing the room, and then ensued a succession of sobs and wails, such as might be caused by a female in deep distress.

In spite of all this they went to bed, and passed the night as best they could. Mrs. X. was dosed with spirits to induce sleep—for her husband was becoming seriously alarmed about her—and the next day they left the house, taking up their quarters in that of a friendly neighbour.

A fortnight later they took the house which they now occupy, and had their furniture removed from the troublesome one. This latter has now been empty for the past two months. I had the opportunity of questioning Mr. and Mrs. X. and the servant separately; their accounts agree pretty accurately . . .

The house is again let, and is to be taken possession of on Monday, November 24th, 1884. The in-coming tenants are aware of the report connected with it, and treat it with scorn. Perhaps the further development of the matter may be safely left in their hands. November 22nd, 1884, Norwich.[347] — G. A. SMITH

☛ CASE #332: TOWARDS the end of August, 1904, somewhat sensational reports appeared in several of the daily papers about a "haunted house" at Upholland, near Wigan, in Lancashire, where "Poltergeist" phenomena were said to be occurring in abundance. The house was tenanted by a widow named Mrs. Winstanley with six children, the eldest son being a French polisher by trade and the younger ones miners. The disturbances occurred in a bedroom occupied by three of the sons, and seemed to be connected with a walled-up window in the room which was close to their bed. From this window and the adjoining parts of the wall of the room, pieces of paper were torn off and stones and mortar were pulled out of the wall and scattered about the room. The wall was repaired, but the same things happened again.

Early in September of the same year, Lieut.-Colonel Le M. Taylor visited Upholland to investigate the case and his report of it would have appeared sooner, but that it was hoped to get further evidence from one of the principal witnesses. He also made plans and drawings of different parts of the house, and obtained photographs of it and of the "haunted" window, which are not reproduced here, but may be seen in our Rooms by members of the Society. Colonel Taylor writes:

I arrived at the village of Upholland at about 11 a.m. on Friday, September 9th, 1904, and at once called on the Rev. G. F. Wills, who told me that the affair at the Winstanleys' had created much stir in the neighbourhood. The Winstanley family consists of Mrs. W. and her six children, namely William, age about 27, Thomas 24, Peter 17, Henry 14, and two little girls under 12 years of age.

Mr. Wills said that they were of good repute; that Peter was not so steady as his brothers the others he thought very trustworthy.

Mr. Wills kindly took me into the village and introduced me to Mr. Baxter as a good witness. He dictated to me the statement herewith, over his signature. We then went and found Mr. Chadwick, who is the local agent for the owner of the "haunted" house; he agreed to come with me to the house in the evening. I then saw Mrs. Winstanley herself, who received me very kindly and offered no objection whatever to my making an investigation in any way I liked. Peter was at home and he and his mother showed me the room and told me their story about what had taken place in it.

At 8 p.m. I returned and found Mr. Chadwick already in the haunted room sitting on the bed. In a few minutes we were joined by William and a Mr. John Corless, and one or two others. The street lamp made the room very far from dark. We sat on the bed in front of the newly plastered wall for about an hour, but as nothing occurred all my companions, except Mr. Corless, went downstairs and he and I went into the back room and sat at the door till 11 o'clock.[348] During this time some other people came and went, partly to see me, I suppose, but they came at once into the backroom and no one attempted to approach the "haunted" wall.

Nothing occult was observed and I returned to Wigan.

On Saturday I went over to Upholland at 11 a.m. and met John Corless and John Winstanley (who is no relation of the other people of that name) at Mr. Baxter's shop; they dictated their statements to me. At 8 p.m. I again went to Mrs. Winstanley's and sat at the door of the back room till 11. I had several visitors but no manifestations.

On Sunday I again returned and watched from 7:30 till 11; again visitors, William, Peter, John Corless, Chadwick and others, but no one attempted to approach the forbidden wall; again no occult manifestation. I was, as I anticipated, too late to get any personal experience in the matter. On Monday I returned to Cheltenham, after being promised three other statements and an assurance that Sergt. Radcliffe of the police would send me his when he returned from his holiday in about ten days.

From what I gathered in conversation during my visits to Upholland the history of the affair seems to be that during the last few days of July, knocks on the wall and bricked-up window were heard, but that it was not till the night of Sunday, August 1st, that they became so insistent as to cause alarm. On this night not only were knocks heard but the wall-paper was torn and pieces of mortar, etc., thrown about the room.

On Monday Mrs. Winstanley secured Mr. Baxter's assistance and called in the police. For something over a fortnight the disturbances continued and every endeavour was made to trace the cause of the phenomena without avail, many people taking part in the investigation, aided in every way by the family.

The agent, Mr. Chadwick, was among the most energetic of the investigators, but was so unfortunate that he did not witness anything which in his opinion excluded human agency. He told me that he was in the room when two pieces of mortar fell at his feet; he is not able to attribute this to the action of any one in the house, but supposes the mortar to have been thrown in through the window of the back room. This explanation is inadequate, for although the ground rises behind the house and thus makes such a thing more possible, the shape and size of the window in my opinion precludes it.

He had the floor of the room taken up, a hole made in the chimney; he examined the wall of Mrs. Peet's house next door, but could find no marks which might indicate operations from that side; he placed pencil marks round the dilapidations to see when pieces of mortar were newly carried away, and finally had the window newly walled up, the window-sill removed and the whole plastered over, making the wall good again. This was done on August 19th, since which time the boys have ceased to sleep in the room and the bed has been placed in its new position in the room (i.e., further away from the window).

Since this date the disturbances seem to have had a tendency gradually to diminish; no more knocks have been heard, or very few, and whereas at first the phenomena recurred every night, now intervals of quiet were interpolated, which have become more and more frequent.

At the date of my visit the last disturbance was noticed on the day before I arrived; still a considerable quantity of mortar and stone has been removed from the wall since the 19th September, also a new place has been attacked.

At first members of the Winstanley (family) were naturally suspected; now the consensus of public opinion has completely acquitted them. I could detect no adequate motive on the part of any one; indeed, the Winstanleys are much exercised about a demand on the part of their landlord that they should make good the damage.

Popular superstition attributes the disturbance to the spirit of a highwayman who was buried in the churchyard near the house about a hundred years ago. Frequent attempts have been made to detect intelligence, with no result; but if the story of the piece of plaster having been balanced on the knob of the bedstead is true, intelligence was certainly present.

I judge that the witnesses in this case were not familiar with, at least, the details of séance room manifestations; still on two occasions things were observed which correlate with these, and similar to phenomena reported to have been observed during other poltergeist manifestations, namely: Once when I was sitting just inside the door of the second room, with the pieces of wood which had formerly constituted the sill of the haunted window behind me against the wall, my two companions at the time—the schoolmaster and another—declared that they saw a light flitting about in the neighbourhood of the boards; they saw it two or three times, as they said, quite plainly; we had not been speaking of "spirit lights" or anything of the sort, our whole attention being directed towards the "haunted window" in the next room which we were watching.

At another time one of the witnesses told me that he considered that the stones he saw come out from the wall travelled more slowly than they could have done if jerked or thrown out and he perceived what looked like a faint light behind them. My informant seemed to lay no stress on this, as if he had no theory of their being removed by a "spirit hand" or anything of that sort. I attach the statements of the various witnesses from whom I was able to get written evidence.

My long delay in making this report is due to the fact that two other men promised me statements,[349] but though I have made several attempts to get them, I am unable; it must therefore be presumed that they are not attainable.

Mrs. Winstanley herself has given no statement, but corroborates, as far as she is concerned, what others informed me of. She told me that on one occasion when she knew that no one was in the house she was standing at the street door with one of her sons when they heard a noise in the room above; it was just getting dark in the evening. They went up to the room at once and found one or more of the stones on the floor; she believed they were in their places when she left the house.

Again, one of the brothers, who has not made a statement in writing, said to me, "Last Sunday week in the evening I was standing outside with Mrs. Peet; we heard what sounded like the stones being thrown on the floor. My brother had just left the house and was a little way down the street. When I heard the sound I called him back and asked him if the stones were in the wall when he left; he said yes. We all went up and found two of the large stones and a third smaller one on the floor."

The last manifestations seem to have shifted their locality, for a hole (about the size of an orange when I saw it) had been made in the plaster of the wall opposite the haunted window and the paper round it much torn only a day or two before my arrival. I should have mentioned that William Winstanley, the eldest brother, is lame, and a French polisher by trade, the other brothers are miners. December 20th, 1904.[350] — G. L. LE M. TAYLOR

☛ CASE #333: It was in September, 1903, that the following abnormal fact occurred to me. Every detail of it has been examined by me very carefully.

I had been on a long journey through the jungle of Palembang and Djambi (Sumatra) with a gang of 50 Javanese coolies for exploring purposes. Coming back from the long trip, I found that my home had been occupied by somebody else and I had to put up my bed in another house that was not yet ready, and had just been erected from wooden poles and lalang or kadjang. The roof was formed of great dry leaves of a kind called "kadjang" in Palembang. These great leaves are arranged one overlapping the other. In this way it is very easy to form a roof if it is only for a temporary house. This house was situated pretty far away from the bore-places belonging to the oil company, in whose service I was working.

I put my bullsack and mosquito curtain on the wooden floor and soon fell asleep. At about one o'clock at night I half awoke hearing something fall near my head outside the mosquito curtain on the floor. After a couple of minutes I completely awoke and turned my head around to see what was falling down on the floor. They were *black stones* from ⅛ to ¾ of an inch long. I got out of the curtain and turned up the kerosene lamp, that was standing on the floor at the foot of my bed. I saw then that the stones were falling through the roof in a parabolic line. They fell on the floor close to my head-pillow. I went out and awoke the boy (a Malay-Palembang coolie) who was sleeping on the floor in the next room. I told him to go outside and to examine the jungle up to a certain distance. He did so whilst I lighted up the jungle a little by means of a small "ever-ready" electric lantern. At the same time that my boy was outside the stones did not stop falling.

My boy came in again, and I told him to search the kitchen to see if anybody could be there. He went to the kitchen and I went inside the room again to watch the stones falling down. I knelt down near (the head of my bed) and tried to catch the stones while they were falling through the air towards me, but I could never catch them; *it seemed to me that they changed their direction in the air as soon as I tried to get hold of them*. I could not catch any of them before they fell on the floor.

Then I climbed up (the partition wall between my room and the boy's) and examined (the roof just above it from which) the stones were flying. They came right through the "kadjang," but there were no holes in the kadjang. When I tried to catch them there at the very spot of coming out, I also failed.

When I came down, my boy had returned from the kitchen and told me there was nobody. But I still thought that somebody might be playing a practical joke, so I took my Mauser rifle and fired 5 sharp cartridges into the jungle from the window of the boy's room. But the stones, far from stopping, fell even more abundantly after my shots than before.

After this shooting the boy became fully awake (it seemed to me that he had been dozing all the time before), and he looked inside the room. When he saw the stones fall down, he told me it was "Satan" who did that, and he was so greatly scared that he ran away in the pitch-dark night.

After he had run away the stones ceased to fall, and I never saw the boy back again.

I did not notice anything particular about the stones except that they were warmer than they would have been under ordinary circumstances.

The next day, when awake again, I found the stones on the floor and everything as I had left it in the night. I examined the roof again, but nothing was to be found, not a single crack or hole in the kadjang. I also found the 5 empty cartridges on the floor near the window. Altogether there had been thrown about 18 or 22 stones. I kept some of them in my pocket for a long while, but lost them during my later voyages.

The worst part of this strange fact was that my boy was gone, so that I had to take care of my breakfast myself, and did not get a cup of coffee nor toast!

At first I thought they might have been meteor-stones because they were so warm, but then again I could not explain how they could get through the roof without making holes!

. . . In the Dutch East Indies this phenomenon seems to happen pretty often; at least every now and then it is reported in the newspaper, generally concerning a house in the city. But I never gave myself the trouble to examine one of these cases, for the simple reason that it is an impossibility to control at the same moment all the people that are living around. . . .

Just because the house where I was sleeping was situated all alone, far away from other houses, I thought that this case might be of more interest than other similar cases.

Let me repeat the following particulars of it.

(1) All around the house was *jungle*, in front, behind, to the left and to the right.

(2) There was no other soul in the house and kitchen than myself and the boy.

(3) The boy certainly did *not* do it, because at the same time that I bent over him, while he was sleeping on the floor, to awake him, there fell a couple of stones. I not only *saw* them fall on the floor in the room, but I also *heard* them fall, the door being at that moment half open.

(4) While the boy was standing *in front of me* and I shot my cartridges, at that same moment I heard them fall behind me.

(5) I climbed up the poles of the roof and I saw quite distinctly that they came right through the "kadjang."

This kadjang is of such a kind that it cannot be penetrated (not even with a needle) without making a hole. Each "kadjang" is one single flat leaf of about 2 by 3 feet in size. It is a speciality of the neighbourhood of Palembang. It is very tough and offers a strong resistance to penetration.

(6) The stones (though not all of them) were hotter than could be explained by their having been kept in the hand or pocket for some time.

(7) All the stones without exception fell down within a certain

radius of not more than 3 feet; they all came through the same kadjang-leaf (that is to say, all the ones I saw) and they all fell down within the same radius on the floor.

(8) They fell rather slowly. Now, supposing that somebody might by trickery have forced them through the roof, or supposing they had not come through it at all,—even then there would remain something mysterious about it, because it seemed to me that they were *hovering* through the air; they described a parabolic line and then came down with a bang on the floor.

(9) The sound they made in falling down on the floor was also abnormal, because considering their slow motion the bang was much too loud.

The same thing had happened to me about a week before; but on that occasion I was standing outside in the open air near a tree in the jungle, and as it was impossible to control it that time (it might have been a monkey that did it), I did not pay much attention to it.

. . . The construction of the house is very different from that of European houses. It is all open, as all houses in the East Indies are. There was no ceiling in the house. The walls forming the rooms did not extend as far up as the roof, so that there was an open space between the walls and the roof. This last circumstance was the reason why I examined the phenomenon so closely and climbed up along the vertical poles of the wall up to the roof, to assure myself that the stones were not thrown over the wall through the open space.

The partition between the place where I was sleeping and the place where the boy was sleeping was continuous all around the four sides of the room, there being a closed door between us two. This partition was a wooden framework, with kadjang nailed on it, forming that way a solid wall, which did not however extend up to the roof (as just described). The only wooden floor was formed of 2 inch boards, nailed together, there being no holes in the floor.

I am sure of the date, 1903, because in June, 1903, my sister died, and after this strange phenomenon occurred to me, I began to ponder whether there might possibly be any connection between my sister's death and the falling stones.

After the phenomenon had taken place, I bought a book about spiritism, to try to find an explanation. Before the phenomenon occurred to me I had read nothing about spiritism, but I had often thought about it. I am not at all convinced that there was any connection between the falling stones and my sister's death. At the moment that the phenomenon occurred to me, I did not think about spiritism.

As I said before, one of my impressions was that the stones might have been meteor-stones, on account of their being hot. I put them in my pocket and carried them about with me for a long time, as there was a geological Professor coming to visit us and to inspect our work. I intended to have the stones inspected by him, but before he came the stones had been lost.

I hope that my plan is plain enough to give you an idea of the way in which I watched the stones coming through the roof. I was inside the room, climbed up along the framework to the top of the wall, held on with one hand to the framework and tried to catch the stones with the other hand, at the same time seeing the boy lying down sleeping outside (in the other room) on the floor behind the door, the space being lit up by means of a lamp in his room. The construction of the house was such that it was impossible to throw the stones through the open space from outside.

I wrote before that it seemed to me that the boy had been dozing all the time after I awoke him. I got that impression because his movements seemed to me abnormally slow; his rising up, his walking around, and everything seemed extraordinarily slow. These movements gave me the same strange impression as the slowly falling stones.

When I think over this last fact (for I remember very well the strange impression the slowly moving boy made on me) I feel now inclined to suggest the hypothesis that there might have been something abnormal in my own condition at the time. For, having read in the *Proceedings* about hallucinations, I dare not state any more that the stones in reality moved slowly; it might have been on account of some condition of my own sensory organs that it seemed to me that they did, though at that time I was not in the least interested in the question of hallucinations or of spiritism. I am afraid that the whole thing will ever remain a puzzle to me.[351] —
MR. W. G. GROTTENDIECK, OF DORDRECHT, HOLLAND

☛ CASE #334: [One of the best documented] supernatural disturbances [occurred] at the house of M. Joller, a well-known lawyer of Lucerne and a member of the Swiss National Council. M. Joller has published a work of ninety-one pages, giving a full account of them.

They consisted of violent rappings and knockings all over the house at all hours day and night. The very wainscot was seen to bend beneath the blows. Sighs, groans, and voices uttering piteous

lamentations, and occasionally, music accompanied with singing, in a melancholy tone, were heard. The rappings responded promptly to questions. Doors and windows were no sooner fastened than they would be suddenly flung open, and those standing open would be as suddenly closed. Showers of stones would fall in the rooms where the family were, though without hurting any one. Furniture was moved about, and articles were conveyed from one part of the house to another.

The spirits at length boldly showed themselves openly and were seen by different people. M. Joller not only felt a soft stroking on the forefinger of his left hand, but he on one occasion seized a hand of one of the spirits. He found it soft, solid, and warm, as a living hand; and felt distinctly the thumb and fingers, which soon, however, drew themselves away.[352] — *THE SPIRITUAL MAGAZINE*

☛ CASE #335: For several nights past immense crowds have been collected in and about the Feathers Hotel, in London-road, Manchester, attracted by a story so singular, and, on the face of it, so incredible, that numbers of people, instead of laughing off the matter as a joke, have been excited by real curiosity.

The new sensation, which is filling the coffers of the landlord of the Feathers, and at the same time mulcting the pockets of the ratepayers for the services of an extra force of policemen—uniform men and detectives—is a ghost which has chosen one of the busiest centres of Manchester, immediately opposite the London road station, for its nocturnal appearances.

The story is (says the *Manchester Examiner*) that for five weeks past the inmates of the hotel have been disturbed at all hours of the night by strange and unaccountable noises. When the weary waiters have gone to sleep, their dreams have been disturbed by the unwelcome tinkle, first of one, then of two and more, and sometimes of all the bells in the house—fourteen in number—clanging together. A strict watch has on several occasions been kept, and when this has been done, the watchers have seen and heard nothing unusual, but so surely as the lights in the inn have been extinguished and quiet has been maintained, the strange noises have commenced.

About a week ago, bellhangers were got in the house, who rearranged the wires and muffled the bells, and by this means it was supposed that the perturbed spirit had been laid at last to rest, an idea which was confirmed by the fact that for six nights thereafter the "ghost" made no manifestation. In the "wee short hour" between Tuesday night and Wednesday morning, however, the sound of bells again broke forth with undiminished violence, and in defiance of bellhangers and special detectives.

An indescribable presence is said to have made itself manifest on the stairs of the hotel, dressed in most unghostly habiliments of black, to a couple of boys and a policeman, who were so much frightened by the sight that they are unable to give any account of the spirit's disappearance.

Of all the inmates of the house the cook, whom one would have thought the most material and unimaginative, has been most affected by the spiritual influence, and on Wednesday resigned her comfortable situation, with all its perquisites, and, we believe, has taken to bed seriously ill.

Meanwhile the house is nightly crowded by hundreds of visitors, who, excited by curiosity, thirst of knowledge, or other desire, have been exorbitant in their demand for spirits, to the no small profit of the landlord, to whom the presence of his singular guest has been as lucky as angels' visits.

At the same time hundreds of people have thronged the streets and lanes outside anxious to obtain sight or hearing of the ghost. Whatever else may be thought of it, this revival of the Cock-lane spirit has been and continues most successful as a sensation in drawing crowded houses. June 4th, 1869.[353] — THE ECHO

☛ CASE #336: In France there is . . . a haunting which is almost official, because the house concerned was that of M. Osmond de Courtisigny, Procureur of the Republic at Cherbourg. About the middle of January it was reported that "every night at a certain hour the lantern over his door is extinguished, stones rattle against all his windows back and front, and when he sits down to dine, gravel and pebbles are thrown by some mysterious agency into his soup. His garret has been invaded, but the visitant there seems to have been material enough to consume wine and viands. Electric traps have been set to catch the intruders, but no discovery has been made.[354]
— THE ANNALS OF PSYCHICAL SCIENCE

☞ CASE #337: [An interesting story is told] of a "haunted house" situated in the environs of Beuvry, a large [French] town of 7,000 inhabitants, about six miles from Béthune. The Lille branch of the Société, Universelle d'Etudes Psychiques, has requested one of its members to make an enquiry into the subject, and he reports as follows:

"We arrived too late to witness any of the phenomena, which had ceased some days before. However, in spite of the proprietor's natural distrust, we were able to enter the house, question the inmates, and inspect the furniture, which bore the marks of violent treatment. The information here given was furnished by M. Sénéchal himself, and we are fully convinced of his good faith.

"M. Sénéchal keeps a small grocer's shop, and lives in the house with his wife, who is aged, and has for years been confined to her chair by paralysis; there is also a girl of about fifteen years of age who acts as servant.

"On January 15th last the furniture began to execute a wild and senseless dance. The chairs flew from one room to another, and smashed themselves against the tables and the walls; vases and household articles fell to the ground in fragments; the counter in the shop was overturned, and boxes of soap were piled on to it; shoes walked up the staircase; a dish of meat came out of the oven and fell in the bedroom; a water-jug fell to the ground without breaking, but on being replaced it fell again and was broken.

"All these things occurred during the daytime, and ceased at nightfall. They always took place in the room where the servant girl was, and never in her absence. While this girl went away for a few days' holiday the house was quiet, but the phenomena began again as soon as she returned.

"Another peculiarity is that no one ever saw the articles move, people heard a noise behind them, and on turning round something was found to have occurred. The servant herself never saw the articles in motion. M. and Mme. Sénéchal have not noticed that the girl was in any special state; she went about her occupations in a normal manner.

"A few days before our arrival M. Sénéchal had dismissed the servant. Since then nothing has happened. We did all we could to find the girl, but without success. The Sénéchals, mortified by what has taken place in their house, refused absolutely to give us the servant's address."[355] — *THE ANNALS OF PSYCHICAL SCIENCE*

☞ CASE #338: The newspapers of Northern France having published an article with regard to a haunted house at Douai

[France], we went to that town on Sunday, January 13th, to enquire into the matter.

The house in question is No. 19, rue des Écoles. It had been uninhabited for some time, but for the last few months it has been occupied by the D. family, consisting of a postman, his wife and five children, also a young servant of 16 or 17 years of age.

The facts which drew attention to this house are as follows:

For about a fortnight Mme. D. had heard the door-bell ring several times a day, and on going to the door she found no one there. At first she thought that it was a hoax, but soon the ringing of the bell increased in frequency and violence, causing much alarm. In the presence of the frightened family the bell rang sharply, while the bell-pull and its handle made corresponding movements. The whole neighbourhood came to see, and more than 300 persons witnessed the phenomenon.

The police were informed, but could not find out the cause. Moreover, three days later, in the very presence of a police officer, the bell came away from the wall while executing a final peal, and broke to pieces on the ground. Such are the facts related by the newspapers.

At Douai we first went to the central police station. The correctness of the facts was there confirmed, but the force confessed that it was unable to discover the cause. We were, unfortunately, not able to question the officer who had seen the breaking of the bell. We also learned that, on that very morning, new phenomena had taken place at the D.'s. We therefore went to the house, and were met by formal orders given by M. D. that nothing was to be said and no one admitted. Despite our insistence, we could not obtain any information from Mme. D. During our short interview with her, we caught a glimpse of the arrangement for ringing the bell—simply a cord which hangs down beside the street-door. The broken bell had been replaced by a new one.

We had to content ourselves with questioning some of the neighbours, who had seen or heard the phenomena. All agreed in confirming the reality and intensity of the manifestations; the bell did not merely tinkle, but rang violent peals; the cord was shaken as though by a hand. A neighbour who lives close to the haunted house gave us the following precise information.

She had several times heard Mme. D. cry out as if in terror; she ran to help her, and found that the bell was ringing of its own accord. One day, to her great alarm, she saw it ring five separate times, and the cord shook frantically. Another day, while talking to Mme. D. on the doorstep, she made an allusion to the bell, and it immediately began to ring. This occurred several times; "one would say it answered back," the woman said. Her opinion, which is that of the neighbourhood, is that the maid is bewitched. The priest was sent for, and he blessed the house and recommended that the bell be changed. The builder came, carefully examined the bell, and assured himself that it could not be rung by any artifice either from that house or from the adjoining houses. In short he found nothing. Finally the police set a watch on the house, but all in vain.

One evening a fresh alarm made Mme. D. resolve to send for a mechanic the next day. But during the morning the final peal occurred, which ended in the breaking of the bell. On replacing it with a new one this trouble ceased.

But the unfortunate tenants were not left in peace.

First of all heavy steps were heard on the floors. Lighted lamps went out of their own accord several times. The servant saw a man in the bed-rooms or on the staircase. These hallucinations recurred frequently. Furniture was moved about. A child's bed was turned over, the mattress thrown to the ground, the sheets carefully rolled up and placed in one corner of the room. Such was the state of affairs in the house when we made our enquiry.

We heard later that the disturbances had ceased after the departure of the young servant girl.

For the sake of truth we must add a very peculiar circumstance: this girl left the D.'s house in company with her father; now it seems that this man has the reputation of being a sorcerer, and that before leaving he performed an incantation "to drive evil spirits from the house." The coincidence is worth noticing, although the hypothesis of an understanding between father and daughter for the purpose of a hoax seems very improbable. Lille, France, February 3rd, 1907.[356] — *THE ANNALS OF PSYCHICAL SCIENCE*

☛ CASE #339: [A] most interesting [case] of these last weeks appears to have been the one at Grenoble, [France,] where a "rapping spirit" has manifested its presence every night in the apartment of Mme. Massot, rue Philis-de-la-Charge.

On January 28th, the manifestation was specially remarkable; the correspondent of the *Journal*, of Paris, thus speaks of it under date January 29th:

"The rapping spirit was officially interrogated yesterday evening by M. de Beylié, formerly president of the tribunal of commerce, who is the owner of the haunted house, in the presence of M. Pelatant, commissioner, and M. Berger, inspector of police. Other police officers had been placed on the roof and in the adjoining rooms, as well as in the street, to prevent any deception.

"Nothing unusual took place until ten o'clock; then the wall was suddenly shaken as though by violent blows with a hammer. The rapping spirit had come home without caring for the presence of the police, who again searched the apartments, but found nothing. The persons present surrounded the wall on which the spirit appeared to strike, and, singularly enough, the blows seemed to sound on both sides of the wall at once.

"M. de Beylié, who is a friend of Col. de Rochas, succeeded in entering into conversation with the spirit, who readily responded.

"'Are you a civilian or a soldier?' asked M. de Beylié. 'If you are a civilian strike one blow; if a soldier, rap twice.'

"Two blows immediately sounded on the wall, and in the same way the spirit was got to say that he was an artilleryman, aged 26, that he had still three years of service to perform, and that before joining his regiment he had been employed by an electrician at Grenoble. The rapping spirit also explained by the same means that he was in love with Mme. Massot's niece. It was now just midnight. Further questions addressed to the mysterious spirit remained unanswered; the spirit had left.

"M. de Beylié, the police commissioner and others who were present, whose good faith is beyond suspicion, then left, absolutely stupefied by this seance. Crowds remained in front of the house and had to be dispersed by the police."

In a telegram the next day the correspondent of the *Journal* observes that the phenomena only take place when Mlle. Alice Cocat, niece of Mme. Massot, is present. There can, however, be no question of fraud on the part of this young lady, who remains among the others and is watched by them while the blows sound. This young lady has for five years been engaged to a nephew of Mme. Massot, who is 26 years of age, is a working electrician, and has served in the second regiment of artillery at Grenoble. These details correspond to those given by the mysterious rapper. As the blows are not understood to come from the spirit of a deceased person, but from that of a living one, it is still more probable than in the majority of other cases, that it is a case of a "subliminal romance" on the part of Mlle. Alice Cocat, who is probably a physical medium.

All this, of course, in no way destroys the genuineness of the phenomenon. "The wall against which the spirit last struck," says the *Journal*, "is not more than four inches thick, and forms a partition between two rooms which were crowded with University professors, high police officers and their men. The Massot family, of course, was present. Now, as it was impossible for anyone to hide in this thin wall, fraud was out of the question. M. de Beylié told the spirit to scratch, and the sound of nails scraping on the wall was very distinctly heard. On being ordered to give blows with the fist the spirit struck violently, and the thin wall shook in a manner which was perfectly evident."[357] — THE ANNALS OF PSYCHICAL SCIENCE

☛ CASE #340: The Rev. Joseph Glanvill, chaplain in ordinary to Charles II, was a writer of great erudition and ability. In his *Sadducismus Triumphatus*, written to show that the phenomena of witchcraft were genuine occurrences, he gives an account of Mr. Mompesson's haunted house at Tedworth, where it was observed that, on beating or calling for any tune, it would be exactly answered by drumming. When asked by some one to give three knocks, if it were a certain spirit, it gave three knocks, and no more. Other questions were put, and answered by knocks exactly. Glanvill himself says, that, being told it would imitate noises, he scratched on the sheet of the bed five, then seven, then ten times; and it returned exactly the same number of scratches each time.

Melancthon relates that at Oppenheim, in Germany, in 1620, the same experiment of rapping, and having the raps exactly answered by the spirit which haunted a house, was successfully tried; and he tells us that Luther was visited by a spirit who announced his coming by "a rapping at his door."[358] — EPES SARGENT

☛ CASE #341: In the famous Wesley case, the haunting of the house of John Wesley's father, the Parsonage at Epworth, Lincolnshire, in 1716, for a period of two months the supposed spirit used to imitate Mr. Wesley's knock at the gate. It responded to the Amen at prayers. Emily, one of the daughters, knocked, and it answered her. Mr. Wesley knocked a stick on the joists of the kitchen; and it knocked again, in number of strokes and in loudness exactly replying. When Mrs. Wesley stamped, it knocked in reply.[359] — EPES SARGENT

☛ CASE #342: In the little village of Hydesville, Wayne County, New York, there stood, in 1847, a small house, which had been occupied by Mr. Michael Weekman. He had been troubled by certain rappings, of which he could give no explanation. But they attracted little attention, and may have had no connection with subsequent developments.

It was reserved for the family of Mr. John D. Fox, of Rochester, a respectable farmer, to have their names inseparably associated with the first development of the modern spiritual movement, based on the phenomena now challenging the regards of all thoughtful persons.

Mr. Fox moved into the house the 11th of December, 1847. His family consisted of himself, his wife, and six children; but only the two youngest were staying with them at the time of the manifestations,—Margaret, twelve years old, and Kate, nine years old. The former of these sisters subsequently became the wife of the celebrated Captain [Elisha Kent] Kane, the Arctic explorer.

From the first, the family were disturbed by noises in the house; but these they attributed for a time to rats and mice. In January, 1848, however, the sounds became loud and startling. Knocks, so violent as to produce a tremulous motion in the furniture and floor, were heard. Occasionally there would be a patter of footsteps. The bed-clothes would be pulled off; and Kate would feel a cold hand passed over her face.

Throughout February, and to the middle of March, the disturbances increased. Chairs and the dining-table were moved from their places. Mr. and Mrs. Fox, night after night, with a lighted candle, explored the house, but in vain. While they stood close to the door, raps would be made on it; and on their opening it no one would be found.

On the night of March 31st, having been broken of their rest for several nights previous, they retired to bed earlier than usual, hoping to sleep without disturbance. The sounds, however, were resumed. They occurred near the bed occupied by Kate and Margaret. Kate attempted to imitate the sounds by the snapping of her fingers. There was the same number of raps in response. She then said, "Now do as I do; count one, two, three, four, five, six," at the same time striking her hands together. The same number of raps responded at similar intervals. The mother of the girls then said, "Count ten!" and ten distinct raps were heard. "Count fifteen!" and that number of sounds followed.

She then said, "Tell us the age of Katie" (the youngest daughter), "by rapping one for each year"; and the number of years was rapped correctly. "How many children have I?" There were seven raps in reply. "Ah," she thought, "it can blunder sometimes. Try again." Still the number of raps was seven. Mrs. Fox was surprised. "Are they all alive?" she asked. No answer. "How many are dead?" There was a single rap. She had lost one child.

"Do as I do," said Kate Fox. Such was the commencement. "Who can tell," asks Owen, "where the end will be?"

... A writer in the *Encyclopædia Metropolitana* (London, 1861), referring to these and similar phenomena, observes:

> "It is, to say the least, a remarkable fact, that such occurrences are to be found in the histories of all ages, and, if inquiries are but sincerely made, in the traditions of nearly all living families. The writer can testify to several monitions of this kind portending death; and the authentic records of such things would make a volume."

In the *Life of Frederica Hauffé, the Seeress of Prevorst*, by Dr. Justinus Kerner, chief physician at Weinsberg" (who died in 1859) almost every phase of the recent spiritual phenomena is described as pertaining to her experience. To these more than twenty credible witnesses testify. They consisted in repeated knockings, noises in the air, a tramping up and down stairs by day and night, the moving of ponderable articles, etc.

But we must return to the experiences of the Fox family.

Startled and somewhat alarmed by the manifestations of intelligence, Mrs. Fox asked if it was a human being that was making the noise, and, if it was, to manifest it by making the same noise. There was no sound. She then said, "If you are a spirit, make two distinct sounds." Two raps were accordingly heard.

The members of the family by this time had all left their beds, and the house was again thoroughly searched, as it had been before, but without discovering anything that could explain the mystery; and, after a few more questions and responses by raps, the neighbours were called in to assist in tracing the phenomenon to its cause. But the neighbours were no more successful than the family had been, and confessed themselves thoroughly confounded.

For several subsequent days, the village was in a turmoil of excitement; and multitudes visited the house, heard the raps, and interrogated the apparent intelligence which controlled them, but without obtaining any clue to the discovery of the agent, further than its own persistent declaration that it was a spirit.

About three weeks after these occurrences, David, a son of Mr. and Mrs. Fox, went alone into the cellar, where the raps were then being heard, and said, "If you are the spirit of a human being who once lived on the earth, can you rap to the letters that will spell your name? and if so, now rap three times." Three raps were promptly given, and David proceeded to call the alphabet, writing down the letters as they were indicated; and the result was the name, "Charles B. Rosma," a name quite unknown to the family, and which they were afterwards unable to trace.

The statement was in like manner obtained from the invisible intelligence, that he was the spirit of a pedlar, who had been murdered in that house some years previously. According to Mr. David Fox, the floor was subsequently dug up, to the depth of more than five feet, when the remains of a human body were found.

Soon after these occurrences, the family removed to Rochester, at which place the manifestations still accompanied them; and here it was discovered, by the rapping of the letters of the alphabet in the manner before described, that different spirits were apparently using this channel of communication; and that, in short, almost any one, in coming into the presence of the two girls, could get a communication from what purported to be the spirits of his departed friends, the same often being accompanied by tests which satisfied the interrogator as to the spirits' identity.

A new phenomenon was also observed in the frequent moving of tables and other ponderable bodies, without appreciable agency, in the presence of these two girls. These manifestations, growing more and more remarkable, attracted numerous visitors, some from long distances; and the phenomenon began, as it were, to propagate itself, and to be witnessed in other families in Rochester and vicinity; while, as coincident therewith, susceptible persons would sometimes fall into apparent trances, and become clairvoyant, and re-affirm these raps and physical movements to be the production of spirits.

In November, a public meeting was called; and a committee appointed to examine into the phenomena. They reported that they were unable to trace the phenomena to any known mundane agency. Of course, the large majority of persons pronounced the whole thing an imposture; and the public press was against it, almost without an exception. There were stories that the Fox girls produced the sounds by their knees and toe-joints; and one of their relations, a Mrs. Culver, declared that Kate Fox had told her how it was done. If the young and mischief-loving Kate had ever told her so, it must have been in sport; for Mrs. Culver's explanation was soon rejected as not covering the phenomena.

The girls were subjected to the examination of a committee of ladies, who had them divested of their clothes, laid on pillows, and watched; still the sounds took place on walls, doors, tables, ceilings, and at quite a distance from the mediums.

We have before us a letter, received by us, dated Rochester, N.Y., Feb. 16, 1850. It is from the pen of a friend, an English gentlemen of high culture, who, at our request, availed himself of a brief stay in Rochester to look into the subject of the mysterious knockings. He made two calls on the Misses Fox, to hear the rappings, and wrote us as follows in regard to them:

> "My opinion of the rappings is that they are human, very human, sinfully human, made to get money by. If really there is a ghost in the matter, then quite certainly he is very fickle, something of a liar, very clumsy, very trifling, and altogether wanting in good taste. It would indeed be painful to me, exceedingly, if I thought that any man on this earth, on dying, had ever turned into such a paltry, contemptible ghost.
>
> "Yet at a distance from this place, as I understand, there are men affecting philosophy, and even a sceptical philosophy, who are ready to believe, and who do believe, that these Rochester knockings are those of a spirit. A very ridiculous spirit! An untrue ghost, a very pretending ghost! a ghost of no reverence or awe whatever! Indeed a ghost that is no ghost at all!
>
> "Here, now I have written what will satisfy your curiosity about this absurd business. My experience in it will be useful to me, in regard to superstition as a disease of the human mind. I have learned something from the errand I have been on. But to me the knockings themselves are not nearly so wonderful as the echoes they make in the city of New York."

The gentleman who wrote this letter subsequently made a very careful investigation of the phenomena, as manifested through the mediumship of the late G. A. Redman, and became fully convinced of their genuineness. He accepted the spiritual hypothesis as to their origin, and is now (1868)—after years of examination and reflection, both in this country and in Europe—an unwavering believer, and one who can give solid reasons for his belief; thus justifying that remark of Novalis, who says, "To become properly acquainted with a truth, we must first have disbelieved it, and disputed against it."

It was soon found that the marvellous phenomena could be

produced through numerous persons of either sex. Mediums for the manifestations began to spring up on all sides; and, as a matter of course, spurious phenomena began to be mixed with the genuine. The raps were soon superseded by more astonishing and inexplicable experiences. Tables, chairs, and other furniture would be moved about, raised from the floor, and, in some cases, so powerfully, that six full-grown men have been known to be carried about a room on a table, the feet of which did not touch the floor, and which no other person touched. Handbells would be rung, guitars floated about the room and played on, tambourines played on, and moved about with marvellous force; and at last spirit-hands would be both seen and felt.

Although these phenomena would be generally produced in the dark, there were enough of them produced in the light to satisfy inquirers that the effects were not imaginary or spurious. Mediums were developed with various powers. There rapidly sprang into notice musical, writing, speaking, drawing, and healing mediums.

The press and the pulpit sneered and fulminated; but the work went on with amazing celerity, until millions were not ashamed to admit their belief in the phenomena.[360] — EPES SARGENT

☛ CASE #343: Nicholas Desbaro, in Hartford, Conn., having unjustly detained a chest of clothes belonging to another man, the former became wonderfully tormented at his own house by various poundings and other phenomena, such as . . . the unaccountable movement of various things about his house. "And it endured for divers months," says Rev. Cotton Mather; "but, upon the restoration of the clothes thus detained, the troubles ceased."[361] — EDWARD COIT ROGERS

☛ CASE #344: [A singular case related is that of] Mr. Philip Smith, aged about fifty years, a son of eminently virtuous parents, a deacon of the church in Hadley, Mass., a member of the General Court, a justice in the county court, a selectman for the affairs of the town, a lieutenant of the troop, a man of devotion, sanctity, gravity, and, in all that is honest, exceeding exemplary. Such a man was, in the winter of the year 1684, murdered with an hideous witchcraft that filled all those parts of New England with astonishment.

He was by his office concerned about relieving the indigence of a wretched woman in the town, who, being dissatisfied at some of his just cares about her, expressed herself to him in such a manner that he declared himself thenceforward apprehensive of receiving mischief at her hands.

[Accordingly we find, that soon after having fallen ill . . . he incessantly talked of the woman, and of her ghost in his room; and how his] gallipots of medicines would be unaccountably emptied. Audible scratchings were made about the bed, when his hands and feet lay wholly still, and were held by others.

[Lights would often appear on his bed, which was sometimes shaken by an unseen force. Soon Mr. Smith passed away, at which time] divers noises were also heard in the room where the corpse lay, as the clattering of chairs and stools, whereof no account could be given. This was the end of so good a man. And I could with unquestionable evidence, relate the tragical death of several good men in this land, attended with such preternatural circumstances.[362]
— REV. COTTON MATHER, 1702

☛ CASE #345: That historic German ghost, the White Lady of the Hohenzollerns, would . . . seem to have more than a legendary basis. Her mission, apparently, is to announce the death of some member of the Hohenzollern family, and her most frequent haunting-place is the royal palace at Berlin. She was seen as early as 1628, and since the time of Frederick the Great her appearance has been regularly chronicled on the eve of the death of the King of Prussia.

For the matter of that, there are not a few families whose ancestral homes, according to tradition, are haunted by death-announcing ghosts. This is particularly the case with certain distinguished British families. Two white owls perching on the roof of the family mansion are taken as a sure omen of death in the Arundel of Wardour family. The Yorkshire Middletons, a Catholic family, are said to be warned of approaching death by the apparition of a Benedictine nun.[363] — HENRY ADDINGTON BRUCE

☛ CASE #346: Of all family ghosts, however, none is so strongly substantiated by documentary evidence as the Knocking Ghost of the Basil Woodds, an old English family. This ghost began operations about the time of the Stuart Restoration, and it is alleged has ever since continued to announce, by three or more loud knocks, the approaching death of a Basil Woodd. First-hand and thoroughly trustworthy accounts are extant of its activity in quite recent times.

December 15, 1893, Mr. Charles H. L. Woodd died at Hampstead, England, after a brief illness. The night before he died the Knocking Ghost was heard by two persons, at Hampstead by his daughter, and in London by his son, the Reverend Trevor Basil Woodd. Both have made statements describing their singular experiences.

"On Thursday evening, December 14, 1893, after church," says the Reverend Mr. Woodd, "I was sitting before my fire. I knew my father was ill, and had a presentiment that he was dangerously ill, though if I had known this I should have remained at Hampstead, where I had been that day. As I sat, I distinctly heard three knocks, perhaps more, like the sound of some one emptying a tobacco pipe upon the bars of my fire grate.

"Thinking it might be a warning, I did not go to bed for an hour, fearing I would be sent for. At one A.M. I was awakened by a ringing of the front door-bell and knocking. It was my father's butler, who told me the doctor had sent for me, as my father was very ill. I said to my housekeeper: 'I must go. I feel sure that my father is dying, because I heard the Woodd knocks, as I sat in my chair before going to bed.'

"On my arrival my first question was: "Is he still alive?" for I believed he must have passed away at the time of the knocking. He died at eight-forty-five next morning."

Mr. Woodd's housekeeper corroborates this statement. As to the knocking heard at Hampstead, the daughter, Mrs. Winifred Dumbell, testifies:

"On December 14, 1893, Thursday morning, hearing my father, Mr. Charles Woodd, was not well, I left Epsom, where I had been staying, for Hampstead, and found my father in bed and very weak, but I was in no way anxious about him, as I did not suppose him to be seriously ill. At eleven o'clock at night, being tired and finding I could not assist my mother or the nurse, I lay down in an adjoining room, leaving the door wide open, and fell asleep.

"In a short time I was suddenly awakened by a loud rapping as if at the door. I jumped up and ran into the passage, thinking my mother had called me. I listened at the door of my father's room, but no one was moving. I lay down again and instantly fell asleep, when exactly the same thing occurred. I did not actually sleep again, and cannot say whether any sound made me get up the third time, but I went in search of the doctor and gathered that he was anxious about my father, who was getting much weaker. We were all aroused, and about eight o'clock a. m. my father died.

"I did not connect this rapping with the Woodd warning, as all was so sudden and unexpected, but on mentioning it at breakfast the next morning to my brother, the Reverend Trevor Basil

Woodd, he told me he also heard a similar warning in his rooms at Vauxhall Bridge Road about the same time."

To mention only one other of the many instances that might be cited, the Knocking Ghost was again heard on June 3, 1895, just twenty-four hours before the death of Mr. Thomas Basil Woodd at Hampstead. Again, too, it was heard by more than one person and in more than one place, by Mr. Woodd's daughters, Fanny and Kate, and by his niece, Miss Ethel G. Woodd, who was at the time visiting friends in Yorkshire, and at first mistook the Knocking Ghost for somebody hammering nails into the wall of the next room.

Oddly enough, this was also the way it sounded to Fanny Woodd, in London, as appears from the following statement signed by her:

"On June 3, 1895, at ten-thirty p.m., Fanny Woodd, staying with Mrs. Stoney, 83 Wharton Road, West Kensington, heard knocks, apparently from next door, as of nails being hammered in and pictures hung, which seemed so unlikely at that hour of night that the next morning she mentioned it to Mrs, Stoney, whose bedroom was just below hers, asking if she had heard it or could account for it."

But Mrs. Stoney had heard nothing, and the next-door neighbor, Mrs. Harriet Taylor, rather tartly declared that:

"There has been no putting up of pictures or knocking of any sort in this house for quite two years. We are also early risers, and are always in bed and asleep by ten p.m."

That same day Miss Woodd rejoined her father and sister in Hampstead, and was astonished to hear that the latter had been awakened about half past ten the previous night by loud knockings against the window shutters. A few hours more and the mystery was solved by the startlingly sudden death of Mr. Woodd, from an attack of apoplexy. The Knocking Ghost of the Basil Woodds had lived up to its reputation.[364] — HENRY ADDINGTON BRUCE

Chapter Eight

TANGIBILITY ACCOUNTS

CASES OF TACTILE SPIRITS

☛ **CASE #347**: In my Northern-Irish home, I received a letter on the 7th November, 1865, from my brother in Warwickshire, saying that my mother was ill, and he wished I would go and see her. I started the same evening by Belfast and Fleetwood.

I had been several hours in my berth, on the Irish Channel, and was half asleep, when I was startled by feeling a hand grasp my shoulder and a voice say, in a loud whisper, "Come quickly." I rose up and sat looking round the cabin, but could see no one. I called to the stewardess, but she was fast asleep, and so were all the other ladies.

I again lay down, but not to sleep, and in a very short time, not 20 minutes afterwards, the same pressure was put on my shoulder and the same words were distinctly uttered close to my ear, "Come quickly." I again called loudly to the stewardess and told her to light the lamp, for I was sure that some one must have been standing by me. She declared that no one had been in the cabin, and all around was so still and quiet.

I reached the station at half-past 12 at noon, when my brother met me. He said, "All is over, mother passed away at 4 this morning."

I ought to have stated that when I called to the stewardess and made her light the lamp, immediately after I heard the voice and felt the hand on my shoulder the second time, I then asked her to tell me what o'clock it was, and she said "Four o'clock." I looked at my own watch and it was the same.

I being an only daughter and my mother having been a widow the last five years of her life, she was much wrapped up in me and in my children, and the tie between us was of no ordinary kind. I have always looked upon this as a direct voice from herself, just as she was dying and passing into the spiritual world. Penarth Lodge, Stoke Bishop, Bristol. April 14th, 1884.[365] — MRS. LUCY HANCOCK

☛ CASE #348: Having been requested to write down the particulars of an event which occurred in the lives of my parents, I do so.

In 1820, my father and mother, both being under 50 years of age, and in perfect health, were staying in Liverpool (their residence being at Whitehaven, in Cumberland), names, Joseph and Ann Mondel.

One night, the latter, sleeping peacefully, was awoke by the former calling out:

"Ann, I feel sure Anthony Mathers is dead."

"What makes you think so?"

"He has just been at the bedside, and laid an icy-cold hand on my cheek."

"You must have been dreaming."

"Oh, but my cheek is still cold."

The old and much-esteemed friend was, at the time, sojourning in one of the West Indian islands. The season was known to be more than usually sickly, so the thought of his danger might have engendered morbid feelings.

My father, as well as my mother, was content to rest in that hope during the weeks that must elapse ere the news of that night's occurrences in Jamaica could reach England. News did arrive, and stated that on the night referred to Mr. Mathers succumbed to a sudden and most severe attack of yellow or other West Indian fever.

As a child, I first heard the tale, but often in my presence was it repeated or referred to, later in life, without any change or amplification of detail.[366] — JANET HARNETT

☛ CASE #349: . . . when a girl of 16, an engagement was formed between myself and a young naval officer, about to sail for the African coast. He had promised my mother and self that he would write us from "Ascension."

It chanced, some time after his departure, I accompanied a friend in a long country walk, when all at once a strange feeling possessed me that this young officer was near. I seemed to feel the clasp of his hand upon my wrist, yet I saw nothing, I only felt a presence. My companion asked why I looked so pale. I made an evasive reply, and on returning home told my mother that "Tom was dead!"

She tried to laugh away my fancy, nevertheless she noted the date of the occurrence, and when a brother of my own, then homeward bound from the coast of Africa, arrived, the first word she spoke, after an exchange of greetings, were, "Oh, that poor fellow you sent letters by for me is dead! He died three days sail from Ascension and is buried on the Island." February 20th, 1885.[367]
— M. W.

☛ CASE #350: In March, 1854, I was up at Oxford, keeping my last term, in lodgings. I was subject to violent neuralgic headaches, which always culminated in sleep.

One evening, about 8 p.m., I had an unusually violent one; when it became unendurable, about 9 p.m., I went into my bedroom, and flung myself, without undressing, on the bed, and soon fell asleep.

I then had a singularly clear and vivid dream, all the incidents of which are still as clear to my memory as ever. I dreamed that I was stopping with the family of the lady who subsequently became my wife. All the younger ones had gone to bed, and I stopped chatting to the father and mother, standing up by the fireplace. Presently I bade them goodnight, took my candle, and went off to bed.

On arriving in the hall, I perceived that my fiancée had been detained downstairs, and was only then near the top of the staircase. I rushed upstairs, overtook her on the top step, and passed my two arms round her waist, under her arms, from behind. Although I was carrying my candle in my left hand, when I ran upstairs, this did not, in my dream, interfere with this gesture.

On this I woke, and a clock in the house struck 10 almost immediately afterwards.

So strong was the impression of the dream that I wrote a detailed account of it next morning to my fiancée.

Crossing my letter, not in answer to it, I received a letter from the lady in question: "Were you thinking about me, very specially, last night, just about 10 o'clock? For, as I was going upstairs to bed, I distinctly heard your footsteps on the stairs, and felt you put your arms round my waist."

The letters in question are now destroyed, but we verified the statement made therein some years later, when we read over our old letters, previous to their destruction, and we found that our personal recollections had not varied in the least degree therefrom. The above narratives may, therefore, be accepted as absolutely accurate.[368] — REV. P. H. NEWNHAM

☛ CASE #351: My sister-in-law, Sarah Eustance, of Stretton, was lying sick unto death, and my wife was gone over to there from Lowton Chapel (12 or 13 miles off), to see her and tend her in her last moments. And on the night before her death (some 12 or 14 hours before) I was sleeping at home alone, and awaking, heard a voice distinctly call me. Thinking it was my niece, Rosanna, the only other occupant of the house, who might be sick or in trouble, I went to her room and found her awake and nervous. I asked her whether she had called me. She answered, "No; but something awoke me, when I heard someone calling!"

On my wife returning home after her sister's death, she told me how anxious her sister had been to see me, "craving for me to be sent for," and saying, "Oh, how I want to see Done once more!" and soon after became speechless. But the curious part was that about the same time she was "craving," I and my niece heard the call.

. . . In answer to your queries respecting the voice or call that I heard on the night of July 2nd, 1866, I must explain that there was a strong sympathy and affection between myself and my sister-in-law, of pure brotherly and sisterly love; and that she was in the habit of calling me by the title of "Uncle Done," in the manner of a husband calling his wife "mother" when there are children, as in this case. Hence the call being "Uncle, uncle, uncle!" leading me to think that it was my niece (the only other occupant of the house that Sunday night) calling to me.

Copy of funeral card: "In remembrance of the late Sarah Eustance, who died July 3rd, 1866, aged 45 years, and was this day interred at Stretton Church, July 6th, 1866."

My wife, who went from Lowton that particular Sunday to see her sister, will testify that as she attended upon her (after the departure of the minister), during the night she was wishing and craving to see me, repeatedly saying, "Oh, I wish I could see Uncle Done and Rosie once more before I go!" and soon after then she became unconscious, or at least ceased speaking, and died the next day; of which fact I was not aware until my wife returned on the evening of the 4th of July.

I hope my niece will answer for me; however, I may state that she reminds me that she thought I was calling her and was coming to me, when she met me in the passage or landing, and I asked her if she called me.

I do not remember ever hearing a voice or call besides the above case. (Summer 1885).[369] — MR. JOHN DONE

Chapter Nine

PARAPHYSICAL & PARAPSYCHOLOGICAL ACCOUNTS

CASES OF UNKNOWN FORCES, MENTAL HEALING, STRANGE POWERS, AND UNUSUAL EXPERIENCES

☛ CASE #352: On Thursday, the 5th of September, 1867, about the hour of 10:45 A.M., on entering my office, I found my clerk in conversation with the porter, and the Rev. Mr. H. standing at the clerk's back. I was just on the point of asking Mr. H. what had brought him in so early (he worked in the same room as myself, but was not in the habit of coming till about mid-day) when my clerk began questioning me about a telegram which had missed me. The conversation lasted some minutes, and in the midst of it the porter gave me a letter which explained by whom the telegram had been sent.

During this scene Mr. R., from an office upstairs, came in and listened to what was going on. On opening the letter, I immediately made known its purport, and looked Mr. H. full in the face as I spoke. I was much struck by the melancholy look he had, and observed that he was without his neck-tie. At this juncture Mr. R. and the porter left the room. I spoke to Mr. H., saying, "Well, what's the matter with you? You look so sour." He made no answer, but continued looking fixedly at me.

I took up an enclosure which had accompanied the letter and read it through, still seeing Mr. H. standing opposite to me at the corner of the table. As I laid the papers down, my clerk said "Here, sir, is a letter come from Mr. H." No sooner had he pronounced the name than Mr. H. disappeared in a second.

I was for a time quite dumbfounded, which astonished my clerk, who (it now turned out) had not seen Mr. H., and absolutely denied that he had been in the office that morning. The purport of the letter from Mr. H., which my clerk gave me, and which had been written on the previous day, was that, feeling unwell, he should not come to the office that Thursday, but requested me to forward his letters to him at his house.

The next day (Friday), about noon, Mr. H. entered the office; and when I asked him where he was on the Thursday about 10:45, he replied that he had just finished breakfast, was in the company of his wife, and had never left his house during the day. I felt shy of mentioning the subject to Mr. R., but on the Monday following I could not refrain from asking him if he remembered looking in on Thursday morning. "Perfectly," he replied; "you were having a long confab with your clerk about a telegram, which you subsequently discovered came from Mr. C."

On my asking him if he remembered who were present, he answered, "The clerk, the porter, you and H." On my asking him further, he said, "He was standing at the corner of the table, opposite you. I addressed him, but he made no reply, only took up a book and began reading. I could not help looking at him, as the first thing that struck me was his being at the office so early, and the next his melancholy look, so different from his usual manner; but that I attributed to his being annoyed about the discussion going on. I left him standing in the same position when I went out, followed by the porter."

On my making known to Mr. R. that Mr. H. was fourteen miles off the whole of that day, he grew quite indignant at my doubting the evidence of his eyesight, and insisted on the porter being called up and interrogated. The porter, however, like the clerk, had not seen the figure.[370] — MR. M. [NAMES WITHHELD BY THE SPR]

☞ CASE #353: After two years of incredulity I am to-day convinced that Reichenbach and Zöllner were correct in affirming that the magnetic needle could be moved by something emanating from the human finger; although only last night I sent a report of my experiments to the Secretary of the Society for Psychical Research, and in this report I stated that I was by no means convinced by my own experiments.

This morning there is a hard frost here which has hardly ever been the case when I have been experimenting. I mounted a small needle on a very delicate pivot without any covering, and pointed a finger of my right hand at it. No result. It then occurred to me to point the left hand index finger—a thing I had never done before—and, lo! the needle was distinctly repelled.

Being by nature very sceptical in such matters, I thought the motion might be caused by my breath, so I bandaged my mouth and nostrils, and held in my breath. There was no doubt about it—the needle became strangely perturbed, being at first attracted and then repelled by the finger.

A curious circumstance was that I could effect this only at the south-seeking pole. I tried to affect the north-seeking pole with the right hand, but without result.

I can throw no light on the cause of the phenomenon, but of its reality I am now at last certain. Whether I shall be able to repeat it I do not know, as I have tried so often before in vain to produce it.

Since writing the foregoing I have successfully repeated the experiment at least a dozen times, but the power has now (for the time at least) gone again. December 31st, 1884.[371] — A. EUBULE-EVANS

☞ CASE #354: A few years since a Mr. Hayward, who came over from Australia to exhibit what he called a circular magnet to the Royal Society and with whom I became myself intimately acquainted, mentioned to me, after detailing numerous magnetic experiments which during many years he had made in the Colony, that he had on several occasions, when in his dark laboratory, seen weak flames around the poles of a large ordinary magnet.

He appeared to be quite unbiassed in his conclusions and observations, so that I have no reason to call in question his testimony. I found too that he had not even heard of Reichenbach's treatise before I mentioned it to him. His evidence, therefore, is strongly in favour of the experiments made by the Society for Psychical Research.[372] — MR. OLLEY

☛ CASE #355: For the purpose of investigating the influence exercised by one mind upon another, apart from the recognised ordinary channels of sensation, I have carried out a series of experiments in the presence of many witnesses, and among them of Professor T_____. These experiments were made with four gentlemen and two ladies. They consisted in the transmission of motor or inhibitory impulses. The experiments, 40 in number, were for the most part successful, except the series with Mr. A_____ (a student of the University). But even in this last case the will of the operator evidently influenced "the subject"; but this subject did not exactly accomplish my orders. For example, when I mentally ordered him to lift his right arm, he raised the left one, etc. The distance between the operator and the subjects varied from three to 50 feet. The experiments were often performed through walls, closed doors, etc. During the experiments the subjects remained quite awake...[373] — DR. A. CHILTOFF

☛ CASE #356: April 30th, 1884. I sitting in the cabinet at my writing-table. Mdlle. T_____ was sitting in the dining-room at the table, and was occupied in embroidering. The doors were open.
Mdlle. T_____ was mentally ordered [by me] to discontinue her work and to go out of the room. She knew nothing of my intentions. The experiment was commenced at 9:20 p.m.
In eight minutes, my wife, who was playing on the piano, came to me and asked if I had not influenced her by my will, for she said that she felt such a fatigue in her hands that she was obliged to discontinue her playing.
But I did not think of her, all my thoughts being concentrated on Mdlle. T_____.
At 9:35 p.m., Mdlle. T_____ went out of the room. She told me afterwards that an irresistible force compelled her, against her own will, to rise off her chair. She felt a great fatigue.[374] — DR. A. CHILTOFF

☛ CASE #357: October 29th, 1884. Present: Professor T_____, Mr. M_____ (a physician) and a student of the University of Kharkoff. In the absence of the subject (Mr. V_____) Professor T_____ proposed the following problem: Mr. V_____ must [be told by mental power only to] seize with his left hand the collar of his uniform. The subject sat with closed eyes in an arm-chair. I was seven feet before him. The witnesses sat near me. The experiment began at 10:5 p.m., and in seven minutes Mr. V_____ had performed the thought-of order.[375] — DR. A. CHILTOFF

☛ CASE #358: November 12th, 1884. I was sitting in the cabinet at my writing-table. The subject, Mr. V_____ was sitting at D in the dining-room at the tea-table. At the same table were also sitting some ladies. The distance between me and Mr. V_____ was about 50 feet.

[Mentally only] Mr. V_____ was ordered to come to me in the cabinet. I had concentrated all my thoughts upon the subject. I could not see the subject. But I heard him distinctly conversing with the ladies. The experiment was commenced at 8:30 p.m.

In three minutes I heard him saying that he felt a great fatigue. The ladies began to laugh at his intention to sleep in their presence. In 15 minutes I did not any longer hear his voice.

At 8:55 my wife came to me, and said to me that Mr. V_____ fell asleep. At 9 p.m. I saw the subject, with closed eyes, marching slowly towards me. Before the writing-table at which I was sitting, he stopped.

Summing up the results of my 40 experiments, I consider:
(1) That there exists an unknown force, acting from the operator to the subjects, and according to the wish of the operator, provoking determined muscular contractions.
(2) That this force acts directly on nervous centres, and not on the groups of muscles thought of.
(3) That the character of the motions provoked by this force shows that they are of a central origin.
(4) That this force acts as well at the distance of three as at the distance of 50 feet.
(5) That this force penetrates through various obstacles, walls, closed doors, etc.
(6) That it acts in all possible directions.
(7) That the intensity of its action upon diverse organisms depends upon the individuality of each organism.[376] — DR. A. CHILTOFF

☛ CASE #359: . . . we think that we have found an answer to the question raised by Sir William Thomson in his last lecture "On the Senses of Man." Have we a special sense for the impressions of magnetism? "It is possible," says the English scientist, "that there is a magnetic sense, and that a magnet of very great power may produce a sensation entirely different from that of heat, force, or any other sensation; at all events, the fact merits profound research."

Let us now touch upon the question of the causes.
So it is evident that the magnet exerts a certain influence upon the nervous system of persons who are predisposed. This

physiological action has been very little studied; there exists, nevertheless, a certain number of experiments relative to the therapeutic action.

Without speaking of Mesmer, it was established as long ago as 1779 by Drs. Andry and Thouret, and confirmed by Becker (1829), Bulmering (1835), Lippic (1846), and especially by Maggiorani (1869-1880). To-day it is placed beyond controversy by Messrs. Charcot, Schiff, Vogt, Benedict, Vigouroux, Debore, Proust, Ballet, and others.

But, while it is incontrovertible, is it really magnetic?

It seems to me that it may be so admitted, [only] in part, since (1) the importance of the action is not in direct relation with the power of the magnet, but rather with the degree of hypnotic sensitiveness of the subject experimented upon; and (2) the north pole has no other influence than the south, although it should necessarily have in the case of an action that was purely and simply magnetic.

Is it, then, a metalloscopic action, as Mr. Pellot has supposed?

This question, which had been already asked at the date at which I made my first communication through Dr. Brown-Sequard, I will answer as follows:

(1) the number of persons who are sensitive to metals is less than that of those sensitive to the magnet, and much less than the number of those who are specially sensitive to steel.

(2) There are persons sensitive to metals (to copper, for example) and insensible to the magnet, and consequently likewise refractory to hypnotisation.

Then is this mysterious action merely imaginary—the effect of suggestion, as one says to-day after the labours of Dr. Bernheim?

No; because (1) it is sometimes (though rarely, it is true) exerted unknown to the subjects under experiment, upon persons asleep, upon animals, etc.; and (2) we may easily distinguish the sensations produced simply by emotion or expectant attention from those produced by [hypnosis]; for imaginary sensations change character or disappear on a new test, while genuine ones always return, preserve their characters, and even become more and more marked. Imaginary sensitiveness becomes effaced, while real sensitiveness is increased by habitude.

Nevertheless, we may grant that the imagination, without being a sufficient cause to explain the phenomena, enters into play in the great majority of cases, as an auxiliary, in preparing the accessibility of the patients. In short, the influence is double-physical and psychical.

Being capable of serving as a physical excitant, does the magnet act directly upon the tissues exposed to its influence, or rather indirectly by reflex way?

It appears that both cases present themselves, but that the last is the more important. It is the vaso-motor nerves that seem to be reached by preference. Are the direct action upon the tissues or the blood and the reflex action upon the nerves identical? It appears not. At all events, magnetism alone does not explain these effects. I rather incline toward the hypothesis that, in the majority of the phenomena, the magnet is merely the substratum of another action, which is so weak, from a psychical point of view, that it hides itself from our instruments, and exhibits itself only through the intermedium of exceptionally sensitive nervous systems.

Is this other physical action due to a new and unknown force?

It is probable that it is not an entirely new force, but only a new and unknown manifestation—a peculiar modification of electric phenomena. This is all that the present state of our knowledge allows us to say.

But the insufficiency of theory in no wise interferes with the practical use of [hypnosis], and, if it is true that it gives us at the same time useful indications as to the state of the nerves in nervous complaints, the importance of the application may be readily seen.

My personal idea goes still further. I see in the revelations of this instrument [hypnosis] the necessity of a future subdivision of therapeutics. It is useless, and even imprudent, to apply the same remedy to sensitive and non-sensitive persons. With a large number of hypnotisable patients, all remedies are equally good or equally bad, according to peculiar nervous influences. We may neutralise strong doses of the most typical medicaments, and reproduce their effect in a most positive manner, by suggestion. In sensitive persons we obtain an improvement that is often almost instantaneous under the influence of various trifling means that hypnotism and magnetism put at our disposal.[377] — DR. J. OCHOROWICZ

☛ CASE #360: In the year 1869 I was Officer of Health in the Hellenic army. By command of the War Office I was attached to the garrison of the Island of Zante. As I was approaching the island in a steamboat, to take up my new position, and at about two hours' distance from the shore, I heard a sudden inward voice say to me over and over again in Italian, "Go to Volterra." I was made almost dizzy by the frequency with which this phrase was repeated. Although in perfectly good health at the time I became seriously alarmed at what I considered as an auditory hallucination. I had no association with the name of M. Volterra, a gentleman of Zante with whom I was not even acquainted, although I had once seen him, ten years before. I tried the effect of stopping my ears, and of trying to distract myself by conversation with the bystanders; but all was useless, and I continued to hear the voice in the same way.

At last we reached land; I proceeded to the hotel and busied myself with my trunks, but the voice continued to harass me. After a time a servant came and announced to me that a gentleman was at the door who wished to speak with me at once.

"Who is the gentleman?" I asked.

"M. Volterra," was the reply.

And M. Volterra entered, weeping violently in uncontrollable distress, and imploring me to follow him at once, and see his son, who was in a dangerous condition.

I found a young man in a state of maniacal frenzy, naked in an empty room, and despaired of by all the doctors of Zante for the last five years. His aspect was hideous, and rendered the more distressing by constantly-recurring choreic spasms, accompanied by hissings, howlings, barkings, and other animal noises. Sometimes he crawled on his belly like a serpent; sometimes he fell into an ecstatic condition on his knees; sometimes he talked and quarrelled with imaginary interlocutors. The violent crises were often followed by periods of profound syncope.

When I opened the door of his room he darted upon me furiously, but I stood my ground and seized him by the arm, looking him fixedly in the face. In a few moments his gaze fell; he trembled all over, and fell on the floor with his eyes shut. I made mesmeric passes over him, and in half an hour he had fallen into the somnambulic state.

The mesmeric cure lasted two months and a half. During that time many interesting phenomena were observed.

1. He became clairvoyant as to his own malady, foreseeing the days and hours of his own attacks, and the nature of each.
2. Sometimes I mesmerised him from my own house, without his previously knowing of it.
3. In the somnambulic state he prescribed for himself; and the exhibition of the remedies prescribed (though these were apparently insignificant) was followed by an improvement in his symptoms.
4. Once, when in the mesmeric trance, he ordered me to let him sleep for eight days continuously, without waking him, but merely causing him to drink one glass of orange-water, and placing in his mouth some morsels of gum. He did, in fact, sleep for eight days, during which time no shouts or pinches from any one could awake him, although he replied at once to questions which I addressed to him from an adjoining room.
5. He used to discern me at a distance during his crises, and once, at my request, he described with great accuracy my house at Corfu.

The cure, however, was not uninterrupted. Often in the mesmeric sleep he seemed to become a different person, expressed hatred for me, spat at me, and tried to abstract himself from my influence. I contended against these moods with all my might, and finally he would become calm again and say "that it was not himself who had thus acted."

A month before his final cure he foresaw its date, but warned me that I should have a severe conflict with him of an hour's duration, at a date which he announced beforehand. After that struggle, if my will prevailed, he would be completely restored to reason.

At the appointed hour I proceeded to mesmerise him, in his father's presence. As soon as he fell under my influence he became wildly excited, called me his assassin, implored his father with tears to turn me out of the house, and gradually became more and more convulsed and haggard, with continual cries of "The doctor is killing me!" I continued to mesmerise him, exerting the whole force of my will, and precisely at the end of an hour the youth became unconscious, and fell on his mattress, dragging me down with him in his fall.

In 20 minutes more he awoke into the mesmeric trance, and said, "Doctor, you have saved me. I am now perfectly cured. Let me sleep another hour and then wake me; there is nothing more to fear." He awoke perfectly well, and has had no return of his terrible malady.[378] — DR. NICOLAS, COUNT DE GONÉMYS

☛ CASE #361: I understand that the Society for Psychical Research invites communications on the above subject, more generally known under what is, in my opinion, the misleading term of "Thought-reading."

For some considerable time I have been engaged at intervals in experiments of this nature, and I have arrived at certain generalisations which I think may be helpful to others engaged in similar experiments. No doubt, here as elsewhere, the "personal equation" will have to be taken into account, but I do not think it will greatly modify the results attained.

My objects have been to ascertain by personal experiments (1) whether it is possible to transfer an impression made on one brain directly to another without the use of any of the ordinary channels of communication, and (2), if so, the conditions under which the transference is made. In almost all cases an ordinary pack of cards was used to supply the brain-pictures.

It did not take long to convince me that this direct transference of a picture from one brain to another was possible. In fact, I was soon struck by the comparative facility of the operation under favourable conditions. I allow that my method of estimating results was not exactly that laid down by other observers. I attached (as I still attach) less importance than others to absolute accuracy in the transference of the picture. In such cases, as it seems to me, the results are to be judged, not by mathematical, but logical laws. . . February 1885.[379] — A. EUBULE-EVANS

☛ CASE #362: In a former paper I had the pleasure of describing to my readers a cure, which I succeeded in effecting in the year 1869, when I was attached to the garrison of Zante. To-day I am going to tell you of another, which I performed in the same year, and which, on account of some singular circumstances connected with it, was of peculiar interest to all concerned, and won for me considerable fame in the neighbourhood in which I then resided.

My patient, in this case, was a girl of about 20, named Denise Zyros, who, since the age of 14, had suffered from that form of hysteria which is generally known by the name of hysterical melancholia. Every kind of treatment during these eight years had been tried for her in vain; the doctors at last pronounced her case hopeless; and the parents could only try to reconcile themselves to the fact that their daughter was incurable.

The poor girl for years had ceased to exist as an animal being; she seemed simply to vegetate, and, but for a few unconnected words which she sometimes muttered in a low voice, one would have supposed every spark of reason in her to have been extinct. Sitting in a chair with closed eyes and bent head, she appeared utterly unconscious of all that took place around her. She had even forgotten how to eat and drink, so that to sustain life her parents were obliged to force open her jaws and compel her to swallow a few mouthfuls of some nutritious substance.

Although, apparently, she was no longer in pain, yet a continuous trembling of the whole body was observable; her eyelids when raised showed only the whites of the eyes, the cornea being lost in the sockets.

From all information I could obtain as to the girl's former state of health, I was confirmed in my opinion that this was a severe case of melancholia, and one, indeed, that was rapidly drawing near its closing scene.

I made a thorough examination of the case and was unable to discover a trace of anything radically wrong in the organic system. This examination took place on the 29th of July, and on that day I mesmerised her for the first time. In the course of half-an-hour she fell into a deep sleep, which sleep was preceded by a relaxation of the limbs, a cessation of the usual trembling, and of the habitual low murmuring. I let her sleep for an hour, and as I saw no change in her expression during that time, I thought it better not to disturb her by addressing her. I certainly had not expected to produce so quick an effect on an organism which, one may almost say, had lost all right of domicile in this physical world, so utterly insensible was it to all surrounding agents.

The next day I mesmerised her again, and this time she not only went to sleep as she had done the previous evening, but she even became clairvoyante. She told me she was sleeping, and that she saw a dazzling light which emanated from my eyes and fingers, and which thrilled her whole body. She asserted that I should succeed in curing her in 17 days, and moreover was able to fix the exact date of her recovery, telling me that I must mesmerise her twice every day, morning and evening, and that she should then be able to walk to Mass on the 15th of August—which would be the Feast of the Assumption—accompanied by her brother, all of which facts did actually take place precisely as she had predicted.

When I left my patient, after first awakening her, I happened to go down to the dispensary, where I found several doctors and other persons assembled. I turned to the former, and asked them if they were acquainted with the case of the afflicted girl Zyros. They replied that they knew her well, that they had used every means in their power to bring about her recovery, and that they had eventually given up her case as hopeless. I told them that I believed them to be mistaken in their opinion, that in 17 days she would be able to go out, that she would be completely cured, and that they might see her at Mass on the Feast of the Assumption. They all burst out laughing at this unexpected assertion, and unanimously agreed that I must be out of my senses.

Gossip spreads quickly in a small town, and in a short time this affair became the subject of general talk in Zante. Opinions varied greatly. Some called me a quack and a humbug, whilst others were inclined to exalt me to the skies; in fact public opinion seemed to know no happy mean.

Meanwhile I continued to mesmerise my patient morning and evening, and found her improving in health daily.

At last the 15th of August, the much-talked of day, arrived. The cathedral bell announced to the faithful the Assumption of the Blessed Virgin, and a crowd collected round the Zyros' house to see Denise walk to church—or rather to see the quack unmasked!

What, then, was their astonishment to see the girl presently walk downstairs, and appear amongst them in perfect health and good spirits. The crowd was electrified; a loud "hurrah" was heard on all sides; whilst I, putting her arm in mine, led her victoriously towards the church, followed by all the bystanders, who cheered us vociferously.

From that date, I am confidently able to affirm that the girl has continued in good health. I do not pretend for a moment to be a partisan of those demonological ideas which must have inspired St. Augustine when he wrote his *Civitas Dei*. At the same time, I feel bound to state openly all that I observed in this case, without deducing from it any conclusions, which might be premature in the present undeveloped state of physiological and psychological science.

The third time I mesmerised the girl, as soon as my influence acted on the nervous system, and even before she was asleep, a great change in her was observable. Her eyes opened wide, she made hideous grimaces, and used excessively coarse language. She defied my mesmeric power, and attempted by such violent efforts and contortions to oppose my actions, that I was obliged to tie her down. As soon, however, as she had fallen into a mesmeric sleep, she would cry bitterly, and excuse herself for what she had just said by assuring me that it was not she who had previously spoken.

Now, we have here before us a case of partial clairvoyance—a clairvoyance, that is to say, relating solely to the patient's own recovery. We know that she had been living for many years in total mental obscurity; that she had lost all idea of time, and all consciousness of outward events; we must, therefore, it seems to me, make a distinction between the two phenomena presented, that is to say, between her prediction as to the duration of her malady, and the sudden awakening of the mind to the consciousness of time, which enabled her to fix the 15th of August as the day on which her sufferings would terminate.

The first of these phenomena I should call subjective, the second entirely objective. The one might be connected with intuition or instinct, the other is independent of any such action. It may be suggested by some that my patient was able to read my mind, that she learnt the day of the month from my thoughts, and was able consequently to make her calculations from this given point.

To this I reply that I was not thinking of the day of the month; that, as a matter of fact, I did not know whether it was the 2nd, 10th, or 20th; neither had I the least idea that the 15th of August was the day of the Assumption. Again, it must be noted that no one was present at these séances. I call attention to this fact, to remove all suspicion from the minds of those who would say that the somnambulist learnt from the bystanders the information she required to enable her to fix the date of her prophecy.[380] — DR. NICOLAS, COUNT GONÉMYS, OF CORFU

☛ CASE #363: On a certain Sunday evening in November 1881, having been reading of the great power which the human will is capable of exercising, I determined with the whole force of my being, that I would be present in spirit in the front bed-room on the second floor of a house situated at 22 Hogarth Road, Kensington, in which room slept two ladies of my acquaintance, viz., Miss L. S. V. and Miss E. C. V., aged respectively 25 and 11 years. I was living at this time at 23 Kildare Gardens, a distance of about three miles from Hogarth Road, and I had not mentioned in any way my intention of trying this experiment to either of the above ladies, for the simple reason that it was only on retiring to rest upon this

Sunday night that I made up my mind to do so. The time at which I determined I would be there was 1 o'clock in the morning, and I also had a strong intention of making my presence perceptible.

On the following Thursday I went to see the ladies in question, and in the course of conversation (without any allusion to the subject on my part) the elder one told me, that on the previous Sunday night she had been much terrified by perceiving me standing by her bedside, and that she screamed when the apparition advanced towards her, and awoke her little sister, who saw me also. I asked her if she was awake at the time, and she replied most decidedly in the affirmative, and upon my inquiring the time of the occurrence, she replied, about 1 o'clock in the morning.

This lady, at my request, wrote down a statement of the event and signed it. This was the first occasion upon which I tried an experiment of this kind, and its complete success startled me very much.

Besides exercising my power of volition very strongly, I put forth an effort which I cannot find words to describe. I was conscious of a mysterious influence of some sort permeating in my body, and had a distinct impression that I was exercising some force with which I had been hitherto unacquainted, but which I can now at certain times set in motion at will.[381] — S. H. B.

☞ CASE #364: La Tour de Peilz, Vaud [Switzerland], October 12th, 1900. This morning I went and paid a visit to a carpenter, Henry Cornaz by name, whom I had heard to be dangerously ill with cancer. I found him very ill indeed with a cancerous tumour in the mouth, cheek, and nose. Our best surgeons in Lausanne told him that it was too late for attempting an operation, and that no remedy would avail anything.

I found him quite cheerful. He is a very good man, a kind of mystic; and he told me that he was sure of recovering.

"One night last week," he said, "while sleeping I heard a voice saying: 'Be of good cheer, thou shalt recover, and still be my witness in this and in other lands.' I awoke, full of joy; and having gone again to sleep, I heard the voice a second time repeating the same words. Hence my confidence."

Supposing he were to recover his health, I would send you certificates of our medical men testifying both to his incurable disease and to his having been restored to health.... But I must add that, for me, I have not the slightest human hope for him. He is about fifty years old, and the disease has brought him down fearfully. — Rev. Aug. Glardon.

Update January 13th, 1901: I believe [the dream occurred] about a week before my letter of October 12th, after that the three medical men seen by Cornaz had agreed in declaring that the disease could not be cured, and that it was too late for an operation.

I have since been talking with one of them, Dr. E. Ceresole (son of the late President of the Swiss Confederation). He confirmed their verdict, and agreed to give me, when and if needed, a written statement about Cornaz's case and a certificate of cure. He still thinks that a cure is not possible, however, in which case his note would not be needed.

Now, I want you to know that since the middle of November Cornaz has been gradually improving, although still far from being recovered. After a few weeks in bed, with hemorrhages in the nose and mouth, he got stronger, was enabled to rise, and finally to go out. He does now sometimes take long walks, has less difficulty in speaking, his face is less swollen, and the cancerous excrescences in his mouth and nose have diminished in size. His faith in the vision has sometimes wavered; just now he is very hopeful, although the doctors refuse to give him remedies, which they deem useless. Dr. Ceresole thinks that *his faith or autosuggestion may be the cause* [my emphasis, L.S.]—is probably the cause of the improvement. . . . I shall write again on the subject, sooner or later according to circumstances. If Cornaz were to die in his prime he would be missed greatly in our religious circles and societies, in which he is much liked. — Rev. Aug. Glardon.

Update January 28th, 1901: I forward Dr. Ceresole's note. As you will perceive, he has not the slightest hope of an ultimate recovery. And the improvement in Cornaz's condition is more apparent than real; not even that. Dr. Ceresole affirms that the tumour has expanded. Well, Cornaz himself says that he feels much better.

I went to see him this morning, and only found his wife; and, in answer to my inquiries, she said: "My husband is certainly better. The 'thing' in the mouth has diminished; he can eat with less difficulty, and feels much stronger. He has just gone out for a walk, notwithstanding the wind and rain."

"Then," said I, "he still believes in a recovery?"

"Most certainly, although ready to submit to the will of God. But, as you know, he had twice the same vision in one night, and believes that the prediction will be realised."

Such is just now the state of things.

Cornaz, whom I have met a few days ago, looks a good deal better, and I have myself ascertained, *de visu*, that if the nostrils have been invaded, the tumour in the mouth is two-thirds smaller. Formerly Cornaz had to keep his mouth open, now he can and does keep it shut. He could hardly speak, now he does speak and make himself understood easily. . . .

Update March 14th, 1901: Henry Cornaz keeps improving wonderfully. He says so, and he looks so.

Update September 9th, 1902: My friend, the carpenter Henri Cornaz, died and was buried a week ago, after a protracted illness and long sufferings. You remember what I told you of his conviction, based on a dream, that his illness would not prove fatal. During about six months he remained steady in his faith; the disease had gone back wonderfully, he seemed in a fair way of recovery, and already the medical men were wondering and almost shaken in their mind about their own dark prognostics. However, during last winter a change for the worse took place. *Cornaz began to waver in his belief* [my emphasis, L.S.]; and during the last four months of his life he gradually prepared himself to die. . . .[382] — REV. AUG. GLARDON

☛ CASE #365: I knew nothing about water-finding until Mr. Houston came here at my request—on Wednesday, 9th July, 1902—to show me how he found water, and to try and find a fresh supply for Charteris, the joiner, who had set the sanitary inspector at me, as his landlord, as the water supply at Bankend had run short on account of the great drouth last spring.

Mr. Houston came over from Barwhillanty, and brought six

twigs of different trees cut out of a hedge, and a twisted wire. In showing me, in my study, how the twigs and wire worked on metal, he discovered that I also had the same power as himself.

We went outside after lunch and found water near the house in several places, both where it was known to exist, and where it was *not* known to exist. We then drove over to Bankend, and again tried for water, and we got a splendid spring of first-class water at the bottom of Mr. Charteris's garden. Mr. Houston stated that the water could be got at 5 feet from the surface. A well was dug, and I measured it. It is 6 feet deep, and the water was standing 14 inches below the surface level of the ground. Charteris says the water is first-class drinking water. We also traced the source of this water in a zig-zag direction from above where the well was sunk.

When it was known through the district that I also had the same power with a twig or wire as Mr. Houston, John Cunningham asked me to go over to Tarbreoch to try and find water near the farm house, as their water supply had failed, and he had a scheme of getting water from a distance, which would be a costly one to carry out. I went over to Tarbreoch with the twisted wire I had got from Mr. Houston, and I tried in the field just above the farm house for water. Very soon the wire began to work, and twisted straight down in my hand, indicating a strong supply of water not far off. I told Cunningham to mark the spot, and dig there. Cunningham turned over a sheep trough to mark the spot, and we then went and tried other places round the farm steading. I found good supplies of water in five or six places, which were marked.

John Cunningham got a man from Kirkpatrick-Durham to dig, and set him to work at the spot marked by the upturned sheep trough. When the workman had dug down 17 feet, he came on a very plentiful supply of water, which has now risen to within 4 or 5 feet of the surface. As water was not known to exist when I indicated this spot to John Cunningham (it was on the brow of a slope in a green grass field), I fail to understand how this can be ascribed to "conscious knavery, or to a more or less unconscious delusion." I had no idea till the wire began to be drawn in my hands towards the spot, and then to twist violently and go straight down, that there was water; but now I can, from practice, blindfolded, and pushed from behind by any one, go about till the wire tells me water is near, and then I can find the spot by attraction. I've done this blindfolded in several places—Shoeburyness, Ashbourne, Hartlip, Llandrindod Wells, etc.

The wires also can tell me that water is running under a house when you are standing, one and sometimes two storeys above the ground. I can find water with forked twigs of the following wood: Willow, hazel, common ash, weeping ash, mountain ash (rowan), whitethorn, blackthorn, holly, laburnum, laurel, and apple. I daresay there are many other kinds of wood that would do as well, that I have not tried yet, and it appears to me that almost any forked twig that is full of sap will do for the purpose of a divining rod.

I never had any interest in water-finding till the sanitary inspector started on me with the threat of setting the County Council at me to get a water supply for Charteris at Bankend, and though I stormed pretty freely at the time, it has turned out a wind that blew me some good, for now I can find water where it exists, and I find I can add materially to the present water supply to this house from springs close to the cistern at Paddock Hall, at present untapped.

I have found some people who have the power much stronger than I have. One man of 82, whom I met at Llandrindod Wells, had this power quite as thoroughly as it lies in myself. My son, Johnny, aged eight on 20th July, 1902, has the power, but none of the rest of the children have it so far. Dorothy can't get either a twig or a wire to work, and she was ten years old on 20th August last.

I have taken hold of people by one hand and made them hold the wires or twigs in their left hand and held the other end in my right hand, and the wires or twigs will work and twist despite what any one does or wishes to do to prevent it. It is quite a simple matter to take a dozen pairs of gloves belonging to twelve different people, lay them at intervals apart, having taken one glove out of any pair, and then blindfolded to go—guided by some one—over every pair till the wire comes over the fellow of the glove you hold in your hand, when the wire will at once twist and go down to the mate of the glove in your hand.

There is no doubt that after using these twigs or wires trying to find water, etc., one gets very much exhausted. I have been taken blindfolded over pipes and taps of water where water was—and was known to be by people to test me—and I could not possibly see these taps or pipes—and the wire has always worked accurately. I've also made sceptics hold one end of the wire or twig, while I held their right hand in my left, and the other end of the wire or twig in my right hand to complete the circle, and the wire or twig will work despite all the sceptic can do to prevent it.

The only place I have ever known the wires or twigs refuse to work was at Norton Hill, Runcorn, Cheshire, where the atmosphere is full of chemicals from the Chemical Works at

Widnes, in Cheshire, and where the upper limbs of all the big trees are destroyed, and the grass is blackened with the chemical soot from the Widnes Works for miles around. . . .

I have gone out of a room and found a sovereign hidden in the room in my absence, and being blindfolded before I was brought into the room—also a hidden glove, while holding the other glove of the pair in my hand. When I hold the wires and am in the vicinity of water, or coal, or metals, one feels the magnetic current strong. I saw the bark twisted off a forked willow held by Tait, the late gardener here, when he tried over a place where I had found water with the wires before him. I've seen two twigs I cut break with a snap in the hands of Colonel Paget, to whom I gave them when at Llandrindod Wells last year, and my hands have been made quite sore by the wires and twigs twisting in them over water. January 21st, 1903.[383] — JAS. WEDDERBURN MAXWELL

☛ CASE #366: My story of the warts is this. A friend had a little girl aged 10 with both hands covered with warts and two on her lip. She was expressing her distress at this when a mutual friend of hers and mine said, "You will laugh at me, but an old man in our village cured one on my hand when I was a girl by charming. He won't say what he does, and does not require to know anything about the person except the number of warts." The mother laughingly asked her to tell "Old Tom," and on the child counting, there were 50.

I forgot all about the incident till about two months after, when my friend was staying with me, and I suddenly said, "How about D____'s warts?"

She answered, "They have nearly disappeared; I expect when I return they will have quite gone."

On her return home she wrote me there was no sign of one. The old man asks no payment, but is very pleased with any present. He is well known in the country round as a doctor for horses, is a herbalist, and a shoemaker, over 80. I have not verified all this as to time, place, etc., but this is the main outline. January 29th, 1904.[384] — BEATRICE GRAVES

☛ CASE #367: [Corroboration of the previous case.] Harry Allen, horse clipper and vet., age over 80, has lived all his life at Attleboro, in Norfolk. Tall, stout, clean shaven, and had around, merry face (very wrinkled with age now).

He was told about the wart charm when a boy of eight; some old man told him, and he must not tell the secret to any one else, or he could not charm the warts away. His wife and son do not know what he does.

Some time back I had a wart on my finger, and stopped him in the road and asked if he could cure it. He looked at the place, and simply said, "Only one, lady? that'll be all right, that will go," and in a short time it did, and has not returned.

I have heard about many children he has cured in the village. In the case of the little girl with the 50 on one hand, 15 on the other, and one on lip, he did not see her. I first asked him if he could do anything in it. He said, "You get the lady just to write the number down on a slip of paper." I think I told him the child lived in Wales, and a girl. I took him the letter, and tore out the piece for him with the number; he asked me to give it him so as not to forget. He seemed very much astonished at the number he had to deal with, and said, "I must get to work at once." He did not say how long it would take for the charm to work—"may be a fortnight or more, as it's a big lot."

The old man is quite a well-known character in the place, and has been very clever with horses; believes in old-fashioned remedies, I think.[385] — IDA K. SALTER

☛ CASE #368: Six years ago I was living with my father and a sister and brother on a farm, 5 miles from the nearest township and about 60 miles from Wellington. My friend, Miss Wilson, was living here in Wellington with her mother, and Miss Wilson and I kept up a regular correspondence.

One morning I awoke very early and felt a strong desire to write a story. I sat up in bed and began at once. I finished it at about noon, and when my sister asked me to read it aloud to her, I said I could not, as the idea was so painful, and that I had put Mrs. Wilson in as one of the characters and that she died of cancer. I felt very depressed. Of course, as far as any of us knew, Mrs. Wilson was quite well and we had never associated this disease with her. Nevertheless I wished I had not written the story.

This happened on a Sunday, and on the next day I received a long letter from Miss Wilson telling me that her mother had been operated on successfully on the preceding day (Sunday) at noon for cancer.

She explained that she and her mother had known of the necessity for the operation for 10 days before, and that she had written me a letter telling me of it as soon as she knew, but that her mother had persuaded her to destroy the letter, because of our living so far from the post and telegraph office, and because our mails were so irregular.

Mrs. Wilson was a thoughtful woman and knew that we would be very nervous, and had no means of communicating quickly with them. Miss Wilson therefore had written just as regularly as usual, but had given us no idea that anything was amiss. A fortnight later Mrs. Wilson died.

Most of my intimate friends know of this incident, and up till quite recently I possessed the manuscript. My sister and my brother knew I had written it, before we had even heard Mrs. Wilson was ill. March 30th, 1904.[386] — MISS BUTLER

☛ CASE #369: [From a letter to a friend.] . . . You remember I told you that I had lost two latch-keys of the outside door here, and was much bothered. After I got back I instituted a drawer to drawer search which went on for several days without success. I felt my subconscious ego knew quite well where they were, as I remembered that I had put them away in some safe place—only keeping one out.

The other night I had a sort of impulse to write and asked where my keys were, and my pen wrote "Dodsworth"—the name of the manager of the flats [apartments]. I thought it most unlikely that he could throw any light on their whereabouts; but as I met him in the lift the next day I said, "Do you remember those three keys you gave me of the outside door?"

"I only gave you one," he said, "you asked me to keep the other two, and I have got them."

I had completely forgotten this, and thought "Dodsworth" so outside the mark that I should not even have asked him but for meeting him just after. March 3rd, 1905.[387] — MRS. A. G. DEW-SMITH

☛ CASE #370: In the summer of 1903 I was staying in a country house in Berkshire. Amongst the guests was a Miss B., the lady superintendent of a home for high-class patients in connection with a large private asylum. I noticed that her hands were covered with warts, and one day she told me that they were a great worry to her, and had been for two years. All the doctors at the asylum, she said, had tried one after the other to cure them, and she had tried many remedies, and been through a good deal of suffering, but in vain; the warts were immoveable.

I had previously been telling my hostess a curious case I had lately heard of some warts being "charmed" away, and she was so much impressed that she begged me to try myself, and see if I could not "charm" her guest's warts. At first I only laughed at the idea, and said it was most unlikely I possessed any such power, and treated it all as a joke; but the day on which Miss B. was to end her visit, my hostess once more begged me at all events to try.

Just to put an end to the matter, and more in fun than anything else, I gave Miss B. a needle in a piece of paper, repeating the formula that I had heard when I was told of the cure that had aroused my hostess's interest. I said: "Take this needle, and keep it safely; do not break it, do not lose it; do not mention it to any one."

She put it away in her purse, saying, "How long do you give me before they go?"

"Six weeks," I said—just because I had to mention some time; not that I had any idea that the warts would disappear at all.

I had forgotten all about the matter, when two months afterwards Miss B. wrote to me, saying she did not know how to thank me enough for having cured her. She had waited until the complete disappearance of the warts before writing, so as to be able to tell me that they were entirely gone. They had begun to die away soon after she saw me.

I told a young doctor about this surprising letter, and he said he thought I ought not to claim the cure until I knew what other influences might have been at work, and furnished me with a list of searching questions: Had there been any fresh water supply to her house? Had she been away for change of air, and become strengthened? Had she used a different kind of soap? Had she taken any medicines or tried any remedies after seeing me; and so on.

She wrote back a very full reply in answer to all these questions, and the answer to each one was absolutely satisfactory; no circumstances had arisen to point to any other possible source of cure. I much regret that I have had no further opportunity of testing my influence, and cannot at all understand how my "charm" succeeded in curing Miss B.[388] — ELLEN MONTAGUE BARRY

☛ CASE #371: Mrs. Mary Jane Roberts, of Pottery Street, Llanelly, has a daughter about 14 years of age, employed by the "Domestic Bazaar Co., Llanelly." Her hands were covered with warts of various sizes, some in groups. She has suffered from them this last 12 months, and various remedies have been tried without success.

Knowing the young lady, and after reading the case of "wart charming" in the July number of *Journal* of the S.P.R., I requested her to let me charm them away, to which she willingly consented, with the result [that all disappeared.] She had 41 on both hands. There is no sign up to date of any reappearance. August 29th, 1904.[389] — J. F. YOUNG

☛ CASE #372: On the evening of January 28th [1850s?], during a somewhat extraordinary display of the Northern Lights, a respectable lady became so highly charged with electricity as to give out vivid electrical sparks from the end of each finger to the face of each of the company present. This did not cease with the heavenly phenomenon, but continued several months, during which time she was constantly charged and giving off electrical sparks to every conductor she approached. This was extremely vexatious, as she could not touch the stove, or any metallic utensil, without first giving off an electrical spark, with the consequent twinge.

The state most favorable to this phenomenon was an atmosphere of about eighty degrees, moderate exercise, and social enjoyment. It disappeared in an atmosphere approaching zero, and under the debilitating effects of fear. When seated by the stove, reading, with her feet upon the fender, she gave sparks at the rate of three or four a minute; and under the most favorable circumstances, a spark, that could be seen, heard, or felt, passed every second. She could charge others in the same way when insulated, who could then give sparks to others. To make it satisfactory that her dress did not produce it, it was changed to cotton and woolen without altering the phenomenon.

The lady is about thirty, of sedentary pursuits and delicate state of health, having for two years previously suffered from acute rheumatism and neuralgic affections, with peculiar symptoms.[390] — JOHN BOVEE DODS

☛ CASE #373: The question has been frequently asked during the ["fraud" trial of spirit photographer William H. Mumler], "Why, if it be not a deception, cannot he produce his pictures in some other establishment than his own?" In answer, I beg space for a brief statement of facts within my own knowledge and experience.

With a desire to fully investigate this subject, I invited Mr. Mumler to visit Poughkeepsie. He accepted, and on the 30th of March last came to our rooms.

I had, previous to his visit, made every arrangement possible for a full investigation, removing all old negatives from my operating rooms, preparing fresh plates from glass never before used, and putting everything in a shape to prevent or detect any attempt at imposture. A reward of $50 was offered by me to any of our employés who should succeed in detecting any trickery or deception.

Mr. Mumler entered our operating rooms without any previous preparation or appliances whatever, and with the camera, chemicals, etc., in daily use by us, and under the closest scrutiny of my operator and myself, produced at once his so-called spirit pictures. In three instances during our experiments my operator performed all the manipulations himself, from the coating of the plate to the developing of the pictures; the result in each case being the same, a second figure appearing upon the plate. In one instance the camera was taken into the developing room by him, the plate-holder there removed and thoroughly examined, and the picture developed. Result the same, no second negative or mechanical arrangement whatever being discovered.

One fact is worth more as evidence than all the theories in existence, and it is a fact that Mr. Mumler's pictures were produced in our rooms, with our instruments, chemicals, etc., without his touching the plates or taking any part in their production whatever; save only that of laying his hand upon the camera box during the time of exposure.

The theories advanced by so-called experts all involve previous preparation of cameras, plate-holders, etc., none of which was it possible for Mr. Mumler to have made upon this occasion. The different processes described by them, by which Mr. M.'s pictures may be imitated, are known to most photographers. They may prove a satisfactory explanation to the minds of said experts, none of whom have investigated Mr. M.'s operations themselves, but are far from satisfying those who have. Messrs. Gilmore, Gurney,

Silver, and myself, with a host of others, know they utterly fail to afford a solution of the problem, or account for the facts within our knowledge. I will pay $100 to any expert who will come to my rooms, and under the same circumstances that Mr. Mumler's pictures were produced there, do the same by natural means without detection. If he succeeds, and can give a satisfactory explanation of the matter, I will promptly acknowledge the fact to the world, and thank him for the solution of a mystery beyond my comprehension.

My operator was present at the trial on Friday last, ready to give his sworn testimony to the facts stated. His testimony was not admitted, on the ground that what occurred in Poughkeepsie was foreign to the case; and yet the question is asked, why cannot Mumler produce his pictures in some other gallery than his own? It would seem, if the desire was to arrive at the facts in the case, and not to condemn the man, innocent or guilty, that any evidence tending to a solution of the matter should not have been ruled out upon mere technical grounds. A sworn statement of the facts mentioned has been made by my operator, and is now in the hands of Mr. M.'s counsel.

Mr. M., while here, was not only thoroughly watched by those immediately about him, but also by our printers, who, stimulated by the reward offered, and believing the whole thing a deception, had loopholes prepared, looking from the printing room above into the developing and dark rooms below; and during the little time Mr. Mumler was left unwatched, or supposed himself to be, his every movement was noted by them. They failed to detect anything in his operations different from the ordinary process.

I have no personal interest in Mr. Mumler, and had no acquaintance with him previous to a casual visit made to his rooms in New York, where, at his invitation, on learning I was a photographer, I investigated the subject as far as possible. Not being fully satisfied there, although unable to detect any sign of imposture, I induced him to visit my rooms, with the above result.[391] — WILLIAM P. SLEE, POUGHKEEPSIE, NY

☛ CASE #374: It is not often, in these prosaic sceptical times, that a miracle comes formally attested by an official Government Report. But the Governor of Aldershot has reported that a prisoner, who—being lately checked on drill by one of the warders—wished, with a blasphemous oath, that the warder "might be struck dumb," was himself "struck dumb on the spot"; all which maybe found solemnly recorded in the recent report on military prisons of Captain Du Cane, inspector general.

Captain Du Cane informs us that the man remained dumb for seven days, and was very much frightened. On recovering his speech it appears that he made great promises of amendment; but we regret to add that he is reported to have been "soon in prison again."[392] — THE SPIRITUAL MAGAZINE

☛ CASE #375: Rising from his seat at the hearth, [famed Scottish medium] Mr. [Daniel D.] Home stepped up quickly to Lord ____ and placing [Joseph] Glanvill's book underneath his extended hand, made several passes over Lord ____'s hand; and, after balancing the book on one finger, gently withdrew his hand.

The book, only just touching Lord ____'s outstretched hand, remained suspended in space for three minutes, and only fell to the ground upon Mrs. J____ passing her hand underneath the book and Lord ____'s hand. My friend described his feeling as if a cushion of steam had held the book in its position.

Fortunately the full clear light of the wax tapers [candles] on the mantelpiece enabled us to watch this phenomenon with the utmost precision, and enabled us to verify the truth of what we were witnessing by our own eyes. This manifestation was repeated twice.[393] — THE SPIRITUAL MAGAZINE

☛ CASE #376: [Continuation of the previous case.]

Mr. [Daniel D.] Home's address (in the trance) now became interrupted, saying, "There are spirits present arguing with Dr. Elliotson and Dr. Jencken; they have brought many here to witness the manifestations, and they are dissatisfied with the result. They want to see the fire test—I will shew it them; they won't believe it possible."

Mr. Home then proceeded to the hearth, and, breaking up the back of burning coal with his hands, placed a lump, the size of a very large orange, on the palm of his hand, and then, still addressing the invisible guests, continued to explain what was going on. After carrying the coal about for three or four minutes on his hand, having allowed each of us to test the intense heat, he put it back on the grate, and, to further satisfy us, showed his hands, which were not even blackened, and, strange to say, emitted a perfume, to which he called attention.

After a moment's pause, in which, evidently, a discussion was going on between the invisibles themselves, Mr. Home said: "They still doubt the phenomenon; I must take another lump of burning coal; they say one side was black."

He then proceeded to the hearth, and selected the hottest incandescent lump of coal, not quite so large as the last, but burning hot; then turning round to us, said, "Only imagine, they will not allow it possible."

He then thrust his head into the grate, holding his face over the burning coals, and receiving the flame points on his hair. To those who have never witnessed this there is something awfully solemn, I might all but say terrible, in this ordeal, the dread fire test, that stands on the highways of the past warning mankind of the horrors of the power of superstition.

Withdrawing his face from the flames, "See," he said [speaking in the third person], "Daniel has not burnt a fibre of the hair of his head."

I cannot conceal that I shuddered.

But the fire test did not terminate here; walking slowly up to Lord _____ who was seated next to me, he said, "I will farther convince you of the truth of the phenomenon. Now, my lord, if you are not afraid, I will place the coal on your hand."

I interrupted and proffered my hand, but was soon warned that my power could not shield me; though I only touched the burning coal on the dark side, and that for a moment I burnt my finger. With singular *sang froid* ["cold blood," that is, fearless] Lord _____ put out his hand, and received the burning coal upon his palm. I closely watched what was passing; the heat of the coal was intense, sufficient to have charred an inch plank right through.

Mr. Home said, "Now, I will further convince them" (meaning the invisible guests), and, taking the other hand of Lord _____, pressed both hands firmly upon the glowing ember. The heat permeated through the back of the hands, which felt as if on fire; I could hardly bear it. After two minutes, the grasp was relaxed, and, on examining the hands of Lord _____, not a trace of injury, or burn, or even blackness was visible.

Fortunately we had a good clear light in the room, and those present, by their quiet and thorough investigation, aided to satisfy beyond doubt that the marvellous fire test applied to a guest who was not a medium was really being witnessed.

Mr. Home then again addressed us, and said: "I have convinced them now; their incredulity is pretty well conquered; but they want some other spirit to try, who does not understand how this is done. Well, let him, but they must not hurt Daniel; but I do not think he (meaning the spirit) knows how to manage the experiment."

He then proceeded to the hearth, and, taking a small piece of coal, not thoroughly hot or glowing, said: " Just see, Daniel has hurt his hand; the coal has blackened the hand—burnt his hand."

Mr. Home now stepped up to a side-table, upon which was placed a flower-stand, and, holding his hand about eighteen inches to two feet above the flowers, extracted the moisture and perfume—the finger tips becoming bedewed with large drops of perfumed liquid. Again, speaking to the spirits, he said: "You see this also can be done; we can extract the perfume from flowers, and carry fluids through space."

He then appeared to be speaking to some of the invisibles, and, opening the door, made the usual parting salute; then, conversing with his spirit friends, he appeared to enjoy a laugh, and reiterated his satisfaction at the result, which had puzzled some of the spirits; after which, he re-seated himself and addressed us:

"Are you aware, do you realise that the phenomena you have seen to-day is what mankind call a miracle; that you have witnessed the fire test—the terrible, traditional fire test? Yet what you have seen is no miracle—no suspending of the laws of nature, of the laws of God. This cannot be; we only passed currents of what you call electricity round the coal, and prevented the heat from attacking Daniel's hand. Mankind do not know their power—they, too, ought to be able to do this; their power over all materiality is boundless, only they do not know how to use their power. Faith is a potent force in nature; how few of you understand this, and yet every page of the history of the past teaches this. We repeat, we performed no miracle, nothing supernatural; all we did was by arranging the electrical currents to shield the hand from injury. Look at the hand; no harm has been done, the epidermis is as uninjured as ever—not hardened nor covered by an artificial coating. From all we have told you, you will learn that it is a natural law that has produced these phenomena—one of the laws God has created."

". . . We made passes over Lord ____'s hand; these shielded him from injury, whilst Mr. J____, though he willingly proffered his hand, burnt it, and yet he only touched the embers for a moment with the point of his finger. In the first instance, preparatory measures had been taken, and all understood this, whilst those who had not been protected were certain to sustain injury by contact. The selfsame coal placed upon an inch plank would have burned a hole through it. Are you now satisfied?"[394] —
THE SPIRITUAL MAGAZINE

☛ CASE #377: The séance [under the guidance of Scottish medium Daniel D. Home] here reported was communicated to M. Piérart by Mr. Gledstanes. It took place in a family circle at Campden Hill. Amongst many of the manifestations at this séance, there was extraordinary music played by the spirits, *The March to Calvary*, amid the sound of the tramp of many feet, and *The Resurrection*, both executed in a manner only to be conceived by those who heard them. Mr. Home was taken up from the floor, wrapped in the window curtains, and suspended for some time in the air. The spirit of a child appeared; presented each of the company with a flower, and asked Mr. Home to go and see his mother. Again, and a third time Mr. Home was floated in the air, and on the last occasion made a cross on the ceiling with a pencil.[395]
—— *THE SPIRITUAL MAGAZINE*

☛ CASE #378: Late in the month of November last [1868?] the Hon. the ____ ____ was engaged sorting papers at the family residence in ____ Square; my friend was alone in his library, and deeply intent on his work, when loud raps aroused his attention; on looking round he noticed that the book-shelf, which was 12 feet by 3, full of books, and must have weighed upwards of half a ton, raised itself horizontally off the ground 12 to 15 inches, and then bumped on the floor as it descended with a crash, so loud as to bring up the housekeeper and servants from the adjoining rooms, who, alarmed at the noise, thought some accident had occurred.

After a short pause raps came, and on asking what was meant the raps spelt out: "Go to [Scottish medium] Daniel [D. Home]." At first the gentleman doubted his senses, but finding the message quite distinct and intelligible, at once went to Ashley House, Victoria Street, where Mr. D. D. Home resides.

On entering the room he found Mr. Home absent, only Lord ____ present, who had been for some time an invalid, confined to the house. Not finding Mr. Home, the Hon. the ____ ____ left, but being strongly impressed, as he describes it, returned about 11 p.m.

By this time Mr. Home had returned, and, strange to say, all but impelled by the strong influence exerted upon him. So strangely brought together, the three seated themselves to see if the influences would produce any manifestation. After the usual preparatory movements of the table, and raps unusually loud, Mr. Home passed into a trance state; suddenly rising up he stepped into the adjoining room, with a bottle of cognac and a wine glass; this he filled with brandy, and then, holding the glass high over his head, proceeded to the window. From the centre of the glass a bluish light appeared, increasing in intensity until finally a flame two or three inches long rose out of the glass, flickering up and down, at times becoming extinguished.

Mr. Home was now raised bodily off the ground, so high that the flame point rising out of the glass appeared to touch the ceiling. After two or three minutes he descended to the floor, and then the phenomenon occurred of the brandy being extracted from the glass. The Hon. the ____ ____ says he could visibly see the brandy as it was extricated, but to satisfy Lord ____ of this, Mr. Home inverted the empty wineglass upon his lordship's hand. The same agency that had removed the liquid now poured it back into the glass, and the fluid, as it filled the glass, could be seen falling.

The manifestation was repeated, accompanied by the click-clack sound of water falling; but this time, in all probability to satisfy Lord ____ the fluid was poured over his hand, then over Mr. Home's hand into the glass.

Mr. H. then said they would extract the alcohol, and which at once took place, filling the room with the unmistakable odour of spirits of wine. Mr. Home had placed himself at the window which he opened, and deliberately stepped upon the ledge outside, looking on to the street, some 80 feet below, with utter unconcern. The Honourable the ____ ____ said he shuddered, alarmed at what he was witnessing. Mr. Home noticing this stepped down and reproached his friend, saying "Little faith, little faith; Daniel will not be injured!"

After a few minutes Mr. Home deliberately stepped down from the ledge and re-entered the room, much to the relief of his two friends. The manifestations now closed, and Mr. Home awoke, as usual, very much exhausted.

The first thing to do was to verify what had occurred with the brandy, and on examining the contents it was found that the alcohol had been completely extracted. This test was so far satisfactory, as it evidenced a former fact of the same kind which had happened to him.[396] — H. D. JENCKEN

☛ CASE #379: [Scottish medium] Mr. [Daniel D.] Home had passed into the trance state so often witnessed; rising from his seat, he laid hold of an arm-chair, which he held at arm's length, and was then lifted about three feet clear off the ground; travelling thus suspended in space, he placed the chair next Lord A____ and made a circuit round those in the room, being lowered and raised as he passed each of us. One of those present measured the elevation, and passed his leg and arm underneath Mr. Home's feet. The elevation lasted from four to five minutes.

On resuming his seat, Mr. Home addressed Captain _____, communicating news to him of which the departed alone could have been cognisant.

The spirit form that had been seen reclining on the sofa now stepped up to Mr. Home and mesmerised him; a hand was then seen luminously visible over his head, about 18 inches in a vertical line from his head. The trance state of Mr. Home now assumed a different character; gently rising he spoke a few words to those present, and then opening the door proceeded into the corridor; a voice then said: "He will go out of this window and come in at that window." The only one who heard the voice was the Hon. _____,

and a cold shudder seized upon him as he contemplated the possibility of this occurring, a feat which the great height of the third floor windows in Ashley Place rendered more than ordinarily perilous.

The others present, however, having closely questioned him as to what he had heard, he at first replied, "I dare not tell you"; when, to the amazement of all, a voice said, "You must tell; tell directly." The Hon. then said, "Yes; yes, terrible to say, he will go out at that window and come in at this; do not be frightened, be quiet."

Mr. Home now re-entered the room, and opening the drawing room window, was pushed out demi-horizontally into space, and carried from one window of the drawing room to the farther most window of the adjoining room. This feat being performed at a height of about 60 feet from the ground, naturally caused a shudder in all present. The body of Mr. Home, when it appeared at the window of the adjoining room, was shunted into the room feet foremost the window being only 18 inches open. As soon as he had recovered his footing he laughed and said, "I wonder what a policeman would have said had he seen me go round and round like a teetotum!"

The scene was, however, too terrible—too strange, to elicit a smile; cold beads of perspiration stood on every brow, while a feeling pervaded all as if some great danger had passed; the nerves of those present had been kept in a state of tension that refused to respond to a joke.

A change now passed over Mr. Home, one often observable during the trance states, indicative, no doubt, of some other power operating on his system. Lord ____ had in the meantime stepped up to the open window in the adjoining room to close it—the cold air, as it came pouring in, chilling the room; when, to his surprise, he only found the window 18 to 24 inches open. This puzzled him, for how could Mr. Home have passed outside through a window only 18 to 24 inches open!

Mr. Home, however, soon set his doubts at rest; stepping up to Lord ____, he said, "No, no; I did not close the window; I passed thus into the air outside." An invisible power then supported Mr. Home all but horizontally in space, and thrust his body into space through the open window, head foremost, bringing him back again feet foremost into the room, shunted not unlike a shutter into a basement below.

The circle round the table having re-formed, a cold current of air passed over those present, like the rushing of winds. This repeated itself several times. The cold blast of air, or electric fluid, or call it what you may, was accompanied by a loud whistle like a gust of wind on the mountain top, or through the leaves of the forest in late autumn; the sound was deep, sonorous, and powerful in the extreme, and a shudder kept passing over those present, who all heard and felt it. This rushing sound lasted quite ten minutes, in broken intervals of one or two minutes.

All present were much surprised; and the interest became intensified by the unknown tongues in which Mr. Home now conversed. Passing from one language to another in rapid succession, he spoke for ten minutes in unknown languages.

A spirit form now became distinctly visible; it stood next to the Hon. ____ clad, as seen on former occasions, in a long robe with a girdle, the feet scarcely touching the ground, the outline of the face only clear, and the tones of the voice, though sufficiently distinct to be understood, whispered rather than spoken. Other voices were now heard, and large globes of phosphorescent lights passed slowly through the room.[397] — *HUMAN NATURE*, FEBRUARY 1869

☛ CASE #380: The party was composed of [Scottish medium] Mr. and Mrs. [Daniel D.] Home and seven other ladies and gentlemen. We sat at the roundtable in the large drawing-room. Mr. Home's hand was moved to write: "The spirit of John is one who was kind to your father during the voyage to America." No one understood this; but Mr. ____ entering the room a minute afterwards, expressed his conviction that it was intended for him, as his father had been to America.

Three loud raps gave assent to what he said. The table then moved away from us, and we enquired if they wished us to draw it to the window. It was answered, "Yes." We accordingly did so, leaving a vacant space against the window, unclosing the shutters, and by their directions extinguishing the candles.

The fire burned brightly. It was spelled out, "There is a little too much light." Mr. screened the fire as much as possible, and the moon and gaslight from the street then alone lighted up the table; but did so completely as the moon was very bright.

The spirit of Albert then took the accordion, and played a beautiful air of unearthly harmony. Mr. Home and I held the accordion together under the table, for the power was very strong, and the music loud; and the instrument at times was nearly carried away from us.

After a short time there rose slowly in the space made by the window a most lovely hand of a female—we saw also part of the beautiful arm as it held it up aloft for some time—we were all greatly amazed. This hand was so transparent and luminous, and so unearthly and angelic, that our hearts were filled with gratitude towards the Creator for permitting so wonderful a manifestation. The hand was visible to us more from the internal light which seemed to stream as it were out of it, than from the external light of the moon.

As soon as it slowly vanished, Mdlle. ____ who sat next to the open space, saw another hand forming itself close to her and a man's hand was raised and placed on the table, far more earthly and life-like in appearance, and one that I thought I recognized, (we were subsequently told that I was right in conjecture).

Then came a dear baby-hand: then the baby (Mrs. L's adopted child) showed its head; and finally, spirit-hands held up the little child, so that all nine of us saw her shoulders and waist. After this, a hand and arm rose luminous and beautiful, covered with a white transparent drapery; and this hand remained visible to us all for at least five minutes, and made us courteous and graceful gestures.

Then spirit-hands held up to us an exquisite wreath of white flowers. I never saw any wreath made by human hands so perfect in form and design; and calling for the alphabet said, "The spirit emblem of William's mother." Then we were told they would shew us "The emblem of superstition"; and a black shrivelled hand arose. On some of us remarking that we could not see it well, the curtains were at once moved aside, and the blind drawn away from the top of the window. It was beyond the reach of any of us; and they then showed us the hand again, so that we all could see it.

The "emblem of truth" was then shewn. This was more beautiful than all the rest—a fairy-like fountain of apparently clear sparkling water which threw up showers of silvery rays, vanishing from our sight like mist, and dwelling on the memory as perfection. After this it was rapped out, "We can do no more."

Mr. Home was put into a trance, and as he fell back in his chair a gleam of the most vivid light fell upon me. This light fell over my shoulders, and gleamed on my right hand, and came from a direction whence no earthly light could have come. It came from a part of the room where the spirit of one who was a friend of mine when on earth has often stood before, and from whence he has communicated to us. This light was seen by no one but myself; but as I turned round in hope of seeing the spirit, Mr. Home said to me, "Yes, he is there"; and added a communication from him.

He then told us that the first hand that we saw had been that of his own mother; the second was my father's, as I had silently expected; and the hand and arm in drapery that remained so long, came for Prudence, and was the same that she had seen one night when alone, several years ago, at Paris, before she had ever heard of spirit-manifestations. He also gave us the full name of the "spirit John," who had gone to America with Mr. A____'s father; and added some private information, which Mr. A____ confirmed as true.

The events of this evening having been so wonderful, I have begged my friends present on the occasion to read over this account, and to sign it as witnesses to the truth of what I have stated. May 1st, 1860.[398] — EDITOR OF *THE SPIRITUAL MAGAZINE*

☛ CASE #381: [Daniel. D. Home on his ability to levitate:] During these elevations, or levitations, I usually experience in my body no particular sensations than what I can only describe as an electrical fullness about the feet. I feel no hands supporting me, and since the first time, above described, I have never felt fear, though should I have fallen from the ceiling of some rooms in which I have been raised, I could not have escaped serious injury.

I am generally lifted up perpendicularly; my arms frequently become rigid and drawn above my head, as if I were grasping the unseen power which slowly raises me from the floor. At times when I reach the ceiling, my feet are brought on a level with my face, and I am as it were in a reclining position. I have frequently been kept so suspended four or five minutes, an instance of which will be seen in an account which is given of occurrences in the year 1857, at a château near Bordeaux.

I have been lifted in the light of day upon only one occasion, and that was in America. I have been lifted in a room in Sloane Street, London, with four gas-lights brightly burning, with five gentlemen present, who are willing to testify to what they saw, if need be, beyond the many testimonies which I shall hereafter adduce. On some occasions the rigidity of my arms relaxes, and I have with a pencil made letters and signs on the ceiling, some of which now exist in London.[399] — DANIEL DUNGLAS HOME

☛ CASE #382: [From Daniel D. Home: "My dearly valued friend, Mr. (James) Wason, who after twenty nine years of outer scepticism, takes pride in dating his new birth to the belief of a spiritual life and a spiritual philosophy, from his observations of the phenomena which he witnessed in my presence, wrote at this time the interesting letter which I now give [below]."]

In July, 1860, I was at a séance at the mansion of a person of distinction, in Hyde Park Terrace, London. Two baronets—one an M.P., and the other the heir and representative of a deceased M.P. of eminent ability; the wife of a distinguished living M.P.; and others, including Mr. [Scottish medium Daniel D.] Home, making eight in number present. The hour was a little after nine, p.m.

Neither of the three first named parties had ever seen any spirit manifestations, and were evidently sceptics: the rest of the party were mediums of greater or less power, and seemed as much interested in watching the effects of the spirit manifestations on the three new comers, as in the manifestations themselves.

We all made a circle round a heavy loo table, capable of seating nine persons comfortably (crinoline included). It was covered with an ordinary damask cloth, (a powerful non-conductor of electricity, completely negativing the theory that spirit manifestations were brought about by electricity); and we were desired by Mr. Home to chat and talk as naturally and cheerfully as we could, and not to be too eager or expectant of spirit manifestation, which he stated had a strong tendency to defeat the object. There were six lights burning in the room.

The floor (a first floor) shook and trembled in a manner that all thought resembled the vibrations or tremulous motion on a small steamer's deck when the paddles are in full work: some said it more nearly resembled the tremulous motion on a screw steamer's deck, in which I concurred. This tremulous motion ceased at intervals and was renewed, and this seemed to strike the new comers very forcibly; it was amusing to notice their startled looks, though they said but little beyond concurring in the observations as to the tremulous movements. The walls also shook at times with a tremulous motion.

The table, which was a very large and heavy one, was frequently lifted a few inches from the ground, and at last it rose from the ground at least three feet, and remained thus suspended 'twixt heaven and earth, like Mahomet's coffin, for a minute or there abouts, probably more than less.

The gentlemen were invited by Mr. Home to ascertain if any machinery was underneath, and the two gentlemen who were new comers swept with their legs under the suspended table, to catch any prop or other machinery that might be applied to raise the table, and they confessed that no such machinery or prop was present.

This séance, wonderful as it will appear—"stranger than fiction"—was not considered to be an entirely successful one; and the lady of the house, with characteristic kindness, after speaking of the meagreness of the manifestations, invited me to another séance on the following evening, an invitation I most gladly accepted, although it kept me in London an extra day, and overthrew my previously arranged movements.

At this second séance we met rather earlier, a little after eight o'clock, p.m., in the same first-floor room. The séance consisted of a barrister of eminence and standing at the bar, and well known to the public, a literary man—an author of established reputation, and others to the number of eight; all on this occasion being believers, except the author [Wason].

The same tremulous motion of the floor and walls as on the preceding evening, took place; and the table was tilted and turned with even greater power than before, and rose perpendicularly from the floor, from three to four feet, and remained in this position suspended (Mahomet's coffin fashion) for about a minute, and then descended to its original place as softly and gently as the fall of a snow flake. An accordion was played by an unseen hand, whilst it was held by one of the party present, and afterwards by myself. I held it over the back of the chair on which I was sitting, using the back of the chair as a rest to my arm, the accordion hanging over the back of the chair. I sat on the opposite side of the table to Mr. Home and the lady of the house. The accordion was also played whilst lying on the floor, and also on the table, and was lifted without visible means from the floor on to the table. The music was of a solemn and impressive character.

A small spirit-hand, warm and soft like that of a child, touched my hand, and placed in it a small hand-bell, and, at my request, took the bell from my hand underneath the table to its mother, who was the lady of the house. She seemed perfectly satisfied that it was the spirit-hand of her little boy, who died three or four years since, aged about eight years, and she received repeated responses, spelt out through the alphabet, such as might be expected from the spirit of a deceased child to its mother.

The bell was carried to several of the parties present and placed in their hands; and lastly, was elevated above our heads, and rung in mid-air, revolving round and touching our heads (my own included). I could see the bell when it passed round my head opposite the window. I could see the bell occasionally as it passed between me and the window, the blinds of which had been drawn down by invisible agency.

Pieces of mignionette and geranium flowers were placed in my hands by spirit hands, and inside my waistcoat. I saw one of the hands distinctly, which, as it came between me and the window was distinctly visible, as the blinds did not altogether exclude the light of a summer evening and of the gas lights in the street.

The curtains at last were drawn by invisible means, and then Mr. Home stated he was being lifted up in the air, and he crossed the table over the heads of the parties sitting around it. I asked him to make a mark with his pencil on the ceiling. He said he had no pencil. I rose up and said I would lend him mine, and by standing and stretching upwards I was enabled to reach his hand, about seven feet distant from the floor, and I placed therein a pencil, and laying hold and keeping hold of his hand, I moved along with him five or six paces as he floated above me in the air, and I only let go his hand when I stumbled against a stool. Mr. Home, as he floated along, kept ringing the small hand-bell to indicate his locality in the room, which was probably forty by thirty feet, and I saw his body eclipse two lines of light issuing from between the top of a door and its architrave—such door leading into an adjoining room that was brilliantly lighted. Mr. Home was replaced, as he stated, with the greatest care and gentleness in the chair from which he rose, but this I could not see.

Previously to Mr. Home's being raised up, the spirit hands of two of the barrister's deceased children touched him. He did not doubt that the hands were the spirit hands of his children.

Questions were asked, and rational answers given by means of the alphabet, in one of the ordinary ways of communicating with spirits. It is right that I should say, that this séance (as in the preceding evening) was commenced with prayer, which I understood was the usual course.

I make no comments on the above, and advance no theory or hypothesis. I have confined myself simply to facts, which I can substantiate by legal evidence in a court of justice; and I add my name, address, and profession, and have only one desire, and that is that truth may prevail. I am, Sir, your obedient Servant, Liverpool, July 1860.[400] — JAMES WASON, SOLICITOR

Chapter Ten
PRECOGNITION ACCOUNTS
Cases of Premonition and Omens

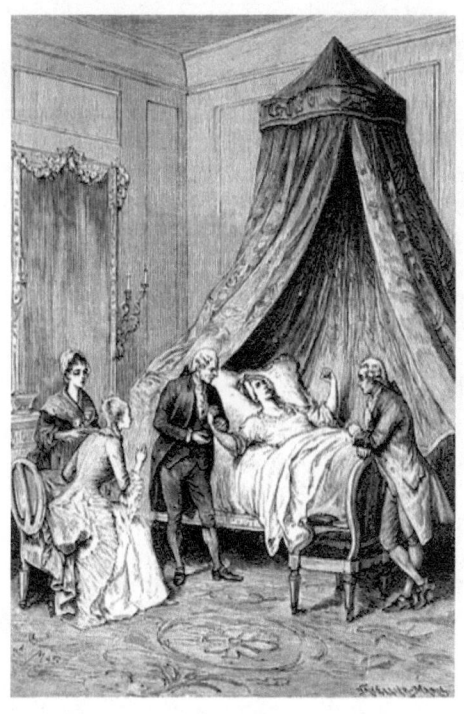

☛ CASE #383: A friend of mine (Dr. Goodall Jones, of Liverpool) related to me the following account of a case of premonition. The names and dates Dr. Jones will give, if required.

He called on a female patient on Sunday afternoon at three o'clock; her husband met him at the door, and said he was about to come for him, as the patient was worse and delirious. On going up-stairs, the doctor found the poor woman in a very excited state, asserting that her brother (a Liverpool pilot) was drowning in the river; "which," said her husband, "is impossible, as he is out at sea, to the best of our knowledge."

The doctor did what he could to soothe his patient, and left, convinced that it was a case of ordinary delirium. But in the next morning's paper he read with surprise the account of the pilot's death by drowning in the river on the previous afternoon at three o'clock.[401] — MR. J. SINCLAIR

☛ CASE #384: In January, 1877, I was on leave of absence in Brooklyn, with my two boys, then on vacation from school. I promised the boys that I would take them to the theatre that night, and I engaged seats for us three. At the same time I had the opportunity to examine the interior of the theatre, and I went over it carefully, stage and all. These seats were engaged the previous day, but on the day of the proposed visit it seemed as if a voice within me was constantly saying, "Do not go to the theatre; take the boys back to school." I could not keep these words out of my mind; they grew stronger and stronger, and at noon I told my friends and the boys that we would not go to the theatre.

My friends remonstrated with me, and said I was cruel to deprive the boys of a promised and unfamiliar pleasure to which they had looked forward, and I partly relented. But all the afternoon the words kept repeating themselves and impressing themselves upon me.

That evening, less than an hour before the doors opened, I insisted on the boys going to New York with me, and spending the night at a hotel convenient to the railroad, by which we could start in the early morning. I felt ashamed of the feeling that impelled me to act thus, but there seemed no escape from it.

That night the theatre was destroyed by fire with a loss of some 300 lives. Had I been present, from my previous examination of the building, I would certainly have taken my children over the stage, when the fire broke out, in order to escape by a private exit, and would just as certainly have been lost as were all those who trusted to it, for that passage, by an accident, could not be used. Had I gone, my sister, who was present, but in another part of the house, would surely have been lost also, for we had arranged to go home together. As it was she left the building before the play was finished and was at home when the fire began.

I have never had a presentiment before or since. I am not in the habit of changing my plans without good reasons, and on this occasion I did so only with the greatest reluctance.

What was it that caused me, against my desire, to abandon the play after having secured the seats and carefully arranged for the pleasure? August 27th, 1884.[402] — CAPTAIN A. B. MACGOWAN

☛ CASE #385: I am an engineer, and have run the engine I am about to speak of nearly six years. On the evening of Oct. 27th, 1868, while receiving a communication (through a medium, Mrs. Glover) she said, "You are in much danger of being killed before many days." She then described a steam-boiler, the inside of which presented a foaming, gaseous appearance, and said the accident would result from that; but my spirit-friends would try to warn me in time to avert it. I knew it meant an explosion.

One week after, while about my work, an impression that seemed an audible voice came to me saying, "Stop it." I obeyed quickly, and stopped the engine, for I remembered the warning; found on examination my pumps choked, and the water in the boiler frothing, so that it appeared to be above the middle gauge. After wetting my fire out, I found my boiler nearly empty.

I cannot too sincerely thank my spirit-friends for this warning. Five minutes later, and I should never have written this article.

Once before I was saved from a similar accident by impressions from spirits through myself. I am at times impressible, and have been used to heal by laying on of hands.[403] — DAVID S. FULLER

396 ∞ YOUR SOUL LIVES FOREVER

APPENDIX A

SPIRITUALISM & THE GOSPEL OF JESUS

by James Burns, 1872

THE RELIGIOUS MIND OF THIS country presents a very strange anomaly. On the one hand we have Christians opposing Spiritualism, and on the other, the Spiritualists claiming kindred with Jesus, the assumed founder of Christianity. All our knowledge of Jesus is derived from the New Testament. Apart from that book, no man has ever succeeded in demonstrating the existence of Jesus as an undeniable historical fact, though much corroborative testimony certainly exists.

In appealing to the Bible, we use it, we treat it, exactly as we would any other book—analysing its matter as we proceed, and crediting it according to the relative value of the various parts as it appears to us. In this way the Bible is on friendly terms with everyone, whatever be their views. It will not quarrel with them if they will not quarrel with it.

What causes difficulty is the action of those who place the Bible in a false relation by imposing it as a thrall and a fetter upon man's intellect and conscience. It is written, "All Scripture is given by inspiration of God," and as all of the Bible is taken for "Scripture," every part is assumed to be of equal value and importance. This syllogism men adopt without ever asking themselves what is meant by the term "Scripture." It signifies "holy writing"; and why "holy writing"?

In those days of Syrian Spiritualism, that which came through prophets, or "mediums" as we would call them—that which was imparted to men from the spirit-world—was called "holy," because it was good, pure, and adapted to elevate men's minds towards that which was eternal and spiritual. It was also the opinion of those ancient Spiritualists that all such utterances came direct from God.

Nowadays we think differently, and know that all truth is from God, but that what comes from spiritual sources is not necessarily or absolutely true. Even though the fountain were pure, the channel is human-faulty; and hence, though "holy writings" may be very good in themselves, they are alike the subject of reason and criticism with any other writings or books. *That and similar terms in the Bible refer to spiritual facts and allusions, and it takes a spiritual student to read their import aright. Without this spiritual light and knowledge, commentators have misjudged the meaning of such passages, and placed the Bible as a bondage upon the minds of men, thus stultifying their mental and spiritual growth, and rendering the*

Bible a curse rather than a benefit to the race [my emphasis, L.S.].

All of the Bible is not "holy writing." Much of it is a mere record of events, the same as may be found in any other history, and has to be judged by its consistency or value. In this light we attribute no authoritative importance to the statements respecting Jesus recorded in the gospels, and we do not profess to endorse them all, or accept them all as of equal value. If we compared them carefully some contradictions might be discovered, on which account we prefer to follow the general portraiture of Jesus as it is depicted in the spirit of the gospels, and form our opinion of his mission from that general view, rather than from the consideration of separate texts and statements.

The records agree in asserting that Jesus was born of poor parents, and that he was brought up to the humble calling of a mechanic. He was a child of intuitive genius, and at the age of twelve years he was discovered in the Temple puzzling the erudite brains of the leading theologians with his questions and answers—a feat which children very readily accomplish at the present day.

Bible history says nothing of him till his thirtieth year, when he entered upon his public career, and displayed such a marked individuality that it would be madness to suppose that he worked passively at the carpenter's bench from the time he was twelve till he "entered on his ministry."

The general supposition is that he left his humble home and wandered forth into the world in search of knowledge; that he visited Egypt—the land of occult philosophy—and, perhaps, India; that he returned to his native land with the full intent of reforming her institutions and enlightening her children, with a mind stored with knowledge, and faculties fully developed and at ready control by careful cultivation and exercise.

Education with the child of spiritual genius is not cramming the memory with a few basketfuls of old books, but a calling out of the Divine powers of the human soul, whereby all knowledge and power is given unto men. Such were at any rate the accomplishments of Jesus. He betrayed remarkable spiritual powers. He was psychometric, clairvoyant, could heal the sick even at a distance, exercised wonderful biological influence over mind and matter, could "summon legions of angels" to his aid, worked by a spiritual power delegated to him by "the Father," and did his mighty works by the "power of the Holy Ghost." We see in this portrait a man with remarkable psychological endowments, and moreover, a medium for superior influences according to his own candid acknowledgment.

We may next notice the positiveness of his character, and the uncompromising opposition which he offered to the ecclesiastical, social, and political institutions and usages of the time. He characterised the priesthood as "whited sepulchres" and pretentious hypocrites, the lawyers as the robbers of the widow and the fatherless, and the political authorities as tyrants. He neither respected the Sabbath nor the man's corn through which he walked and helped himself to. He abrogated in his person all religion except trust in the Divine Father, all social usages except brotherly love, and all law except the "new commandment" which he made the basis of his social intercourse. No wonder that all classes of society were against him—that the respectable people held him as of no repute that the rich despised him, the sanctimonious reviled him, the theologians thought he had "a devil," and the authorities put him to death as a political offender.

He had his friends. The lowly and erring were particularly dear to him: "publicans and sinners" were his associates, and he chose his followers from the most ignorant and humble rank in society. These understood him very imperfectly. When in danger, they all deserted him: Peter denied him, Judas betrayed him, Thomas doubted him, and Philip was so hopelessly stupid that he could not comprehend the purport of his Master's mission. Yet this strange man, poorly circumstanced as he was, identified himself with his Divine Parent as the loving child would with his father and mother. His motive was truth, his means love, and his aim goodness to his brother man; and he realised thereby the glorious fact that He and his Father were one. In doing this, he arrogated no special privileges to himself, but in the name of humanity asserted his Divine Sonship, and that no power, either in heaven or earth, had a right to come between a man's soul and his sense of right and duty.

He said, "The kingdom of heaven is within you," and as God makes "heaven his dwelling place," therefore God is within the innermost of every man, and thus he taught that man was essentially spiritual, divine. The objects of existence were also spiritual. "My kingdom is not of this world, but the great mission of my life is spiritual; and so is yours, for you are also the sons of God."

He did not set himself up as superior, or as an object of adoration and worship. On the contrary, he promised that those who should follow him and perform the necessary duties should do even greater things than he himself accomplished. He was the first fruits the forerunner of a mighty Spiritual Brotherhood; and, as an everlasting member of that sacred compact, he promised to visit them in spirit after his bodily decease. It is recorded that he did so in a tangible physical manner which Spiritualists can well understand.

He enforced on no one any belief or creed, but tolerated every man's inability to comprehend his teachings or motives. He enjoined all to adopt his method or example; and what was that? From the professions of his modern followers, we would suppose that Jesus was a copyist, for they pretend to copy his character, though they miserably fail in all their attempts to do so.

Jesus was no copyist—no imitator of others. Many good men had preceded him, the paragon of his people, with whose renown he was no doubt acquainted; but we do not read of him imitating Moses, David, or Isaiah, but he truthfully and diligently lived out *himself*; and the spiritual light within him, which "lighteth every man that cometh into the world," was his pattern and teacher. He asked his friends to follow his example—it was that of a self-reliant, original genius; and if we would achieve any success in spiritual gifts, intellect, or morals, we must try to be like ourselves—not like Jesus, which would be a sheer impossibility, as no two men can be alike; but every man will make the most of life by self-knowledge and self-development.

What, then, was the Gospel or gladdening teachings of Jesus?

He lived in an age when hollow ceremony was called religion, when government was tyranny, and when society was a seething mass of passional corruption and selfishness—when scepticism on the one hand, and fanatical piety on the other, either openly denied man's spiritual nature, or rendered it ridiculous. Jesus taught a practical religion of the highest morality, that God is spirit, and that man is the child of his bosom; but he left everyone to think as their capabilities permitted them in all philosophical matters. He demonstrated the truth that the child might act in harmony with the parent—that man might be one with God. He exhibited the fact that man in the flesh could be the instrument of spiritual powers and beings for the enlightenment of man on spiritual matters; and, finally, that after physical death man assumed an immortal body, in which he lived in a spiritual world, and could, in accordance with certain conditions, return to those with whom he was in mutual sympathy.

This is, in short, the Gospel of Jesus, and it is nothing but pure Spiritualism, the essence and form of all religion.

It is not "Christianity," however, with its doctrines, theologies, and dogmatic assumptions. Where did these proceed from?

They have existed in the world from the earliest dawn of idolatrous priestcraft. The Fall and the Devil—the immaculate conception by a virgin—the birth, life, and acts of a God-man—the angry God—the Hell torments—the vicarious Sacrifice, and the Trinity are to be found in nearly every form of idolatry or Paganism that has existed or is now to be found upon the face of the earth. These beliefs were in the minds of the people, who adopted certain notions from the spiritual lights of ancient days, which they engrafted upon their own idolatrous dogmas.

If space permitted, we might profitably refer to history, and point out the career of all the Pagan myths that are now taught in our churches as popular Christianity.[404]

What, then, is the duty of Spiritualists in the present crisis?

The position of the true Spiritualist is the same as that of Jesus in every sense of the word. The genuine Spiritualist is a man who follows his reason and his intuitions—so did Jesus. The Spiritualist follows truth, and lives by the application of truth to all the relations of life—so did Jesus. The Spiritualist is a self-reliant original—so was Jesus. The Spiritualist is a reformer in every sense of the term—so was Jesus. The Spiritualist is unpopular—so was Jesus. The Spiritualist exercises spirit-power—so did Jesus. In every aspect we have a parallel, all of which are avowedly ignored by Christian Churches, as is seen by their blind hostility to Spiritualism.

The Spiritualist is doing the same work now that Jesus did in his day. It is nothing new now, and was nothing new then. It had all been enacted over and over again in the world's history, but each time had got contaminated by the selfishness [and innate Paganism] of priesthoods, and so required renewing.

The great practical question now is, How shall we make it pure, and keep it pure?

By having no compact whatever with the prevailing forms of priestcraft. Jesus did not betray his God by claiming kinship with any of the religious bodies of his time, and scorned to wear their name, enjoy their privileges, or conform to their requirements. Let us do likewise, and, with all the power we possess, oppose every effort to Christianise, Mormonise, Mohammedanise, or otherwise pollute Spiritualism. To do so would be to accept the opinions of men—opinions that have been blindly or designedly thrust upon their minds to serve certain selfish ends and shut out from mankind the great spiritual light which comes to every man according to his needs.

Spiritualists! surely we may call our souls our own?

Let us resist as traitors and dangerous foes those who would enthral our minds by their personal opinions under the term of "Christian Spiritualism," or any other authoritarian bondage whatever. Jesus brought, "not peace, but a sword," and yet he said, "My peace give I unto you." What is this "peace" which the world cannot take away? It is, that every man be in harmony with his own sense of right and truth, but not with fashionable religion. If Jesus had tried to be at peace with the "Scribes and Pharisees," he might have occupied a high position in the Synagogue, but would he have been at peace?

Let every soul answer and be guided by the result of its questioning.[405]

Dublin, Ireland.

APPENDIX B

ASHES TO ASHES, DUST TO DUST
The Spiritual Magazine, 1869

IT IS ASSERTED BY SCIENTIFIC writers that the number of persons who have existed on our globe since the beginning of time, amounts to 36,627,853,273,075,256 [that is, 36.6 quadrillion people. L.S.]. These figures, when divided by 3,095,000—the number of square leagues on the globe—leave 11,320,689,732 square miles of land; which being divided as before, give 1,314,622,076 persons to each square mile.

If we reduce these miles to square rods, the number will be 1,853,174,600,000; which, divided in like manner, will give 1,283 inhabitants to each square rod, and these being reduced to feet, will give about five persons to each square foot of terra firma. It will thus be perceived that our earth is a vast cemetery. On each square rod of it 1,283 human beings lie buried, each rod being scarcely sufficient for ten graves, with each grave containing 128 persons. The whole surface of our globe, therefore, has been dug over 128 times to bury its dead!

These facts may well make us pause and think.

If the resurrection of the spirit were dependent on and bound up with that of the physical body, its chances were small indeed. The Apostle might well say to the churches: "Our teachings were vain, and your faith were also vain!"

It is evidence how material—how unspiritual, must be our conceptions when such views can be held by a large section of the Christian world—when it is apparently believed that flesh and blood shall inherit the kingdom of heaven; that at some future, though it may be distant day, we are to reanimate and retain for ever "this muddy vesture of decay." A dismal prospect we should think—not one calculated to inspire the soul with hope and joy!

We need not wonder at French Spiritists believing in reincarnation when the belief of so many sincere and earnest, if not very enlightened Christians, is only another and not an improved version of the same old pagan doctrine. Both need to learn that true Christianity and sound philosophy alike teach not the resurrection of the body, but the resurrection out of the body—and the clothing of the spirit with another—a more glorious, a spiritual body,

> "So, when this corruptible shall have put on incorruption, and this mortal shall have put on immortality, then shall be brought to pass the saying that is written, Death is swallowed up in victory. O Death! where is thy sting? O Grave! where is thy victory?" [1 Corinthians 15:54-55][406]

Dublin, Ireland.

NOTES

ALL FOOTNOTES, ENDNOTES, & NOTES IN GENERAL ARE MINE, UNLESS OTHERWISE INDICATED. L.S.

1. Burns, No. 3, p. 4.
2. *The Spiritual Magazine*, Vol. 4, 1869, pp. 386-388.
3. In mystical Christianity the word-name "Jesus" actually means "Spiritual Law"—to the wise a "key to the Kingdom" that unlocks many biblical secrets. To learn more, see my numerous books on Jesus, Christ, and spirituality; in particular, *Seabrook's Bible Dictionary of Traditional and Mystical Christian Doctrines*.
4. John 14:12.
5. Mark 11:24.
6. For more on this topic see my books, *Jesus and the Law of Attraction*, and *The Bible and the Law of Attraction*.
7. Leviticus 19:31.
8. 1 Corinthians 12:8,11.
9. Doyle, *The New Revelation* (L. Seabrook, editor; Sea Raven Press, publisher), p. 51. (See my bibliography. L.S.)
10. *Light*, Vol. 15, January-December 1895, p. 19.
11. See, for example, *Extra-Sensory Perception After Sixty Years*, by Rhine, Pratt, Smith, Stuart, and Greenwood. And also, *Parapsychology: Frontier Science of the Mind; a Survey of the Field, the Methods, and the Facts of ESP and PK Research*, by Rhine and Pratt.
12. Bruce, p. 137.
13. Ephesians 5:13.
14. *Proceedings of the Society for Psychical Research*, Vol. 1, 1883, pp. 121-122.
15. *Proceedings of the Society for Psychical Research*, Vol. 1, 1883, p. 124.
16. *Proceedings of the Society for Psychical Research*, Vol. 1, 1883, pp. 124-125.
17. *Proceedings of the Society for Psychical Research*, Vol. 1, 1883, pp. 125-126.
18. *Proceedings of the Society for Psychical Research*, Vol. 1, 1883, p. 126.
19. *Proceedings of the Society for Psychical Research*, Vol. 1, 1883, pp. 126-127.
20. *Proceedings of the Society for Psychical Research*, Vol. 1, 1883, pp. 127-128.
21. *Proceedings of the Society for Psychical Research*, Vol. 1, 1883, p. 128.
22. *Proceedings of the Society for Psychical Research*, Vol. 1, 1883, pp. 128-129.
23. *Proceedings of the Society for Psychical Research*, Vol. 1, 1883, pp. 129-130.
24. *Proceedings of the Society for Psychical Research*, Vol. 1, 1883, p. 130.
25. *Proceedings of the Society for Psychical Research*, Vol. 1, 1883, pp. 130-131.
26. *Proceedings of the Society for Psychical Research*, Vol. 1, 1883, p. 131.
27. *Proceedings of the Society for Psychical Research*, Vol. 1, 1883, pp. 131-132.
28. *Proceedings of the Society for Psychical Research*, Vol. 1, 1883, p. 132.
29. *Proceedings of the Society for Psychical Research*, Vol. 1, 1883, p. 133.
30. *Proceedings of the Society for Psychical Research*, Vol. 1, 1883, pp. 134-135.
31. *Proceedings of the Society for Psychical Research*, Vol. 1, 1883, p. 135.
32. *Proceedings of the Society for Psychical Research*, Vol. 1, 1883, pp. 138-139.
33. *Proceedings of the Society for Psychical Research*, Vol. 1, 1883, p. 146.
34. *Proceedings of the Society for Psychical Research*, Vol. 1, 1883, p. 103.
35. *Proceedings of the Society for Psychical Research*, Vol. 1, 1883, pp. 103-104.
36. *Proceedings of the Society for Psychical Research*, Vol. 1, 1883, pp. 106-107.
37. *Proceedings of the Society for Psychical Research*, Vol. 1, 1883, pp. 108-113.
38. Brewster, pp. 40-41.
39. Brewster, pp. 41-42.
40. Brewster, pp. 42-43.
41. Brewster, pp. 43-44.

42. Brewster, p. 44.
43. Brewster, pp. 44-45.
44. Brewster, p. 45.
45. Brewster, p. 46.
46. Brewster, p. 46.
47. *Journal of the Society for Psychical Research*, Vol. 1, 1884-1885, pp. 94-95.
48. *Journal of the Society for Psychical Research*, Vol. 1, 1884-1885, pp. 116-117.
49. *Journal of the Society for Psychical Research*, Vol. 1, 1884-1885, p. 126.
50. *Journal of the Society for Psychical Research*, Vol. 1, 1884-1885, p. 127.
51. *Journal of the Society for Psychical Research*, Vol. 1, 1884-1885, pp. 127-128.
52. *Journal of the Society for Psychical Research*, Vol. 1, 1884-1885, p. 129.
53. *Journal of the Society for Psychical Research*, Vol. 1, 1884-1885, p. 129.
54. *Journal of the Society for Psychical Research*, Vol. 1, 1884-1885, p. 159.
55. *Journal of the Society for Psychical Research*, Vol. 1, 1884-1885, p. 160.
56. *Journal of the Society for Psychical Research*, Vol. 1, 1884-1885, pp. 161-162.
57. *Journal of the Society for Psychical Research*, Vol. 1, 1884-1885, pp. 162-163.
58. *Journal of the Society for Psychical Research*, Vol. 1, 1884-1885, pp. 164-165.
59. *Journal of the Society for Psychical Research*, Vol. 1, 1884-1885, p. 246.
60. *Journal of the Society for Psychical Research*, Vol. 1, 1884-1885, pp. 247-248.
61. *Journal of the Society for Psychical Research*, Vol. 1, 1884-1885, pp. 249-252.
62. *Journal of the Society for Psychical Research*, Vol. 1, 1884-1885, pp. 252-253.
63. *Journal of the Society for Psychical Research*, Vol. 1, 1884-1885, pp. 282-283.
64. *Journal of the Society for Psychical Research*, Vol. 1, 1884-1885, p. 297.
65. *Journal of the Society for Psychical Research*, Vol. 1, 1884-1885, pp. 298-300.
66. *Journal of the Society for Psychical Research*, Vol. 1, 1884-1885, pp. 301-302.
67. *Journal of the Society for Psychical Research*, Vol. 1, 1884-1885, pp. 302-303.
68. *Journal of the Society for Psychical Research*, Vol. 1, 1884-1885, pp. 305-306.
69. *Journal of the Society for Psychical Research*, Vol. 1, 1884-1885, pp. 306-307.
70. *Journal of the Society for Psychical Research*, Vol. 1, 1884-1885, p. 325.
71. *Journal of the Society for Psychical Research*, Vol. 1, 1884-1885, p. 326.
72. *Journal of the Society for Psychical Research*, Vol. 1, 1884-1885, pp. 327-328.
73. *Journal of the Society for Psychical Research*, Vol. 1, 1884-1885, p. 328.
74. *Journal of the Society for Psychical Research*, Vol. 1, 1884-1885, pp. 329-330.
75. *Journal of the Society for Psychical Research*, Vol. 1, 1884-1885, pp. 331-332.
76. *Journal of the Society for Psychical Research*, Vol. 1, 1884-1885, p. 333.
77. *Journal of the Society for Psychical Research*, Vol. 1, 1884-1885, pp. 334-335.
78. *Journal of the Society for Psychical Research*, Vol. 1, 1884-1885, p. 337.
79. *Journal of the Society for Psychical Research*, Vol. 1, 1884-1885, pp. 337-338.
80. *Journal of the Society for Psychical Research*, Vol. 1, 1884-1885, pp. 339-340.
81. *Journal of the Society for Psychical Research*, Vol. 1, 1884-1885, pp. 358-359.
82. *Journal of the Society for Psychical Research*, Vol. 1, 1884-1885, pp. 363-364.
83. *Journal of the Society for Psychical Research*, Vol. 1, 1884-1885, pp. 379-380.
84. *Journal of the Society for Psychical Research*, Vol. 1, 1884-1885, pp. 381-382.
85. *Journal of the Society for Psychical Research*, Vol. 1, 1884-1885, p. 383.
86. *Journal of the Society for Psychical Research*, Vol. 1, 1884-1885, pp. 385-386.
87. *Journal of the Society for Psychical Research*, Vol. 1, 1884-1885, pp. 438-439.
88. *Journal of the Society for Psychical Research*, Vol. 1, 1884-1885, p. 443.
89. *Journal of the Society for Psychical Research*, Vol. 1, 1884-1885, pp. 445-446.
90. *Journal of the Society for Psychical Research*, Vol. 1, 1884-1885, pp. 446-447.
91. *Journal of the Society for Psychical Research*, Vol. 1, 1884-1885, p. 447.
92. *Journal of the Society for Psychical Research*, Vol. 1, 1884-1885, p. 471.
93. *Journal of the Society for Psychical Research*, Vol. 1, 1884-1885, p. 472.
94. *Journal of the Society for Psychical Research*, Vol. 1, 1884-1885, p. 473.
95. *Journal of the Society for Psychical Research*, Vol. 1, 1884-1885, pp. 473-474.

96. *Journal of the Society for Psychical Research*, Vol. 1, 1884-1885, p. 476.
97. *Journal of the Society for Psychical Research*, Vol. 1, 1884-1885, pp. 476-477.
98. *Journal of the Society for Psychical Research*, Vol. 1, 1884-1885, p. 478.
99. Bruce, *The Riddle of Personality*, pp. 140-141.
100. Bruce, *The Riddle of Personality*, pp. 141-142.
101. Bruce, *The Riddle of Personality*, pp. 142-143.
102. Bruce, *The Riddle of Personality*, pp. 118-121.
103. Bruce, *The Riddle of Personality*, p. 121.
104. Bruce, *The Riddle of Personality*, p. 122.
105. Bruce, *The Riddle of Personality*, pp. 122-125.
106. Myers, Vol. 1, pp. 282-283.
107. Myers, Vol. 1, p. 285.
108. Myers, Vol. 1, pp. 255-256.
109. Myers, Vol. 1, p. 261.
110. Myers, Vol. 1, p. 262.
111. Myers, Vol. 1, p. 266.
112. Myers, Vol. 1, p. 269.
113. Myers, Vol. 1, pp. 270-271.
114. Myers, Vol. 1, p. 272.
115. *Journal of the Society for Psychical Research*, Vol. 11, 1903-1904, pp. 135-136.
116. *Journal of the Society for Psychical Research*, Vol. 11, 1903-1904, p. 187.
117. *Journal of the Society for Psychical Research*, Vol. 11, 1903-1904, pp. 187-188.
118. *Journal of the Society for Psychical Research*, Vol. 11, 1903-1904, pp. 191-193.
119. *Journal of the Society for Psychical Research*, Vol. 11, 1903-1904, p. 214.
120. *Journal of the Society for Psychical Research*, Vol. 12, 1905-1906, pp. 18-19.
121. *Journal of the Society for Psychical Research*, Vol. 12, 1905-1906, pp. 119-120.
122. *Journal of the Society for Psychical Research*, Vol. 12, 1905-1906, pp. 121-122.
123. *Journal of the Society for Psychical Research*, Vol. 12, 1905-1906, pp. 173-174.
124. *Journal of the Society for Psychical Research*, Vol. 12, 1905-1906, pp. 193-194.
125. *Journal of the Society for Psychical Research*, Vol. 12, 1905-1906, pp. 290-291.
126. On May 1st, 1905, Mrs. D. told J. G. P. her sister knew of her approaching confinement. The blue dressing-gown had been made a few days before specially for the confinement, and her sister could not have known about it. In all respects Mrs. C.'s hallucination corresponded with the real facts. [S.P.R.'s note.] *Journal of the Society for Psychical Research*, Vol. 12, 1905-1906, pp. 310-311.
127. *Journal of the Society for Psychical Research*, Vol. 12, 1905-1906, pp. 317-318.
128. *Journal of the Society for Psychical Research*, Vol. 12, 1905-1906, pp. 323-325.
129. *The Spiritual Magazine*, Vol. 4, 1869, p. 83.
130. *The Spiritual Magazine*, Vol. 4, 1869, p. 96.
131. *The Spiritual Magazine*, Vol. 4, 1869, pp. 512-515.
132. *The Spiritual Magazine*, Vol. 4, 1869, pp. 520-522.
133. *The Spiritual Magazine*, Vol. 4, 1869, pp. 556-557.
134. *The Spiritual Magazine*, Vol. 4, 1869, pp. 561-563.
135. *The Spiritual Magazine*, Vol. 4, 1869, pp. 409-414.
136. *The Spiritual Magazine*, Vol. 4, 1869, pp. 425-426.
137. *The Theosophist Magazine*, Vol. 1, 1879-1880, p. 31.
138. *The Theosophist Magazine*, Vol. 1, 1879-1880, p. 31.
139. *The Annals of Psychical Science*, Vol. 5, January-June 1907, pp. 215-216.
140. Olcott, pp. 66-67.
141. Reichenbach, p. 48.
142. Bruce, *Historic Ghosts and Ghost Hunters*, pp. 106-109.
143. Bruce, *Adventurings in the Psychical*, pp. 4-8.
144. In a prefatory note to the book, *An Adventure*, in which these ladies detail their experience, their publishers, Messrs. Macmillan and Company, of London, guarantee "that the authors have put down what happened to them as faithfully and accurately as was in their power." Their good faith is also vouched for by

a reviewer in *The Spectator*. [Bruce's note.]
145. Bruce, *Adventurings in the Psychical*, pp. 8-12.
146. Bruce, *Adventurings in the Psychical*, pp. 22-26.
147. Bruce, *Adventurings in the Psychical*, pp. 26-27.
148. Bruce, *Adventurings in the Psychical*, pp. 27-29.
149. Bruce, *Adventurings in the Psychical*, pp. 29-31.
150. Bruce, *Adventurings in the Psychical*, pp. 31-32.
151. Gurney, Myers, and Podmore, Vol. 1, pp. 205-206.
152. Gurney, Myers, and Podmore, Vol. 1, p. 207.
153. Gurney, Myers, and Podmore, Vol. 1, p. 209.
154. Gurney, Myers, and Podmore, Vol. 1, pp. 210-211.
155. Gurney, Myers, and Podmore, Vol. 1, p. 213.
156. Gurney, Myers, and Podmore, Vol. 1, pp. 218-219.
157. Podmore, *Apparitions and Thought-transference*, pp. 236-237.
158. Podmore, *Modern Spiritualism*, p. 71.
159. Owen, p. 266.
160. Owen, pp. 278-279.
161. Howitt, pp. 363-364.
162. Anonymous, pp. 146-150.
163. *Proceedings of the Society for Psychical Research*, Vol. 1, 1883, p. 133.
164. *Proceedings of the Society for Psychical Research*, Vol. 1, 1883, pp. 133-134.
165. *Proceedings of the Society for Psychical Research*, Vol. 1, 1883, p. 134.
166. *Journal of the Society for Psychical Research*, Vol. 1, 1884-1885, p. 101.
167. *Journal of the Society for Psychical Research*, Vol. 1, 1884-1885, p. 102.
168. *Journal of the Society for Psychical Research*, Vol. 1, 1884-1885, p. 99.
169. *Journal of the Society for Psychical Research*, Vol. 1, 1884-1885, pp. 114-115.
170. *Journal of the Society for Psychical Research*, Vol. 1, 1884-1885, p. 116.
171. *Journal of the Society for Psychical Research*, Vol. 1, 1884-1885, pp. 119-120.
172. *Journal of the Society for Psychical Research*, Vol. 1, 1884-1885, p. 122.
173. *Journal of the Society for Psychical Research*, Vol. 1, 1884-1885, pp. 122-123.
174. *Journal of the Society for Psychical Research*, Vol. 1, 1884-1885, p. 144.
175. *Journal of the Society for Psychical Research*, Vol. 1, 1884-1885, p. 146.
176. *Journal of the Society for Psychical Research*, Vol. 1, 1884-1885, p. 147.
177. *Journal of the Society for Psychical Research*, Vol. 1, 1884-1885, p. 147.
178. *Journal of the Society for Psychical Research*, Vol. 1, 1884-1885, p. 148.
179. *Journal of the Society for Psychical Research*, Vol. 1, 1884-1885, pp. 149-150.
180. *Journal of the Society for Psychical Research*, Vol. 1, 1884-1885, pp. 150-151.
181. *Journal of the Society for Psychical Research*, Vol. 1, 1884-1885, p. 152.
182. *Journal of the Society for Psychical Research*, Vol. 1, 1884-1885, pp. 357-358.
183. *Journal of the Society for Psychical Research*, Vol. 1, 1884-1885, pp. 387-388.
184. *Journal of the Society for Psychical Research*, Vol. 1, 1884-1885, p. 388.
185. *Journal of the Society for Psychical Research*, Vol. 1, 1884-1885, p. 436.
186. *Proceedings of the Society for Psychical Research*, Vol. 1, 1883, p. 134.
187. *Proceedings of the Society for Psychical Research*, Vol. 1, 1883, p. 137.
188. *Journal of the Society for Psychical Research*, Vol. 1, 1884-1885, pp. 97-99.
189. *Journal of the Society for Psychical Research*, Vol. 1, 1884-1885, p. 99.
190. *Proceedings of the Society for Psychical Research*, Vol. 1, 1883, pp. 139-140.
191. *Proceedings of the Society for Psychical Research*, Vol. 1, 1883, pp. 30-31.
192. *Proceedings of the Society for Psychical Research*, Vol. 1, 1883, p. 31.
193. *Proceedings of the Society for Psychical Research*, Vol. 1, 1883, p. 31.
194. *Proceedings of the Society for Psychical Research*, Vol. 1, 1883, p. 32.
195. *Proceedings of the Society for Psychical Research*, Vol. 1, 1883, p. 58.
196. *Proceedings of the Society for Psychical Research*, Vol. 1, 1883, p. 59.
197. *Journal of the Society for Psychical Research*, Vol. 1, 1884-1885, p. 95.

198. *Proceedings of the Society for Psychical Research*, Vol. 1, 1883, pp. 59-60.
199. *Proceedings of the Society for Psychical Research*, Vol. 1, 1883, p. 60.
200. *Proceedings of the Society for Psychical Research*, Vol. 1, 1883, pp. 62-63.
201. *Proceedings of the Society for Psychical Research*, Vol. 1, 1883, p. 63.
202. *Proceedings of the Society for Psychical Research*, Vol. 1, 1883, p. 119.
203. *Proceedings of the Society for Psychical Research*, Vol. 1, 1883, p. 120.
204. *Proceedings of the Society for Psychical Research*, Vol. 1, 1883, p. 120.
205. *Journal of the Society for Psychical Research*, Vol. 1, 1884-1885, p. 45.
206. *Journal of the Society for Psychical Research*, Vol. 1, 1884-1885, pp. 54-55.
207. *Journal of the Society for Psychical Research*, Vol. 1, 1884-1885, p. 55.
208. *Journal of the Society for Psychical Research*, Vol. 1, 1884-1885, p. 77.
209. *Journal of the Society for Psychical Research*, Vol. 1, 1884-1885, p. 78.
210. *Journal of the Society for Psychical Research*, Vol. 1, 1884-1885, pp. 78-79.
211. *Journal of the Society for Psychical Research*, Vol. 1, 1884-1885, pp. 79-80.
212. *Journal of the Society for Psychical Research*, Vol. 1, 1884-1885, pp. 81-82.
213. *Journal of the Society for Psychical Research*, Vol. 1, 1884-1885, pp. 365-366.
214. *Journal of the Society for Psychical Research*, Vol. 1, 1884-1885, pp. 366-367.
215. *Journal of the Society for Psychical Research*, Vol. 1, 1884-1885, p. 368.
216. *Journal of the Society for Psychical Research*, Vol. 1, 1884-1885, pp. 384-385.
217. *Journal of the Society for Psychical Research*, Vol. 1, 1884-1885, pp. 391-392.
218. *Journal of the Society for Psychical Research*, Vol. 1, 1884-1885, pp. 399-400.
219. *Journal of the Society for Psychical Research*, Vol. 1, 1884-1885, p. 433.
220. *Journal of the Society for Psychical Research*, Vol. 1, 1884-1885, pp. 485-486.
221. *Journal of the Society for Psychical Research*, Vol. 1, 1884-1885, pp. 486-487.
222. Bruce, *The Riddle of Personality*, pp. 127-129, 131.
223. Bruce, *The Riddle of Personality*, p. 130.
224. *Journal of the Society for Psychical Research*, Vol. 11, 1903-1904, pp. 278-281.
225. *Journal of the Society for Psychical Research*, Vol. 11, 1903-1904, p. 323.
226. *Journal of the Society for Psychical Research*, Vol. 12, 1905-1906, p. 22.
227. Podmore, *Apparitions and Thought-transference*, p. 194.
228. *Proceedings of the Society for Psychical Research*, Vol. 1, 1883, p. 141.
229. *Proceedings of the Society for Psychical Research*, Vol. 1, 1883, p. 141.
230. *Journal of the Society for Psychical Research*, Vol. 11, 1903-1904, pp. 145-146.
231. *Proceedings of the Society for Psychical Research*, Vol. 1, 1883, pp. 141-142.
232. *Proceedings of the Society for Psychical Research*, Vol. 1, 1883, pp. 142-143.
233. *Journal of the Society for Psychical Research*, Vol. 1, 1884-1885, p. 229.
234. *Journal of the Society for Psychical Research*, Vol. 1, 1884-1885, p. 229.
235. *Journal of the Society for Psychical Research*, Vol. 1, 1884-1885, p. 230.
236. *Journal of the Society for Psychical Research*, Vol. 1, 1884-1885, p. 230.
237. *Journal of the Society for Psychical Research*, Vol. 1, 1884-1885, p. 230.
238. *Journal of the Society for Psychical Research*, Vol. 1, 1884-1885, pp. 295-296.
239. *Journal of the Society for Psychical Research*, Vol. 11, 1903-1904, p. 138.
240. *Journal of the Society for Psychical Research*, Vol. 1, 1884-1885, pp. 303-304.
241. *Journal of the Society for Psychical Research*, Vol. 1, 1884-1885, pp. 307-308.
242. *Journal of the Society for Psychical Research*, Vol. 1, 1884-1885, p. 308.
243. *Journal of the Society for Psychical Research*, Vol. 1, 1884-1885, pp. 341-342.
244. *Journal of the Society for Psychical Research*, Vol. 1, 1884-1885, pp. 342-343.
245. *Journal of the Society for Psychical Research*, Vol. 1, 1884-1885, pp. 343-344.
246. *Journal of the Society for Psychical Research*, Vol. 1, 1884-1885, p. 347.
247. *Journal of the Society for Psychical Research*, Vol. 1, 1884-1885, p. 348.
248. *Journal of the Society for Psychical Research*, Vol. 1, 1884-1885, pp. 350-351.
249. *Journal of the Society for Psychical Research*, Vol. 1, 1884-1885, pp. 351-353.
250. *Journal of the Society for Psychical Research*, Vol. 1, 1884-1885, pp. 353-357.
251. *Journal of the Society for Psychical Research*, Vol. 1, 1884-1885, pp. 364-365.

252. *Journal of the Society for Psychical Research*, Vol. 1, 1884-1885, pp. 377-378.
253. *Journal of the Society for Psychical Research*, Vol. 1, 1884-1885, pp. 390-391.
254. *Journal of the Society for Psychical Research*, Vol. 1, 1884-1885, pp. 393-394.
255. *Journal of the Society for Psychical Research*, Vol. 1, 1884-1885, pp. 394-395.
256. *Journal of the Society for Psychical Research*, Vol. 1, 1884-1885, p. 396.
257. *Journal of the Society for Psychical Research*, Vol. 1, 1884-1885, p. 397.
258. *Journal of the Society for Psychical Research*, Vol. 1, 1884-1885, pp. 397-398.
259. *Journal of the Society for Psychical Research*, Vol. 1, 1884-1885, pp. 441-442.
260. *Journal of the Society for Psychical Research*, Vol. 1, 1884-1885, p. 484.
261. *Journal of the Society for Psychical Research*, Vol. 1, 1884-1885, p. 485.
262. *Journal of the Society for Psychical Research*, Vol. 11, 1903-1904, pp. 64-66.
263. *Journal of the Society for Psychical Research*, Vol. 11, 1903-1904, pp. 86-89.
264. *Journal of the Society for Psychical Research*, Vol. 11, 1903-1904, p. 99.
265. *Journal of the Society for Psychical Research*, Vol. 11, 1903-1904, p. 118.
266. *Journal of the Society for Psychical Research*, Vol. 11, 1903-1904, p. 123.
267. *Journal of the Society for Psychical Research*, Vol. 11, 1903-1904, pp. 177-178.
268. *Journal of the Society for Psychical Research*, Vol. 11, 1903-1904, p. 144.
269. *Journal of the Society for Psychical Research*, Vol. 11, 1903-1904, p. 181.
270. *Journal of the Society for Psychical Research*, Vol. 11, 1903-1904, p. 223.
271. *Journal of the Society for Psychical Research*, Vol. 11, 1903-1904, p. 228.
272. *Journal of the Society for Psychical Research*, Vol. 11, 1903-1904, pp. 269-271.
273. *Journal of the Society for Psychical Research*, Vol. 12, 1905-1906, pp. 99-100.
274. *Journal of the Society for Psychical Research*, Vol. 12, 1905-1906, pp. 102-103.
275. *Journal of the Society for Psychical Research*, Vol. 12, 1905-1906, pp. 146-148.
276. *Journal of the Society for Psychical Research*, Vol. 12, 1905-1906, pp. 303-305.
277. *Journal of the Society for Psychical Research*, Vol. 12, 1905-1906, pp. 312-313.
278. *Journal of the Society for Psychical Research*, Vol. 12, 1905-1906, p. 328.
279. *Journal of the Society for Psychical Research*, Vol. 12, 1905-1906, pp. 340-341.
280. *The Spiritual Magazine*, Vol. 4, 1869, p. 4.
281. *The Spiritual Magazine*, Vol. 4, 1869, pp. 550-552.
282. *The Spiritual Magazine*, Vol. 4, 1869, p. 553.
283. *The Spiritual Magazine*, Vol. 4, 1869, p. 554.
284. *The Spiritual Magazine*, Vol. 4, 1869, p. 556.
285. *The Theosophist Magazine*, Vol. 1, 1879-1880, p. 31.
286. Podmore, *Apparitions and Thought-transference*, p. 196.
287. *Journal of the Society for Psychical Research*, Vol. 1, 1884-1885, pp. 338-339.
288. *Journal of the Society for Psychical Research*, Vol. 1, 1884-1885, p. 479.
289. *Journal of the Society for Psychical Research*, Vol. 1, 1884-1885, p. 475.
290. Brewster, pp. 39-40.
291. Brewster, p. 43.
292. *Journal of the Society for Psychical Research*, Vol. 1, 1884-1885, pp. 184-186.
293. *Journal of the Society for Psychical Research*, Vol. 1, 1884-1885, p. 187.
294. *Journal of the Society for Psychical Research*, Vol. 1, 1884-1885, p. 190.
295. *Journal of the Society for Psychical Research*, Vol. 1, 1884-1885, pp. 190-191.
296. *Journal of the Society for Psychical Research*, Vol. 1, 1884-1885, pp. 192-193.
297. *Journal of the Society for Psychical Research*, Vol. 1, 1884-1885, p. 308.
298. *Journal of the Society for Psychical Research*, Vol. 1, 1884-1885, pp. 359-360.
299. *Journal of the Society for Psychical Research*, Vol. 1, 1884-1885, p. 380.
300. *Journal of the Society for Psychical Research*, Vol. 1, 1884-1885, p. 381.
301. *Journal of the Society for Psychical Research*, Vol. 1, 1884-1885, p. 382.
302. *Journal of the Society for Psychical Research*, Vol. 1, 1884-1885, p. 389.
303. *Journal of the Society for Psychical Research*, Vol. 1, 1884-1885, pp. 433-435.
304. *Journal of the Society for Psychical Research*, Vol. 1, 1884-1885, pp. 444-445.
305. *Journal of the Society for Psychical Research*, Vol. 1, 1884-1885, pp. 479-480.

306. *Journal of the Society for Psychical Research*, Vol. 1, 1884-1885, p. 480.
307. *Journal of the Society for Psychical Research*, Vol. 1, 1884-1885, p. 481.
308. *Journal of the Society for Psychical Research*, Vol. 1, 1884-1885, pp. 482-483.
309. Bruce, *The Riddle of Personality*, pp. 125-126.
310. *Journal of the Society for Psychical Research*, Vol. 11, 1903-1904, pp. 60-61.
311. *Journal of the Society for Psychical Research*, Vol. 11, 1903-1904, pp. 80-81.
312. *Journal of the Society for Psychical Research*, Vol. 11, 1903-1904, pp. 214-215.
313. *Journal of the Society for Psychical Research*, Vol. 11, 1903-1904, pp. 320-321.
314. *Journal of the Society for Psychical Research*, Vol. 12, 1905-1906, p. 14.
315. *Journal of the Society for Psychical Research*, Vol. 12, 1905-1906, pp. 24-27.
316. *Journal of the Society for Psychical Research*, Vol. 12, 1905-1906, pp. 54-55.
317. *Journal of the Society for Psychical Research*, Vol. 12, 1905-1906, p. 57.
318. *Journal of the Society for Psychical Research*, Vol. 12, 1905-1906, pp. 57-58.
319. *Journal of the Society for Psychical Research*, Vol. 12, 1905-1906, pp. 184-185.
320. *Journal of the Society for Psychical Research*, Vol. 12, 1905-1906, pp. 196-197.
321. *The Spiritual Magazine*, Vol. 4, 1869, pp. 554-555.
322. *The Spiritual Magazine*, Vol. 4, 1869, p. 48.
323. Bruce, *Adventurings in the Psychical*, pp. 13-17.
324. Gurney, Myers, and Podmore, Vol. 1, p. 221.
325. Gurney, Myers, and Podmore, Vol. 1, pp. 222-224.
326. *Journal of the Society for Psychical Research*, Vol. 12, 1905-1906, pp. 188-189.
327. *Journal of the Society for Psychical Research*, Vol. 1, 1884-1885, pp. 292-293.
328. *Journal of the Society for Psychical Research*, Vol. 1, 1884-1885, pp. 293-294.
329. *Proceedings of the Society for Psychical Research*, Vol. 1, 1883, pp. 122-123.
330. *Journal of the Society for Psychical Research*, Vol. 1, 1884-1885, pp. 118-119.
331. Brewster, pp. 131-132.
332. Brewster, pp. 132-133.
333. Brewster, pp. 134-135.
334. Brewster, pp. 135-136.
335. Brewster, pp. 136-138.
336. Brewster, pp. 142-144.
337. Brewster, p. 144.
338. Brewster, pp. 144-145.
339. *Journal of the Society for Psychical Research*, Vol. 1, 1884-1885, p. 163.
340. *Journal of the Society for Psychical Research*, Vol. 1, 1884-1885, pp. 361-362.
341. *Journal of the Society for Psychical Research*, Vol. 11, 1903-1904, p. 126.
342. *Journal of the Society for Psychical Research*, Vol. 11, 1903-1904, pp. 157-158.
343. *Journal of the Society for Psychical Research*, Vol. 12, 1905-1906, pp. 308-310.
344. *Journal of the Society for Psychical Research*, Vol. 12, 1905-1906, p. 342.
345. *Journal of the Society for Psychical Research*, Vol. 11, 1903-1904, pp. 26-31.
346. *Journal of the Society for Psychical Research*, Vol. 1, 1884-1885, pp. 206-210.
347. *Journal of the Society for Psychical Research*, Vol. 1, 1884-1885, pp. 313-315.
348. Colonel Taylor's plan of the house shows that the back room opens out of the front ("haunted") room, so that a full view of the latter can be obtained from the doorway of the former. [S.P.R.'s note.]
349. One of these was a Mr. Bibby, who is cited as one of the principal witnesses in an illustrated article on "The Haunted House at Upholland," which appeared in *The Wide World Magazine* for February, 1905. [S.P.R.'s note.]
350. *Journal of the Society for Psychical Research*, Vol. 12, 1905-1906, pp. 124-128.
351. *Journal of the Society for Psychical Research*, Vol. 12, 1905-1906, pp. 261-265.
352. *The Spiritual Magazine*, Vol. 4, 1869, p. 314.
353. *The Spiritual Magazine*, Vol. 4, 1869, pp. 423-424.
354. *The Annals of Psychical Science*, Vol. 5, January-June 1907, pp. 216-217.
355. *The Annals of Psychical Science*, Vol. 5, January-June 1907, pp. 217-218.
356. *The Annals of Psychical Science*, Vol. 5, January-June 1907, pp. 218-219.

357. *The Annals of Psychical Science*, Vol. 5, January-June 1907, pp. 220-221.
358. Sargent, p. 4.
359. Sargent, p. 4.
360. Sargent, pp. 3-6.
361. Rogers, p. 289.
362. Rogers, p. 290.
363. Bruce, *Adventurings in the Psychical*, pp. 12-13.
364. Bruce, *Adventurings in the Psychical*, pp. 17-22.
365. *Journal of the Society for Psychical Research*, Vol. 1, 1884-1885, p. 241.
366. *Journal of the Society for Psychical Research*, Vol. 1, 1884-1885, pp. 360-361.
367. *Journal of the Society for Psychical Research*, Vol. 1, 1884-1885, p. 476.
368. Gurney, Myers, and Podmore, Vol. 1, pp. 225-226.
369. Gurney, Myers, and Podmore, Vol. 1, pp. 227-228.
370. *Proceedings of the Society for Psychical Research*, Vol. 1, 1883, pp. 145-146.
371. *Journal of the Society for Psychical Research*, Vol. 1, 1884-1885, pp. 255-256.
372. *Journal of the Society for Psychical Research*, Vol. 1, 1884-1885, p. 83.
373. *Journal of the Society for Psychical Research*, Vol. 1, 1884-1885, p. 275.
374. *Journal of the Society for Psychical Research*, Vol. 1, 1884-1885, pp. 275-276.
375. *Journal of the Society for Psychical Research*, Vol. 1, 1884-1885, p. 276.
376. *Journal of the Society for Psychical Research*, Vol. 1, 1884-1885, p. 276.
377. *Journal of the Society for Psychical Research*, Vol. 1, 1884-1885, pp. 279-282.
378. *Journal of the Society for Psychical Research*, Vol. 1, 1884-1885, pp. 310-311.
379. *Journal of the Society for Psychical Research*, Vol. 1, 1884-1885, pp. 318, 320.
380. *Journal of the Society for Psychical Research*, Vol. 1, 1884-1885, pp. 467-469.
381. Myers, Vol. 1, pp. 292-293.
382. *Journal of the Society for Psychical Research*, Vol. 11, 1903-1904, pp. 49-52.
383. *Journal of the Society for Psychical Research*, Vol. 11, 1903-1904, pp. 86-89.
384. *Journal of the Society for Psychical Research*, Vol. 11, 1903-1904, p. 274.
385. *Journal of the Society for Psychical Research*, Vol. 11, 1903-1904, pp. 274-275.
386. *Journal of the Society for Psychical Research*, Vol. 11, 1903-1904, pp. 315-316.
387. *Journal of the Society for Psychical Research*, Vol. 12, 1905-1906, p. 104.
388. *Journal of the Society for Psychical Research*, Vol. 12, 1905-1906, pp. 313-315.
389. *Journal of the Society for Psychical Research*, Vol. 12, 1905-1906, p. 316.
390. Dods, pp. 31-32.
391. *The Spiritual Magazine*, Vol. 4, 1869, pp. 264-266.
392. *The Spiritual Magazine*, Vol. 4, 1869, p. 559.
393. *The Spiritual Magazine*, Vol. 4, 1869, p. 44.
394. *The Spiritual Magazine*, Vol. 4, 1869, pp. 44-46.
395. *The Spiritual Magazine*, Vol. 4, 1869, p. 50.
396. *The Spiritual Magazine*, Vol. 4, 1869, pp. 82-83.
397. *The Spiritual Magazine*, Vol. 4, 1869, pp. 176-178.
398. Home, pp. 142-144.
399. Home, p. 39.
400. Home, pp. 149-153.
401. *Proceedings of the Society for Psychical Research*, Vol. 1, 1883, pp. 137-138.
402. *Journal of the Society for Psychical Research*, Vol. 1, 1884-1885, pp. 283-284.
403. *The Spiritual Magazine*, Vol. 4, 1869, pp. 83-84.
404. For more on the overt Paganism in modern Christianity, see my many books on spirituality, Jesus, and Church history. L.S.
405. Burns, No. 2, pp. 1-4.
406. *The Spiritual Magazine*, Vol. 4, 1869, pp. 426-427.

BIBLIOGRAPHY
And Suggested Reading

Anonymous. *Ghost-Stories; Collected With a Particular View to Counteract the Vulgar Belief in Ghosts and Apparitions and to Promote a Rational Estimate of the Nature of the Phenomena Commonly Considered as Supernatural*. London, UK: self-published, 1823.
Ashburner, John. *Notes and Studies in the Philosophy of Animal Magnetism and Spiritualism*. London, UK: Hippolyte Bailliere, 1867.
Blavatsky, Helena Petrovna. *The Theosophist*. Vol. 1, 1879-1880. Madras, India: The Theosophical Society, 1880.
Bloomfield, Lady Georgiana. *Lady Bloomfield's Reminiscences*. 2 vols. London, UK: Kegan Paul, Trench, and Co., 1883.
Brewster, David. *Natural Magic*. London, UK: John Murray, 1832.
Bruce, Henry Addington. *Historic Ghosts and Ghost Hunters*. New York: Moffat, Yard, and Co., 1908.
——. *The Riddle of Personality*. New York: Moffat, Yard, and Co., 1908.
——. *Scientific Mental Healing*. Boston, MA: Little, Brown, and Co., 1911.
——. *Adventures in the Psychical*. Boston, MA: Little, Brown, and Co., 1914.
Burns, James. *Seed Corn: Spiritualist Tracts*. London, UK: self-published, 1872.
Bushnell, Horace. *Nature and the Supernatural as Together Constituting the One System of God*. New York: Charles Scribner, 1859.
Carpenter Edward. *Angel's Wings: A Series of Essays on Art and Its Relation to Life*. London, UK: Swan Sonnenschein, 1898.
Crowe, Catherine. *The Night-side of Nature; Or, Ghosts and Ghost-seers*. New York: J. S. Redfield, 1850.
Dameron, James P. *Spiritism: The Origin of All Religions*. San Francisco, CA: self-published, 1885.
Das, Bhagavan. *The Essential Unity of All Religions*. Wheaton, IL: Theosophical Publishing House, 1932.
Dods, John Bovee. *Spirit Manifestations Examined and Explained*. New York: De Witt and Davenport, 1854.
Doyle, Arthur Conan. *The New Revelation* (reprint—Lochlainn Seabrook, editor). Springhill, TN: Sea Raven Press, 2021.
Fechner, Gustav Theodore. *On Life After Death*. (Hugo Wernekke, trans.). London, UK: Sampson Low, Marston, Searle, and Rivington, 1882.
Figuier, Louis. *Les Mystères de la Science: Aujourd'hui*. Paris, France: A La Librairie Illustrée, 1881.

Finch, Laura I. *The Annals of Psychical Science*. Vol. 5, January-June 1907. London, UK: self-published, 1907.
Fitzpatrick, William J. *History of the Dublin Catholic Cemeteries*. Dublin, Ireland: self-published, 1900.
Gurney, Edmund, Frederic W. H. Myers, and Frank Podmore. *Phantasms of the Living*. 2 vols. London, UK: The Society for Psychical Research, 1886.
Hall, Spencer Timothy. *Mesmeric Experiences*. London, UK: Hippolyte Bailliere, 1845.
——. *Days in Derbyshire*. London, UK: Simpkin, Marshall, and Co., 1863.
Home, Daniel Dunglas. *Incidents in My Life*. London, UK: Longman, Green, Longman, Roberts, and Green, 1863.
Howitt, William. *The History of the Supernatural in All Ages and Nations, and in All Churches, Christian and Pagan: Demonstrating a Universal Faith*. 2 vols. London, UK: Longman, Green, Longman, Roberts, and Green, 1863.
James, William. *The Varieties of Religious Experience: A Study in Human Nature*. 1902. New York: Longmans, Green, and Co., 1903 ed.
Journal of the Society of Psychical Research. 1882-present. London, UK: The Society's Rooms (self-published).
Jung-Stilling, Johann Heinrich. *Theory of Pneumatology: In Reply to the Question, What Ought to be Believed or Disbelieved Concerning Presentiments, Visions, and Apparitions, According to Nature, Reason, and Scripture*. London, UK: Longman, Rees, Orme, Brown, Green, and Longman, 1834.
Kilner, Walter John. *The Human Atmosphere (The Aura)*. London, UK: Kegan Paul, Trench, and Co., 1920.
Lasserre, Henri. *Notre-Dame de Lourdes*. Paris, France: Victor Palme, 1869.
Lecky, William Edward Hartpole. *History of the Rise and Influence of the Spirit of Rationalism in Europe*. 2 vols. London, UK: Longmans, Green, and Co., 1865.
Light: A Journal of Psychical, Occult, and Mystical Research. London, UK: self-published (founded in 1881).
Longfellow, Henry Wadsworth. *Longfellow's Poetical Works—Vol. 10: Birds of Passage*. London, UK: George Routledge and Sons, 1878.
Myers, Frederic William Henry. *Human Personality and Its Survival of Bodily Death*. 2 vols. Longmans, Green, and Co., 1903.
Olcott, Henry Steel. *A Collection of Lectures on Theosophy and Archaic Religions, Delivered in India and Ceylon*. Madras, India: The Theosophical Society, 1883.
Owen, Robert Dale. *Footfalls on the Boundary of Another World*. London, UK: Trübner and Co., 1860.
Podmore, Frank. *Apparitions and Thought-transference: An Examination of*

the Evidence for Telepathy. London, UK: Walter Scott, 1894.
———. *Modern Spiritualism: A History and a Criticism.* 2 vols. London, UK: Methuen and Co., 1902.
Potter, William Bailey. *Spiritualism as it is: Or, The Results of a Scientific Investigation of Spirit Manifestations.* New York: French and Wheat, 1865.
Pratt, J. G., J. B. Rhine, Burke M. Smith, Charles E. Stuart, and Joseph E. Greenwood. *Extra-Sensory Perception After Sixty Years.* 1940. Boston, MA: Bruce Humphries, 1966 ed.
Proceedings of the Society for Psychical Research, Vol. 1, 1882-1883. London, UK: Trubner and Co., 1883.
Reichenbach, Karl Ludwig Freiherr von. *Researches on Magnetism, Electricity, Heat, Light, Crystallization, and Chemical Attraction, in Their Relation to the Vital Force.* London, UK: Taylor, Walton, and Maberly, 1850.
———. *Odic-Magnetic Letters.* (John S. Hittell, trans.) New York: Calvin Blanchard, 1860.
Rhine, J. B., and J. G. Pratt. *Parapsychology: Frontier Science of the Mind; a Survey of the Field, the Methods, and the Facts of ESP and PK Research.* Springfield, IL: Charles C. Thomas, 1957 ed.
Rogers, Edward Coit. *Philosophy of Mysterious Agents, Human and Mundane.* Boston, MA: John P. Jewett and Co., 1853.
Samson, George Whitefield. *Physical Media in Spiritual Manifestations: The Phenomena of Responding Tables and the Planchette, and Their Physical Cause in the Nervous Organism.* Philadelphia, PA: J. B. Lippincott and Co., 1869.
Sargent, Epes. *Communications from Another World.* Melbourne, Australia: George Robertson, 1869.
Seabrook, Lochlainn. *The Goddess Dictionary of Words and Phrases: Introducing a New Core Vocabulary for the Women's Spirituality Movement.* 1997. Franklin, TN: Sea Raven Press, 2010 ed.
———. *Britannia Rules: Goddess-Worship in Ancient Anglo-Celtic Society - An Academic Look at the United Kingdom's Matricentric Spiritual Past.* 1999. Franklin, TN: Sea Raven Press, 2010 ed.
———. *The Book of Kelle: An Introduction to Goddess-Worship and the Great Celtic Mother-Goddess Kelle, Original Blessed Lady of Ireland.* 1999. Franklin, TN: Sea Raven Press, 2010 ed.
———. *UFOs and Aliens: The Complete Guidebook.* Spring Hill, TN: Sea Raven Press, 2005.
———. *Carnton Plantation Ghost Stories: True Tales of the Unexplained from Tennessee's Most Haunted Civil War House!* 2005. Franklin, TN, 2016 ed.
———. *Christmas Before Christianity: How the Birthday of the "Sun" Became the Birthday of the "Son."* Franklin, TN: Sea Raven Press, 2010.
———. *Jesus and the Law of Attraction: The Bible-Based Guide to Creating*

Perfect Health, Wealth, and Happiness Following Christ's Simple Formula. Franklin, TN: Sea Raven Press, 2013.

———. *The Bible and the Law of Attraction: 99 Teachings of Jesus, the Apostles, and the Prophets*. Franklin, TN: Sea Raven Press, 2013.

———. *Christ Is All and In All: Rediscovering Your Divine Nature and the Kingdom Within*. Franklin, TN: Sea Raven Press, 2014.

———. *Jesus and the Gospel of Q: Christ's Pre-Christian Teachings As Recorded in the New Testament*. Spring Hill, TN: Sea Raven Press, 2014.

———. *Seabrook's Bible Dictionary of Traditional and Mystical Christian Doctrines*. Spring Hill, TN: Sea Raven Press, 2016.

———. *The Martian Anomalies: A Photographic Search for Intelligent Life on Mars*. Cody, WY: Sea Raven Press, 2022.

———. (editor) *Mysterious Invaders: Twelve Famous 20th-Century Scientists Confront the UFO Phenomenon*. Cody, WY: Sea Raven Press, 2024.

Searcher After Truth. *The Rappers: Or, The Mysteries, Fallacies, and Absurdities of Spirit-rapping, Table-tipping, and Entrancement*. New York: H. Long and Brother, 1854.

Sinnett, Alfred Percy. *The Rationale of Mesmerism*. London, UK: Kegan Paul, Trench, and Co., 1892.

Smucker, Samuel M. *A History of All Religions*. Philadelphia, PA: Duane Rulison, 1859.

The Annals of Psychical Science (Laura Finch, ed.). Vol. 5, January-June 1907. London, UK: self-published, 1907.

The Bhagavad Gita. Reprint. Yogi Ramacharaka, (ed.). Chicago, IL: Yogi Publication Society, 1907.

The Holy Bible (King James Version). 1611. Reprint. Oxford, UK: Oxford University Press, 1833.

The Spiritual Magazine. London, UK: James Burns, 1869.

The Zoist: A Journal of Cerebral Physiology and Mesmerism, and Their Applications to Human Welfare. Vol. 9, March 1851-January 1852. London, UK: Hippolyte Bailliere, 1852.

Wallace, Abraham. *Jesus of Nazareth*. Manchester, UK: The Two World's Publishing Co., 1920.

INDEX

INCLUDES TOPICS, PEOPLE OF NOTE, KEYWORDS, SPELLING VARIATIONS, & KEY PHRASES

Aaron's rod, 18
Affectional Source, 15
affidavits, 11
Africa, 51, 211, 258, 351
Alabama, 151
alcohol, 384
angel, 18, 121, 148, 161
angelic beings, 14
angels, 13, 179
animal, 36, 114, 204-207, 209, 239, 261, 362, 365, 413
animals, 20, 167, 207, 208, 360
Antarctica, 429
Antoinette, Marie, 144, 146
Appalachia, 429
apparitions, 9, 20, 23, 25, 119, 120, 125, 156, 210, 260, 316, 413, 414
Armour, Jean, 257
army, 33, 129, 132, 172, 322, 362
Ashmolean, 105
asleep, 28, 29, 52, 56, 61, 64, 66, 73, 75, 90, 93-95, 99, 113, 116, 128, 142, 143, 165, 170, 174, 175, 193, 210, 212, 221, 233, 237, 245, 249, 254, 257, 273, 277, 278, 287-289, 296, 299-301, 323, 329, 347-349, 351, 359, 360, 366
atheists, 17
Atkins, Chet, 429
attic stairs, 89
aunt, 28, 29, 54, 79, 80, 84, 109, 119, 124, 125, 148, 174, 178, 186, 193, 217, 221, 226, 250, 255, 270
Australia, 69, 220, 221, 232, 233, 267, 357, 415
autonomous lights, 20
ball-room, 34
Banshee, 296
Barnard, Edward E., 253
Bay of Biscay, 71
beach, 58
beard, 116, 226
bed-curtains, 48, 266
bedroom, 23, 24, 26, 28, 31, 39, 40, 60, 61, 64, 73, 85, 100, 130, 132, 133, 155, 158, 191, 212, 221, 239, 257, 259, 264, 268, 276, 281, 285, 286, 289, 309, 315-318, 323, 325, 336, 348, 351
bedside, 25, 66, 79, 87, 91, 102, 118, 133, 148, 173, 187, 190, 194, 222, 288, 350, 368
Beethoven, Ludwig van, 279
bell, 47, 102, 125, 135, 160, 163, 185, 192, 238, 280, 337, 338, 347, 366, 391, 392
bells, 40, 52, 126, 334, 335
Bermuda, 32
Beyrout, 33
Bible, 3, 15, 18, 19, 68, 194, 195, 243, 264, 397, 398, 415, 416, 429, 431
Bible history, 398
biblical warnings, 19
bird, 36, 253
birds, 3, 94, 253, 295, 414
Birmingham Town Hall, 52
birth, 8, 13, 18, 116, 122, 133, 243, 389, 400
blacksmith, 112
blasphemous oaths, 40
blood, 2, 135, 163, 169, 173, 198, 205-207, 246, 250, 295, 361, 381, 403
boat, 35, 52, 58, 60, 98, 168, 171, 172, 240, 241, 244
bodies, 8, 25, 126, 213, 233, 343, 401
body, 3, 12, 13, 26, 34, 35, 87, 92, 96, 99, 106, 113, 114, 130, 150, 180, 204-207, 209, 218, 228, 242, 246, 249, 257, 259, 264, 268, 287, 343, 365, 368, 385, 386, 389, 392, 400, 403
Bolling, Edith, 429
bonnet, 31, 73, 74, 153, 256
Book of Revelation, 17
bookcase, 58, 96, 295
Boone, Pat, 429
boots, 59, 211, 237
boy, 24, 27, 34, 35, 50, 54, 61, 66, 84, 87, 106, 124, 149, 154, 169, 178, 197, 201, 211, 231, 236, 241, 286, 330-333, 373, 391

Boyle, Mrs. Cavendish, 143
boys, 2, 24, 64, 65, 163, 194, 198, 212, 285, 286, 315, 318, 327, 335, 393, 394
breakfast, 40, 62, 65, 67, 81, 83, 88, 98, 107, 118, 163, 182, 183, 187, 189, 205, 209, 219, 238, 243, 244, 247, 255, 276, 278, 282, 286, 290, 294, 295, 331, 347, 356
Brewster, David, 39
brooch, 64
brother, 24-26, 32, 35, 36, 43-45, 49, 51, 53, 54, 60, 61, 64, 66-68, 70, 81, 83, 93, 98, 99, 103, 104, 115, 138, 140, 149, 151-153, 156, 158, 159, 164, 169-172, 174, 175, 179, 187, 188, 191, 193, 203, 204, 211, 212, 214, 220, 221, 223-225, 232, 233, 236, 237, 246, 247, 249, 259, 262-265, 267, 278, 309, 310, 329, 347, 349, 351, 366, 374, 375, 393, 399, 416
brothers, 20, 115, 185, 326, 329
Brougham, Henry P., 141
Bruce, H. Addington, 20
Buchanan, Patrick J., 429
Buddha, 19
burning bush, 18
Burns, Robert, 257
California, 65, 166-168
Camp Independence, 65
Campbell, Joseph, 429
Canada, 32, 33, 74, 146
candle, 29, 39, 44, 58, 73, 94, 120, 122, 123, 125, 136, 144, 161, 181, 187, 265, 276, 278, 279, 319, 320, 322, 341, 351
candles, 47, 141, 320, 387
candlestick, 102, 319, 320
candlesticks, 103, 322
carriage and four, 49
Carson, Martha, 429
Cash, Johnny, 429
castle, 209, 291-293, 305-307
cat, 46, 47
cats, 3, 47
Ceresole, E., 369
chain of causation, 15
chair, 24, 29, 41, 46-49, 68, 75, 76, 80, 90, 91, 94, 108, 116, 124, 139-141, 148, 155, 321, 324, 336, 347, 358, 365, 384, 388, 391, 392
chairs, 74, 160, 336, 341, 345, 346

chapel, 106, 121-123, 146, 352
character, 13, 14, 29, 46, 62, 93, 122, 123, 180, 252, 263, 279, 281, 290, 294, 308, 323, 359, 360, 374, 385, 391, 398, 400
Charles II, King, 340
chemistry, 122
child, 24, 27, 28, 31, 55, 56, 67, 78, 81, 86, 96, 102, 121, 125, 139, 146-148, 178, 185, 193, 195, 198, 201, 222, 227, 241, 257, 270, 279, 282, 287, 309, 320, 341, 350, 373, 374, 383, 387, 391, 398-400, 429
children, 3, 23, 24, 27, 29, 30, 32, 55, 64, 79, 85, 86, 98, 99, 121, 136, 168, 175, 177, 185, 186, 193, 222, 227, 236, 239, 240, 254, 267, 271, 272, 284, 287, 289, 308, 320, 321, 325, 326, 337, 341, 349, 352, 372, 374, 392, 394, 398
Christ, 3, 18, 19, 416, 431
Christian, 3, 5, 7, 17-19, 21, 80, 268, 271, 293, 313, 401, 403, 414, 416, 431
Christian Bible, 18
Christian Churches, 401
Christian mystic, 5, 21
Christian researchers, 7
Christianity, 3, 15, 18, 19, 82, 397, 401, 403, 415, 431
Christians, 18-20, 397, 403
Christmas, 3, 38, 41, 52, 105, 156, 242, 244, 286, 292, 315, 415, 431
Christmas Eve, 38
church, 13, 19, 53, 88, 91, 92, 101, 102, 105, 115, 129, 146, 150, 154, 186, 187, 193, 197, 202, 214, 216, 219, 222, 240-242, 266, 274, 345, 347, 352, 366, 401
cigar, 97, 294
clairvoyance, 9, 19, 196, 201, 311, 318, 367
clairvoyante, 316, 365
clergy, 122, 163
clergyman, 25, 85, 94, 96, 117, 146, 149, 177-179, 237, 242, 275
cloak, 59, 73, 74, 87
clothes, 24, 46, 47, 49, 57, 61, 67, 113, 131, 132, 138, 141, 150, 165, 171, 176, 183, 190, 235, 341, 344, 345
coat, 38, 63, 72, 94, 98, 116, 205,

248, 323
coat-of-arms, 72
coffin, 31, 53, 68, 102, 218, 220, 255, 287, 299, 300, 390, 391
collier, 54
Combs, Bertram T., 429
communion, 13
confirmation bias, 20
Connecticut, 148
consciousness, 3, 5, 6, 14, 17, 20, 82, 113, 141, 163, 204, 213, 278, 285, 367
conventional science, 20, 21
Corinthians, Book of First, 403
corporeal body, 13
corpse, 78, 125, 127, 128, 158, 263, 346
corpses, 47
corroborative letters, 11
cottages, 107
country home, 117
Courtisigny, M. Osmond de, 335
Crawford, Cindy, 429
creeds, 13, 429
cries, 40, 220, 363
Crimea, 26
Cruise, Tom, 429
cryings, 40
cryptids, 20
cupboard, 70, 96, 118, 248, 320
curtains, 46, 48, 78, 110, 117, 120, 137, 228, 257, 266, 295, 312, 383, 388, 392
cyclist, 112
cyclists, 111
Cyrus, Miley, 429
death, 3, 5, 6, 8, 11, 13, 17, 20, 23, 25, 26, 28-32, 40, 42, 43, 49, 50, 52-55, 57, 58, 66-70, 77, 78, 80, 82-84, 87-89, 91-93, 95, 97-100, 103-106, 118-120, 126, 127, 129, 134, 137, 141, 142, 146, 148, 149, 151-153, 156, 158, 159, 167, 169, 174, 175, 177, 178, 183, 192, 193, 196, 203, 205, 206, 208, 216, 218, 219, 221, 224, 225, 227, 233, 234, 238-241, 246, 247, 251, 254, 256, 257, 260, 262, 264, 267, 268, 270, 276-279, 286, 287, 289, 292-294, 301, 319, 320, 332, 342, 346, 348, 352, 393, 399, 400, 403, 413, 414
death-bed, 55, 178, 192
deathbed visitors, 20
deferred percipience, 93

delusion, 83, 164, 187, 268, 371
demonic beings, 14
despair, 40, 269
development, 14, 135, 325, 341, 400
dinner, 44, 61, 68, 85, 168, 170, 171, 185, 186, 191, 193, 195, 224, 292, 312, 319
disharmony, 15
ditch, 112
divine economy, 14
Divine Essence, 15
divine law, 13
Divine Sonship, 399
divinity, 15
doctor, 36, 71, 109, 146-150, 156, 165, 169, 172, 173, 180, 204, 247, 254, 272, 278, 287, 288, 306, 309, 315, 347, 363, 373, 376, 393
doctors, 227, 235, 362, 365, 366, 369, 375
dog, 47, 49, 185, 186, 204-208, 219, 264, 296, 302, 321
dogs, 208, 321
door, 24-29, 31, 33, 38-45, 51, 53, 56, 57, 60, 64, 68, 70, 72-75, 80, 81, 84-86, 89, 91, 94-96, 100-102, 110, 113-115, 118, 125, 130, 131, 133-136, 139, 141, 143-147, 150, 154, 155, 157, 158, 161, 165, 168, 173, 180, 185, 187, 190, 203, 211, 214, 219, 223, 224, 239, 243, 256, 259, 262, 264, 265, 271, 272, 276, 278, 279, 281, 286, 289, 301, 302, 316, 318-324, 326-329, 331-333, 335, 337, 340, 341, 347, 348, 362, 375, 382, 385, 392, 393
doors, 16, 40, 42, 74, 75, 77, 110, 129, 190, 191, 240, 262, 265, 266, 290, 296, 334, 344, 358, 359, 394
döppelganger, 318
downstairs, 31, 44, 45, 61, 73, 90, 100, 155, 156, 193, 208, 253, 256, 285, 289, 315, 317-319, 326, 351, 366
Doyle, Arthur C., 19
Drab Room, 60-63
dragging furniture, 41
drawing-room, 44
dread, 30, 86, 195, 229, 381
dream, 27, 30, 37, 67, 68, 75, 79, 83, 86, 87, 93, 95, 113, 137, 141, 142, 151, 165, 170-172, 174,

183, 187, 188, 190, 199, 204-207, 211-213, 215-227, 231-259, 268, 272, 278, 296, 301, 351, 369, 370
dreaming, 25, 27, 30, 66, 75, 86, 91, 97, 165, 181, 183, 211, 228, 230, 236, 237, 243, 246, 248, 254, 275, 288, 350
dreams, 9, 20, 50, 98, 113, 114, 174, 182, 187, 191, 211, 221, 226-231, 235, 244-246, 249-251, 255, 260, 272, 334
dress, 27, 29, 31, 34, 43-45, 47, 48, 63, 64, 69, 70, 72, 75, 86, 90, 101-103, 106, 107, 109, 110, 114, 135-137, 139, 140, 144, 146, 151, 153, 157, 191, 221, 234, 251, 262, 278, 317, 318, 377
dressing glass, 47
dressing-closet, 64, 65
dressing-room, 61-63, 73, 152, 157
drinking, 107, 310, 371
drowned, 33, 34, 55, 69, 78, 79, 98, 99, 111, 171, 178, 211, 244, 267, 276, 277
drowning, 69, 98, 104, 204, 232, 393
drunk, 78, 112, 180
dusk, 43, 44, 61, 88, 111
Duvall, Robert, 429
dying, 23, 28, 52, 57, 96, 97, 167, 173, 178, 183-185, 193-195, 204, 207, 211, 213, 220, 231, 235, 238, 257, 261, 270, 272, 289, 309, 344, 347, 349
dysentery, 66
Earl of Oxford, 429
Early Christian Church, 19
earth, 8, 13, 86, 109, 132, 204, 304, 342, 344, 388, 390, 399, 400, 403
Eastlake, Lady, 143
Edward VI, King, 142
Egypt, 18, 288
electricity, 104, 377, 382, 389, 390, 415
electro-biology, 231
Elijah, 18
England, 28, 29, 32, 48, 56, 71, 75, 76, 85, 86, 120, 146, 152, 156, 158, 177, 178, 192, 194, 202, 203, 215, 218, 224, 230, 255, 256, 258-260, 274, 294, 301, 304, 345, 346, 350
enlightened individuals, 21
eschatology, 17, 21

ESP, 9, 20, 163, 415
eternal life, 17, 18, 21, 254
eternity, 11
Europe, 414
European countries, 36
European royalty, 429
evil, 15, 39, 133, 163, 170, 181, 264, 338
expansion, 205
experience, 13, 36, 59, 66, 72, 76, 82, 83, 94-96, 98, 104, 106, 114, 118, 142, 143, 145, 149, 150, 156, 164, 173, 176, 179, 182, 183, 185, 189, 248-252, 255, 256, 275, 283-286, 297, 316, 317, 324, 327, 342, 344, 377, 388, 414
experiences, 10, 14, 17, 20, 21, 113, 145, 172, 227, 231, 250, 252, 297, 309, 342, 345, 347, 355, 414
extra-dimensional reality, 21
eye, 54, 101, 122, 149, 152, 154, 182, 189, 213, 216, 251, 253, 268, 283, 285, 304, 306
eyes, 8, 17, 23, 25-27, 29, 32, 33, 37, 39, 46-49, 52, 53, 59, 61-63, 67, 70, 81, 90-93, 96, 99, 104, 109, 112, 115, 118, 123, 139, 140, 148, 157, 165, 175, 179, 185, 186, 188, 190, 196, 224, 226-228, 236, 247, 251, 283, 284, 299, 300, 319, 358, 359, 363, 365, 366, 380
Ezekiel, 18
fall of Jericho, 18
familiar spirits, 18
father, 2, 15, 24-28, 30, 32, 34, 40, 41, 50, 53-55, 60, 67, 68, 70-72, 80, 88-90, 97, 98, 112, 118, 119, 130, 131, 136, 137, 140, 156, 167, 172, 173, 177, 180, 187, 192, 195, 203, 211, 214, 217, 218, 222, 225, 227, 231-235, 240, 255, 256, 259, 260, 264-269, 271-273, 277, 278, 286, 293, 299, 301, 308, 309, 338, 340, 347, 348, 350, 351, 363, 374, 387, 388, 398, 399, 429
Fechner, Gustav T., 8
fever, 86, 102, 165, 173, 279, 287, 350
field, 20, 77, 86, 110, 184, 240, 253, 274, 294, 300, 371, 415
fire, 30, 35, 41, 42, 46, 48, 49, 55,

61, 76, 80, 136, 158, 160, 183, 208, 214, 249, 262, 267, 308, 310, 313, 320, 321, 347, 380-382, 387, 394, 395
flannel petticoat, 102
float, 113, 126
floating, 16, 188, 205, 230, 233, 256
Florida, 173
flying saucer, 18
Foote, Shelby, 429
footfalls, 45, 414
footsteps, 40, 41, 108, 279, 295, 296, 323-325, 341, 351
forest, 244, 386
Forming Principle, 15
Fox girls, 343
Fox, David, 342
Fox, John D., 341
Fox, Kate, 341
Fox, Margaret, 341
France, 30, 52, 146, 220, 261, 283, 304, 335, 336, 338, 413, 414
Frederick the Great, 346
Friday, 54, 67, 105, 115, 117, 150, 153, 205, 214, 233, 247, 313, 317-319, 326, 356, 379
funeral, 53, 88, 91, 151, 219, 247, 312, 352
funeral procession, 53
furniture, 41, 45, 74, 99, 112, 143, 175, 266, 325, 334, 336, 338, 341, 345
gardener, 96, 153, 373
Gayheart, Rebecca, 429
Georgia, 165
Germany, 159, 193, 280, 340
ghost, 3, 15, 30, 41, 42, 44, 56, 63, 93, 109-111, 135-138, 141-144, 146, 148, 151, 159, 216, 269, 291, 292, 334, 335, 344, 346, 348, 398, 413, 415
ghost stories, 20
ghosts, 9, 16, 19, 23, 25, 39, 44, 52, 64, 106, 135, 138, 142, 144, 146, 346, 413
Gibraltar, 120
girl, 28, 29, 44, 55, 57, 78, 80, 85, 103, 106, 108-110, 121, 122, 136, 146-148, 168, 175, 198, 205, 214, 218, 225, 239, 255-257, 267, 287, 317-319, 321, 324, 336, 338, 350, 364-366, 373, 374
girls, 29, 44, 56, 57, 317, 326, 341, 343, 344
Glanvill, Joseph, 340, 380

gloom, 87, 128, 139
God, 2, 3, 13, 17, 18, 21, 27, 53, 63, 68, 78, 98, 107, 149, 150, 158, 165, 184, 195, 240, 271, 288, 289, 370, 382, 397, 399-401, 413
Godfrey, Clarence, 94
goffered cap, 118, 119
good health, 35, 44, 50, 55, 99, 109, 154, 175, 197, 234, 253, 262, 264, 277, 362, 366
Gospel of Jesus, 10, 397, 400
Gospel of Mark, 18
gown, 32, 39, 40, 48, 109, 116, 145, 222
grandfather, 29, 39, 40, 149, 192
grandmother, 24, 26, 27, 29, 30, 32, 87, 88, 118, 119, 200, 242
granite, 107, 108
grave, 19, 26, 47, 49, 128, 133, 135, 139, 140, 157, 218, 403
grave-clothes, 47
Graves, Robert, 429
Greece, 116
Griffith, Andy, 429
groanings, 40
groans, 63, 333
growth, 13, 14, 204, 206, 397
guitars, 345
gun, 2, 3, 53, 59, 429
gun-carriage, 53
gunpowder, 96
hallucination, 39, 72, 88, 93, 116, 152, 154, 156, 268, 271, 276, 286, 362
hallucinations, 115, 174, 333, 338
handkerchief, 48, 89, 144, 278
happiness, 3, 13, 14, 140, 194, 416, 431
harbour, 55, 99, 304
Harding, William G., 429
Harmonial Philosophy, 15
harmonium, 101
harmony, 14, 15, 280, 387, 400, 401
Hartwig, Carl E. A., 253
hat, 38, 59, 102, 107, 110, 111, 153, 202, 235, 278
haunt, 137, 222, 292, 323
haunted, 3, 9, 16, 41, 44, 63, 64, 127, 133-135, 137, 142-144, 180, 193, 224, 227, 233, 234, 246, 255, 266, 291, 315, 326, 328, 329, 336-338, 340, 346, 415
haunted house, 144, 291, 328, 336-338, 340

haunted houses, 9, 16, 142, 315
haunting, 128, 292, 335, 340, 346
hauntings, 20
healing, 10, 14, 19, 20, 345, 355, 413
healing of the sick, 14
health, 3, 27, 28, 31, 32, 35, 44, 47, 50, 54-56, 65, 82, 84, 86, 93, 99, 107, 109, 122, 137, 154, 166, 174, 175, 178, 180, 184, 195, 197, 221, 224, 226, 227, 231, 234, 235, 251, 253, 254, 258, 259, 262-264, 267, 277, 282, 288, 293, 301, 302, 350, 362, 365, 366, 368, 377, 416, 429, 431
heaven, 14, 121, 161, 194, 239, 390, 399, 403
hell, 2, 14, 400
Henry VIII, King, 60, 142
hide-and-seek, 89
hideous figures, 49
Highlanders, 35
hills, 8, 174, 282, 307, 308
hoaxing, 11
Hodgson, Richard, 203
Holmes, Sherlock, 19
Holy Ghost, 15, 398
holy ministries, 19
Holy Virgin, 121, 123
Home, Daniel D., 124, 126, 380-384, 386-389, 391, 392
horror, 60, 129, 150, 168, 170, 190, 195, 247, 255, 268, 295
horse, 43, 103, 107, 114, 166, 167, 172, 227, 232, 233, 242, 243, 301, 302, 373
horses, 195, 209, 223, 243, 302, 308, 373, 374
hospital, 98, 100, 175, 188, 223, 235, 236, 248
house, 3, 16, 19, 23-26, 28, 29, 33, 36, 38-45, 47, 49, 51, 53, 55, 58, 60, 61, 64, 65, 67, 70-73, 77, 80, 82, 85, 87-93, 96-99, 102-109, 112, 114, 115, 119, 125, 127-130, 133, 135-140, 144, 146, 147, 149, 153-157, 159-161, 164, 165, 168-171, 175, 176, 183-186, 189-191, 195, 198, 200, 212, 214, 217-220, 223, 225, 228, 232, 234, 235, 238-240, 242, 244, 248-250, 254-257, 259, 261-267, 270-272, 275, 279-281, 284-287, 290, 291, 294, 296, 301, 302, 309, 311, 312, 315-318, 320-329, 331-343, 345, 348, 351, 352, 356, 363, 366, 367, 371, 372, 375, 376, 383, 390, 391, 394, 413, 415
houses, 9, 16, 58, 142, 212, 265, 294, 296, 315, 319, 331, 332, 335, 338
Howard, Catharine, 142
Hugo, Victor, 244
human soul, 398
human spirit, 14
human spirits, 14
hunt, 192, 278
hunter, 30-32
hunting, 54, 294
husband, 23, 26, 30, 31, 38, 46, 49, 52, 58, 60, 62-64, 73, 80, 85, 86, 96-98, 102, 115, 129, 160, 161, 165, 167, 171, 176, 184-187, 192, 193, 210, 211, 216, 218, 220, 222, 223, 232, 233, 237, 239-241, 247, 249, 253, 257, 261, 267, 269, 271, 272, 276-278, 280, 288, 289, 301, 302, 310, 325, 352, 370, 393

icy chill, 52, 153
idolatrous dogmas, 401
idolatry, 400
ill, 23, 24, 28, 33, 36, 50, 52, 59, 65, 71, 73, 74, 81, 84, 87, 88, 92, 102, 105, 106, 112, 113, 117, 118, 120, 124, 125, 147, 148, 157, 164, 172, 173, 178, 180, 183-185, 191, 193, 195, 196, 198, 214, 219, 221, 223-225, 228, 233-235, 237-239, 244, 246, 247, 254, 256, 262, 269, 270, 275, 281, 288, 289, 293, 311, 320, 324, 325, 335, 346, 347, 349, 368, 375
Illinois, 149
illness, 27, 28, 35, 53, 65, 71, 88, 100, 106, 127, 148, 149, 164, 165, 169, 171, 174, 175, 177, 191, 194, 198, 200, 254, 261, 263, 272, 285-288, 346, 370
illusion, 39, 46, 47, 50, 64, 118, 135, 263, 269, 306
Immaculate Conception, 121
immortal, 13, 17, 20, 400
immortal life, 17, 20
immortality, 21, 128, 403
incorruption, 403
India, 31, 35, 52, 53, 69, 74, 81, 113,

120, 141, 142, 156, 174, 192, 198, 202, 225, 259, 278, 286, 287, 294, 398, 413, 414
Indian mutiny, 35, 225
infallible truth, 14
infant, 300
Infinite Parent, 15
infinite spirit, 13, 15
inspirations, 14
invisible touching, 20
Ireland, 3, 40, 54, 93, 192, 225, 402, 404, 414, 415
Isle of France, 52
Italy, 136, 137, 178, 230, 303, 311
James, William, 202
Jefferson Davis Historical Gold Medal, 429
Jericho, 18
Jesus, 3, 7, 10, 18, 19, 21, 397-401, 415, 416, 431
Job, 18, 153
John, Saint, 7
Judd, Ashley, 429
Judd, Naomi, 429
Judd, Wynonna, 429
Kane, Elisha K., 341
Kentucky, 299, 301, 429
Keough, Riley, 429
kindness, 98, 99, 174, 223, 390
kingdom of heaven, 399, 403
Knocking Ghost of the Basil Wooods, 346
labour pains, 116
lake, 103, 178, 244
lamp, 41, 42, 95, 96, 104, 130, 136, 139, 151, 295, 312, 322, 326, 330, 333, 349
lamps, 338
landing-net, 100, 101
laughter, 31, 284
lavatory, 96
law of affinity, 14
Law of Attraction, 3, 19, 415, 416, 431
laws of physics, 17
laying on of hands, 14, 395
letter-box, 100
levitate, 388
levitation, 20
library, 6, 36, 89, 95, 96, 101, 102, 163, 182, 198, 255, 383
life after death, 11, 17, 20, 413
light, 16, 19, 21, 25, 27, 29, 30, 36, 37, 39, 41, 42, 44, 46, 47, 53, 61, 64, 66, 67, 71, 75, 78, 85, 86, 90, 91, 93, 102, 104, 110, 124, 126-128, 130, 134, 136, 137, 139, 141-146, 156, 177, 181, 183, 187, 236, 237, 246, 248, 250, 256, 261, 265, 268, 280, 281, 284, 285, 291, 295, 299, 304, 315, 316, 319, 328, 345, 349, 357, 365, 375, 380, 381, 384, 387-389, 392, 397, 398, 400, 401, 414, 415
Lodge, Oliver, 203, 204
Longfellow, Henry W., 16
Lord, 18, 19, 28, 31, 141, 154, 217, 242, 292, 293, 380-384, 386
Lot's wife, 18
Louisiana, 151
love, 2, 3, 15, 106, 111, 123, 176, 180, 200, 227, 228, 239, 296, 339, 352, 399
Loveless, Patty, 429
lunch, 74, 99, 175, 189, 371
luncheon, 111, 209, 299, 301
luncheon party, 111
Luther, Martin, 340
Madagascar, 51
mainstream Christians, 18, 19
manna, 18
mansion, 346, 389
marriage, 3, 27, 30, 52, 73, 91, 216, 224, 225, 234, 269, 272, 323
Martyrs' Memorial, 105
Marvin, Lee, 429
Mary, 18, 24, 88, 175, 276, 284, 288, 376
Massachusetts, 15, 166, 167
materialists, 17
Mather, Cotton, 346
McGraw, Tim, 429
meadows, 8
medicine, 102, 103, 152, 169, 322
mediums, 19, 138, 202, 344, 345, 389
memories, 11
memory, 23, 39, 48, 50, 68, 70, 104, 105, 119, 138, 141, 146, 165, 171, 180, 201, 217, 220, 285, 289, 351, 388, 398
mental healing, 10, 20, 355, 413
mental impressions, 14, 51
mental telepathy, 21
mesmerism, 61, 316, 416
mess-room, 100, 101
miracle, 14, 122, 258, 379, 382
miracles, 14, 19, 122, 123
mirage, 308
mirages, 9, 20, 299
mirror, 43, 47, 196

mirrors, 87, 200
misery, 14, 134, 231
misidentifications, 11
misinterpretation, 14
Mississippi, 151
Missouri, 97
mists, 16
modern mainstream Christians, 18, 19
modern science, 19
Monday, 25, 67, 115, 117, 152, 164, 169, 179, 181, 191, 205-207, 213, 214, 219, 233, 240, 241, 245, 246, 250, 252, 288, 291, 318, 325, 327, 356
money, 53, 90, 130, 132, 198, 217, 269, 274, 344
moon, 3, 16, 25, 90, 108, 118, 119, 127, 137, 256, 276, 295, 387
moonlight, 25, 32, 33, 39, 56, 90, 118, 119, 125, 127, 237, 256, 277, 282, 299
moral growth, 14
mortification, 262
Mosby, John S., 429
Moses, 18, 133, 400
mother, 3, 15, 23-29, 32-36, 41, 48, 50, 52, 53, 55, 57, 64-68, 70-72, 79-81, 84-86, 90-92, 97, 102, 103, 105, 106, 109-111, 118-120, 125, 136, 140, 142, 149, 151, 155, 156, 164, 165, 172, 173, 179, 183-185, 187, 189, 198, 214, 220-223, 226, 227, 235, 238, 246, 248, 251, 252, 258, 259, 261, 264-271, 273, 277-279, 286, 301, 309, 315, 326, 341, 347, 349-351, 373, 374, 383, 388, 391, 399, 415, 429
mountain, 122, 302, 303, 372, 386
mountains, 12, 138, 307, 429
music, 139, 150, 151, 198, 199, 227, 280, 292, 334, 383, 387, 391, 429
Myers, Frederic W. H., 95, 196, 203
mystical Christianity, 18
mystical Christians, 20
Napoleon I, 126
Napoleon III, 126
neckcloth, 64
nephew, 50, 148, 246, 339
nescience, 20
Nevada, 166
New Hampshire, 219
New Jersey, 151
New York, 78, 79, 133, 166-168, 340, 344, 379, 394, 413-416
news, 26, 28, 31, 32, 55, 57, 58, 72, 73, 79, 84, 93, 107, 116, 120, 148, 149, 151, 159, 164, 171, 174, 187, 192, 193, 198, 211, 217, 218, 221, 222, 224-226, 240, 246, 247, 258, 259, 265, 268, 275, 293, 309, 350, 385
newspaper, 57, 58, 157, 196, 197, 212, 216, 232, 233, 242, 243, 331
newspapers, 57, 137, 225, 268, 322, 336, 337
Newton, A. E., 15
niece, 150, 225, 233, 339, 348, 352, 353
night, 16, 24-27, 29-32, 34-37, 39, 40, 42, 44-47, 49, 50, 52, 56, 57, 61-66, 69, 70, 73, 76, 77, 79, 83-85, 87, 90, 93, 98, 102, 104, 107-109, 112, 113, 116-120, 124-127, 132-134, 136-138, 140, 141, 143, 147, 148, 155, 156, 161, 164, 170, 173, 176, 179-187, 189, 192-195, 198, 199, 204-206, 208, 212-215, 217, 223, 225, 227, 228, 231, 233, 234, 237, 238, 241-245, 247-254, 256, 258, 260-272, 277-280, 282, 285-288, 290, 291, 293-295, 301, 308, 310, 315-319, 323-325, 327-330, 333-335, 338, 341, 342, 346-348, 350-352, 357, 368, 370, 375, 388, 393, 394, 413
nightcap, 73
nightfall, 336
nightmare, 62, 135, 143, 204
non-physical beings, 18
North Carolina, 429
Nova Scotia, 158
nurse, 28, 30, 31, 64, 85, 103, 148, 164, 201, 222, 223, 244, 245, 257, 272, 287, 308, 309, 347
nursery, 31, 85, 86, 89, 90, 99, 111, 175, 192, 236, 309
nurses, 178, 227
occult formula, 18
ocean, 107
odors, 20
officers, 26, 32, 33, 52, 100, 158, 159, 172, 184, 218, 339, 340
Old Testament, 19
omens, 10, 20, 393
Onset Bay, MA, 15

opiates, 228
other realities, 17
other-worldly forces, 18
Pagan, 18, 114, 401, 403, 414
Pagan myths, 401
Paganism, 400, 401
pain, 17, 112, 113, 116, 122, 163, 165, 166, 170, 172, 188, 210, 220, 261, 365
painter, 106
palace, 27, 142-145, 184, 244, 346
palaces, 303, 304
papillotes, 47
parade, 101
paranormal, 7, 9, 11, 17-19, 21, 297, 315, 429
paranormal abilities, 18
paranormal experiences, 17
parlour, 43, 67, 158, 257
Parton, Dolly, 429
Paul, Saint, 7, 19, 21
peace, 131, 138, 194, 338, 401
Peebles, James M., 13, 19
Penn, Sybil, 142
percipience, 93
phantasm, 94, 299
phantasms, 9, 23, 414
phantoms, 16
Pharisees, 401
philistinism, 20
physical body, 403
physical death, 13, 400
physical phenomena, 19
physics, 17, 20, 122
physiological rationales, 17
piano, 88, 195, 280, 311-313, 358
pillow, 2, 63, 75, 76, 263, 330
pillows, 30, 266, 344
Piper, Leonora F., 202
plagues, 18
plagues on Egypt, 18
pneumatology, 21
poltergeist, 319, 328
poltergeist manifestations, 328
poltergeists, 9, 20, 315
Porter, Anna M., 157
postillions, 49
powers, 10, 18-20, 228, 273, 345, 355, 398, 400
pray, 18, 86, 194
prayer, 26, 92, 123, 194, 271, 392
premonition, 10, 65, 393
premonitary dreams, 20
premonitions, 225
preservationist, 429
Presley, Elvis, 429

Presley, Lisa M., 429
priesthood, 19, 399
priesthoods, 401
primitive Christians, 19
procession, 12, 53
progression, 14
prophecy, 19, 367
psychic powers, 18
psychological explanations, 17
punkah, 93
purity, 128
Pyrenees, 120
quantum physics, 20
railway station, 106, 114, 264, 294
rappings, 333, 334, 340, 344
rationalists, 17
rats, 41, 42, 62, 183, 208, 341
rectory, 35, 40, 41, 71, 89, 90, 101, 102, 266, 267
Red Sea, 18
Redman, G. A., 344
Reichenbach, Karl L. F. von, 141, 182, 357
religious Spiritualists, 19
resurrection, 17, 383, 403
resurrection of the spirit, 403
Rhine, J. B., 20
river, 34, 58-60, 99, 110, 111, 206, 240, 276, 308, 393
rocking-chair, 116
room, 24, 25, 27-31, 33-36, 38-49, 53, 56-58, 60-66, 69, 71-76, 80, 84, 85, 87-91, 93-97, 99-102, 104, 107, 110, 112-114, 116-120, 124-128, 130, 131, 134-139, 141, 143, 144, 148, 150-152, 154-159, 164, 165, 169, 171, 173, 175, 176, 179, 180, 183, 187-191, 194, 195, 197, 199, 200, 204, 208, 210, 211, 214, 219, 224, 225, 229, 236, 237, 246, 252, 255, 256, 258, 259, 261, 262, 264, 265, 267, 270, 271, 278, 279, 281, 284, 286, 287, 289, 291, 294-296, 299, 301, 309-312, 316, 317, 319-333, 336, 338, 345-348, 352, 355, 358, 359, 362, 363, 367, 373, 378, 379, 381, 383-392
rooms, 41, 42, 44, 100, 120, 129, 136-138, 160, 191, 228-230, 264, 266, 277, 285-287, 290, 294, 317, 326, 332, 334, 338, 339, 348, 377-379, 383, 389, 414

Royal Artillery, 32
Royal Fusiliers, 24, 26
Rucker, Edmund W., 429
sacrament, 25, 53
sailor, 54, 66, 70, 78, 235, 268
salt, 18, 319
salvation, 322
Saturday, 61, 63, 88, 112, 117, 127, 151-153, 169, 179, 191, 201, 204, 206, 239, 245, 247, 276, 281, 310, 326
sceptic, 372
sceptics, 121, 372, 389
scientific method, 17
Scotland, 23, 47, 141, 149, 201, 231, 239, 251, 252
Scott, George C., 429
scream, 30, 31, 239, 249, 296
screams, 266, 268
sea, 3, 5, 6, 12, 16, 18, 19, 32, 69, 163, 171, 209, 211, 216, 217, 235, 240, 267, 303-306, 308-310, 393, 413, 415, 416, 431
Seabrook, Lochlainn, 11, 21, 429
séance, 199, 251, 252, 328, 383, 389-392
séance room, 328
séances, 20, 123, 252, 367
second sight, 175, 176, 201, 231
sedatives, 228
serpent, 18, 362
servant, 28, 35, 36, 38, 43-45, 53, 73, 85, 87, 157, 175, 192, 205, 211, 214, 221-223, 239, 242, 256, 278, 289, 302, 324, 325, 336-338, 362, 392
servants, 27, 33, 39, 41-45, 60, 64, 73, 81, 90, 169, 266, 272, 383
settee, 74, 75
Seymour, Jane, 142
shadowy figure, 113
shadowy light, 78
ship, 66, 69, 71, 79, 141, 163, 172, 173, 202, 216, 256, 258, 268, 269, 307, 308
shrieks, 63, 161
sighs, 63, 173, 286, 324, 333
singing, 96, 97, 139, 227, 334
sister, 24, 26, 28-30, 33-35, 41, 42, 44, 45, 48, 50, 51, 55-57, 69-72, 74, 81, 84, 87, 89, 92, 93, 97, 99, 101-104, 106, 112, 113, 116, 118, 119, 123, 140, 150, 153, 156, 160, 161, 164, 175, 184, 187, 188, 190-193,
195, 208, 209, 215, 220-222, 226, 228, 229, 231, 234, 243, 245-247, 250, 252, 256, 261-265, 270, 277, 283-285, 317, 332, 348, 352, 368, 374, 375, 394
sisters, 20, 33, 41, 43, 45, 56, 57, 90, 99, 136, 173, 175, 198, 215, 227, 233, 316, 341, 429
sitting-room, 114, 278, 296, 323
Skaggs, Ricky, 429
skeletons, 49
skeptic, 17, 141
sleep, 8, 26, 32, 33, 56, 57, 60-63, 65, 66, 71, 75, 87, 90, 94, 112, 113, 116, 118, 125, 134, 141, 165, 166, 170, 172-174, 176, 179, 180, 182, 185, 187, 191, 195, 205, 207, 208, 220, 221, 227, 228, 233, 244, 247, 252, 255, 262, 267, 268, 270, 273, 276, 279, 280, 286, 290, 321, 323, 327, 334, 341, 347, 349, 351, 359, 363-365, 367, 368
sleeping, 8, 28, 29, 35, 45, 61, 62, 73, 78, 82, 86, 87, 90, 104, 112, 120, 141, 143, 147, 170, 183, 184, 211, 227, 228, 255, 264, 267, 276, 281, 286, 287, 330-333, 350, 352, 365, 368
smells, 9, 297
Society of Friends, 23
Sons of Confederate Veterans, 429
soul, 1, 3, 5, 6, 19, 21, 37, 87, 121, 258, 268, 273, 279, 331, 398, 399, 401, 403
souls, 8, 11, 138, 165, 273, 401
sounds, 9, 16, 20, 42, 44, 63, 131, 133, 261, 263, 268, 290, 291, 317, 323, 324, 341-344
spectral illusion, 39, 46
spectral voices, 9, 20, 261
spectre, 33, 134, 135, 159, 266
spell-bound, 49, 125
Spirit, 3, 8, 12-18, 21, 37, 55, 83, 87, 105, 124, 128, 132-135, 138, 142, 153, 158, 161, 190, 194, 202, 207, 216, 257, 279, 285, 290, 328, 335, 338-340, 342-345, 367, 377, 378, 381-383, 385-392, 394, 395, 397-401, 403, 413-416
spirit beings, 18
spirit hand, 328
spirit lights, 328
spirit manifestations, 389, 413, 415

spiritism, 279, 332, 333, 413
spiritistic hypothesis, 203
spirits, 8, 10, 13, 14, 16, 19, 20, 24, 35, 44, 99, 124, 126, 140, 152, 157, 175, 181, 184, 197, 221, 239, 258, 267, 291, 318, 325, 334, 335, 338, 343, 349, 366, 380, 382-384, 392, 395
spiritual beings, 14
spiritual body, 403
spiritual leaders, 19
spiritual nature, 13, 400
spiritual realm, 14
spiritual signs, 17
spiritual state, 13, 14
spiritual world, 13, 14, 194, 349, 400
Spiritualism, 9, 10, 13, 15, 18-20, 124, 126, 135, 151, 157, 257, 397, 400, 401, 413, 415
Spiritualist camp meeting, 15
Spiritualists, 13, 19, 123, 128, 134, 397, 399, 401
steamer, 99, 211, 239
Stephens, Alexander H., 429
strange noises, 39, 41, 61, 335
strange sounds, 44, 133
Stuart Restoration, 346
suffering, 13, 62, 112-114, 130, 152, 169, 171, 219, 220, 279, 293, 375
Sumatra, 66, 165, 329
summer dress, 102
sun, 97, 107, 141, 165, 166, 253, 303, 305
Sunday, 38, 61-63, 67, 77, 80, 88, 106, 115, 117, 121, 127, 150, 153, 164, 168, 169, 186, 189, 193, 197, 198, 205, 206, 209, 217, 221, 238-242, 251, 252, 254, 262, 286, 290, 312, 327, 329, 337, 352, 367, 368, 374, 393
Sunshine Sisters, the, 429
supernatural, 18, 20, 46, 50, 59, 62, 106, 122, 123, 139, 142, 254, 267, 269, 271, 316, 333, 382, 413, 414
supernatural activities, 17
supernatural events, 18
supernatural power, 122
superstition, 54, 89, 123, 124, 195, 266, 278, 328, 344, 381
supper, 68, 102, 160, 267
sweets, 118
Synagogue, 401
Syria, 33

Syrian Spiritualism, 397
tea, 41-43, 54, 98, 157, 243, 274, 320, 322, 324, 359
telegram, 51, 74, 98, 116, 118, 124, 156, 178-180, 187, 191, 192, 195, 196, 231, 232, 234, 235, 249, 253, 260-262, 272, 277, 278, 288, 339, 355, 356
telegraph, 33, 55, 259, 374
telepathic phantasm, 94
Tennessee, 3, 429
terror, 61, 75, 92, 161, 170, 228, 229, 256, 266, 337
thanatology, 21
theologians, 398, 399
Thompson, Isaac C., 203
thought transference, 9, 20, 163
Thursday, 61, 62, 77, 88, 99, 116, 152, 175, 182, 191, 205, 206, 212, 213, 239, 254, 275, 319, 347, 355, 356, 368
Timsbury Ghosts, 64
travels, 100, 175, 308
tree, 58, 209, 211, 215, 332
trees, 58, 60, 89, 103, 160, 192, 281, 308, 371, 373
trousers, 90, 100, 296
truth, 12, 14, 19, 82, 122, 133, 142, 146, 182, 187, 188, 226, 241, 269, 279, 309, 311, 317, 338, 344, 380, 381, 388, 392, 397, 399-401, 416
Tuesday, 80, 106, 114, 151, 180, 182, 213, 214, 241, 252, 254, 318, 335
typhoid fever, 102, 287
uncle, 52, 79, 119, 124, 125, 174, 178, 193, 203, 216-218, 273, 352
United States of America, 2, 6
universal laws, 14
universe, 13, 208
unknown forces, 10, 20, 355
unseen world, 18, 19
unusual powers, 20
upstairs, 38, 41, 43-45, 51, 61, 67, 100, 131, 139, 154, 155, 191, 208, 211, 214, 276, 296, 315-317, 319, 325, 351, 355
Valois, Marguerite de la, 254
vapours, 16
veridical hallucination, 93
Vermont, 138, 148
vertigo, 98
virgin birth, 18
Virginia, 429

vision, 29, 31, 33, 48, 52, 53, 66, 67, 70-72, 75, 77-79, 83, 84, 87, 88, 95, 98, 103, 104, 119, 121, 122, 128, 141, 142, 149, 161, 169-174, 181, 188, 196, 204, 222, 223, 225, 236, 245, 250-252, 254, 258, 259, 288, 289, 300-302, 308, 309, 311, 369, 370
visions, 9, 19, 20, 48, 121, 123, 218, 228, 285, 299, 414
visitation, 97, 134, 146
visitations, 227
voice, 27, 35, 36, 86, 87, 104, 107, 113, 115, 120, 139, 144, 164, 168, 182, 184, 190, 204, 207, 236-238, 247, 251, 252, 261-263, 270-276, 280-285, 287, 288, 293, 349, 352, 353, 359, 362, 365, 368, 385, 386, 394, 395
voices, 9, 20, 65, 261, 324, 333, 387
waistcoat, 64, 323, 391
Waldegrave, Lady, 102
Wales, 72, 221, 282, 374
walking, 32, 36, 40, 51, 54, 55, 58, 77, 81, 86, 89, 90, 92, 100, 101, 113, 153, 176, 199-201, 214, 215, 221, 237, 245, 250, 286, 290, 302, 309, 324, 333, 381
war, 2, 3, 217, 218, 362, 415, 429
wardrobe-closet, 65
washing stand, 74
Washington, 6
Wason, James, 389, 392
water, 18, 31, 35, 48, 63, 69, 94, 103, 104, 107, 108, 110, 111, 116, 122, 123, 147, 165-168, 170, 171, 179, 184, 204-207, 232, 233, 256, 258, 267, 274, 296, 303, 306, 309, 310, 336, 363, 370-373, 376, 384, 388, 395
wedding, 81, 244
Wednesday, 94, 105, 112, 151, 178, 182, 212-214, 219, 233, 242, 279, 304, 319, 335, 370
Wesley, John, 340
West Virginia, 429
whirlwind, 18
whisperings, 65
White Lady of the Hohenzollerns, 346
white magic, 18
white mist, 109
whited sepulchres, 399
wife, 18, 23, 24, 28, 33, 39, 51, 55, 60, 62, 63, 65, 67, 72, 73, 81, 84, 85, 91-93, 96, 104, 107, 117, 124, 129, 130, 136, 149, 152-156, 160, 161, 170, 171, 176, 177, 179, 180, 184, 185, 187, 189, 194, 200, 201, 204, 207, 213, 219, 221, 224, 238, 243, 254, 259, 263, 264, 266, 268, 269, 276-278, 282, 284, 286, 289, 290, 293-296, 318-320, 322-325, 336, 337, 341, 351, 352, 356, 358, 359, 370, 374, 389, 429
Wilson, Woodrow, 429
window, 24, 25, 27, 32, 35, 36, 38, 43, 46, 48, 49, 51, 58, 60, 61, 63, 71, 72, 75, 78, 80, 81, 90, 92, 94, 104, 114, 119, 125, 134, 139, 188, 212, 221, 237, 239, 262, 268, 270, 276, 280, 292, 295, 296, 310, 312, 323-331, 348, 383-388, 391
window blind, 78
windows, 43-45, 80, 200, 281, 293, 294, 296, 303, 334, 335, 385
wine, 18, 160, 228, 335, 383, 384
wisdom, 15
Witherspoon, Reese, 429
witness, 72, 138, 170, 210, 234, 279, 304, 323, 326, 327, 336, 368, 380
witnesses, 11, 119, 121, 126, 128, 195, 245, 258, 268, 326, 328, 342, 358, 388
Womack, Lee Ann, 429
woods, 146
Wyoming, 5, 6, 21
yacht, 34
Your Soul Lives Forever (Seabrook), 21

MEET THE AUTHOR-EDITOR

NEO-VICTORIAN SCHOLAR LOCHLAINN SEABROOK, a descendant of the families of Alexander Hamilton Stephens, John Singleton Mosby, Edmund Winchester Rucker, and William Giles Harding, is a 7th generation Kentuckian and one of the most prolific and widely read writers in the world today. Known by literary critics as the "new Shelby Foote," the "American Robert Graves," the "Southern Joseph Campbell," and by his fans as the "Voice of the Traditional South," he is a recipient of the United Daughters of the Confederacy's prestigious Jefferson Davis Historical Gold Medal. A lifelong writer, the Sons of Confederate Veterans member has authored and edited books ranging in topics from history, politics, science, religion, spirituality, astronomy, entertainment, military, and biography, to nature, music, humor, gastronomy, etymology, onomastics, alternative health, genealogy, and the paranormal; books that his readers describe as "game changers," "transformative," and "life altering."

One of the world's most popular living historians, he is a 17th generation Southerner of Appalachian heritage who descends from dozens of patriotic Revolutionary War soldiers and Confederate soldiers from Kentucky, Tennessee, North Carolina, and Virginia. Also a history, wildlife, and nature preservationist, the well-respected polymath began life as a child prodigy, later maturing into an archetypal Renaissance Man. Besides being an accomplished and esteemed author, historian, biographer, creative, and Bible authority, the influential litterateur is also a Kentucky Colonel, eagle scout, entrepreneur, screenwriter, nature, wildlife, and landscape photographer and videographer, artist, graphic designer, content creator, genealogist, former history museum docent, and a former ranch hand, zookeeper, and wrangler. A songwriter (of some 3,000 songs in a dozen genres), he is also a film composer, multi-instrument musician, vocalist, session player, and music producer who has worked and performed with some of Nashville's top musicians and singers.

Currently Seabrook is the multi-genre author and editor of nearly 100 adult and children's books (totaling some 30,000 pages and 15,000,000 words) that have earned him accolades from around the globe. His works, which have sold on every continent except Antarctica, have introduced hundreds of thousands to vital facts that have been left out of our mainstream books. He has been endorsed internationally by leading experts, museum curators, award-winning historians, bestselling authors, celebrities, filmmakers, noted scientists, well regarded educators, TV show hosts and producers, renowned military artists, venerable heritage organizations, and distinguished academicians of all races, creeds, and colors.

Of northern, western, and central European ancestry, he is the 6th great-grandson of the Earl of Oxford and a descendant of European royalty through his Kentucky father and West Virginia mother. His modern day cousins include: Johnny Cash, Elvis Presley, Lisa Marie Presley, Billy Ray and Miley Cyrus, Patty Loveless, Tim McGraw, Lee Ann Womack, Dolly Parton, Pat Boone, Naomi, Wynonna, and Ashley Judd, Ricky Skaggs, the Sunshine Sisters, Martha Carson, Chet Atkins, Patrick J. Buchanan, Cindy Crawford, Bertram Thomas Combs (Kentucky's 50th governor), Edith Bolling (second wife of President Woodrow Wilson), Andy Griffith, Riley Keough, George C. Scott, Robert Duvall, Reese Witherspoon, Lee Marvin, Rebecca Gayheart, and Tom Cruise.

A constitutionalist, avid outdoorsman, and gun rights advocate, Seabrook is the author of the international blockbuster, *Everything You Were Taught About the Civil War is Wrong, Ask a Southerner!* He lives with his wife and family in the magnificent Rocky Mountains, heart of the American West, where you will find him hiking, filming, and writing.

For more information on author Mr. Seabrook visit
LochlainnSeabrook.com

LOCHLAINN SEABROOK ∾ 431

If you enjoyed this book, you will be interested in Mr. Seabrook's other popular related titles:

☞ SEABROOK'S BIBLE DICTIONARY OF TRADITIONAL AND MYSTICAL CHRISTIAN DOCTRINES
☞ JESUS & THE LAW OF ATTRACTION: THE BIBLE-BASED GUIDE TO CREATING PERFECT HEALTH, WEALTH, AND HAPPINESS FOLLOWING CHRIST'S SIMPLE FORMULA
☞ JESUS & THE GOSPEL OF Q: CHRIST'S PRE-CHRISTIAN TEACHINGS AS RECORDED IN THE NEW TESTAMENT
☞ CHRIST IS ALL & IN ALL: REDISCOVERING YOUR DIVINE NATURE & THE KINGDOM WITHIN
☞ CHRISTMAS BEFORE CHRISTIANITY: HOW THE BIRTHDAY OF THE "SUN" BECAME THE BIRTHDAY OF THE "SON"
☞ BRITANNIA RULES: GODDESS-WORSHIP IN ANCIENT ANGLO-CELTIC SOCIETY

Available from Sea Raven Press and wherever fine books are sold

ALL OF OUR BOOK COVERS ARE AVAILABLE AS 11" X 17" POSTERS, SUITABLE FOR FRAMING.

SeaRavenPress.com

www.ingramcontent.com/pod-product-compliance
Lightning Source LLC
Chambersburg PA
CBHW021758220426
43662CB00006B/103